STATISTICS
FOR THE
BEHAVIORAL
AND
SOCIAL SCIENCES

STATISTICS
FOR THE
BEHAVIORAL
AND
SOCIAL SCIENCES

A BRIEF COURSE

Arthur Aron
Elaine N. Aron

State University of New York at Stony Brook

Prentice Hall, Upper Saddle River, NJ 07458

Library of Congress Cataloging-in-Publication Data

ARON, ARTHUR.
   Statistics for the behavioral and social sciences : a brief course
     / Arthur Aron, Elaine N. Aron.
     p.   cm.
   Includes bibliographical references and index.
   ISBN 0–13–458902–5
   1. Social sciences—Statistical methods.   2. Social sciences—
     Data processing.   I. Aron, Elaine.   II. Title.
HA39.A745   1997
300'.1'5195—dc20   96–41285
                               CIP

Acquisition Editor: *Pete Janzow*
Editorial Assistant: *Ilene Kalish*
Director of Production and Manufacturing: *Barbara Kittle*
Managing Editor: *Bonnie Biller*
Project Manager: *Fran Russello*
Production Coordination: *PublisherStudio*
Manufacturing Manager: *Nick Sklitsis*
Prepress and Manufacturing Buyer: *Tricia Kenny*
Creative Design Director: *Leslie Osher*
Interior Design: *Maureen Eide/Judith A. Matz-Coniglio*
Art Director and Cover Design: *Anne Bonanno Nieglos*
Cover Art: *Horned Puffin, Alaska, John Worden/Tony Stone Images*
Photo Research: *Sherry Cohen*
Line Art Coordinator: *Michele Giusti*
Director, Image Resource Center: *Lori Morris-Nantz*
Photo Research Supervisor: *Melinda Lee Reo*
Image Permission Supervisor: *Kay Dellosa*
Supervisor of Production Services: *Lori Clinton*
Electronic Art Creation: *NK Graphics*

This book was set in 11 point Times Roman by NK Graphics
and was printed and bound by Courier Westford.
The cover was printed by Phoenix Color Corp.

Printed in the United States of America
10 9 8 7 6 5 4

ISBN 0-13-458902-5

Prentice-Hall International (UK) Limited, *London*
Prentice-Hall of Australia Pty. Limited, *Sydney*
Prentice-Hall Canada Inc., *Toronto*
Prentice-Hall Hispanoamericana, S.A., *Mexico*
Prentice-Hall of India Private Limited, *New Delhi*
Prentice-Hall of Japan, Inc., *Tokyo*
Prentice-Hall Asia Pte. Ltd., *Singapore*
Editora Prentice-Hall Do Brasil, Ltda., *Rio de Janeiro*

Brief Contents

Contents

2 The Mean, Variance, Standard Deviation, and Z Scores 22

3 Correlation and Prediction 44

4 Some Key Ingredients for Inferential Statistics: The Normal Curve, Probability, and Population Versus Sample 74

5 Introduction to Hypothesis Testing 90

6 Hypothesis Tests With Means of Samples 108

7 Making Sense of Statistical Significance: Error, Power, and Effect Size 126

8 The *t* Test for Dependent Means 152

9 The *t* Test for Independent Means 178

10 Introduction to the Analysis of Variance 198

11 Chi-Square and Strategies When Population Distributions Are Not Normal 230

12 Making Sense of Advanced Statistical Procedures in Research Articles 264

Appendix

Tables   287

Preface to the Instructor

The heart of this book was written over a summer in a small apartment near the Place Saint Ferdinand, having been outlined in nearby cafés and on walks in the Bois de Boulogne. It is based on our 30 years of experience teaching, doing research, and writing. We believe that this book is as different from the conventional lot of statistics books as Paris is from Calcutta, yet still comfortable and stimulating to the long-suffering community of statistics instructors.

The approach embodied in this text has been developed over three decades of successful teaching—successful not only in the sense that students have consistently rated the course (a statistics course, remember) as a highlight of their undergraduate years but also in the sense that students come back to us years later saying, "I was light-years ahead of my fellow graduate students because of your course," or "Even though I don't do research, your course has really helped me understand statistics that I read about in my field."

What We Have Done Differently

We continue to do what the best of the other current books are already doing well: emphasizing the intuitive, deemphasizing the mathematical, and explaining everything in clear, simple language. What we have done differs from these other books in nine key respects.

   1. *The definitional formulas are brought to center stage* because they provide a concise symbolic summary of the logic of each particular procedure.

All our explanations, examples, practice problems, and test bank items, are based on these definitional formulas. (The numbers involved in practice problems and test items are reduced appropriately to keep computations manageable.)

Why this change? To date, statistics books have failed to adjust to technologic reality. What is important is not that the students learn to calculate a correlation coefficient with a large set of numbers—computers can do that for them. What is important is that students remain constantly aware of the underlying logic of the procedure. For example, consider the population variance—the average of the squared deviations from the mean. This concept is immediately clear from the definitional formula (once the student is used to the symbols): Variance $= \Sigma (X - M)^2/N$. Working problems using this formula constantly engrains the meaning in the student's mind. In contrast, the usual computational version of this formula serves only to obscure this meaning: Variance $= [\Sigma X^2 - (\Sigma X)^2/N]/N$. Working problems using this formula does nothing but teach the student the difference between ΣX^2 and $(\Sigma X)^2$!

Teaching computational formulas today is an anachronism. Researchers do their statistics on computers now. At the same time, the use of statistical software makes the understanding of the basic principles, as they are symbolically expressed in the definitional formula, more important than ever.

It is a mystery to us why statistics textbooks have not changed their methods with the advent of statistical software, but we are convinced that the change is overdue. Of course, because computational formulas are both historically interesting and occasionally needed—and because some instructors may feel naked without them—we still provide them in a brief footnote wherever a computational formula would normally be introduced.

2. *Each procedure is taught both verbally and numerically—and usually visually as well—with the same examples being described in each of these ways.* Practice exercises and test bank items, in turn, require the student to calculate results and make graphs or illustrations and also to write a short explanation in layperson's language of what the statistic means. The chapter material completely prepares the student for these kinds of exercises and test questions.

It is our repeated experience that these different ways of expressing an idea are very important for permanently establishing a concept in a student's mind. Many students in the social and behavioral sciences are more at ease with words than with numbers. In fact, some have a positive fear of all mathematics. Writing the lay language explanation gives them an opportunity to do what they do best and, if they are having trouble, forces them to put the procedures in front of them in the verbal form they process best.

3. A main goal of any introductory statistics course in the social and behavioral sciences is to *prepare students to read research articles.* In fact, the way a procedure such as a *t* test or chi-square is described in a research article is often quite different from what the student expects on the basis of standard textbook discussions. Therefore, as this book teaches a statistical method, it also gives examples of how that method is reported in the journals. The practice problems and test bank items also include excerpts from articles for the student to explain.

4. The book is unusually *up-to-date.* For some reason, most of the introductory statistics textbooks we have seen read as if the authors were writing in the 1950s. The basics are still the basics. The subtleties of the way statisticians and researchers think about those basics today has changed radically. The basics today are undergirded by a different appreciation of issues like effect size and power, the central role of models, the underlying unity of difference and association statistics, and a whole host of new orientations arising from the prominent role of the computer in our analyses. We are very much engaged in the latest developments in theory and application of statistics and we believe the writing of this book reflects that engagement. One not-so-subtle example is our major emphasis on effect size and power. Most other texts, when they treat this at all, tack it on in one place, never to be brought up again. Another example is our treatment of assumptions and how to handle situations in which they are violated, which is rooted in recent Monte Carlo and theoretical treatments results plus actual research practice. (One of the authors, A. A., is currently an editor of a major social science journal.) Most other texts tend to teach these topics in a kind of all-or-none doctrinaire manner that puts the students at odds with what they read in their nonstatistics courses.

5. *The final chapter looks at advanced procedures* without actually teaching them in detail. It explains in simple terms how to make sense out of these statistics when they are encountered in research articles. Most research articles today use methods such as hierarchical and stepwise multiple regression, factor analysis, structural equation modeling, analysis of covariance, and multivariate analysis of variance. Students completing the ordinary introductory statistics course are ill-equipped to comprehend most of the articles they must read to prepare a paper or study for a course. This chapter makes use of the basics that students have just learned to give a cursory understanding of these advanced procedures. It also serves as a reference guide that they can keep and use in the future when reading such articles.

6. The book is written to *capitalize on the students' motivations.* We try to do this in two ways. First, our examples, while attempting to represent the diversity of social and behavioral science research, emphasize topics or populations that students seem to find most interesting. The very first is from a real study in which 151 students in their first week of an introductory statistics class rate how much stress they feel they are under. Also, in our examples, we continually emphasize the usefulness of statistical methods and ideas as tools in the research process, never allowing students to feel that what they are learning is theory for the sake of theory.

Second, we have tried to make the book extremely straightforward and systematic in its explanation of basic concepts so that students can have frequent "aha" experiences. Such experiences bolster self-confidence and motivate further learning. So often textbooks constantly beat their readers over the head with just how oversimplified everything they are learning is. Instead, we try to inspire readers with the depth of what can be learned, even in an introductory course. It is really quite inspiring to *us* to see even fairly modest students glow from having mastered some concept like negative correlation, the distinction between failing to reject the null hypothesis and supporting the null hypothesis, or the idea of independence in a chi-square analysis.

7. The accompanying *Student's Study Guide and Computer Workbook* focuses on mastering concepts and also includes instructions and examples for working problems using a computer. Most study guides focus on plugging numbers into formulas and memorizing rules (which is consistent with the emphasis of the textbooks they accompany). For each chapter, our *Student's Study Guide and Computer Workbook* provides learning objectives, a detailed chapter outline, the chapter's formulas (with all symbols defined), and summaries of steps of conducting each procedure covered in the chapter, plus a set of self tests, including multiple-choice, fill-in, and problem/essay questions. In addition, for each procedure covered in the chapter, the study guide furnishes a thorough outline for writing an essay explaining the procedure to a person who has never had a course in statistics.

Especially important, our *Student's Study Guide and Computer Workbook* provides the needed support for teaching students to conduct statistical analyses on the computer. First, there is a special appendix introducing the language and procedures of SPSS/for Windows. Then, in each chapter corresponding to the text chapters, there is a section showing in detail how to carry out the chapter's procedures on the computer (including step-by-step instructions, examples, and illustrations of how each step of input and output appears on the computer screen), plus special activities for using the computer to deepen understanding. As far as we know, no other statistics textbook package provides this much depth of explanation.

8. We have written an *Instructor's Manual* that really helps teach the course. The *Instructor's Manual* begins with a chapter summarizing what we have gleaned from our own teaching experience and from a review of the research literature on effectiveness in college teaching. The next chapter discusses alternative organizations of the course, including tables of possible schedules and a sample syllabus. Then each chapter, corresponding to the text chapters, provides full lecture outlines and worked-out examples not found in the text (in a form suitable for copying onto transparencies or for student handouts). These worked-out examples are particularly useful in that creating examples is one of the most difficult parts of preparing statistics lectures.

Also, we have developed a teaching technique students really enjoy: We administer an anonymous questionnaire on the first day, on a topic of interest to them, and then analyze the class's responses throughout the quarter using the techniques of each chapter. The *Instructor's Manual* provides the questionnaire we have used for this purpose. (Or you can always develop one of your own—or even let the students help develop one with questions that would interest them.) If you do not wish to administer a questionnaire, for each text chapter the *Instructor's Manual* provides transparency masters based on results obtained with our classes, analyzed with whatever procedure is being studied in the text, following the steps described there. If you use our questionnaire, we provide SAS and SPSS code to help you analyze these data for each transparency example.

9. Our *Test Bank and Answers to Practice Problems* makes preparing good exams easy. We supply approximately 40 multiple-choice, 25 fill-in, and 10 to 12 problem/essay questions for each chapter. Considering that the emphasis of the course is so conceptual, the multiple-choice questions will be particularly useful for those of you who do not have the resources to grade essays. This supplement also includes answers to each textbook chapter's practice problems which are not given in the text. (The textbook provides answers to selected practice problems, including at least one example answer to an essay-type question for each chapter.)

About the x

We were thrilled by the enthusiastic response of instructors and students to our *Statistics for Psychology* (Aron & Aron, 1994). This *Brief Course* is our answer to the many requests we have received from instructors and students for a textbook using our approach that is (a) more general in its focus than psychology alone and (b) shorter, to accommodate less comprehensive courses. Of course, we have tried to retain all the qualities that have endeared the original to our readers. At the same time, this is not a cosmetic revision. The broadening of focus has meant using examples from the entire range of the social and behavioral sciences, from anthropology to political science, with many in education especially (a field with many students and which is relevant to students in all fields, since they are all in school). Most important, the broadening informs the relative emphasis (and inclusion) of different topics and the tenor of the discussion of these topics. The shortening has also been dramatic: This book is about half the length of the original, making it quite feasible to do the whole book, even in a quarter-length course. In addition to the refocusing and shortening, this *Brief Course* is sharpened by our own and other instructor's experience with the original, reflects developments in statistics in the last three years, and benefits from a thorough rewriting to make the language even simpler and the explanations even more direct.

Keep in Touch

Our goal is to do whatever we can to help you make your course a success. If you have any questions or suggestions, please write or contact us by email (**ARON@PSYCH1.PSY.SUNYSB.EDU** will do for both of us). Indeed, if you let us know you are teaching the course with this book, we will add you to our network of folks to be kept informed of any suggestions or comments we receive from others teaching the course (and our replies). If you should find an error somewhere, we promise that we will (a) try to fix it in the very next printing, (b) send out the details to everyone on the network, and (c), if you are the first to find it, include your name with our thanks in the Introduction to the next edition.

Acknowledgments

First and foremost, we are grateful to our students through the years, who have guided our approach to teaching by encouraging us with their appreciation for what we have done well, as well as their various means of discouraging us from persisting in what we have done not so well.

We remain grateful to all of those who helped us with the original version of the text. For their very helpful input on the development of this *Brief Course,* we want to thank Dr. Nicholas P. Maxwell, University of Washington; Dr. Robert J. Schneider, Metropolitan State College; Dr. Miriam Goldstein, Washington University; Dr. Carol Randey, LA Pierce Community College; Dr. Paul Yarnold, Northwestern University; Professor Robert Reynolds, Weber State; Dr. Alvaro Nieves, Wheaton College; Dr. Lee

Griffith, Anderson University. We are also particularly grateful to Sheri Koplow for her assistance in locating many of the education and other social science examples. Finally we are grateful to all the folks at PublisherStudio for their fine work on the production side.

Arthur Aron

Elaine Aron

Credits

Data in tables 3-9, 3-10, 8-7, 8-8, 9-4, 9-5, 10-6, 10-7, 11-7, 11-8, and 11-9 are based on tables in Cohen, J. (1988). *Statistical power analysis for the behavioral sciences* (2nd Ed.). Copyright © 1988 by Lawrence Erlbaum Associates, Inc. Reprinted by permission.

Introduction to the Student

The goal of this book is to help you *understand* statistics. We emphasize meaning and concepts, not just symbols and numbers.

This emphasis plays to your strength. Most social and behavioral science students are not lovers of calculus but are keenly attuned to ideas. We want to emphasize the following, based on our experience of 30 years of teaching: *We have never had a student who could do well in other college courses who could not also do well in this course.* (However, we will admit that doing well in this course may require more work than doing well in others.)

In this introduction, we discuss why you are taking this course and how you can gain the most from it.

Why Learn Statistics? (Besides It Being Required)

1. *Understanding statistics is crucial to being able to read research results.* In most of the social and behavioral sciences, nearly every course you will take emphasizes the results of research studies, and these are usually expressed in statistics. If you do not understand the basic logic of statistics—if you cannot make sense of the jargon, the tables, and the graphs that are at the heart of any research report—your reading of research will be very superficial.

2. *Understanding statistics is crucial to doing research yourself.* Many students eventually go on to graduate school. Graduate study in the social and behavioral sciences almost always involves *doing* research. Often learning to do research on your own is the entire focus of graduate school, and doing research almost always involves statistics. (This is increasingly true of even much "qualitative" research.) This course gives you a solid foundation in the statistics you need for doing research. Further, by mastering the basic logic and ways of thinking about statistics, you will be unusually well prepared for the advanced courses, which focus on the nitty-gritty of analyzing research results.

Many universities also offer opportunities for undergraduates to do research. The main focus of this book is understanding statistics, not using statistics. Still, you will learn the skills you need to do some of the most common statistics used in the kinds of research you are likely to do.

3. *Understanding statistics develops your analytic and critical thinking.* Social and behavioral science majors are often most interested in people and in improving things in the practical world. This does not mean that you avoid abstractions. In fact, the students we know are exhilarated most by the almost philosophical levels of abstraction where the secrets of human experience so often seem to hide. Even this kind of abstraction often is grasped only superficially at first, as slogans instead of useful knowledge. Of all the courses you are likely to take in the social and behavioral sciences, this course will probably do the most to help you learn to think precisely, to evaluate information, and to apply logical analysis at a very high level.

How to Gain the Most from This Course

There are five things we can advise:

1. *Keep your attention on the concepts.* Treat this course less like a math course and more like a course in logic. When you read a section of a chapter, your attention should be on grasping the principles. When working the exercises, think about why you are doing each step. If you simply try to memorize how to come up with the right numbers, you will have learned very little of use in your future studies—nor will you do very well on the tests in this course.

2. *Be sure you know each concept before you go on to the next.* Statistics is cumulative. Each new concept is built on the last one. Even within a chapter, if you have read a section and you do not understand it—*stop*. Reread it, rethink it, ask for help. Do whatever you need to do to grasp it. (If you think that you have understood a section but are not sure, try working a relevant practice problem at the end of the chapter.)

Having to read the material in this book over and over does not mean that you are stupid. Most students have to read each chapter several times. Each reading is much slower than reading an ordinary textbook. Statistics reading has to be pored over with clear, calm attention for it to sink in. Allow plenty of time for this kind of reading and rereading.

3. *Keep up.* Again, statistics is cumulative. If you fall behind in your reading or miss lectures, the lectures you then attend will be almost meaningless. It will get harder and harder to catch up.

4. *Study especially intensely in the first half of the course.* It is especially important to master the material thoroughly at the start of the course. This is because everything else in statistics is built on what you learn at the start. Yet the beginning of the semester is often when students study least seriously.

If you have mastered the first half of the course—not just learned the general idea, but really know it—the second half will be easier than the first. If you have not mastered the first half, the second half will be close to impossible.

5. *Help each other.* There is no better way to solidify and deepen your understanding of statistics than to try to explain it to someone who is having a harder time. (Of course, this explaining has to be with patience and respect.) For those of you who are having a harder time, there is no better way to work through the difficult parts than by learning from another student who has just learned it.

We strongly suggest that you form study teams with one to three other students. It is best if your team includes some members who expect this material to come easy and some who do not. Those who learn statistics easily will really get the very most from helping others who have to struggle with it—the latter will tax the former's supposed understanding enormously. For those who fear trouble ahead, you need to work with those who do not—the blind leading the blind is no way to learn. Pick teammates who live near you so that it is easy for you to get together. Meet often—between each class, if possible.

A Final Note

Believe it or not, we love teaching statistics. Time and again, we have had the wonderful experience of having beaming students come to us to say, "Professor Aron, I got a 90% on this exam. I can't believe it! Me, a 90 on a statistics exam!" Or the student who tells us, "This is actually fun. Don't tell anyone, but I'm actually enjoying . . . statistics, of all things!" We hope you will have these kinds of experiences in this course.

Arthur Aron
Elaine N. Aron

1

Displaying the Order in a Group of Numbers

Welcome to *Statistics for the Behavioral and Social Sciences.* We imagine you to be like other social science students we have known. Some of you are highly scientific sorts; others are more intuitive. Some of you are fond of math; others may be less so or even afraid of it. Whichever category you fall into, we welcome you. We want to assure you that if you give this book some special attention (perhaps a little more than most textbooks require), you *will* learn statistics. The approach used in this book has taught successfully all sorts of students before you, including people who had taken statistics previously and done poorly. With this book, and your instructor's help, you will learn statistics and learn it well.

Even if you feel you have been forced to study statistics because it is a requirement in your major, this course is not a waste of time. Soon you will be better able to read research articles in your major, do your own research if you so choose, and use both your reason and your intuition.

Think of statistics as a tool that extends a basic thinking process that every human employs: We observe a thing; we wonder what it means or what caused it; we have an insight or make an intuitive guess; we observe again, but now in detail, or we try making some little changes in the process to test our intuition. Then, we face the eternal problem: Was our hunch really confirmed or not? What are the chances that what we have observed this second time will happen again and again, so that we can announce our insight to the world as something probably true?

In other words, statistics is a method of pursuing truth. At least statistics can tell you the likelihood that your hunch is true in this time and place, with these sorts of people. (The truth of statistics also depends on how carefully you have collected your statistics, but good research design is another topic altogether.) This pursuit of truth, or at least future likelihood, is the essence of science, and of human evolution. Think of the first hypotheses: What will the mammoths do next spring? What will happen if I eat this root? It is easy to see how the accurate have survived. You are among them. Statistics is one good way to pursue accuracy and truth.

The Two Branches of Statistical Methods

There are two main branches of statistical methods:

1. Descriptive statistics. Social and behavioral scientists use descriptive statistics to summarize and make understandable, to describe, a group of numbers from a research study.

2. Inferential statistics. Social and behavioral scientists use inferential statistics to draw conclusions and inferences, which are based on the numbers from a research study, but go beyond these numbers.

The first three chapters of this book focus on descriptive statistics. This topic is important in its own right, but it also prepares you to understand inferential statistics. Inferential statistics are the focus of Chapters 4 through 12.

Frequency Tables

In this chapter, you learn to use tables and graphs to describe a group of numbers. The purpose of descriptive statistics is to make a group of numbers easy to understand. Tables and graphs help a great deal.

An Example

Aron, Paris, and Aron (1995), as part of a larger study, gave a questionnaire to 151 students in an introductory statistics class during the first week of the course. One of the questions asked, "How stressed have you been in the last 2 1/2 weeks, on a scale of 0 to 10, with 0 being not at all stressed and 10 being as stressed as possible?" The 151 students' ratings were as follows:

4, 7, 7, 7, 8, 8, 7, 8, 9, 4, 7, 3, 6, 9, 10, 5, 7, 10, 6, 8, 7, 8, 7, 8, 7, 4, 5, 10, 10, 0, 9, 8, 3, 7, 9, 7, 9, 5, 8, 5, 0, 4, 6, 6, 7, 5, 3, 2, 8, 5, 10, 9, 10, 6, 4, 8, 8, 8, 4, 8, 7, 3, 8, 8, 8, 8, 7, 9, 7, 5, 6, 3, 4, 8, 7, 5, 7, 3, 3, 6, 5, 7, 5, 7, 8, 8, 7, 10, 5, 4, 3, 7, 6, 3, 9, 7, 8, 5, 7, 9, 9, 3, 1, 8, 6, 6, 4, 8, 5, 10, 4, 8, 10, 5, 5, 4, 9, 4, 7, 7, 7, 6, 6, 4, 4, 4, 9, 7, 10, 4, 7, 5, 10, 7, 9, 2, 7, 5, 9, 10, 3, 7, 2, 5, 9, 8, 10, 10, 6, 8, 3

It takes a while just to read all these ratings. Looking through them gives some sense of the overall tendencies. This is hardly an accurate method. One solution is to make a table showing how many students used each of the 11 values the ratings can have (0, 1, 2, and so on, through 10). We have done this in Table 1–1. We also figured the percentages each value's frequency is of the total number of scores.

Table 1–1 is called a **frequency table** because it shows how frequently (how many times) each rating occurred. A frequency table makes the pattern of numbers very easy to see. In this example, you can see that most of these students rated their stress around 7 or 8, with few rating it very low.

descriptive statistics

inferential statistics

TABLE 1–1
Number of Students Rating Each Value of the Stress Scale

Stress Rating	Frequency	Percent
10	14	9.3
9	15	9.9
8	26	17.2
7	31	20.5
6	13	8.6
5	18	11.9
4	16	10.6
3	12	7.9
2	3	2.0
1	1	.7
0	2	1.3

Note: Data from Aron, Paris, & Aron (1995).

frequency table

Frequency tables sometimes give only the raw-number frequencies and not the percentages, or only the percentages and not the raw-number frequencies.[1]

Variables, Values, and Scores

Another way of saying what a frequency table does is to say that it shows the frequency of each **value** of a particular **variable.** A value is simply a number, such as 4, –81, or 367.12. A value can also be a category, such as male or female or a person's religion.

    value
    variable

A variable is a characteristic that can have different values. In short, it can vary. In our stress example, the variable is level of stress. It can have values of 0 through 10. Height is a variable, social class is a variable, score on a creativity test is a variable, number of people absent from work is a variable, dosage of a medication is a variable, political party preference is a variable, and class size is a variable.

On any variable, each person has a particular number or **score** that is that person's value on the variable. For example, Chris's score on the stress variable might have a value of 6; Pat's score might have a value of 8. We often use the word score for a particular person's value on a variable. This is because much social science research involves scores on some type of test.

    score

Social science research is about variables, values, and scores. We will be using this terminology throughout the book. The formal definitions are a bit abstract. In practice, you will find that what we mean when we use these words usually is obvious.

Numeric and Nominal Variables

Most of the variables social scientists use are like those in the example of the stress ratings. The scores are numbers that tell you the degree or amount of what is being measured. In the stress rating example, the higher the number the more stress. We refer to this kind of variable as a **numeric variable.** Numeric variables also are referred to as *quantitative variables.*[2]

    numeric variable

---

[1]In addition, some frequency tables include for each value the total number of scores with that value and all values preceding it. These are called *cumulative frequencies* because they tell how many scores are accumulated up to this point on the table. If Table 1–1 included a cumulative frequency column, the first cumulative frequency (for a stress rating of 10) would be 14, the same as the frequency, because there are no values preceding it. The second cumulative frequency (for a stress rating of 9) would be 29, the sum of the frequency of 15 for this value plus the 14 for the preceding value. The frequency for the last value (a stress rating of 0) would be 151, the total number of scores. Sometimes the cumulative frequencies are accumulated going from lowest to highest value. Thus, Table 1–1 would have cumulative frequencies of 2 for a rating of 0, 3 for a rating of 1, 6 for a rating of 2, and so forth, up to 151 for a rating of 10.

    If percentages are used, cumulative percentages also may be included. Cumulative percentages would give, for each value, the percentage of scores up to and including that value. Thus, if a value had a cumulative percentage of 48%, this would mean that 48% of the scores have this value or the values preceding it. The cumulative percentage for any given value also is called a *percentile.* Thus, if a particular person had a stress rating with a cumulative frequency of 48%, that person would be in the "48th percentile" for stress ratings.

[2]There are actually several kinds of numeric variables. In the social sciences, the most important distinction is between (a) variables in which the numbers stand for about equal amounts of what is being measured versus (b) variables in which the numbers only stand for relative rankings. For example, grade point average (GPA) is a roughly equal-interval variable because the difference between a GPA of 2.5 and 2.8 means about as much of a difference as the difference between ratings of 3.0 and 3.3. (Both are a difference of .3 of a GPA.) An example of a rank-order variable

The other major type of variable is a **nominal variable** (also called a *categorical variable*). Nominal variables are variables, such as gender or religion, in which the values are names or categories. (The term *nominal* comes from the idea that its values are names.) For example, the values for gender are female and male. A person's score on the variable gender is one of these two values. Similarly, religion has values, such as Catholic, Muslim, and so forth.

In this book, we focus mostly on numeric variables. However, nominal variables also are quite common; we discuss some procedures specifically designed for nominal variables in Chapter 11.

How to Make a Frequency Table

The four steps for making a frequency table follow:

1. Make a list down the page of each possible value, starting from the highest and ending with the lowest. In the stress rating results, the list goes from 10, the highest possible rating, down through 0, the lowest possible rating. (Even if one of the ratings between 10 and 0 had not been used, you would still include that value of the stress variable in the listing, showing it as having a frequency of 0. For example, if no one in the class had given stress a 2 rating, you would still include 2 as one of the values on the frequency table.)

2. Go one by one through the scores. For each score, make a mark next to its value on your list. This is shown in Figure 1–1. It is a good idea to cross off each score as you mark it on the list.

3. Make a table showing how many times each value on your list occurs. To do this, add up the number of marks beside each value. It also is wise to cross-check the accuracy of your work by adding up these totals. You want to be sure that their sum equals the total number of scores.

4. Figure the percentage of scores for each value. Do this by taking the frequency for that value and dividing it by the total number of scores. You

FIGURE 1–1

Creating a frequency table of stress ratings. (Data from Aron et al., 1995)

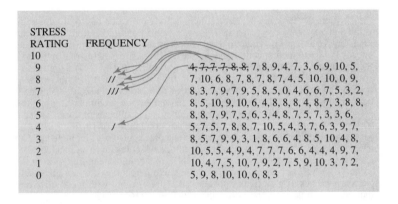

would be rank in ones graduating class. The difference between being second and third in class standing could be a very unlike amount of difference in underlying GPA than the difference between being eighth and ninth. There is somewhat less information in the rank-order variable. It is less precise. (Rank-order variables are also commonly referred to as *ordinal variables*.) We will discuss rank-order variables in Chapter 11. This whole topic is called *levels of measurement*.

usually will need to round off the percentage. There is no fixed rule about how many decimals to use when rounding off the percentages. A rough guideline would be with less than 10 values, round to the nearest whole percentage; with 10 to 20 values, round to one decimal place; with more than 20 values, round to two decimal places. Note that because of the rounding, the total of your percentages will not usually be exactly 100%. However, it should be close.

A Second Example

Martha Moorehouse and Paul Sanders (1992) conducted a study of children's attitudes toward learning and work. As part of that study, these researchers had the teachers of 153 grade school students fill out a questionnaire. The questionnaire asked the teachers to rate the students' attitudes toward achievement. Example items were "Prefers new and challenging problems over easy problems" and "Is easily frustrated." The highest possible score on the test was 120. This would be a very positive attitude toward achievement. The lowest possible score was 24. This would be the most negative possible attitude toward achievement. The scores for the 153 students were as follows:

> 77, 78, 98, 85, 59, 59, 59, 108, 86, 104, 111, 67, 77, 66, 70, 74, 65, 108, 92, 68, 95, 56, 87, 92, 73, 92, 106, 74, 97, 109, 69, 103, 113, 119, 45, 99, 111, 78, 95, 54, 68, 42, 65, 84, 80, 115, 44, 32, 107, 57, 118, 107, 30, 50, 63, 74, 76, 43, 25, 73, 115, 40, 45, 86, 113, 115, 111, 114, 94, 110, 96, 90, 112, 103, 108, 110, 82, 73, 101, 72, 61, 75, 67, 74, 55, 74, 69, 109, 87, 74, 112, 97, 91, 101, 105, 97, 107, 92, 100, 109, 114, 103, 107, 100, 117, 74, 120, 86, 105, 108, 115, 96, 97, 106, 110, 112, 95, 113, 71, 88, 94, 104, 95, 62, 104, 70, 64, 117, 116, 65, 82, 119, 115, 81, 107, 111, 118, 63, 53, 104, 112, 90, 74, 65, 79, 53, 115, 84, 93, 68, 70, 114, 91

Now, let's follow our four steps for making a frequency table.

1. Make a list of each possible value down the left edge of a page, starting from the highest and ending with the lowest. In this study, the values ranged from a possible high score of 120 to a possible low score of 24. Thus, the first step is to list these values down a page. (It might be good to use several columns so that you can have all the scores on a single page.)

2. Go one by one through the scores. For each score, make a mark next to its value on your list. Figure 1–2 shows this.

3. Make a table showing how many times each value on your list occurred. Table 1–2 is the result.

4. Figure the percentages of scores for each value. We have *not* done so in this example because it would not help much for seeing the pattern of scores. However, if you want to check your understanding of this step, the first six percentages would be .65%, 1.31%, 1.31%, 1.31%, .65%, and 3.92%. (These are the percentages for frequencies of 1, 2, 2, 2, 1, and 6. We have rounded to two decimal places.)

Grouped Frequency Tables

Sometimes there are a great many possible values and a frequency table is too awkward to give a simple picture of the scores. The last example was a

120 - /	80 - /	40 - /
119 - //	79 - /	39 -
118 - //	78 - //	38 -
117 - //	77 - //	37 -
116 - /	76 - /	36 -
115 - ᵀᕼᏞ /	75 - /	35 -
114 - ///	74 - ᵀᕼᏞ ///	34 -
113 - ///	73 - ///	33 -
112 - ////	72 - /	32 - /
111 - ////	71 - /	31 -
110 - ///	70 - ///	30 - /
109 - ///	69 - //	29 -
108 - ////	68 - ///	28 -
107 - ᵀᕼᏞ	67 - //	27 -
106 - //	66 - /	26 -
105 - //	65 - ////	25 - /
104 - ////	64 - /	24 -
103 - ///	63 - //	
102 -	62 - /	
101 - //	61 - /	
100 -	60 -	
99 - /	59 - ///	
98 - /	58 -	
97 - ////	57 - /	
96 - //	56 - /	
95 - ////	55 - /	
94 - //	54 - /	
93 - /	53 - //	
92 - ////	52 -	
91 - //	51 -	
90 - //	50 - /	
89 -	49 -	
88 - /	48 -	
87 - //	47 -	
86 - //	46 -	
85 - /	45 - //	
84 - //	44 - /	
83 -	43 - /	
82 - //	42 - /	
81 - /	41 -	

FIGURE 1–2
Creating a frequency table of teachers' ratings of 153 grade school students' attitudes toward achievement. (Data from Moorehouse & Sanders, 1992)

TABLE 1–2
Frequency Table for Teachers' Ratings of 153 Grade School Students' Attitudes Toward Achievement

Score	Frequency	Score	Frequency	Score	Frequency
120	1	88	1	56	1
119	2	87	2	55	1
118	2	86	3	54	1
117	2	85	1	53	2
116	1	84	2	52	0
115	6	83	0	51	0
114	3	82	2	50	1
113	3	81	1	49	0
112	4	80	1	48	0
111	4	79	1	47	0
110	3	78	2	46	0
109	3	77	2	45	2
108	4	76	1	44	1
107	5	75	1	43	1
106	2	74	8	42	1
105	2	73	3	41	0
104	4	72	1	40	1
103	3	71	1	39	0
102	0	70	3	38	0
101	2	69	2	37	0
100	2	68	3	36	0
99	1	67	2	35	0
98	1	66	1	34	0
97	4	65	4	33	0
96	2	64	1	32	1
95	4	63	2	31	0
94	2	62	1	30	1
93	1	61	1	29	0
92	4	60	0	28	0
91	2	59	3	27	0
90	2	58	0	26	0
89	0	57	1	25	1
				24	0

Note: Data from Moorehouse & Sanders (1992).

bit like that, wasn't it? The solution is to make groupings of values that include all values within a certain interval. For example, consider our stress example. Instead of having a separate frequency figure for the students who rated their stress as 8 and another for those who rated it as 9, you could have a combined category of 8 and 9. This combined category is an interval including two values. This interval would have a frequency of 41 (the 26 scores with a value of 8 and the 15 scores with a value of 9).

grouped frequency table

A frequency table that uses intervals is a **grouped frequency table.** Table 1–3 is a grouped frequency table for the stress ratings example. (However, in this example, the full frequency table has only 11 different values. Thus, a grouped frequency table was not really necessary.) Table 1–4 is a grouped frequency table for the teachers' ratings of 153 students' attitudes toward achievement.

intervals

Making a grouped frequency table involves combining values into **intervals.** There are some rules about how this is done. Most important, there should be about 5 to 15 intervals and all intervals should be of the same size.

(Sometimes researchers make an exception for the highest and lowest interval.) If you study the examples closely, you will see that we have followed some additional principles. The low end of each interval is always a multiple of the interval size. (For example, if the interval size is 3, then the low end of the intervals contains multiples of 3, such as 0, 3, 6, 9, and so on.) It also is standard to make the intervals a round number, such as 2, 3, 5, 10, or a multiple of 10. (Table 1–3 uses an interval size of 2. Table 1–4 uses an interval size of 10.)

The big question in actually designing a grouped frequency table is determining the interval size and the number of intervals. There are various guidelines to help researchers with this, but in practice it is done automatically by the researcher's computer. Thus, we will not focus on it in this book. However, should you have to make a grouped frequency table on your own, the key thing is to experiment with the interval size until you come up with an interval size that is a round number and that creates about 5 to 15 intervals. Then when actually setting up the table, be sure you set the low end of each interval to a multiple of the interval size and the top end of each interval to the number that is just below the low end of the next interval.

Histograms

A graph is another good way to make a large group of scores easy to understand. "A picture is worth a thousand words"—and sometimes a thousand numbers. One way to graph the information in a frequency table is to make a special kind of bar chart called a **histogram.** In a histogram, the height of each bar is the frequency of each value in the frequency table, and all the bars are put next to each other with no space in between. A histogram looks a bit like a city skyline. Figure 1–3 shows two histograms based on the stress ratings example (one based on the ordinary frequency table and one based on the grouped frequency table).

histogram

How to Make a Histogram

The four steps for making a histogram follow:

1. Make a frequency table.
2. Place the scale of values along the bottom of a page. The numbers should go from left to right, from lowest to highest. For a grouped frequency table, the histogram is of the intervals. Mark only the midpoint of each interval, under the center of each bar. (The midpoint is the middle of the interval. To get the midpoint, take the bottom of the next interval minus the bottom of this interval, divide by 2, and add this to the bottom of this interval.)
3. Make a scale of frequencies along the left edge of the page. The scale should run from 0 at the bottom to the highest frequency for any value.
4. Make a bar for each value. The height of each bar is the frequency of the value it is placed over.

Making a histogram is easiest if you use graph paper.

Additional Histogram Example

Figure 1–4 shows a histogram based on the grouped frequency table for the students' attitudes toward achievement example.

TABLE 1–3
Grouped Frequency Table for Stress Ratings

Stress Rating Interval	Frequency	Percent
10–11	14	9
8–9	41	27
6–7	44	29
4–5	34	23
2–3	15	10
0–1	3	2

Note: Data from Aron, Paris, & Aron (1995).

TABLE 1–4
Grouped Frequency Table for Teachers' Ratings of 153 Grade School Students' Attitudes Toward Achievement

Interval	Frequency	Percent
120–129	1	.6
110–119	30	19.6
100–109	27	17.6
90–99	23	15.0
80–89	13	8.5
70–79	23	15.0
60–69	17	11.1
50–59	10	6.5
40–49	6	3.9
30–39	2	1.3
20–29	1	.6

Note: Data from Moorehouse & Sanders (1992).

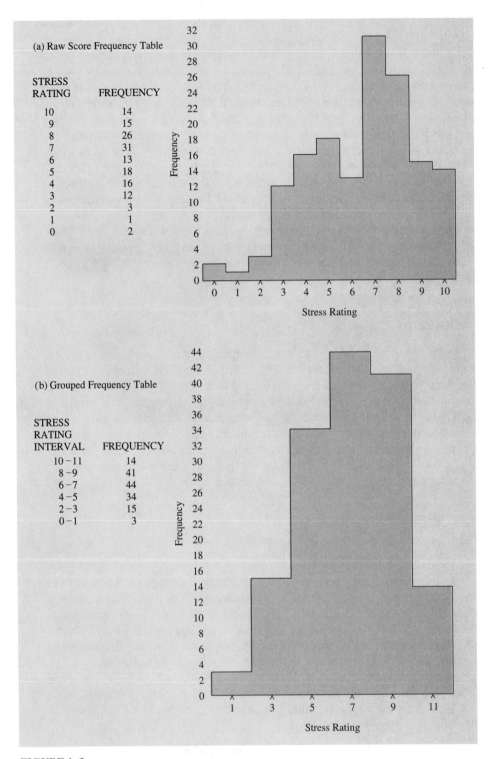

(a) Raw Score Frequency Table

STRESS RATING	FREQUENCY
10	14
9	15
8	26
7	31
6	13
5	18
4	16
3	12
2	3
1	1
0	2

(b) Grouped Frequency Table

STRESS RATING INTERVAL	FREQUENCY
10 – 11	14
8 – 9	41
6 – 7	44
4 – 5	34
2 – 3	15
0 – 1	3

FIGURE 1–3

Histograms based on (a) a frequency table and (b) a grouped frequency table for the Aron et al. (1995) data.

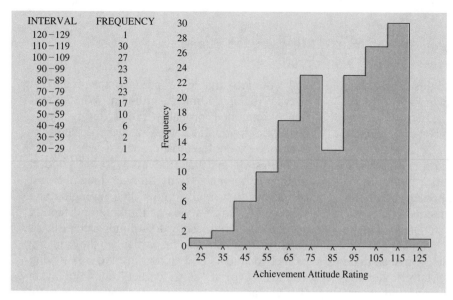

INTERVAL	FREQUENCY
120–129	1
110–119	30
100–109	27
90–99	23
80–89	13
70–79	23
60–69	17
50–59	10
40–49	6
30–39	2
20–29	1

FIGURE 1–4
Histogram for teachers' ratings of 153 students' attitudes toward achievement, based on grouped frequencies. (Data from Moorehouse & Sanders, 1992)

Frequency Polygons

Another way to graph the information in a frequency table is to make a special kind of line graph called a **frequency polygon.** In a frequency polygon, the line moves from point to point. The height of each point shows the number of scores that have that value. This creates a kind of mountain-peak skyline. Figure 1–5 shows the frequency polygons for the frequency tables in the

frequency polygon

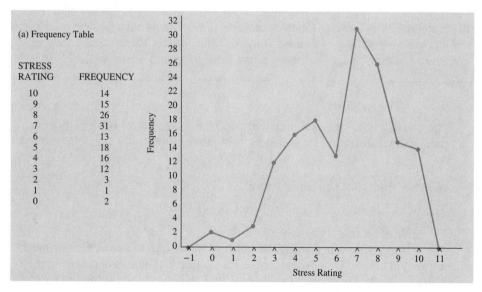

(a) Frequency Table

STRESS RATING	FREQUENCY
10	14
9	15
8	26
7	31
6	13
5	18
4	16
3	12
2	3
1	1
0	2

FIGURE 1–5
Frequency polygon based on a frequency table for the Aron et al. (1995) data.

BOX 1-1

Math Anxiety, Statistics Anxiety, and You: A Message for Those of You Who Truly Are Worried About This Course

Let's face it: Many of you dread this course, even to the point of having a full-blown case of "statistics anxiety" (Zeidner, 1991). If you become tense the minute you see numbers, we need to talk about that right now.

First, this course is a chance for a fresh start with the digits. Your past performance in (or avoidance of) geometry, trigonometry, calculus, or similar horrors need not influence in any way how well you comprehend statistics. This is largely a different subject.

Second, if your worry persists, you need to decide where it is coming from. Math or statistics anxiety, test anxiety, general anxiety, and general low self-confidence each seem to play their own role in students' difficulties with math courses (Cooper & Robinson, 1989; Dwinell & Higbee, 1991).

1. If math anxiety is your problem, we highly recommend Sheila Tobias's (1987) *Succeed with Math: Every Student's Guide to Conquering Math Anxiety.* Tobias, a former math avoider herself, suggests that your goal be "math mental health," which she defines as "the willingness to learn the math you need when you need it" (p. 12). (Could it be that this course in statistics is one of those times?)

Tobias explains that math mental health is usually lost in elementary school, when you are called to the blackboard, your mind goes blank, and you are unable to produce the one right answer to an arithmetic problem. What confidence remained probably faded during timed tests, which you did not realize were difficult for everyone except the most proficient few.

Tobias claims that students who are good at math are not necessarily smarter than the rest of us, but they really know their strengths and weaknesses, their styles of thinking and feeling around a problem. They do not judge themselves harshly for mistakes. In particular, they do not expect to understand things instantly. Allowing yourself to be a "slow learner" does not mean that you are less intelligent. It shows that you are growing in math mental health.

2. If test anxiety is your problem, you need to understand anxiety better. Any kind of anxiety produces arousal, and one of the best understood relationships in psychology is between arousal and performance. Whereas moderate arousal helps performance, too much or too little dramatically reduces performance. When arousal is the root of the problem, there is nothing wrong with the "hardware"—nothing wrong with your brain, your intelligence, or your studying of the material. When arousal exceeds a certain level, performance must go down. Things you have learned become harder to recall. Your mind starts to race, and this creates more anxiety, more arousal, and so on. Because some of your anxiety during a test may be that you are "no good and never will be," it is

stress ratings example. (Notice that two peaks merged into one in this example, so that information was lost by grouping scores.)

How to Make a Frequency Polygon

The five steps for making a frequency polygon follow:

1. Make a frequency table.
2. Place the values along the bottom. Be sure to include one extra value above and one extra value below the values that actually have scores in them. The extra values are needed so that the line starts and ends along the baseline of the graph, at zero frequency. This creates a closed or "polygon" figure.

important to reduce that additional source of arousal. Realize that your difficulty with tests is no indication of your real abilities.

There are many ways to reduce anxiety and arousal, such as learning to breathe properly and to take a quick break to relax deeply. Your counseling center should be able to help you or direct you to some good books on the subject.

Test anxiety specifically is reduced by over-preparing for a few tests, so that you go in with the certainty that you cannot possibly fail, no matter how aroused you become. The best time to begin applying this tactic is the first test of this course: There will be no old material to review, success will not depend on having understood previous material, and it will help you do better throughout the course. (You also might enlist the sympathy of your instructor or teaching assistant. Bring in a list of what you have studied, state why you are being so exacting, and ask if you have missed anything.) Your preparation must be ridiculously thorough, but only for a few exams. After these successes, your test anxiety should decline.

Also, create a practice test situation as similar to a real test as possible, making a special effort to duplicate the aspects that bother you most. If feeling rushed is the troubling part, once you think you are well prepared, set yourself a time limit for solving some homework problems. Make yourself write out answers fully and legibly. This may be part of what makes you feel slow during a test. If the presence of others bothers you, the sound of their scurrying pencils while yours is frozen in midair, do

your practice test with others in your course. Even make it an explicit contest to see who can finish first.

3. If you suspect that your problem is a general lack of confidence, or if there is something else in your life causing you to worry, we suggest that it is time you tried your friendly college counseling center.

A final word about anxiety and arousal. About 15 to 20% of humans (and all higher animals) are the sort that pick up on subtle stimulation more easily, often making them highly intuitive or even gifted. They are also easily overaroused by levels of stimulation that do not bother others (Eysenck, 1981; Kagan, 1994). This is an inborn difference in temperament (Thomas & Chess, 1977). You just have to learn to live with it.

We are in the process of doing research on this issue of highly sensitive people (Aron, 1996), but one thing we have seen already is that it helps to appreciate the helpful aspects of your trait and to make allowances for the disadvantage, like your tendency to be overaroused. It has to affect your performance on tests. What matters is what you actually know, which is probably quite a bit. This simple act of self-acceptance—that you are *not* less smart but *are* more sensitive—may in itself help ease your arousal when trying to express your statistical knowledge.

So good luck to all of you. We wish you the best while taking this course and in your lives.

3. Along the left side of the page, make a scale of frequencies that goes from 0 at the bottom to the highest frequency in any value.

4. Mark a point above each value corresponding to the frequency of that value.

5. Connect the points with lines.

Additional Frequency Polygon Example

Figure 1–6 shows the five steps in constructing a frequency polygon based on the grouped frequency table for the attitude toward achievement example.

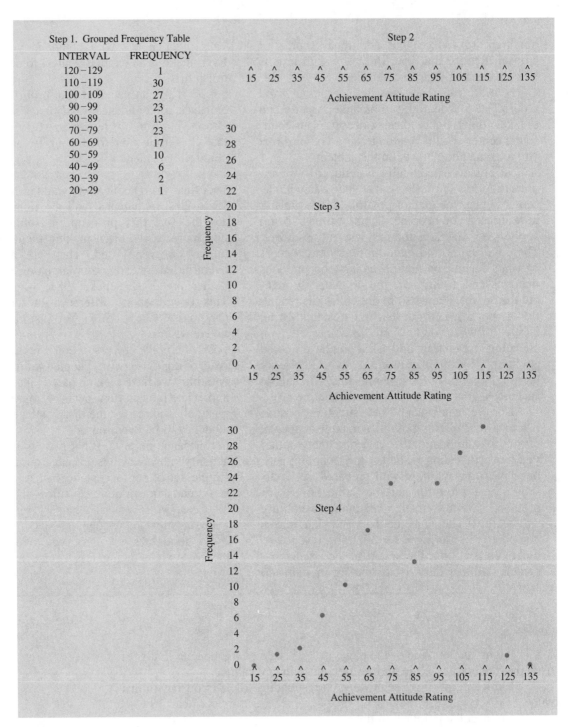

Step 1. Grouped Frequency Table

INTERVAL	FREQUENCY
120–129	1
110–119	30
100–109	27
90–99	23
80–89	13
70–79	23
60–69	17
50–59	10
40–49	6
30–39	2
20–29	1

FIGURE 1–6

Five steps in making a frequency polygon based on the grouped frequency table for teachers' ratings of 153 students' attitudes toward achievement. (Based on data from Moorehouse & Sanders, 1992) Step 1: Make a frequency table. Step 2: Place the values along the bottom. Step 3: Along the left side of the page, make a scale of frequencies that goes from 0 at the bottom to the highest frequency in any interval. Step 4: Mark a point above the center of each interval corresponding to the frequency of that interval. Step 5: Connect the points with lines.

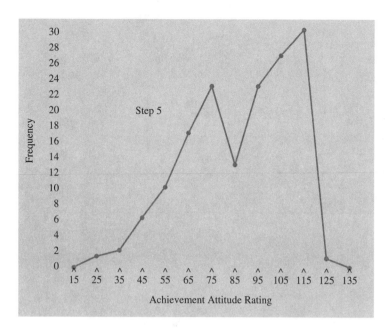

FIGURE 1–6 (*cont.*)

Shapes of Frequency Distributions

A frequency table, histogram, or frequency polygon describes a **frequency distribution.** That is, these show the pattern of how the frequencies are spread out, or "distributed."

Social scientists also find it useful to describe in words the pattern of how the frequency of scores is distributed. In general, these descriptions are of aspects of the shape of the pattern you see in a histogram or frequency polygon. These aspects and their special terminology are considered in this section.

frequency distribution

unimodal
bimodal
multimodal
rectangular

Unimodal and Bimodal Frequency Distributions

One important aspect of the shape of a frequency distribution is whether it has only one main high point (one high "tower" in the histogram or one main "peak" in the frequency polygon). For example, in the stress ratings, the most frequent score is a 7, giving a graph with only one very high area. Such a distribution is called **unimodal.** A distribution with two fairly equal high points is **bimodal.** Any distribution with two or more high points is called **multimodal.** Finally, a distribution in which all the values have about the same frequency is called **rectangular.** These frequency distributions are illustrated in Figure 1–7.

The information we collect in social science research is usually approximately unimodal. Bimodal and other multimodal distributions occasionally appear. A bimodal example would be the distribution of number of employees whose names have come to the attention of higher-level managers. If you made a frequency distribution for the quality of work of such employees, the high points in a graph of these would be at the values indicating that the quality of work was either very poor or very high. An example of a rectangular distribution is the number of children at each grade level attending an elementary school. There would be about the same number in first grade, second grade, and so on. These examples are illustrated in Figure 1–8.

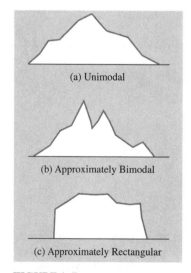

FIGURE 1–7
Examples of (a) unimodal, (b) approximately bimodal, and (c) approximately rectangular frequency polygons.

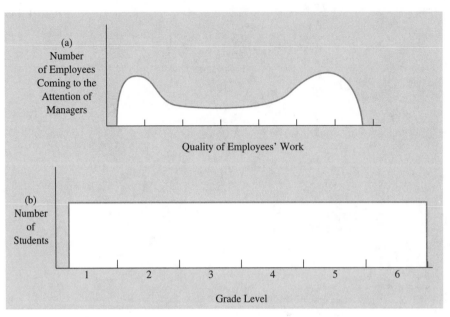

FIGURE 1–8
Fictional examples of distributions that are not unimodal: (a) A bimodal distribution showing the possible frequencies for different levels of quality of work of employees who come to the attention of higher-level managers. (b) A rectangular distribution showing the possible frequencies of students at different grade levels in an elementary school.

Symmetrical and Skewed Distributions

Another aspect of the stress ratings example is that the distribution was uneven, with more cases near the high end. This is somewhat unusual. Most things we measure in the social sciences have about equal numbers on both sides of the middle. That is, most distributions are approximately **symmetrical.** (If you folded them in half, the two halves would look the same.)

symmetrical

skewed

Distributions that clearly are not symmetrical are called **skewed.** The stress ratings distribution is an example of a skewed distribution. A skewed distribution has one side that is long and spread out, somewhat like a tail. The side with the fewer cases (the side that looks more like a tail) is the side that is what we use to describe the direction of the skew. Thus a distribution with too few cases to the right of the peak is said to be "skewed to the right." A distribution like the stress example, with too few cases at the low end, is skewed to the left. The other example we have examined in this chapter, the distributions of students' attitudes toward achievement, is skewed slightly to the left as well. Figure 1–9 illustrates symmetrical and skewed distributions.

FIGURE 1–9
Examples of frequency polygons of distributions that are (a) approximately symmetrical, (b) skewed to the right (positively skewed), and (c) skewed to the left (negatively skewed).

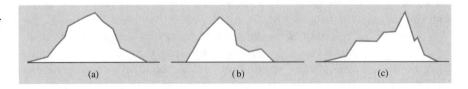

A distribution that is skewed to the right is also called positively skewed. A distribution skewed to the left is also called negatively skewed.

In practice, strongly skewed distributions come up in the social and behavioral sciences mainly when what is being measured has some upper or lower limit. For example, the distribution of the number of children in U.S. families is skewed to the right (see Figure 1–10) because it is not possible to have fewer than zero children! The situation in which many scores pile up at the low end because it is impossible to have a lower score is called a **floor effect.**

An example of a skewed distribution caused by an upper limit is illustrated in Figure 1–11. This is a distribution of adults' scores on a multiplication table test. This distribution is highly skewed to the left. Most of the scores pile up at the right, the high end (a perfect score). This is an example of a **ceiling effect.** The stress example also shows a mild ceiling effect. This is because many students had high levels of stress, the maximum rating was 10, and people often do not like to use ratings right at the maximum.

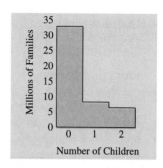

FIGURE 1–10
A distribution skewed to the right: number of children in U.S. families in 1988. (Data from U.S. Bureau of the Census, 1990)

floor effect
ceiling effect

Normal, Heavy-Tailed, and Light-Tailed Distributions

Finally, a distribution can be described in terms of whether its tails are particularly heavy (thick, with many cases in them) or light (thin, with few cases in them). These are called **heavy-tailed distributions** and **light-tailed distributions.** The standard of comparison is a bell-shaped curve. In social and behavioral science research and nature generally, distributions often are quite similar to this bell-shaped standard. It is called the **normal curve.** We will discuss this curve in some detail in later chapters. For now, however, the important thing is that the normal curve is a unimodal, symmetrical curve with average sort of tails—the sort of bell shape shown in Figure 1–12a. Both of

heavy-tailed distributions
light-tailed distributions

normal curve

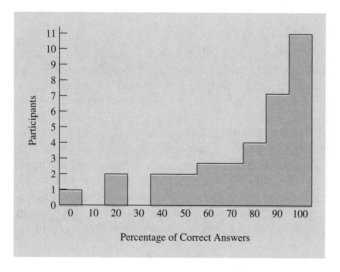

FIGURE 1–11
A distribution skewed to the left: fictional distribution of adults' scores on a multiplication table test.

Gender, Ethnicity, and Math Performance

From time to time, someone tries to argue that because some groups of people excel at math, on the average, this means that these groups are inherently better at math (or statistics). Other groups are said or implied to be worse. The issue comes up about men versus women, about members of social classes, and about ethnic groups.

Regarding gender, in spite of an occasional claim to the contrary, there is no support for the idea that men genetically are better at math (Tobias, 1982). It is true that the very top performers in math have tended to be male. However, the differences are slight, and the lowest performers are not more likely to be female, as would probably be the case if there were a genetic difference.

Tobias (1982) cites numerous studies providing nongenetic explanations for why women might not make it to the very top in math. For example, in a study of students identified by a math talent search, it was found that few parents arranged for their daughters to be coached before the talent exams. Sons were almost invariably coached. In another study of talented youths, parents of mathematically gifted girls were not even aware of their daughters' abilities, whereas parents of boys invariably were. In general, girls tend to avoid math classes, according to Tobias, especially accelerated classes, because parents, peers, and even teachers often advise them against pursuing too much math. So even though women are earning more PhDs in math than ever before, it is not surprising that math is the field with the highest dropout rate for women.

As for women's performance in statistics, we checked the grades in our own introductory statistics classes and simply found no reliable difference for gender. Neither did Buck (1985), in an analysis of 13 semesters of elementary and advanced undergraduate statistics courses.

Turning to the topic of ethnic differences, by the year 2000 fully 30% of U.S. youth will be African-American or Hispanic; yet, in 1986 only 9 African-Americans and Hispanics received doctoral degrees in mathematics, and only a handful of the top 10,000 college freshmen in these populations indicated an interest in math as their major. There are plenty of obvious reasons for this situation that have nothing to do with genetics. Like women, people of color are frequently not encouraged to study higher math. Worse, the schools serving them typically have fewer advanced math courses, qualified math teachers, and resources for teaching math and science. The lack of PhDs from within these communities is likely to perpetuate the disadvantage. All of this makes it clear that the real problem is not genes, but the attitudes that have fostered these inequalities in education.

our main examples in this chapter are roughly like a normal curve, except that both are somewhat skewed to the left and each of them has a secondary high point. In our experience, most distributions that result from social and behavioral science research are actually closer to the normal curve than these examples.

Figures 1–12b and 1–12c show examples of heavy-tailed and light-tailed distributions. Heavy-tailed distributions usually also have a low central peak compared to the normal curve. This is because in a heavy-tailed distribution more of the scores are at the two tails, so there are fewer left for the middle. An extreme case of a heavy-tailed distribution would be a rectangular distribution. In contrast, a light-tailed distribution usually has a high, narrow peak compared to a normal curve because fewer scores are in the two tails.

What can you do? One thing is to battle as best as you can this idea that math is "naturally" harder for you. It is harder only because you were told it would be, because you were discouraged from taking higher math courses, because your math instruction was probably not as good as it could have been. Catching up may be difficult, but if you need to work harder, that says nothing at all about your potential to learn statistics.

In changing the wrong ideas you have heard about your own abilities, it may help to know that you are participating in a widespread mistaken and crippling belief that math ability is innate, something you either have or lack. (So the conclusion too often is, why study a subject that you have no hope of mastering?) There is no evidence for innate ability but much evidence for performance differences due to effort.

Tobias (1987) cites a study comparing students in Asia and the United States on an international mathematics test. The U.S. students were thoroughly outperformed, but more important was why: Interviews revealed that Asian students saw math as an ability fairly equally distributed among people and thought that differences in performance were due to hard work. U.S. students persisted in this idea that mathematical ability is a rare, inborn talent.

Because, in fact, math almost never comes easily to anyone, thinking otherwise must work particularly against students who, because of gender or racial stereotypes or difficulty with English, are discouraged by lack of success early in their career with numbers.

There is simply no evidence for any inherent difference, and the performance differences that do exist need not predict anything at all about you. You are an individual, with your own brain and determination. It may take much more work for you to do well in this class than it will for others. However, it may be especially satisfying when you succeed in that hard work, when you have proved to yourself that you can master this subject matter and have modeled that achievement for others who will follow you.

Consider these words, from the former president of the Mathematics Association of America:

> The paradox of our times is that as mathematics becomes increasingly powerful, only the powerful seem to benefit from it. The ability to think mathematically—broadly interpreted—is absolutely crucial to advancement in virtually every career. Confidence in dealing with data, skepticism in analyzing arguments, persistence in penetrating complex problems, and literacy in communicating about technical matters are the enabling arts offered by the new mathematical sciences. (Steen, 1987, p. xviii)

Do not be left out because someone gave you the impression you could not or would not want to learn these "enabling arts."

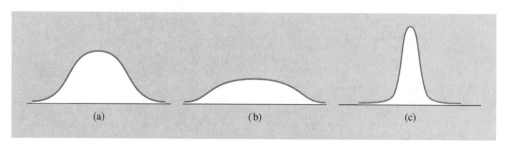

FIGURE 1–12
Examples of (a) normal, (b) heavy-tailed, and (c) light-tailed distributions.

Frequency Tables, Histograms, and Frequency Polygons in Research Articles

Frequency tables, histograms, and frequency polygons are used by researchers mainly as a step in more elaborate statistical procedures. They usually are not shown in research articles. When they are provided, it is often to give background information on the group studied. For example, Robert Bowman and Vicki Bowman (1995) conducted a survey of colleges about whether they offer courses to train resident assistants. Table 1–5, which is from their Table 1, describes the colleges that responded to their survey. There are actually four grouped frequency tables here, one each for private and public colleges for enrollments and housing capacity. The table makes it clear, for example, that the largest single group of public colleges that responded had enrollments in the 7,501 to 15,000 range while for the private colleges, the most common range was 2,501 to 7,500. (Notice, incidentally, that these researchers did not use equal intervals in their groupings. The advantage of the groupings they used is that they give more detail for the smaller enrollment and housing capacity schools. On the other hand, the lack of equal interval sizes makes it harder to get a clear idea of the shape of the distribution.)

Most often, frequency tables that appear in articles are for studies of nominal variables. Often, the tables give additional information, such as the rank of a particular category. (That is, the first ranked category is the one with the most cases.) Here is an example. This study was conducted by Hemant Shah and Gati Gayatri (1994). Shah is a professor of Journalism in the United States and Gayatri is a research officer in the Indonesian government. This study focused on the content of newspaper stories related to economic and social development in Indonesia. Specifically, the researchers examined two major Indonesian newspapers, analyzing for each paper one day's issue per week over a 16-week period. One of the newspapers, *Kompas,* was selected

TABLE 1–5
Demographic Information on Respondent Institutions

Descriptor	Public ($n = 92$) N%		Private ($n = 32$) N%	
Total Enrollment				
< 2,500	5	(5.4%)	12	(35.2%)
2,501–7,500	15	(16.3%)	15	(44.1%)
7,501–15,000	33	(35.8%)	3	(8.8%)
15,000–30,000	15	(16.3%)	0	
30,000+	10	(10.8%)	1	(2.9%)
Not Reported	14	(15.2%)	3	(8.8%)
Housing Capacity				
< 1,000	12	(13.0%)	11	(32.3%)
1,001–2,500	16	(17.3%)	13	(38.2%)
2,501–5,000	42	(45.6%)	4	(11.7%)
5,000+	15	(16.3%)	4	(11.7%)
Not Reported	7	(7.6%)	0	

Note: Data from Bowman & Bowman (1995).

as an example of an "elite" newspaper. *Kompas* is widely read by well-educated and influential people in the country. The other, *Poskota,* was selected as an example of a "nonelite" paper. It has a less well-educated readership who is generally of a lower economic status. Table 1–6 is taken from their article. It shows, for each paper, the number of news items in each development category, the percentage of news items in each category, and the rank of each category's frequency. Looking at the table, one finding that pops out is that the elite paper (*Kompas*) heavily emphasizes news on agriculture. Agriculture is the number one category, accounting for more than 13% of the development news items. The nonelite paper (*Poskota*), on the other hand, gives relatively little emphasis to agriculture. Agriculture is the number 10 category and accounts for about 3 1/2% of the development news items.

TABLE 1–6
Topics in Development News Items in *Kompas* and *Poskota*

	Kompas			*Poskota*		
	N	%	Rank	N	%	Rank
1. Agriculture	81	13.24	(1)	16	3.52	(10)
2. Industry	31	5.07	(7)	12	2.64	(14)
3. Mining	8	1.31	(23)	—	—	(28)
4. Energy	16	2.61	(14)	7	1.54	(22)
5. Transportation	37	6.05	(6)	68	14.98	(1)
6. Tourism	10	1.63	(22)	9	1.98	(18)
7. Trade	41	6.70	(5)	13	2.86	(13)
8. Cooperation	15	2.45	(15)	9	1.98	(18)
9. National Business	22	3.59	(11)	21	4.63	(6)
10. Manpower	18	2.94	(12)	18	3.96	(7)
11. Transmigration	3	0.49	(26)	—	—	(28)
12. Regional Development	44	7.19	(3)	46	10.13	(2)
13. Natural Resources, the Environment	15	2.45	(15)	9	1.98	(18)
14. Religion, Belief in One Supreme God	14	2.29	(19)	15	3.30	(11)
15. Education	50	8.17	(2)	27	5.95	(4)
16. Culture	12	1.96	(21)	6	1.32	(23)
17. Science, Technology, and Research	14	2.29	(19)	4	0.88	(25)
18. Health	15	2.45	(14)	17	3.74	(9)
19. Demography and Family Planning	2	0.33	(27)	6	1.32	(23)
20. Housing and Settlement	24	3.92	(9)	43	9.47	(3)
21. Social Welfare	5	0.82	(25)	12	2.64	(14)
22. Young Generation	2	0.33	(27)	3	0.66	(26)
23. Women's Role	2	0.33	(27)	3	0.66	(26)
24. Politics	43	7.03	(4)	27	5.95	(4)
25. Government Apparatus	7	1.14	(24)	10	2.20	(16)
26. Law	25	4.08	(8)	10	2.20	(16)
27. Information and Mass Media	23	3.76	(9)	18	3.96	(7)
28. Foreign Relations	18	2.94	(12)	8	1.76	(21)
29. Defense and National Security	15	2.45	(14)	14	3.08	(12)
Totals	612	100.01*		454	99.29*	

*rounding error
Note: Data from Shah & Gayatri (1994).

Summary

Social scientists use descriptive statistics to describe—to summarize and make understandable—a group of numbers from a research study.

A frequency table organizes the numbers into a table in which each of the possible values is listed from highest to lowest, along with the number of scores that have that value.

When there is a large number of different values, a grouped frequency table will be more useful. It is like an ordinary frequency table except that the frequencies are given for intervals that include a range of values.

The pattern of frequencies can be illustrated with a histogram, a kind of bar graph in which the height of each bar is the frequency for a particular value and there are no spaces between the bars. An alternative is a frequency polygon, in which a line connects dots, the height of each of which is the frequency for a particular value.

The general shape of the histogram or frequency polygon can be unimodal (having a single peak), bimodal, multimodal (including bimodal), or rectangular (having no peak); it can be symmetrical or skewed (having a long tail) to the right or the left; and compared to the bell-shaped normal curve, it can be light tailed or heavy tailed.

Frequency tables rarely appear in research articles. When they do, they often involve frequencies (and percentages) for various categories of a nominal variable rather than for the different numeric values of a numeric variable. Histograms and frequency polygons almost never appear in articles, though the shapes of distributions (normal, skewed, and so on) occasionally are described in words.

Key Terms

bimodal distribution	heavy-tailed distribution	numeric variable
ceiling effect	histogram	rectangular distribution
descriptive statistics	inferential statistics	score
floor effect	interval	skewed distribution
frequency distribution	light-tailed distribution	symmetrical distribution
frequency polygon	multimodal distribution	unimodal distribution
frequency table	nominal variable	value
grouped frequency table	normal curve	variable

Practice Problems

These problems involve computation (with the assistance of a calculator). Most real-life statistics problems are done on a computer. Even if you have a computer, do these by hand to ingrain the method in your mind.

For practice in using a computer to solve statistics problems, refer to the computer section of each chapter of the Student's Study Guide and Computer Workbook *that accompanies this text.*

All data are fictional (unless an actual citation is given).

Answers to selected problems are given at the back of the book.

1. Suppose that 50 students were asked how many hours they had studied last weekend and they responded as follows:

11, 2, 0, 13, 5, 7, 1, 8, 12, 11, 7, 8, 9, 10, 7, 4, 6, 10, 4, 7, 8, 6, 7, 10, 7, 3, 11, 18, 2, 9, 7, 3, 8, 7, 3, 13, 9, 8, 7, 7, 10, 4, 15, 3, 5, 6, 9, 7, 10, 6

(a) Make a frequency table; (b) make a frequency polygon based on the frequency table; and (c) describe the shape of the distribution.

2. The number of children in each of 30 classrooms in an elementary school follows.

24, 20, 35, 25, 25, 22, 26, 28, 38, 15, 25, 21, 24, 25, 25, 24, 25, 20, 32, 25, 22, 26, 26, 28, 24, 22, 26, 21, 25, 24

(a) Make a frequency table; (b) make a histogram based on the frequency table; and (c) describe the shape of the distribution.

3. Draw an example of each of the following distributions: (a) symmetrical, (b) rectangular, and (c) skewed to the right.

4. Explain to a person who has never had a course in statistics what is meant by (a) a symmetric, unimodal distribution and (b) a negatively skewed unimodal distribution. (Be sure to explain in your first answer what is meant by a distribution as well.)

5. Indicate a book and page number of your choice. (Choose a page with at least 30 lines.) Make a list of the number of words in each line; then use that list as your data set. (a) Make a frequency table; (b) make a histogram; (c) make a frequency polygon; and (d) describe the general shape of the distribution.

6. Give an example of something having these distribution shapes: (a) bimodal, (b) approximately rectangular, and (c) positively skewed. Do not use an example given in this book or in class.

2 The Mean, Variance, Standard Deviation, and Z Scores

As we noted in Chapter 1, the purpose of descriptive statistics is to make a group of scores understandable. We looked at some ways of providing that understanding through tables and graphs. In this chapter, we consider the main statistical techniques for describing a group of scores with numbers. These numbers are the mean, the variance, the standard deviation, and Z scores. The mean is the average score. The variance and standard deviation are about the amount of variation in the scores. A Z score describes a particular score in terms of how much that score varies from the average.

The Mean

Usually, the best single number for describing a group of scores is the ordinary average, the sum of all the scores divided by the number of scores. In statistics, this is called the **mean (M).**

mean (M)

Suppose that a political scientist does a study on experience in elected office. As part of this research, the political scientist determines the number of years served by mayors of the 10 largest cities in a particular region. The numbers of years served were as follows:

7, 8, 8, 7, 3, 1, 6, 9, 3, 8

The mean of these 10 scores is 6 (the sum of 60 years served divided by 10 mayors). That is, on the average, these 10 mayors had served 6 years in office. The information for the 10 mayors is thus summarized by this single number.

Many students find it helpful to visualize the mean as a kind of balancing point for the distribution of scores. Try it by visualizing a board balanced over a log, like a rudimentary teeter-totter. On the board, imagine piles of blocks distributed along the board according to their values, one for each score in the distribution. (This is a little like a histogram made of blocks.) The mean would be the point on the board where the weight of the blocks on each side would balance exactly. Figure 2–1 illustrates this for the case of our imaginary 10 mayors.

Some other examples are shown in Figure 2–2. Note that there need not even be a block right at the balance point. That is, the mean need not correspond to a value actually in the distribution. The mean is simply the average of the values, the balance point. The mean could even be a number that cannot possibly occur in the distribution. For example, a mean could be a decimal number when all the numbers in the distribution have to be whole numbers (2.3 children, for example). Also notice that the blocks can be very spread out or very close together and that they need not be spread out evenly. In any of these examples, it is still quite possible to mark a balance point. (By the way, this analogy to blocks balanced on a board on a log would, in reality, work precisely only if the board had no weight of its own.)

Formula for the Mean and Statistical Symbols

The rule for computing the mean we have seen is to add up all the scores and divide by the number of scores. This can be stated as the following formula:

$$M = \frac{\Sigma X}{N} \tag{2-1}$$

M is a symbol for the mean. (An alternative symbol, $\bar{X}$, sometimes called "X-bar," is widely used also.)

Σ

Σ, the capital Greek letter "sigma," is the symbol for "sum of." It means "add up all the numbers" for whatever follows. It is the most common special arithmetic symbol used in statistics.

X refers to scores in the distribution of the variable X. We could have selected any letter; however, if there is only one variable, it usually is called X. If you are dealing with two variables in the same formula, sometimes a second letter, Y, is used. Also, sometimes subscripts are used, as in X_1 and X_2. (In later chapters, we will be dealing with more than one distribution at a time.)

ΣX means "the sum of X." That is, this tells you to add up all the scores in the distribution of the variable X. Suppose X refers to the number of years in office in our example of 10 mayors: ΣX would equal 60, the sum of $7 + 8 + 8 + 7 + 3 + 1 + 6 + 9 + 3 + 8$.

N

N stands for number. It is used in statistics to mean the number of scores in a distribution. In our example, there are 10 scores. Thus, N equals 10.

FIGURE 2–1
Mean of the numbers of years in office for 10 mayors, illustrated through an analogy using blocks on a board balanced on a log.

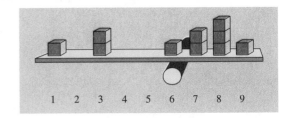

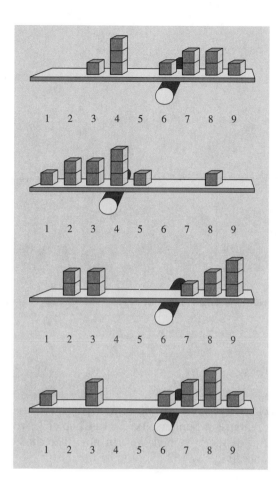

FIGURE 2–2
Means of various fictional distributions illustrated using the analogy of blocks on a board balanced on a log.

Overall, the formula says to divide the sum of all the scores in the distribution of the variable X by the total number of scores, N. In our example, this means we are to divide 60 by 10. Put in terms of the formula,

$$M = \frac{\Sigma X}{N} = \frac{60}{10} = 6$$

Additional Examples of Computing the Mean

Consider the examples from Chapter 1. The mean of the 151 statistics students' stress ratings (from Aron et al., 1995) is figured by adding up all the ratings and dividing by the number of ratings.

$$M = \frac{\Sigma X}{N} = \frac{975}{151} = 6.46$$

This tells you that the average stress rating on the 10-point scale was 6.46. This is a figure clearly well above the middle of that scale. This can also be illustrated with a graph. Think again of the histogram as a pile of blocks on a board and the mean of 6.46 as the point where the board balances on a fulcrum. (See Figure 2–3.) This single number much simplifies the information in the 151 stress scores.

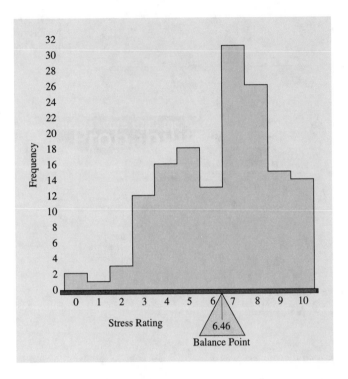

Similarly, consider the teachers' ratings of grade school students' attitudes toward achievement (Moorehouse & Sanders, 1992). In Chapter 1, we organized the original data into a frequency table. We can now take those same 153 scores, add them up, and divide by 153 to compute the mean:

$$M = \frac{\Sigma X}{N} = \frac{13,366}{153} = 87.36$$

This is illustrated in Figure 2–4.

Other Measures of the Typical or Representative Value of a Group of Scores

mode

The mean is only one of several ways of describing the typical or representative value in a group of scores. One alternative is the **mode.** The mode is the most common single number in a distribution. In our mayors' example, the mode is 8 because there are three cases of 8 years served in office and no other number of years served in office with as many cases. Another way to think of the mode is that it is the value with the largest frequency in a frequency table, the high point or peak of a distribution's frequency polygon or histogram (as shown in Figure 2–5).

In a perfectly symmetrical unimodal distribution, the mode is the same as the mean. However, when it is not the same, the mode is not really what we would usually think of as a good representative value. Also, it is possible to change some of the scores in a distribution (see Figure 2–6) without affecting the mode. The mean may be affected by many changes. The mean is more representative of all the numbers in the distribution. For these and other reasons, researchers use the mode only in very special situations.

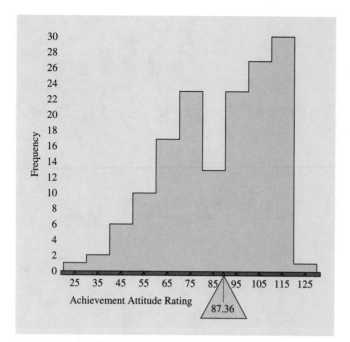

FIGURE 2–4
Analogy of blocks on a board balanced on a fulcrum (using a histogram) illustrating the mean for teachers' ratings of 153 grade school students' attitudes toward achievement. (Data from Moorehouse & Sanders, 1992)

Another alternative to the mean is the **median.** If you line up all the scores from highest to lowest, the middle score is the median. As shown in Figure 2–7, if you line up the numbers of years served in office from highest to lowest, the fifth and sixth scores (the two middle ones), are both 7s. Either way, the median is 7.

median

When you have an even number of scores, the median can fall between two different numbers. In that situation, you use the average of the two.

In certain cases, the median is better than the mean as a typical or representative value for a group of scores. This happens when there are a few extreme scores that would strongly affect the mean but would not affect the median. For example, suppose that among the 100 families on a banana plantation in Central America, 99 families have an annual income of $100 and 1 family (the owner's) has an annual income of $90,100. The mean family income on this plantation would be $1,000 ($99 \times 100 = 9,900$; $9,900 + 90,100 = 100,000$; $100,000/100 = 1,000$). That is, no family has an income even close to $1,000, so this number is completely misleading. The median income in this case would be $100—a figure much more typical of whomever you would meet if you walked up to someone randomly on the plantation.

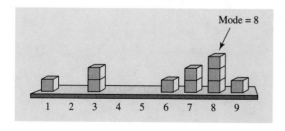

FIGURE 2–5
Illustration of the mode as the high point in a distribution's histogram, using the fictional example of the number of years in office served by 10 mayors.

The Mean 27

FIGURE 2–6
Illustration of the effect on the mean and on the mode of changing some scores, using the fictional example of the number of years in office served by 10 mayors.

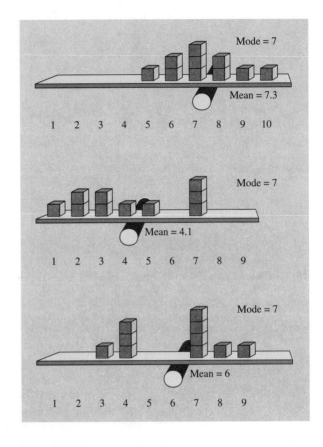

The median is used occasionally in the social sciences as a descriptive statistic. Again, it is most likely to be used in situations in which there are a few extreme scores, called **outliers,** that would make the mean unrepresentative of most of the scores.

outliers

The Variance and the Standard Deviation

Researchers also want to know how spread out a distribution is. For example, suppose you were asked, "How old are the students in your statistics class?" At a city-based university with many returning and part-time students, the mean age might turn out to be 38. So you could tell whoever asked you, "The average age is 38." However, this would not tell the whole story. It would be possible, for example, to have a mean of 38 because every student in the class was exactly 38 years old. Or, you could have a mean of 38 because exactly half the class was 18 and the other half was 58. These would be two quite different situations.

FIGURE 2–7
Illustration of the median as the middle score when scores are lined up from highest to lowest, using the fictional example of the number of years in office served by 10 mayors.

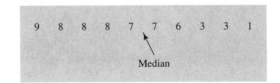

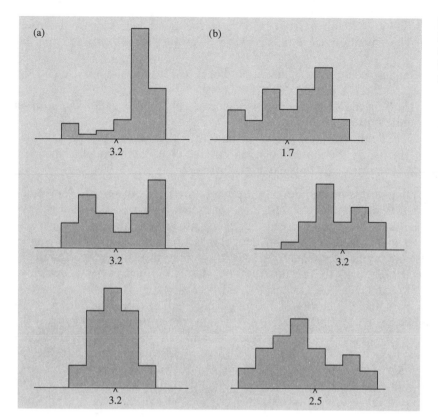

FIGURE 2–8
Examples of distributions with (a) the same mean but different amounts of spread and (b) different means but the same amount of spread.

Figure 2–8 shows three different frequency distributions with the same mean but different amounts of spread around the mean, and three with different means but the same amount of spread.[1]

The Variance

The **variance** (SD^2) of a group of numbers tells how spread out the scores are around the mean. To be precise, the variance is the average of each score's squared difference from the mean.[2] These are the steps to compute the variance:

variance (SD^2)

[1]There is also another way to describe the spread of a group of scores. You can just subtract—take the highest score minus the lowest score. This is called the *range* of a group of scores. For example, suppose that for a particular class the highest score on a midterm is 98 and the lowest score on the midterm is 60. The range is 38 (that is, 98 − 60 = 38). However, the range rarely is used by researchers because it is a very crude way of describing the spread. It is crude because it does not take into account how clumped together the scores are within the range.

[2]You may wonder why we do not just use the deviation scores themselves, simply making all deviations positive, and use the average of these. This was actually done in the past and gives a statistic called the *average deviation*. Unfortunately, however, in spite of its simplicity, the average deviation does not work out very well as part of more complicated statistical procedures. This is because it is hard to do algebraic manipulations with a formula that ignores the signs of some of its numbers.

There is also a deeper reason why we use the squared approach. Using the squared deviations gives more influence to large deviations (squaring a deviation of 4 gives a squared deviation of 16; squaring a deviation of 8 gives a squared deviation of 64). Deviation scores often are thought of as "errors": The mean is expected, and deviations from it are errors from what is expected. Thus using squared scores has the effect of "penalizing" large errors to a greater extent than small errors.

1. Subtract the mean from each score; this gives each score's **deviation score.** The deviation score tells how far away the actual score is from the mean.

2. Square each of these deviation scores. (Multiply each by itself.) This gives each score's **squared deviation score.**

3. Add up the squared deviation scores. This total is called the **sum of squared deviations.**

4. Divide the sum of squared deviations by the number of squared deviations (that is, by the number of scores). This gives the average or mean of squared deviations, which is called the variance.

Although this procedure may seem a bit awkward or hard to remember at first, it works quite well. Suppose one distribution is more spread out than another. The more spread-out distribution has a larger variance because being spread makes the deviation scores bigger. If the deviation scores are bigger, the squared deviation scores also are bigger, and the variance bigger. In the example of the class in which everyone was exactly 38 years old, the variance would be exactly 0. That is, there would be no variance. (In terms of the numbers, each person's deviation score would be $38 - 38 = 0$; 0 squared is 0. The average of a bunch of zeros is 0.) By contrast, the class of half 18-year-olds and half 58-year-olds would have a rather large variance of 400. (The 18-year-olds would each have deviation scores of $18 - 38 = -20$. The 58-year-olds would have deviation scores of $58 - 38 = 20$. In both cases, the squared deviation scores, which are -20 squared or 20 squared, would come out to 400. The average of all 400s is 400.)

The variance is important in many other statistical procedures. However, the variance is used only occasionally as a descriptive statistic. This is because the variance is based on squared deviation scores and squared deviation scores do not give a very easy-to-understand sense of how spread out the actual, nonsquared scores are. For example, it is clear that a class with a variance of 400 has a more spread-out distribution than one whose variance is 200. However, the number 400 does not give an obvious insight into the actual variation among the ages, none of which are anywhere near 400.

The Standard Deviation

The statistic most widely used for describing the spread of a group of scores is the **standard deviation (*SD*).** The standard deviation is the positive square root of the variance: To find the standard deviation, you first compute the variance and then take its square root. If the variance of a distribution is 400, the standard deviation is 20. If the variance is 9, the standard deviation is 3. If the variance is 100, the standard deviation is 10; and so on.

The variance is about squared deviations from the mean. Therefore, its square root, the standard deviation, is about direct, ordinary, not-squared deviations from the mean. *Roughly speaking, the standard deviation is the average amount that scores differ from the mean.* For example, consider a class where the ages have a standard deviation of 20 years. This would tell us that the ages are spread out, on the average, about 20 years in each direction from the mean. Knowing the standard deviation gives you a general sense of the degree of spread.

The standard deviation is not exactly the average amount that scores differ from the mean. To be precise, the standard deviation is the square root of the average of the scores' squared deviations from the mean. This squaring, averaging, and then taking the square root gives a slightly different result from simply averaging the scores' deviations from the mean. Still, the result of this approach has technical advantages to outweigh this slight disadvantage of giving only an approximate description of the average variation from the mean.

Formulas for the Variance and the Standard Deviation

We have seen that the variance is the average squared deviation from the mean. In symbols, this is how it looks:

$$SD^2 = \frac{\Sigma(X - M)^2}{N}$$

(2–2)

SD^2 is the symbol for the variance. (Shortly, you will learn another symbol, S^2. This other symbol is for a slightly different kind of variance.) SD is short for *standard deviation*. The symbol SD^2 emphasizes that the variance is the standard deviation squared.

The top part of the formula describes the sum of squared deviations. X is for each score and M is the mean. Thus, $X - M$ is the score minus the mean, or the deviation score. The exponent, 2, tells you to square each deviation score. Finally, the sum sign (Σ) tells you to add together all these squared deviation scores. The bottom part of the formula tells you to divide the sum of squared deviation scores by N, the number of scores.[3]

---

[3]In actual research situations, researchers must often figure the variance and the standard deviation for distributions with a great many scores, often involving decimals or large numbers. This can make the whole process quite time-consuming, even with a calculator. To deal with this problem, over the years, a number of shortcut formulas were developed to simplify the computation. A shortcut formula of this type is called a *computational formula*. The computational formula for the variance is

$$SD^2 = \frac{\Sigma X^2 - (\Sigma X)^2 / N}{N}$$

(2–6)

Note that ΣX^2 means that you square each score and then take the sum of these squared scores. However, $(\Sigma X)^2$ means that you first add up all the scores and then take the square of this sum. This formula is easier to use if you are computing the variance for a lot of numbers by hand because you do not have to first find the deviation score for each raw score.

However, these days computational formulas are mainly of historical interest and are used by researchers only when computers are not readily available to do the computations. In fact, when it comes to figuring the variance and the standard deviation, even many hand calculators are set up so that you need only enter the scores and press a button or two to get the variance and the standard deviation.

We give a few computational formulas in footnotes in this book, just so they will be available in case a student is doing a research project involving a lot of numbers and does not have access to a computer. We do not feel that the computational formulas are useful for learning statistics. Rather they tend to obscure the meaning of the computations. It is much better when carrying out the practice problems to use the formulas we give in the main text, which are designed to help strengthen your understanding of what the computations mean. The formulas we give in the main text are called *definitional formulas*.

The standard deviation is the square root of the variance. So, if you already know the variance, the formula is

$$SD = \sqrt{SD^2}$$

(2–3)

Example of Computing the Variance and the Standard Deviation

Table 2–1 shows the computation of the variance and standard deviation for our example of mayors. (The table assumes we already have figured out the mean to be 6 years in office.) Usually, it is easiest to do your figuring using a calculator, especially one with a square root key.

Additional Example of Computing the Variance and the Standard Deviation

Table 2–2 shows the arithmetic for figuring the variance and standard deviation for the teachers' ratings of grade school students' attitudes toward achievement, which was discussed in Chapter 1. (To save space, the table shows only the first few and last few scores.)

Roughly speaking, this result means that a student's attitude toward achievement varies from the mean by an average of 22.55 points. This can also be shown on a histogram (Figure 2–9).

The Variance as the Sum of Squared Deviations Divided by N – 1

Researchers often use a slightly different kind of variance. We have defined the variance as the average of the squared deviation scores. That means

TABLE 2–1
Computation of Variance and Standard Deviation in the Example of Number of Years Served in Office by the 10 Mayors of a Particular Region

Score (Number of Years Served)	–	Mean Score (Mean Number of Years Served)	=	Deviation Score	Squared Deviation Score
7		6		1	1
8		6		2	4
8		6		2	4
7		6		1	1
3		6		–3	9
1		6		–5	25
6		6		0	0
9		6		3	9
3		6		–3	9
8		6		2	4
				Σ: 0	66

$$\text{Variance} = SD^2 = \frac{\Sigma(X - M)^2}{N} = \frac{SS}{N} = \frac{66}{10} = 6.6$$

$$\text{Standard deviation} = SD = \sqrt{SD^2} = \sqrt{6.6} = 2.57$$

TABLE 2–2
Computation of Variance and Standard Deviation for Children's Attitudes Toward Achievement (Showing Only First Few and Last Few Scores)

Attitude Score	−	Attitude Score Mean	=	Deviation Score	Squared Deviation Score
77		87.36		−10.36	107.33
78		87.36		−9.36	87.61
98		87.36		10.64	113.21
85		87.36		−2.36	5.57
59		87.36		−28.36	804.29
59		87.36		−28.36	804.29
.		.		.	.
.		.		.	.
.		.		.	.
93		87.36		5.64	31.81
68		87.36		−19.36	374.81
70		87.36		−17.36	301.37
114		87.36		26.64	709.69
91		87.36		3.64	13.25
				Σ:0.00	77,807.84

$$\text{Variance} = SD^2 = \frac{\Sigma(X-M)^2}{N} = \frac{77{,}807.84}{153} = 508.55$$

$$\text{Standard deviation} = SD = \sqrt{SD^2} = \sqrt{508.55} = 22.55$$

Note: Data from Moorehouse & Sanders (1992).

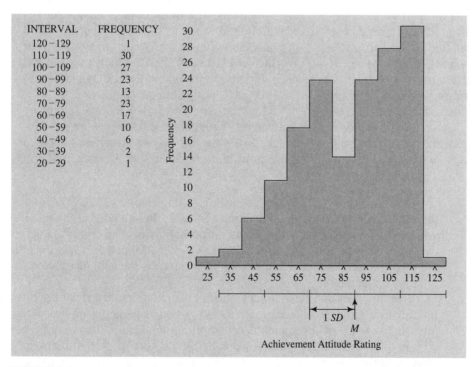

INTERVAL	FREQUENCY
120–129	1
110–119	30
100–109	27
90–99	23
80–89	13
70–79	23
60–69	17
50–59	10
40–49	6
30–39	2
20–29	1

FIGURE 2–9
Graphic description of the standard deviation as the distance along the base of a histogram, using teachers' ratings of grade school students' attitudes toward achievement. (Data from Moorehouse & Sanders, 1992)

BOX 2–1

The Psychology of Statistics and the Tyranny of the Mean

Looking in the leading journals of psychology, you would think that statistical methods are that field's sole tool and language. Psychology has also initiated several rebellions against the reign of statistics. One of the most unexpected came from the leader of behaviorism, the school of psychology most dedicated to keeping the field strictly scientific.

Behaviorism opposed the study of inner states because inner events are impossible to observe objectively. (Today most research psychologists claim to measure inner events indirectly but objectively.) Behaviorism's most famous advocate, B. F. Skinner, was quite opposed to statistics. Skinner even said, "I would much rather see a graduate student in psychology taking a course in physical chemistry than in statistics. And I would include [before statistics] other sciences, even poetry, music, and art" (Evans, 1976, p. 93).

Skinner was constantly pointing to the information lost by averaging the results of a number of cases. For instance, Skinner (1956) cited the example of three overeating mice—one naturally obese, one poisoned with gold, and one whose hypothalamus had been altered. Each had a different curve for learning to press a bar for food. If these learning curves had been summed or merged statistically, the result would have represented no actual eating habits of any real mouse at all. As Skinner said, "These three individual curves contain more information than could probably ever be generated with measures re-

quiring statistical treatment, yet they will be viewed with suspicion by many psychologists because they are single cases" (p. 232).

A different voice of caution was raised by another school of psychology, humanistic psychology, which began in the 1950s as a "third force" in reaction to Freudian psychoanalysis and behaviorism. The point of humanistic psychology was that human consciousness should be studied intact, as a whole, as it is experienced by individuals. Although statistics can be usefully applied to ascertain the mathematical relationships between phenomena, including events in consciousness, human conscious experience can never be fully explained by reducing it to numbers (any more than it can be reduced to words). Each individual's experience is unique.

This viewpoint existed in psychology even before humanistic psychology. In clinical psychology and the study of personality, voices have always been raised in favor of the in-depth study of one person instead of or as well as the averaging of persons. The philosophical underpinnings of the in-depth study of individuals can be found in phenomenology, which began in Europe after World War I (Husserl, 1970). This viewpoint has been important throughout the social and behavioral sciences, not just in psychology.

Today, the rebellion is led in psychology by qualitative research methodologies (e.g., McCracken, 1988), an approach which is much more prominent in other social and behavioral

dividing the sum of squared deviation scores by the number of scores. But you learn in Chapter 8 that for many purposes it is instead correct to define the variance as the sum of squared deviation scores divided by 1 less than the number of scores. In these situations, the variance is the sum of squared deviations divided by $N - 1$.

The variances and standard deviations given in research articles are often figured using the $N - 1$ approach. Also, when calculators or computers give the variance or the standard deviation automatically, they may be figured in this way. The approach you are learning in this chapter of dividing by N is entirely correct for the purposes for which we have been using it (describing the variation in a particular group of scores). It is also entirely correct for the material covered in the rest of this chapter (Z scores of the kind we are using), and for the material in Chapters 3 through 7. We

sciences. The qualitative research methods were developed mainly in anthropology and typically involve long interviews or observations of a few subjects. The highly skilled researcher decides, as the event is taking place, what is important to remember, record, and pursue through more questions or observations. The mind of the researcher is the main tool because, according to this approach, only that mind can find the important relationships among the many categories of events arising in the respondent's speech.

Many in psychology who favor qualitative methods argue for a blend: First, discover the important categories through a qualitative approach. Then, determine their incidence in the larger population through quantitative methods. Too often, these advocates would argue, quantitative researchers jump to conclusions about a phenomenon without first exploring the human experience of it through free-response interviews or observations.

Finally, Carl Jung, founder of Jungian psychology, sometimes spoke of the "statistical mood" and its effect on a person's feeling of uniqueness. The Jungian analyst Marie Louise von Franz (1979) wrote about Jung's thoughts on this subject: When we walk down a street and observe the hundreds of blank faces and begin to feel diminished, or even so overwhelmed by overpopulation that we are glad that humans don't live forever, this is the statistical mood. We feel how much we are just part of the crowd, ordinary. Yet von Franz points out that if some catastrophe were to happen, each person would respond uniquely. There is at least as much irregularity to life as ordinariness. As she puts it,

> The fact that this table does not levitate, but remains where it is, is only because the billions and billions and billions of electrons which constitute the table tend statistically to behave like that. But each electron in itself could do something else. (pp. IV–17)

Likewise, when we are in love, we feel that the other person is unique and wonderful. Yet in a statistical mood, we realize that the other person is ordinary, like many others.

Jung did not cherish individual uniqueness just to be romantic about it, however. He held that the important contributions to culture tend to come from people thinking at least a little independently or creatively, and their independence is damaged by this statistical mood.

Further, von Franz argues that a statistical mood is damaging to love and life. "An act of loyalty is required towards one's own feelings" (pp. IV–18). Feeling "makes your life and your relationships and deeds feel unique and gives them a definite value" (pp. IV–19). In particular, feeling the importance of our single action makes immoral acts—war and killing, for example—less possible. We cannot count the dead as numbers but must treat them as persons with emotions and purposes, like ourselves.

In short, there are definite arguments for limiting our statistical thinking to its appropriate domains and leaving our heart free to rule in others.

mention this $N - 1$ approach here only so you will not be confused when you read about variance or standard deviation in other places or if your calculator or a computer program gives a surprising result. To keep things simple, we wait to discuss the $N - 1$ approach until it is needed, starting in Chapter 8.

Z Scores

So far you have learned about describing a group of scores in terms of its mean and variation. In this section, you learn how to describe a particular score in terms of where it fits into the overall group of scores. That is, you learn to describe a score in terms of whether it is above or below the average and how much above or below the average.

Suppose that you were told that a particular mayor, the Honorable Julia Hernandez, has served in this office in her town for 9 years. Now, suppose we did not know anything about the number of years served in office by other mayors in the region. In that case, it would be hard to tell whether this mayor had served a lot or a few years in relation to other mayors in her region. However, suppose we do know that for the 10 mayors in her region, the mean is 6 and the standard deviation is 2.57. With this knowledge, it is clear that Ms. Hernandez has served an above-average number of years. It is also clear that the amount she has served more than the average (3 years in office more than average) was a bit more than the amount mayors in her region typically vary from the average. This is all illustrated in Figure 2–10.

What Is a Z Score?

Z score

A **Z score** is an ordinary score converted so that it better describes that score's place in its distribution. Specifically, a Z score is the number of standard deviations the score is above the mean (if it is positive) or below the mean (if it is negative). The standard deviation now becomes a kind of yardstick, a unit of measure in its own right. In our mayoral example, Ms. Hernandez, who has served 9 years in office, has a Z score of +1.17 because she was 1.17 standard deviations above the mean (a little more than 1 standard deviation of 2.57 years in office above the mean). Another mayor, the Honorable Samuel Phillips has served 6 years in office. He has a Z score of 0 because his score is exactly the mean. That is, his score is 0 standard deviations above or below the mean. What about a mayor who had served only 1 year in office? That mayor has served 5 less than average. This would be nearly 2 standard deviations below the mean (a Z score of –1.95). This mayor would be about twice as far below average as mayors in this region typically vary from the average.

Z Scores as a Scale

raw scores

Figure 2–11 shows, for our mayoral example, a scale of Z scores lined up against a scale of **raw scores.** (A raw score is an ordinary score, as opposed to a Z score.) The two scales are something like a ruler with inches lined up on one side and centimeters on the other or like a thermometer with Fahrenheit scale on one side and the Celsius scale on the other.

FIGURE 2–10
Relation of the number of years in office served by a particular mayor (Ms. Hernandez) to the overall distribution of number of years in office served by all mayors in a particular (fictional) region.

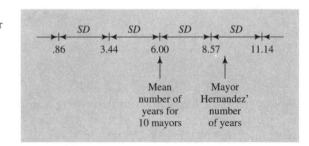

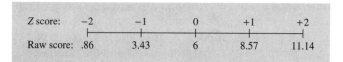

FIGURE 2–11
Scales of Z scores and raw scores in the mayoral example.

Additional Examples

Z scores have many practical uses. They also are important for many of the statistical procedures you learn later in this book. It is important that you become very familiar with them.

Let us take another example. Suppose that a developmental specialist observed 3-year-old Peter in a standardized laboratory situation playing with other children of the same age. During the observation, the specialist counted the number of times Peter spoke to the other children. The result, over several observations, is that Peter spoke to other children about 8 times per hour of play. Without any standard of comparison, it would be hard to draw any conclusions from this. Suppose, however, that it was known from previous research that under similar conditions the mean number of times children speak is 12, with a standard deviation of 4. Clearly, Peter spoke less often than other children in general, but not extremely less often. Peter would have a Z score of –1. (If $M = 12$ and $SD = 4$, a score of 8 is 1 SD below M.) Suppose Ian was observed speaking to other children 20 times in an hour. Ian would clearly be unusually talkative, with a Z score of +2. Ian would speak not merely more than the average but more by twice as much as children tend to vary from the average! (See Figure 2–12.)

Z Scores as Providing a Generalized Standard of Comparison

Another advantage of Z scores is that scores on completely different variables can be converted to Z scores and compared. With Z scores, the mean is always 0 and the standard deviation is always 1.[4] (Because Z scores have these standard values, they are also sometimes called *standard scores*.)

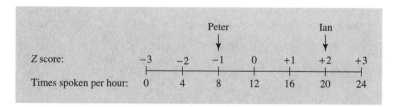

FIGURE 2–12
Number of times each hour that two children spoke, expressed as raw scores and Z scores (fictional data).

[4]As an example, suppose you have three scores: 1, 2, and 6.

$$M = \frac{1+2+6}{3} = 3 \quad SD^2 = \frac{(1-3)^2 + (2-3)^2 + (6-3)^2}{3} = \frac{14}{3} = 4.67$$

$$SD = \sqrt{4.67} = 2.16$$

Z scores: $(1-3)/2.16 = -.93 \quad (2-3)/2.16 = -.46 \quad (6-3)/2.16 = 1.39$

M of Z scores: $\frac{-.93 + -.46 + 1.39}{3} = \frac{0}{3} = 0$

SD^2 of Z scores: $\frac{(-.93 - 0)^2 + (-.46 - 0)^2 + (1.39 - 0)^2}{3} = \frac{3}{3} = 1 \quad SD = 1$

If the same children in our example were also measured on a test of language skill, we could directly compare the Z scores on language skill to the Z scores on speaking to other children. Suppose that Peter had a score of 100 on the language skill test. If the mean on that test was 82 and the standard deviation was 6, then clearly Peter is much better than average at language skill, with a Z score of +3. It seems unlikely that Peter's less than usual amount of speaking to other children is due to poorer than usual language skill. (See Figure 2–13.)

Notice in this latest example that by using Z scores, we can directly compare the results of both the specialist's observation of the amount of talking and the language skill test. This is almost as wonderful as being able to compare apples and oranges!

Converting a number to a Z score is a bit like converting the words for measurement in various obscure languages into one language that everyone can understand—inches, cubits, and zinqles (we made that last one up), for example, into centimeters. It is a very valuable tool.

Converting a Raw Score to a Z Score

An ordinary score is called a raw score. As we noted, a Z score is the number of standard deviations the raw score falls above (or, if negative, below) its mean. To figure a Z score, subtract the mean from the raw score, giving the deviation score. Then, divide the deviation score by the standard deviation. In symbols, the formula is

$$Z = \frac{X - M}{SD} \tag{2–4}$$

For example, using the formula for the child who scored 100 on the language test,

$$Z = \frac{X - M}{SD} = \frac{100 - 82}{6} = \frac{18}{6} = 3$$

Converting a Z Score to a Raw Score

To change a Z score back to a raw score, the process is reversed: You multiply the Z score by the standard deviation and then add the mean. The formula is

$$X = (Z)(SD) + M \tag{2–5}$$

FIGURE 2–13
Scales of Z scores and raw scores for number of times spoken per hour and language skill, showing the first child's score on each (fictional data).

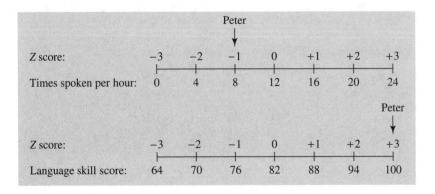

(Remember that when two symbols, or two parentheses, are next to each other in formulas, this means you are supposed to multiply them. If we used "$\times$" to mean multiply in a formula like this, it might be confused with the X meaning the score.)

For example, if a child has a Z score of -1.5 on the language ability test, then the child is 1.5 standard deviations below the mean. Because a standard deviation in this example is 6 raw score points, the child is 9 raw score points below the mean. The mean is 82, so 9 points below this is 73. Using the formula,

$$X = (Z)(SD) + M = (-1.5)(6) + 82 = -9 + 82 = 73$$

Additional Examples of Computing Z Scores from Raw Scores and Vice Versa

Consider the stress ratings' example we used in Chapter 1. The mean of that distribution was 6.46, and the standard deviation was 2.30. Figure 2–14 shows the relationship of the raw score and Z score scales. If a student's stress raw score was 9, the student is clearly above the mean. Specifically, using the formula,

$$Z = \frac{X - M}{SD} = \frac{9 - 6.46}{2.3} = \frac{2.54}{2.3} = 1.10$$

In comparison, a student with a Z score of -2.5 has a stress raw score well below the mean. Using the formula, the raw stress score is computed as

$$X = (Z)(SD) + M = (-2.5)(2.3) + 6.46 = -5.75 + 6.46 = .71$$

Consider some examples from the study of childrens' attitudes toward achievement (Moorehouse & Sanders, 1992). Recall that the mean was 87.36 and the standard deviation was 22.55. A child who scored 87 had a deviation score of $-.36$ (that is $87 - 87.36 = -.36$). The Z score is then $-.02$ (that is $-.36/22.55 = -.02$). This score is just under the mean. Similarly, a child who scored 120 had a deviation score of 32.64 (that is, $120 - 87.36 = 32.64$). The Z score is 1.45 (that is $32.64/22.55 = 1.45$). This child is 1.45 standard deviations above the mean.

To go the other way, suppose that you knew that a child's Z score was 0.56. This child's raw score would be the Z score times the standard deviation, plus the mean: $(.56)(22.55) + 87.36 = 99.99$. These relationships are illustrated in Figure 2–15.

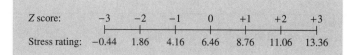

FIGURE 2–14
Raw score and Z score scales for 151 statistics students' ratings of their stress level (data from Aron et al., 1995), showing the scores of two sample individuals.

FIGURE 2–15
Raw score and Z score scales for teachers' ratings of 153 grade school students' attitudes toward achievement (Moorehouse & Sanders, 1992), showing scores of three sample individuals.

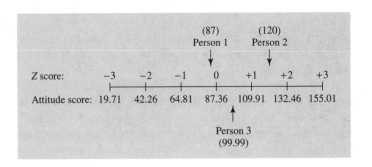

The Mean, Variance, Standard Deviation, and Z Scores as Used in Research Articles

The mean and the standard deviation (and occasionally the variance) are commonly reported in research articles. Sometimes mean and standard deviation are included in the text of an article. For example, our fictional political scientist, in a research article about the mayors of this region, would write, "At the time of the study, the mean number of years in office for the 10 mayors in this region was 6.0 ($SD = 2.57$)."

More commonly, however, means and standard deviations are given in tables. This is especially likely to be the case if there are different groups studied, or several variables are involved. For example, Goidel and Langley (1995) conducted a study of the relation of positivity and negativity of newspaper accounts of economic events in the period just before the 1992 U.S. Presidential election. As part of their study, they presented a table showing the monthly means and standard deviations for numbers of front-page articles on economic news in the *New York Times* for the 23 months preceding the election. (See Table 2–3.) (Note that their table also gives the number of articles in the month with the fewest articles and the number in the month with the most articles.) The table also gives the total number of all articles (whether on economic events or not). After presenting this table, Goidel and Langley commented as follows:

> As can be seen in Table 1 [our Table 2–3], during the average month, we would expect roughly six front-page articles devoted to the economy. In addition, we would expect one or two of these articles to have a positive tone and one or two of the articles to have a negative tone (and two or three of the articles to be neutral). Also worth noting in Table 1 is that there is considerable variation regard-

TABLE 2–3

Descriptive Statistics for News Coverage Variables Aggregated by Month, *New York Times Index*, January 1981–November 1992.

	Mean	Standard Deviation	Range	Total
Total Front-Page Articles	5.84	4.10	0–22	835
Positive Front-Page Articles	1.64	1.33	0–6	261
Negative Front-Page Articles	1.83	1.92	0–11	234

Source: *New York Times Index.*

Note: Data from Goidel & Langley (1995).

ing the total number of articles within any given month as well as the general tone of these articles. (p. 318)

What about Z scores? They are used widely when figuring more complicated statistics. Z scores are only rarely discussed directly in published research articles. Occasionally, however, if an article talks about individuals, comparisons to other individuals or to the general population will be made using Z scores. Also, in studies in which several different measures are used, the various kinds of raw scores may be converted to Z scores so that comparisons between measures will be more readily understood. For example, Huber (1991) compared supervisors' and employees' ratings of five aspects of the various jobs performed at a major television station. The five aspects of the jobs were measured on different scales, with different means and different standard deviations. Thus, as shown in Table 2–4, in addition to using raw scores, Huber converted the scores for all participants in the study on each scale to Z scores and then computed the means and standard deviations of these Z scores separately for supervisors and employees ("incumbents" on her table). Notice that the two groups tended to give about the same ratings for skill (a fairly objective aspect of a job), but in the other categories, supervisors tended to rate the jobs considerably lower than the employees did. Z scores make such comparisons much easier.

TABLE 2–4
Means and Standard Deviations of Supervisors' and Incumbents' Job Evaluation Ratings

Compensable Factor	Supervisors		Incumbents	
	Points	*Z score*	*Points*	*Z score*
Skill				
M	217.78	.06	213.41	− .04
SD	76.01	.94	81.75	1.03
Problem Solving				
M	107.50	−.32	123.01	.17
SD	28.38	.88	32.96	.88
Impact				
M	103.13	−.13	111.12	.10
SD	29.63	.82	103.13	1.02
Environment				
M	60.92	−.20	66.50	.11
SD	16.51	.90	18.95	1.04
Supervision				
M	157.78	−.16	175.88	.09
SD	61.31	.95	67.11	1.02
Total				
M	647.10	−.14	689.93	.07
SD	157.79	.91	186.60	1.04

Note: From Huber, V. L. (1991), tab. 1. Comparison of supervisor-incumbent and female-male multidimensional job evaluation ratings. *Journal of Applied Psychology, 76,* 115–121. Copyright, 1991, by the American Psychological Association. Reprinted by permission of the author.

Summary

The mean is the ordinary average—the sum of the scores divided by the number of scores. Expressed in symbols, $M = \Sigma X/N$.

Some less commonly used alternative descriptors of the typical value of a group of scores are the mode—the most common single value—and the median—the value of the middle score if all the scores were lined up from highest to lowest.

The variation among a group of scores can be described by the variance—the average of the squared deviation of each score from the mean. Expressed in symbols: $SD^2 = \Sigma (X - M)^2/N$.

The standard deviation is the square root of the variance. In symbols, $SD = \sqrt{SD^2}$. It can be best understood as, approximately, the average amount that scores differ from the mean.

A Z score is the number of standard deviations a raw score is above or below the mean. Among other uses, with Z scores you can compare scores on variables that have different scales.

Means and standard deviations are often given in research articles in the text or in tables. Z scores rarely are reported in research articles.

Key Terms

deviation score	outlier	variance (SD^2)
mean (M)	raw score	Z score
median	squared deviation score	Σ
mode	standard deviation (SD)	
N	sum of squared deviations	

Practice Problems

These problems involve computation (with the assistance of a calculator). Most real-life statistics problems are done on a computer. Even if you have a computer, do this by hand to ingrain the method in your mind.

For practice in using a computer to solve statistics problems, refer to the computer section of each chapter of the Student's Study Guide and Computer Workbook *that accompanies this text.*

All data are fictional (unless an actual citation is given).

Answers to selected problems are given at the back of the book.

1. For each data set, determine the following: (a) mean, (b) median, (c) variance, and (d) standard deviation. Be sure to show your work.

Set A: 32, 28, 24, 28, 28, 31, 35, 29, 26

Set B: 6, 1, 4, 2, 3, 4, 6, 6

2. The temperature on December 26 in Montreal was measured, in degrees Celsius, at 10 random times. They were –5, –4, –1, –1, 0, –8, –5, –9, –13, and –24. Describe the typical temperature and the amount of variation to a person who has never had a course in statistics. Give three ways of describing the typical temperature and two ways of describing its variation, explaining the differences and how you computed each. (You will learn more if you try to write your own answer first, before reading our answer. Your own answer need not be quite so thorough as the sample answer in the book.)

3. A researcher interested in political behavior measured the square footage of the desks in the official office of four U.S. governors and of four chief executive officers (CEOs) of major U.S. corporations. The figures for the governors were 44, 36, 52, and 40 square feet. The figures for the CEOs were 32, 60, 48, and 36 square feet. Compute the mean and the standard deviation for the governors and for the CEOs, and explain what you have done to a person who has never had a course in statistics. Also, note the ways in which the means and standard deviations differ, and speculate on the possible meaning of these differences, presuming that they are rep-

resentative of U.S. governors and large corporations' CEOs in general.

4. A study involves measuring the number of days absent from work for 216 employees of a large company during the preceding year. As part of the results, the researcher reports, "The number of days absent during the preceding year ($M = 9.21$; $SD = 7.34$) was . . ." Explain the material in parentheses to a person who has never had a course in statistics.

5. Six months after a divorce, the former wife and husband each take a test that measures divorce adjustment. The wife's score is 63, and the husband's score is 59. Overall, the mean score for divorced women on this test is 60 ($SD = 6$); the mean score for divorced men is 55 ($SD = 4$). Which of the two has adjusted better to the divorce in relation to other divorced people of their own gender? Explain your answer to a person who has never had a course in statistics.

6. A person scores 81 on a test of verbal ability and 6.4 on a test of quantitative ability. For the verbal ability test, the mean for people in general is 50 and the standard deviation is 20. For the quantitative ability test, the mean for people in general is 0 and the standard deviation is 5. Which is this person's stronger ability, verbal or quantitative? Explain your answer to a person who has never had a course in statistics.

3

Correlation and Prediction

A group of 208 college students was asked about their closest personal relationship (Aron, Aron, & Smollan, 1992). Consider one of the findings for men students: The longer they had been in a romantic relationship, the closer they felt to their partner. That is, in general, men who had high levels of length of time with their partner tended to report high levels of closeness with their partner. Men who had low levels of length of time with their partner tended to report low levels of closeness with their partner. (The results for women appear later.)

You can also see this pattern visually. Figure 3–1 is a graph of the men's results of this study. Scores on the closeness measure are on the vertical axis. Scores on the length-of-relationship measure are on the horizontal axis. Each man's score is shown as a dot. The general pattern is that the dots go from the lower left corner to the upper right corner. That is, lower scores on one variable more often go with lower scores on the other variable, and higher with higher. Even though the pattern is far from one to one, you can see a general trend.

The pattern of high scores on one variable going with high scores on the other variable, low scores going with low scores, and moderate with moderate, is an example of a **correlation.**

correlation

There are countless examples of correlation: In children, there is a correlation between age and coordination skills; among students, there is a correlation between amount of time studying and amount learned; in the marketplace, between price and quality—that higher prices go with higher quality and lower with lower.

This chapter explores the nature of correlation, including how it is described graphically, different types of correlations, how to compute the

FIGURE 3–1
Scatter diagram showing the correlation for men between relationship length and closeness. (Data from Aron, Aron, & Smollan, 1992)

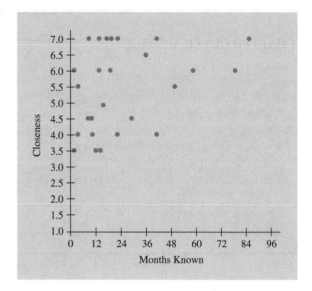

correlation coefficient (a measure of the degree of correlation), the relation of correlation to causality, and how you can use correlation to predict the level of one variable from knowledge of a person's score on another correlated variable (such as predicting college grades from high school grades). In considering correlation and prediction, we move on from the descriptive statistics for a single variable (Chapters 1 and 2) to the relationship between two or more variables.

Independent or Predictor Variables and Dependent Variables

Before going into correlation, however, we first need to introduce some important terms. When considering the relation of two variables, we often think of one variable as a *cause* and the other variable as an *effect.* For example, we might think of relationship length as causing the degree of closeness. The variable that is considered a cause is called the **independent variable,** and the one that is considered an effect is called the **dependent variable.** (The dependent variable has this name because its value depends on the value of the independent variable; the independent variable's score, by contrast, has this name because its value does not depend on the dependent variable. In this little world of only two variables, in which one is the cause of the other, one is independent and the other one depends on it.) In our example, relationship length (the cause) would be the independent variable and closeness (the effect) the dependent variable.

In this example, as in many examples in the social sciences, it is possible to reverse which variable is considered the cause and which the effect. The only major exception is in true experiments, where the experimenter controls the level of the independent variable, for example, by randomly assigning people to different levels of a variable. In such cases, researchers can be quite confident about which is cause and which is effect. But out in the world, closeness, for example, could cause a relationship to last just as much as a long relationship could cause closeness.

independent variable
dependent variable

Researchers are often a bit uncomfortable using the terms *independent variable* and *dependent variable* in studies in which two variables are simply measured as they exist in a group of people. Nevertheless, even if we cannot say with certainty what is cause and what is effect, it is still possible to use knowledge about one variable to *predict* scores on the other variable. For example, in daily life, we may assume that if people have been in a relationship a long time, they are probably closer than people who have been in a relationship only a short time. In this case, we are using relationship length to predict closeness. The underlying cause and effect do not really matter as long as relationship length and closeness consistently go together.

When examining two variables that go together, some researchers prefer to call the one they are predicting from the **predictor variable.** However, the other one is usually still called the dependent variable. (The proper term for the predicted variable is the *criterion variable,* but this is seldom used in the social sciences except in some statistics textbooks.) Following custom, in this book we will usually refer to one of the two variables being correlated as the predictor variable and the other as the dependent variable. Also following custom, we will use X for the independent or predictor variable and Y for the dependent variable.

predictor variable

Graphing Correlations: The Scatter Diagram

Figure 3–1, showing the correlation between relationship length and closeness, is an example of a **scatter diagram.** A scatter diagram permits you to see at a glance the degree and pattern of relation of the two variables.

scatter diagram

How to Make a Scatter Diagram

There are three steps to making a scatter diagram:

1. Draw the axes, and determine which variable should go on which axis. The independent or predictor variable goes on the horizontal axis, the dependent variable on the vertical axis. In Figure 3–1, we put relationship length (months known) on the horizontal axis and closeness on the vertical axis because in the context of the study, we were interested in seeing if relationship length might be a cause of the degree of closeness.

2. Determine the range of values to use for each variable, and mark them on the axes. Your numbers should go upward on each axis, starting from where the axes meet. Ordinarily, begin with the lowest value your measure can possibly have (usually 0), and continue to the highest value your measure can possibly have. When there is no obvious or reasonable lowest or highest possible value, begin or end at a value that is as high or low as people ordinarily score in the group of people of interest for your study.

In Figure 3–1, the horizontal axis starts at 0 months together and the vertical axis starts at 1, which is the lowest possible score on the closeness test used. The highest value on the horizontal axis is 96 months, which is a reasonable maximum length for most romantic relationships among college students. The highest value on the vertical axis is 7, which is the highest possible value on the closeness test.

3. Mark a dot for the pair of scores for each case. Locate the place on the horizontal axis for that person's score on the predictor variable. Then move up to the height on the vertical axis that represents the person's score on that variable, and mark a clear dot.

If there are two cases in one place, you can either put the number 2 in that place or locate a second dot as near as possible to the first—touching, if possible—but making it clear that there are, in fact, two dots in the one place.

An Example

Suppose that a company is considering increasing the number of people managed by each of its floor managers but is concerned about the stress that this might create for these managers. The company expects that the more people managed, the higher a manager's stress. To examine the question, a research consultant suggests studying five managers randomly selected from all the company's floor managers. (In practice, a much larger group should be used, but we will use five cases for simplicity.) The five managers are given a stress questionnaire on which the possible scores range from 0 (no stress at all) to 10 (extreme stress). The results might look like those shown in Table 3–1.

1. Draw the axes, and determine which variable should go on which axis. Because the company is interested in the effect of number of employees supervised on stress level, we consider number of employees supervised to be the predictor variable and put it on the horizontal axis; stress level is the dependent variable and goes on the vertical axis. (See Figure 3–2a.)
2. Determine the range of values to use for each variable, and mark them on the axes. For the horizontal axis, we do not know the maximum possible, but let us assume that in this company no manager is permitted to supervise more than 12. Thus the horizontal axis goes from 0 to 12. The vertical axis goes from 0 to 10, the limits of the questionnaire in this example. (See Figure 3–2b.)
3. Mark a dot for the pair of scores for each case. For the first case, the number of employees supervised is 6. Move across to 6 on the horizontal axis. Then, move up to the point across from the 7 (the stress level for the first manager) on the vertical axis. Place a dot at this point. (See Figure 3–2c.) Do the same for each of the other four managers. The result should look like Figure 3–2d.

TABLE 3–1
Employees Supervised and Stress Level (Fictional Data)

Employees Supervised	Stress Level on Questionnaire
6	7
8	8
3	1
10	8
8	6

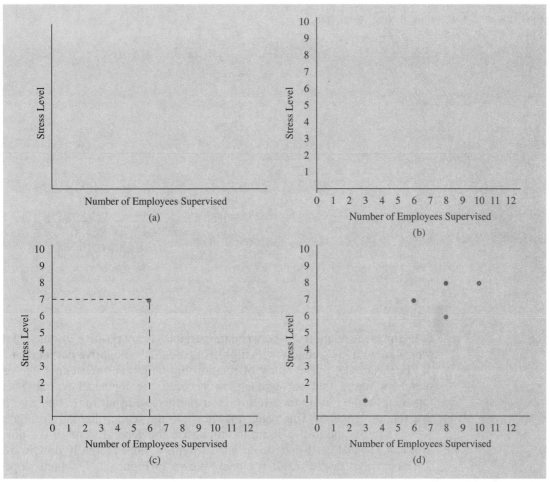

FIGURE 3–2
How to make a scatter diagram. (a) The axes are set up—the predictor variable (employees supervised) on the horizontal axis, the dependent variable (stress level) on the vertical axis. (b) The range of values has been marked on the axes. (c) A dot has been placed for the pair of scores for the first manager. (d) A dot has been placed for the pair of scores for all five managers.

Patterns of Correlation

So far we have examined the situation in which highs go with highs, lows with lows, and mediums with mediums. This situation is called a **positive correlation.** Because the pattern in the scatter diagram roughly approximates a straight line, it is also an example of a **linear correlation.**

positive correlation

linear correlation

For example, in the scatter diagram of Figure 3–1, you could draw a line showing the general trend of the dots, as we have done in Figure 3–3. Similarly, you could draw such a line in our second example, as shown in Figure 3–4. (One reason why these examples of linear correlations are called "positive" is that in geometry, the slope of a line is positive when it goes up and to the right on a graph like this.)

FIGURE 3–3
The scatter diagram of Figure 3–1 with a line drawn in to show the general trend. (Data for men from Aron et al., 1992)

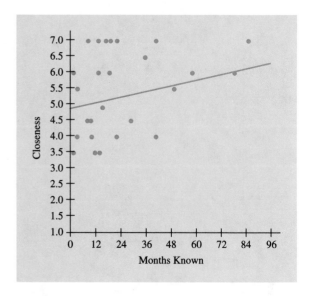

Negative Correlations

negative correlation

Sometimes the relationship between the variables is not positive. Instead, high scores go with low and low with high. This is called a **negative correlation.**

For example, in the study of relationship length and closeness, the researchers found that for women, in general, the longer they had been together, the less close they felt to their partner—a result quite opposite to that found for males! This pattern is shown in the scatter diagram in Figure 3–5. We put a line in the figure to emphasize the general trend of the dots. You can see that as it goes from left to right, it slopes slightly downward. (Compare this to the result for men, shown in Figure 3–3, which slopes upward.)

Another study (Mirvis & Lawler, 1977) also illustrates a negative correlation. That study found that absenteeism from work had a negative linear correlation with "intrinsic satisfaction" with the job. That is, the higher the

FIGURE 3–4
The scatter diagram of Figure 3–2d with a line drawn in to show the general trend.

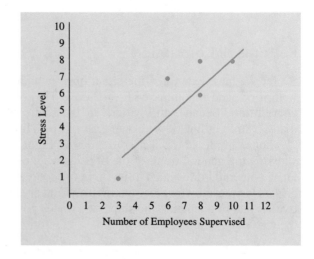

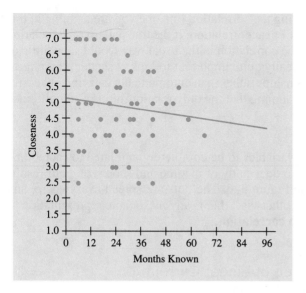

FIGURE 3–5
Scatter diagram with the line drawn in to show the general trend for negative correlation between two variables—longer length of relationship goes with less closeness for women. (Data from Aron et al., 1992)

level of job satisfaction, the lower the level of absenteeism. Put another way, the lower the level of job satisfaction, the higher the absenteeism.

Curvilinear Correlations

Sometimes the relationship between two variables does not follow any kind of straight line, positive or negative, but instead follows the more complex pattern of a **curvilinear correlation.**

For example, it is known that up to a point, more physiological arousal makes you do better on almost any kind of task (such as on a math test). Beyond that point, still greater physiological arousal makes you do worse. That is, going from being nearly asleep to a moderate level of arousal makes you more effective. Beyond that moderate level, further increases in arousal may make you too "keyed up" to do well. This particular curvilinear pattern is illustrated in Figure 3–6. Notice that you could not draw a straight line to describe this pattern.

curvilinear correlation

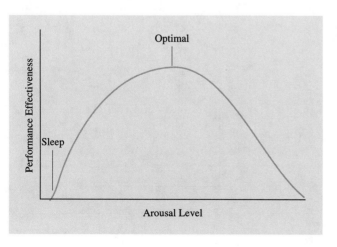

FIGURE 3–6
Example of a curvilinear relationship: task performance and arousal.

The usual way of figuring the correlation (the one you are learning in this chapter) gives the degree of linear correlation. If the true pattern of association is curvilinear, computing the correlation in the usual way would show little or no correlation. Thus, it is really quite important to look at scatter diagrams to unearth these richer relationships rather than automatically carrying out correlations in the usual way, assuming that the only relationship is a straight line.

No Correlation

It is also possible for two variables to be completely unrelated to each other. For example, if you were to do a study of income and shoe size, your results might appear as shown in Figure 3–7. The dots are spread everywhere, and there is no line, straight or otherwise, that is any reasonable representation of a trend. There is simply **no correlation.**

no correlation

Computing the Degree of Linear Correlation: The Pearson Correlation Coefficient

Looking at a scatter diagram gives a rough indication of the type and degree of relationship between two variables. It is obviously not a very precise approach. A number representing the precise degree of correlation is needed.

Degree of Correlation

What we mean by the *degree of correlation* is the extent to which there is a clear pattern of some particular relationship between two variables. For example, we saw that a positive linear correlation is when high scores go with highs, mediums with mediums, lows with lows. The degree of such a correlation, then, is how much highs go with highs, and so on. Similarly, the degree of negative linear correlation is how much highs on one variable go with lows on the other, and so forth. In terms of a scatter diagram, a high degree of

FIGURE 3–7
Two variables with no association with each other: income and shoe size.

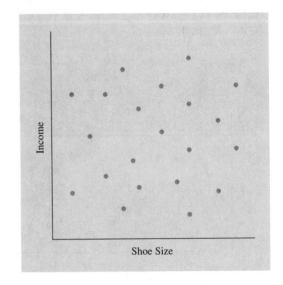

linear correlation means that the dots all fall very close to a straight line (the line sloping up or down depending on whether the linear correlation is positive or negative). A perfect linear correlation means all the dots fall exactly on the straight line.

Figuring the Degree of Linear Correlation

The first thing we need to figure the degree of correlation is some way of gauging what is a high and what is a low score—and how high is a high and how low a low. This means comparing scores on different variables in a consistent way. This kind of problem of comparing apples and oranges, as we saw in Chapter 2, is best solved by using Z scores.

To review, a Z score is the number of standard deviations a score is from the mean. Whatever the scale on which you have measured something, if you convert your raw scores to Z scores, a raw score that is high (that is, above the mean of the other scores on that variable) will always have a positive Z score, and a raw score that is low (below the mean) will always have a negative Z score. Furthermore, regardless of the particular measure used, Z scores give a standard indication of just how high or low each score is. A Z score of 1 is always exactly 1 standard deviation above the mean, and a Z score of 2 is twice as many standard deviations above the mean. Z scores on one variable are directly comparable to Z scores on another variable.

There is an additional reason why Z scores are used when we figure the degree of correlation. It has to do with what happens if you multiply a score on one variable times a score on the other variable, which is called a cross-product. When using Z scores, this is called a **cross-product of Z scores.** If you multiply a high Z score by a high Z score, you will always get a positive cross-product. This is because no matter what the scale, scores above the mean become positive Z scores, and a positive times a positive is a positive. Further—and here is where it gets interesting—if you multiply a low Z score by a low Z score, you also always will get a positive cross-product. This is because no matter what the scale, scores below the mean become negative Z scores, and a negative times a negative gives a positive.

cross-product of Z scores

If highs on one variable go with highs on the other and lows on the one go with lows on the other, the cross-products of Z scores always will be positive. Considering a whole distribution of scores, suppose you take each person's Z score on one variable and multiply it by that person's Z score on the other variable. The result of doing this when highs go with highs and lows with lows is that the multiplication for each person will come out positive. If you sum up these cross-products of Z scores for all the people in the study, which are all positive, you will end up with a big positive number.

On the other hand, with a negative correlation, highs go with lows and lows with highs. In terms of Z scores, this would mean positives with negatives and negatives with positives. Multiplied out, that gives all negative cross-products. If you add all these negative cross-products together, you get a large negative number.

Finally, suppose there is no linear correlation. In this case, for some people highs on one variable would go with highs on the other variable (and some lows would go with lows), making positive cross-products. For others, highs on one variable would go with lows on the other variable (and some lows would go with highs), making negative cross-products. Adding up these cross-products for all the people in the study would result in the positive cross-products and the negative cross-products canceling each other out, giving a number around 0.

In each situation, we changed all the scores to Z scores, multiplied the two Z scores for each person times each other, and added up these cross-products. The result is you get a large positive number if there is a positive correlation, a large negative number if there is a negative correlation, and a number near 0 if there is no linear correlation.

However, you are still left with the problem of figuring the degree of a positive or negative correlation. Obviously, the larger the number, the bigger the correlation. But how large is large, and how large is not very large? You cannot judge from the sum of the cross-products alone, which increases rapidly just by adding the cross-products of more cases together. (That is, a study with 100 people would have a bigger sum of cross-products than the same study with only 25 people.)

perfect correlation

The solution is to divide this sum of the cross-products by the number of cases. That is, you compute the *average of the cross-products of Z scores*. It turns out that this average can never be more than +1—a positive linear **perfect correlation.** Its minimum is –1, which is a negative linear perfect correlation. In the case of no linear correlation, it will be 0.

For a positive linear correlation that is not perfect, which is the usual case, the average of the cross-products of Z scores will be between 0 and +1. To put it another way, if the general trend of the dots is upward and to the right, but they do not fall exactly on a single straight line, this number is between 0 and +1. The same rule holds for negative correlations: They fall between 0 and –1.

The Correlation Coefficient

correlation coefficient (*r*)

The average of the cross-products of Z scores thus serves as an excellent way of figuring the degree of linear correlation. It is called the **correlation coefficient (*r*).** It also is called the Pearson correlation coefficient (or the Pearson product-moment correlation coefficient, to be very traditional). It is named after Karl Pearson (whom you meet in Box 11–1). Pearson, along with Francis Galton (see Box 3–1), played a major role in developing the correlation coefficient. The correlation coefficient is abbreviated by the letter *r,* which is short for *regression,* a concept closely related to correlation. (We discuss regression later in the chapter.)

Figure 3–8 shows scatter diagrams and the correlation coefficient for several examples.

Formula for the Correlation Coefficient

The correlation coefficient, as we have seen, is the average of the cross-product of Z scores. Stated as a formula in symbols,

$$r = \frac{\Sigma \ Z_X Z_Y}{N}$$

(3–1)

r is the correlation coefficient. Z_X is the Z score for each person on the X variable and Z_Y is the Z score for each person on the Y variable. $Z_X Z_Y$ is Z_X times

BOX 3–1

Galton: Gentleman Genius

Francis Galton is credited with inventing the correlation statistic, although Karl Pearson and others worked out the formulas. Pearson was a student of Galton and gave him all the credit for the discovery of correlation. As you may be sensing, statistics at this time was a tight little British club. (In fact, most of science was an only slightly larger club. Galton also was influenced greatly by his own cousin, Charles Darwin.)

Of the members of this club, Galton was a typical, eccentric, independently wealthy, gentleman scientist. Aside from his work in statistics, he possessed a medical degree, had explored "darkest Africa," invented glasses for reading underwater, experimented with stereoscopic maps, dabbled in meteorology and anthropology, and wrote a paper about receiving intelligible signals from the stars.

Above all, Galton was a compulsive counter. Some of his counts are rather infamous. Once while attending a lecture, he counted the fidgets of an audience per minute, looking for variations with the boringness of the subject matter. While twice having his picture painted, he counted the artist's brush strokes per hour, concluding that each portrait required an average of 20,000 strokes. While walking the streets of various towns in the British Isles, he classified the beauty of the female inhabitants by fingering a recording device in his pocket to register "good," "medium," or "bad."

Galton's consuming interest, however, was the counting of geniuses, criminals, and other types in families. He wanted to understand how each type was produced so that science could improve the human race by encouraging governments to enforce eugenics—selective breeding for intelligence, proper moral behavior, and other qualities—to be determined, of course, by the eugenicists. (Eugenics has since been generally discredited.) The concept of correlation came directly from his first simple efforts in this area, the study of the relation of the height of children to their parents.

At first, Galton's method of exactly measuring the tendency for "one thing to go with another" seemed almost the same as proving the cause of something. For example, if it could be shown mathematically that most of the brightest people came from a few highborn British families and most of the least intelligent people came from poor families, that would prove that intelligence was caused by the inheritance of certain genes (provided that you were prejudiced enough to overlook the differences in educational opportunities). The same study might prove more convincingly that if you were a member of one of those better British families, history would make you a prime example of how easy it is to misinterpret the meaning of a correlation.

References: Peters (1987); Tankard (1984).

Z_Y (the cross-product of the Z scores) for each person and $\Sigma Z_X Z_Y$ is the sum of the cross-products of Z scores over all the people in the study. N is the number of people in the study. Putting it all together, $\Sigma Z_X Z_Y$ divided by N is the average of the cross-products of Z scores.[1]

---

[1]There is also a "computational" version of this formula, which is mathematically equivalent and thus gives the same result but does not require you to first figure out Z scores:

$$r = \frac{N\Sigma(XY) - \Sigma X \Sigma Y}{\sqrt{[N\Sigma X^2 - (\Sigma X)^2]}\ \sqrt{[N\Sigma Y^2 - (\Sigma Y)^2]}}$$

(3-2)

However, as we noted in Chapter 2, researchers rarely use computational formulas like this any more because most actual computations are done by computer. As a student learning statistics, it is better to use the definitional formula (3-1) because when solving problems using the definitional formula you are strengthening your understanding of what the correlation coefficient means. In all examples in this chapter, we use the definitional formula and we urge you to use it in doing the chapter exercises.

FIGURE 3–8

Scatter diagrams and correlation coefficients for fictional studies with different correlations.

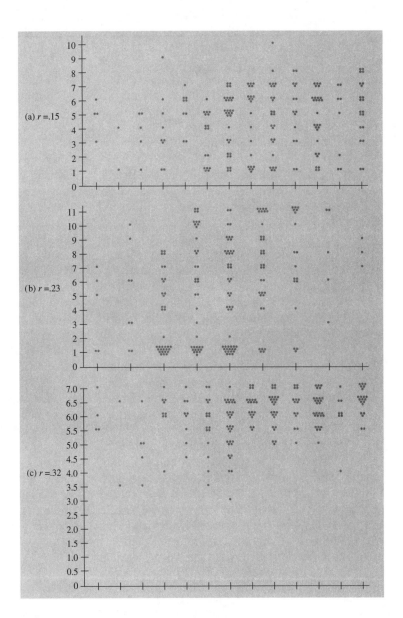

(a) r = .15

(b) r = .23

(c) r = .32

Steps for Computing the Correlation Coefficient

The four steps for computing the correlation coefficient follow:

1. Convert all scores to Z scores. This requires figuring the mean and the standard deviation of each variable, then figuring the Z score for each raw score.

2. Compute the cross-product of the Z scores for each person. That is, for each person, multiply the Z score for one variable times the Z score for the other variable.

3. Sum the cross-products of the Z scores.

4. Divide by the number of people in the study.

An Example

Let us try these steps with the managers' stress example.

FIGURE 3–8 (*cont.*)

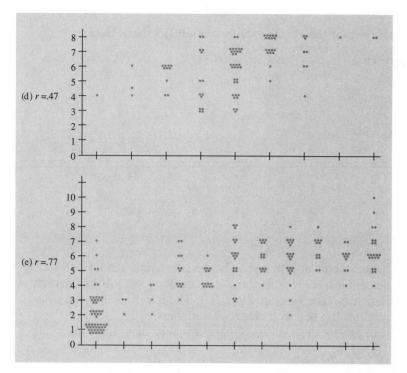

(d) r = .47

(e) r = .77

1. Convert all scores to Z scores. Starting with the number of employees supervised, the mean is 7 (sum of 35 divided by 5 managers), and the standard deviation is 2.37 (sum of squared deviations, 28, divided by 5 managers, for a variance of 5.6, the square root of which is 2.37). For the first manager, then, a score of 6 is 1 below the mean of 7, and 1 divided by 2.37 is .42. Thus the first score is .42 standard deviations below the mean, or a Z score of −.42. We compute the rest of the Z scores in the same way and show them in the appropriate columns in Table 3–2.

2. Compute the cross-product of the Z scores for each case. For the first manager, multiply −.42 times .38. This gives −.16. The cross-products for all the managers are shown in the last column of Table 3–2.

3. Sum the cross-products of the Z scores. Adding up all the cross-products of Z scores, as shown in Table 3–2, gives a sum of 4.38.

4. Divide by the number of cases. Dividing 4.38 by 5 (the number of managers in the study) gives a result of .876, rounded off to .88—the correlation coefficient. In terms of the correlation coefficient formula,

$$r = \frac{\Sigma\ Z_X Z_Y}{N} = \frac{4.38}{5} = .88$$

Because this correlation coefficient is positive and near 1, the highest possible value, this is a very strong positive linear correlation.

An Example of Graphing and Computing a Correlation

In this example, we put together the steps of making a scatter diagram and computing the correlation coefficient.

TABLE 3–2
Figuring the Correlation Coefficient for the Managers' Stress Study (Fictional Data)

Number of Employees Supervised (X)				Stress Level (Y)				Cross-Products	
X	$X-M$	$(X-M)^2$	Z_X	Y	$Y-M$	$(Y-M)^2$	Z_Y	$Z_X Z_Y$	
6	−1	1	− .42	7	1	1	.38	−.16	
8	1	1	.42	8	2	4	.77	.32	
3	−4	16	−1.69	1	−5	25	−1.92	3.24	
10	3	9	1.27	8	2	4	.77	.98	
8	1	1	.42	6	0	0	0.00	0.00	

$\Sigma = 35$ $SS = 28$ $\Sigma = 30$ $SS = 34$ $\Sigma Z_X Z_Y = 4.38$
$M = 7$ $SD^2 = 5.60$ $M = 6$ $SD^2 = 6.80$ $r = .88$
$SD = 2.37$ $SD = 2.61$

Suppose that an educational researcher had the average class size and average achievement test score from the five elementary schools in a particular small school district, as shown in Table 3–3. The question she then asks is, what is the relationship between these two variables?

The first thing she must do is to make a scatter diagram. This requires three steps.

1. Draw the axes, and determine which variable should go on which axis. Because it seems reasonable to think of class size as affecting achievement test scores rather than the other way around, we can draw the axes with class size along the bottom.

2. Determine the range of values to use for each variable, and mark them on the axes. We will assume that the achievement test scores go from 0 to 100. Class size has to be at least 1 and in this example we guessed that it would be unlikely to me more than 50.

3. Mark a dot for the pair of scores for each case. The completed scatter diagram is shown in Figure 3–9.

In any correlation problem, before going on to figure the correlation coefficient, it is a good idea to look at the scatter diagram to be sure that the pattern is roughly a straight line. In this example, it is. It is also wise to make a rough estimate of the direction and degree of correlation. This serves as a check against making a major mistake in figuring. In this case, the basic pat-

TABLE 3–3
Average Class Size and Achievement Test Scores in Five Elementary Schools (Fictional Data)

Elementary School	Class Size	Achievement Test Score
Main Street	25	80
Casat	14	98
Harland	33	50
Shady Grove	28	82
Jefferson	20	90

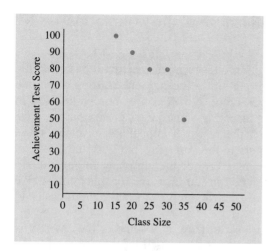

FIGURE 3–9
The last step in making a scatter diagram for the data in Table 3–3. A dot has been placed for each pair of scores for each of the five schools.

tern is one in which the dots go down and to the right fairly consistently, suggesting a fairly strong negative correlation. Now we can proceed to compute the correlation coefficient, following the usual steps.

1. Convert all scores to Z scores. The mean for class size is 24, and the standard deviation is 6.54. The Z score for the first class size, of 25, is $(25 - 24)/6.54 = 0.15$. All of the Z scores are shown in the appropriate columns of Table 3–4.

2. Compute the cross-product of the Z scores for each case. The first cross product is .15 times 0, which is 0. The second is –1.53 times 1.10, which equals –1.68. All of the cross-products of Z scores are shown in the rightmost column of Table 3–4.

3. Sum the cross-products of the Z scores. The total is –4.52.

4. Divide by the number of cases. The sum –4.52 divided by 5 is –.90; that is, $r = -.90$.

Note that a correlation coefficient of –.90 corresponds well to our original estimate of a fairly strong negative correlation.

TABLE 3–4
Figuring the Correlation Coefficient for Average Class Size and Achievement Test Scores in Five Elementary Schools (Fictional Data)

School	Class Size		Achievement Test Score		Cross-Product
	X	Z_X	Y	Z_Y	$Z_X Z_Y$
Main Street	25	.15	80	0.00	0.00
Casat	14	–1.53	98	1.10	–1.68
Harland	33	1.38	50	–1.84	–2.53
Shady Grove	28	.61	82	.12	.08
Jefferson	20	– .61	90	.61	– .38
Σ:	120		400		–4.52
M:	24		80		$r = -.90$
$SD = \sqrt{214/5} = 6.54$			$\sqrt{1{,}328/5} = 16.30$		

Testing the Statistical Significance of the Correlation Coefficient

The correlation coefficient, by itself, is a descriptive statistic. It describes the degree and direction of linear correlation in the particular group of people studied. However, when doing research, we often are more interested in a particular group of scores as representing some larger group that we have not studied directly. For example, the research consultant gave the stress questionnaires to only five managers in the company, but with the intention that they would be typical of the managers of the company in general. (In practice, one would want a much larger group than five for this purpose. We have used small groups of people in our examples to make them easier to follow.)

The problem, however, is that by studying only some of the cases, it is possible to pick by chance just those cases in which highs happened to go with highs and lows with lows, even though, had we studied all the cases, there might really be no correlation. We say that a correlation is significant if it is unlikely that we could have gotten a correlation this big if, in fact, the overall group had no correlation. Specifically, we figure out whether that likelihood is less than some small degree of probability (p), such as 5% or 1%. If it is that small, we say that the correlation is "statistically significant" with "$p < .05$" or "$p < .01$."

statistical significance

The method and logic of figuring **statistical significance** is the main focus of this book starting with Chapter 4, and we would be jumping ahead if we were to try to explain it now. However, by the time you have completed the later chapters, the details will be quite clear. (The needed information is in the appendix to this chapter, but we suggest that you leave this appendix until you have completed Chapter 8.) We only mention this now so that you will have a general idea of what is meant if you see mentions of statistical significance, "$p < .05$," or some such phrase when reading a research article that reports correlation coefficients.

Causality and Correlation

direction of causality

If two variables have a significant correlation, we normally assume that there is something causing that relationship. However, the **direction of causality** (just what is causing what) cannot be figured out from the correlation alone. For any correlation between variables X and Y, there are three possible directions of causality: X could be causing Y, Y could be causing X, or some third factor could be causing both X and Y. It is also possible (and often likely) that there is more than one direction of causality.

Take the managers' stress example. The study began with the implied notion that supervising more people (X) causes an increase in stress level (Y). The result of the study was a strong positive correlation between X and Y. This result certainly fits the idea that X causes Y. But the result fits just as well with the idea that Y causes X. (Perhaps managers who appear stressed are seen as working hard, and their superiors give them more people to supervise.) It also is possible that the correlation results from some third factor causing X and Y to go together. For example, certain sections of the factory may both need more people and thus create more stress.

Prediction

One important use of correlations is to help in making predictions. A college admissions officer might want to use a person's score on one variable, such as the person's SAT score, to predict the person's score on another variable, such as the person's college grade point average. Similarly, a personnel manager might want to use the score on a job application examination to predict whether the applicant will be successful on the job; a parole officer might want to use number of rule violations to predict whether a prisoner would commit a crime if released; a public health official might want to use tomorrow's expected high temperature to predict the number of people likely to have heat-related health problems; and so forth. In each case, if there is a high correlation between the variable used as the basis for the prediction, such as SAT scores, and the variable whose value is being predicted, such as college grades, then the prediction will be more accurate. If there is no correlation, then there is no basis for prediction.

Prediction Using *Z* Scores

It simplifies learning about prediction if we first consider prediction using Z scores. The **prediction model,** or formula, that we use to make predictions with Z scores is as follows: A person's predicted Z score on the dependent variable is found by multiplying a particular number, called a **regression coefficient,** times that person's Z score on the predictor variable.

    Because we are working with Z scores, which are also called standard scores, the regression coefficient in this case is called a **standardized regression coefficient;** it is symbolized by the Greek letter "beta" (β). In symbols,

$$\text{Predicted } Z_Y = (\beta)(Z_X)$$

(3–3)

In this formula, predicted Z_Y is the predicted value of the Z score for the particular person's score on the dependent variable Y.[2] β is the standardized regression coefficient. Z_X is the known Z score for the particular person's score on the predictor variable X. Thus, $(\beta)(Z_X)$ means multiplying the standardized regression coefficient times the person's Z score on the predictor variable.

    For example, suppose that at your school the beta for predicting college GPA (at graduation) from SAT (at admission) is .3. A person applying to your school has an SAT score that is 2 standard deviations above the mean (that is, a Z score of +2). The predicted Z score for this person's GPA would be .3 times 2, which is .6. That is, this person's predicted Z score for their college GPA is .6 standard deviations above the mean. In symbols,

$$\text{Predicted } Z_Y = (\beta)(Z_X) = (.3)(2) = .6$$

    It can be proved mathematically (using methods that are beyond the level of this book) that when predicting using Z scores, the best number to use for

prediction model

regression coefficient

standardized regression coefficient, (β)

---

[2]The predicted value of a score often is written with a hat symbol. Thus $\hat{Z}_Y$ means Predicted Z_Y.

beta is the correlation coefficient. That is, when predicting one variable from another using Z scores, $\beta = r$.

An Example

Consider again the managers' stress example. In this example, the correlation between employees supervised and managers' stress level was .88. Thus $\beta = .88$, and the model for predicting a manager's Z score for stress is to multiply .88 times the Z score for the number of employees that the manager will supervise. Suppose a new manager were going to be supervising 10 employees. This would be a Z score of +1.27 on employees supervised. (We changed 10 to a Z score using the procedure you learned in Chapter 2 for converting raw scores to Z scores: $Z = (X - M)/SD$.) We would predict a Z score on stress level by multiplying .88 times 1.27, which comes out to 1.12. This means that a manager who supervised 10 employees is predicted to have a stress level that is slightly more than 1 standard deviation above the mean. In terms of the formula,

$$\text{Predicted } Z_Y = (\beta)(Z_X) = (.88)(1.27) = 1.12$$

By contrast, if the new manager were going to supervise only three employees, the model would predict a Z score stress level of .88 times −1.69 (the Z score when the number supervised is three), which is −1.49. That is,

$$\text{Predicted } Z_Y = (\beta)(Z_X) = (.88)(-1.69) = -1.49$$

Why Prediction Is Also Called Regression

Statisticians usually refer to prediction of the kind we are doing as *regression*. The term comes from the fact that when there is less than a perfect correlation between two variables, the dependent variable Z score is some fraction (the value of r) of the predictor variable Z score. As a result, the dependent variable Z score is closer to its mean. (That is, it regresses or returns toward a Z of 0.)

For example, in the managers' stress example, the new manager who was going to supervise 10 employees has a Z score for employees to be supervised of 1.27, but the predicted stress level Z score has regressed to only 1.12.

Prediction Using Raw Scores

Based on what you have learned, you can now make predictions involving raw scores as follows:

1. Convert the raw score on the predictor variable to a Z score.
2. Multiply beta (the correlation coefficient) times this Z score to get the predicted Z score on the dependent variable.
3. Convert the predicted Z score on the dependent variable to a raw score.[3]

[3]In practice, if one is going to make a number of predictions for different people, a *raw-score prediction formula* may be used that allows you to just plug in a particular person's raw score on the predictor variable and then solve directly to get the person's predicted raw score on the dependent variable. What the raw score prediction formula amounts to is taking the usual Z-score prediction formula, but substituting for the Z scores the formula for getting a Z score

For example, in the managers' stress study, when we wanted to predict the stress level of a manager supervising 10 employees, we first converted 10 to a Z score (1.27). This was Step 1. We then found the predicted stress-level Z score by multiplying beta times this Z score (.88 times 1.27 gave a predicted Z score of 1.12). This was Step 2. Step 3 (which we did not do earlier) is to convert this predicted Z score of 1.12 to a raw score. Using the formula from Chapter 2 for converting a Z score to a raw score, this comes out to 8.92). That is, using the regression procedure, we predict that a manager supervising 10 employees will have a stress level of 8.92.

These steps are laid out in Table 3–5 for the other example prediction we made (for the manager who will be supervising three people).

In using these steps, be careful when changing raw scores to Z scores and Z scores to raw scores to use the mean and standard deviation for the correct variable. In Step 1, you are working only with the score, mean, and standard deviation for the predictor variable (X). In Step 3, you are working only with the score, mean, and standard deviation for the dependent variable (Y).

Multiple Regression and Correlation

So far we have predicted a person's score on a dependent variable using the person's score on a single predictor variable. What if you also could use additional predictor variables? For example, in predicting a managers' stress, all we had to work with was the number of employees the manager supervised. Suppose that we also knew something about noise level and number of deadlines managers had to meet each month. This added information might allow us to make a much more accurate prediction of stress level.

The association between a dependent variable and two or more predictor variables is called **multiple correlation.** Making predictions in this situation is called **multiple regression.**

We will explore these topics only very briefly because the details are beyond the level of an introductory book. However, since multiple regression and correlation are frequently used in research articles in the social and behavioral sciences it will be useful for you to have a general understanding of them.

multiple correlation
multiple regression

TABLE 3-5
Summary, Using Formulas, of Steps for Making Raw Score Predictions With Raw-to-Z and Z-to-Raw Conversions, With an Example

Step	Formula	Example
1	$Z_X = (X - M_X)/SD_X$	$Z_X = (3 - 7)/2.37 = -1.69$
2	Predicted $Z_Y = (\beta)(Z_X)$	Predicted $Z_Y = (.88)(-1.69) = -1.49$
3	Predicted $Y = (SD_Y)$ Predicted $(Z_Y) + M_Y$	Predicted $Y = (2.61)(-1.49) + 6 = 2.11$

from a raw score. If you know the mean and standard deviation for both variables and the correlation coefficient, this whole thing can then be reduced algebraically to give the raw-score prediction formula. This raw-score prediction formula is of the form predicted $Y = a + (b)(X)$, where a is called the *regression constant* (because this number that is added into the prediction does not change regardless of the value of X) and b is called the *raw-score regression coefficient* (because it is the number multiplied by the raw-score value of X and then added to a to get the predicted value of Y). You will sometimes see these terms referred to in research reports. However, since the logic of regression and its relation to correlation is most directly appreciated from the Z score prediction formula, that is our emphasis in this introductory text.

In multiple regression, each predictor variable has its own regression coefficient. The predicted Z score of the dependent variable is found by multiplying the Z score for each predictor variable times its beta (standardized regression coefficient) and then adding up the results. For example, the Z-score multiple regression formula with three predictor variables follows:

$$\text{Predicted } Z_Y = (\beta_1)(Z_{X_1}) + (\beta_2)(Z_{X_2}) + (\beta_3)(Z_{X_3})$$

(3–4)

β_1 is the standardized regression coefficient for the first predictor variable. Similarly, β_2 and β_3 are the standardized regression coefficients for the second and third predictor variables. Z_{X_1} is the Z score for the first predictor variable. Similarly, Z_{X_2} and Z_{X_3} are the Z scores for the second and third predictor variables. $(\beta_1)(Z_{X_1})$ means multiplying β_1 times Z_{X_1}; and so forth.

For example, in the managers' stress situation, a multiple regression model for predicting stress level (Y) using the predictor variables of number of employees supervised, which we will now call X_1, and also noise level (X_2) and number of deadlines per month (X_3) might turn out to be as follows:

$$\text{Predicted } Z_Y = (.51)(Z_{X_1}) + (.11)(Z_{X_2}) + (.33)(Z_{X_3})$$

Suppose that you were asked to predict the stress level of a potential manager who had a Z score of 1.27 for number of employees to be supervised (a fairly high number of employees supervised), a Z score of -1.81 for noise of working conditions (a low noise level), and a Z score of .94 for number of deadlines per month (a somewhat high number of deadlines). Your predicted Z score for stress level would be computed by multiplying .51 times the employees supervised Z score, .11 times the noise Z score, and .33 times the deadlines Z score, then adding up the results:

$$
\begin{aligned}
\text{Predicted } Z_Y &= (.51)(1.27) + (.11)(-1.81) + (.33)(.94) \\
&= \quad .65 \quad + \quad -.20 \quad + \quad .31 \quad = .76
\end{aligned}
$$

So under these conditions, you would predict a stress-level Z score of .76, which means a stress level about three-fourths of a standard deviation above the mean.

In multiple regression, the overall correlation between the dependent variable and all the predictor or independent variables is called the **multiple correlation coefficient (R)** and is symbolized as capital R.

multiple correlation coefficient (R)

There is one particularly important difference between multiple regression and prediction when only using one predictor variable. In ordinary correlation, $\beta = r$. But in multiple regression, the beta for a predictor variable is not the same as the ordinary correlation coefficient (r) of that predictor variable with the dependent variable. In most cases, the beta will be lower (closer to 0) than r. The reason for this is that usually part of what makes any one predictor variable successful in predicting the dependent variable will overlap with what makes the other predictor variables successful in predicting the dependent variable. In multiple regression, beta is related to the unique, distinctive contribution of the variable, excluding any overlap with other predictor variables.

Consider the managers' stress example. When we were predicting stress using just the number of employees supervised, beta was the same as the correlation coefficient of .88. Now, in our example with the multiple regression model, beta for employees supervised is only .51. It is less because part of what makes number of employees supervised predict stress overlaps with what makes noise and number of deadlines predict stress. (For example, part of what makes the number of people supervised predict stress is that the number of people supervised adds to the noise.)

Because of this overlap among the predictor variables, the multiple correlation (R) is usually smaller than the sum of the individual rs of each predictor variable with the dependent variable.

The Correlation Coefficient and the Proportion of Variance Accounted For

A correlation coefficient tells you the strength of a linear relationship. Bigger rs (values farther from 0) mean a higher degree of correlation. That is, an r of .4 is a stronger correlation than an r of .2. However, an r of .4 is *not* twice as strong as an r of .2. To compare correlations with each other, you have to square each correlation (that is, you use r^2 instead of r). The correlation squared is called the **proportion of variance accounted for (r^2).**[4]

For example, a correlation of .2 is equivalent to an r^2 of .04, and a correlation of .4 is equivalent to an r^2 of .16. A correlation of .2 actually means a relationship between X and Y that is only one-quarter as strong as a correlation of .4.

This all works the same way in multiple regression. In multiple regression, the proportion of variance in the dependent variable accounted for by all the predictor variables taken together is the multiple correlation squared, R^2.

proportion of variance accounted for (r^2)

Correlation and Prediction as Described in Research Articles

Research articles give correlation coefficients either in the text of research articles or in tables. (Sometimes the "significance level," such as $p < .05$, will also be reported.) The result we started the chapter with would be described as follows: Men had a positive correlation ($r = .46$) between length of relationship and closeness.

Tables of correlation are very common when several variables are involved. Usually, the table is set up so that each variable is listed both at the top and at the left side; the correlation of each pair of variables is shown inside the table. This is called a **correlation matrix.**

Table 3–6 is from a study of grades in different classes of a group of nursing students (Drake & Michael, 1995). Notice that the correlation of a

correlation matrix

---

[4]The reason r^2 is called proportion of variance accounted for can be understood as follows: Suppose you used the prediction formula to predict each person's score on Y. Unless the correlation between X and Y was perfect (1.0), the variance of those predicted Y scores would be smaller than the variance of the original Y scores. There is less variance in the predicted Y scores because these predicted scores are on the average closer to the mean than are the original scores. (We discussed this in this section on why prediction is called regression.) However, the more accurate the prediction, the more the predicted scores are like the actual scores. Thus, the more accurate the prediction, the closer the variance of the predicted scores is to the variance of the actual scores. Now suppose you divide the variance of the predicted Y scores by the variance of the original Y scores. The result of this division is the proportion of variance in the actual scores "accounted for" by the variance in the predicted scores. This proportion turns out (for reasons beyond what we can cover in this book) to be r^2.

TABLE 3–6
Intercorrelations of Grades in 14 Courses of the Nursing Curriculum ($N = 235$) (Decimal Points Omitted)

Courses in the Nursing Curriculum	(1)	(2)	(3)	(4)	(5)	(6)	(7)	(8)	(9)	(10)	(11)	(12)	(13)	(14)
1. Fundamentals of Nursing Theory	—	63	30	44	07	62	22	35	08	52	22	52	25	25
2. Intermediate Nursing Theory	63	—	29	49	15	58	22	32	05	48	22	58	27	26
3. Intermediate Nursing Laboratory	30	29	—	08	23	25	32	06	15	24	22	30	39	15
4. Maternity Nursing Theory	44	49	08	—	09	51	19	33	22	35	21	46	14	34
5. Maternity Nursing Laboratory	07	15	23	09	—	03	29	08	12	–02	15	18	19	16
6. Advanced Medical-Surgical Theory	62	58	25	51	03	—	19	44	13	50	19	53	27	30
7. Advanced Medical-Surgical Laboratory	22	22	32	19	29	19	—	18	29	14	19	29	31	10
8. Mental Health Nursing Theory	35	32	06	33	08	44	18	—	20	40	07	40	16	35
9. Mental Health Nursing Laboratory	08	05	15	22	12	13	29	20	—	01	05	16	16	10
10. Advanced Medical-Surgical Nursing Theory	52	48	24	35	–02	50	14	40	01	—	17	55	28	28
11. Advanced Medical-Surgical Nursing Laboratory	22	22	22	21	15	19	19	07	05	17	—	21	25	16
12. Pediatric Nursing Theory	52	58	30	46	18	53	29	40	16	55	21	—	28	41
13. Pediatric Nursing Laboratory	25	27	39	14	19	27	31	16	16	28	25	28	—	08
14. Leadership in Nursing Theory	25	26	15	34	16	30	10	35	10	28	16	41	08	—

Note: The four courses identified as Biology 20: Anatomy; Biology 22; Physiology; Anatomy & Physiology; and Microbiology did not enter into the intercorrelations or factor analysis because of the relatively large numbers of missing cases.
Data from Drake & Michael (1995).

variable with itself is not given (a short line is put in instead). Also, notice that the lower left triangle of the table contains exactly the same information as the upper right triangle of the table. For example, the correlation between grades in (1) Fundamentals of Nursing Theory and (2) Intermediate Nursing Care is .63. This is exactly the same as the correlation between (2) Intermediate Nursing Care and (1) Fundamentals of Nursing Theory. In fact, usually a correlation matrix reported in a research article only gives one of these two triangles and leaves the other area blank.

When prediction models are given in research articles, they are usually for multiple regression. Multiple regression is quite common in the social and behavioral sciences. Table 3–7 shows the results of a multiple regression analysis. This table is from a study (Bankston, Thompson, Jenkins, & Forsyth, 1990) of 1,177 drivers in Louisiana in which the dependent variable was whether or not the driver carried a firearm in his or her car. As can be seen from the table, the betas show an especially strong link with gender and cultural factors (French-English ratio and location size). The table also includes a number of other statistics, which you do not have to fully understand to appreciate the main result. (The "Unstandardized Coefficient" column and the "Constant" near the bottom of the table refer to raw-score prediction of the type described in footnote 3. "Standard Error, "Significance of t," and "F" all have to do with statistical significance.)

TABLE 3–7
Regression Results for State Sample ($N = 1,177$)

Variable	Unstandardized Coefficient	Standard Error	Beta	Significance of t
French-English ratio	−.061*	.018	−.099*	.001
Fear index	.014	.008	.049	.105
Income	.022	.012	.034	.304
Gender	−.256*	.060	−.126*	.000
Victim experience	.090	.060	.044	.133
Age	−.003	.002	−.047	.118
Location size	−.041*	.015	−.085*	.006
Education	−.027	.017	−.052	.113

Constant = 1.077
$R^2 = .034$
$F = 5.21$
Significance of $F = .000$

Note: *$p < .05$. Unstandardized coefficients that have an absolute value at least twice the standard error are significant at the .05 level. Data from Bankston, W., Thompson, C., Jenkins, Q., & Forsyth, C. (1990). The influence of fear of crime, gender, and southern culture on carrying firearms for protection. *Sociological Quarterly, 31,* 287–305. Copyright, 1990, by JAI Press, Inc. Reprinted by permission.

Summary

A scatter diagram shows the relation between two variables. The lowest to highest possible values of the independent or predictor variable are marked on the horizontal axis, and the lowest to highest possible values of the dependent variable are marked on the vertical axis. Each individual pair of scores is shown as a dot.

When the dots in the scatter diagram generally follow a straight line, this is called a linear correlation. In a positive linear correlation, the line goes upward to the right (so that low scores go with low and high with high). In a negative linear correlation, the line goes downward to the right (so that low scores go with high and high with low). In a curvilinear correlation, the dots follow a line other than a simple straight line. No correlation exists when the dots do not follow any kind of line.

The correlation coefficient (r) gives the degree of linear correlation. It is the average of the cross-products of Z scores. The correlation coefficient is highly positive when there is a strong positive linear correlation. This is because positive Z scores are multiplied by positive, and negative Z scores by negative. The correlation coefficient is highly negative when there is a strong negative linear correlation. This is because positive Z scores are multiplied by negative and negative Z scores by positive. The coefficient is 0 when there is no linear correlation. This is because positive Z scores are sometimes multiplied by positive and sometimes by negative Z scores and negative Z scores are sometimes multiplied by negative and sometimes by positive. Thus, positive and negative cross-products cancel each other out.

The maximum positive value of r is +1. $r = +1$ when there is a perfect positive linear correlation. The maximum negative value of r is −1. $r = −1$ when there is a perfect negative linear correlation.

A correlation usually is based on scores from a particular group that is intended to represent some larger group. When statistical procedures (to be taught later) support the idea that a correlation does exist in the larger group, too, we say that the correlation is statistically significant.

Correlation does not tell you the direction of causation. If two variables, X and Y, are correlated, this could be because X is causing Y, Y is causing X, or a third factor is causing both X and Y.

Prediction (or regression) makes predictions about scores on a dependent variable based on scores on a predictor variable. The best model for predicting a person's Z score on the dependent variable is to multiply a number called the standardized regression coefficient (beta) times the person's Z score on the predictor variable. The best number to use for the standardized regression coefficient in this situation is the correlation coefficient.

Predictions with raw scores can be made by converting the person's score on the predictor variable to a Z score, multiplying it by beta, and then converting the resulting predicted Z score on the dependent variable to a raw score.

In multiple regression, a dependent variable is predicted using two or more predictor variables. In a multiple regression model, each predictor variable is multiplied by its own regression coefficient (beta), and the results are added up to make the prediction. However, because the predictor variables overlap in their influence on the dependent variable, each of the regression coefficients generally is smaller than the variable's correlation coefficient with the dependent variable. The multiple correlation coefficient (R) describes the overall degree of association between the dependent variable and the predictor or independent variables taken together.

Comparisons of the degree of linear correlation are considered most accurate in terms of the correlation coefficient squared (r^2 or R^2), the proportion of variance accounted for.

Correlational results are usually presented in research articles either in the text with the value of r (and sometimes the significance level) or in a special table (a correlation matrix) showing the correlations among several variables. Multiple correlation results typically report betas and overall R (or R^2), as well as other statistics.

Key Terms

correlation	multiple correlation	predictor variable
correlation coefficient (r)	multiple correlation coefficient	proportion of variance accounted
correlation matrix	(R)	for (r^2)
cross-product of Z scores	multiple regression	regression coefficient
curvilinear correlation	negative correlation	scatter diagram
dependent variable	no correlation	standardized regression coeffi-
direction of causality	perfect correlation	cient (β)
independent variable	positive correlation	statistical significance
linear correlation	prediction model	

Practice Problems

These problems involve computation (with the assistance of a calculator). Most real-life statistics problems are done on a computer. Even if you have a computer, do this by hand to ingrain the method in your mind.

For practice in using a computer to solve statistics problems, refer to the computer section of each chapter of the Student's Study Guide and Computer Workbook *that accompanies this text.*

All data are fictional (unless an actual citation is given).

Answers to selected problems are given at the back of the book.

For Problems 1 through 4, do the following: (a) Make a scatter diagram of the raw scores; (b) describe in words the general pattern of association, if any; (c) compute the correlation coefficient; (d) explain the logic of what you have done, writing as if you were speaking to someone who has never had a statistics course (but who does understand the mean, standard deviation, and Z scores); (e) give three logically possible directions of causality, indicating for each whether it was a reasonable direction in light of the variables involved (and why); (f) make raw score predictions on the dependent variable for persons with Z scores on the predictor variable of –2, –1, 0, +1, and +2; and (g) give the proportion of variance accounted for.

1. An instructor asked five students how many hours they had studied for an exam. (For part f, assume that hours studied is the predictor variable.) Here are the number of hours studied and the students' grades:

Hours Studied	Test Grade
0	52
10	95
6	83
8	71
6	64

2. Four young children were monitored closely over several weeks to measure how much they watched violent television programs and their amount of violent behavior toward their playmates. (For part f, assume that hours watching violent television is the predictor variable.) The results were as follows:

Child's Code Number	Weekly Viewing of Violent TV (hours)	Number of Violent or Aggressive Acts Toward Playmates
G3368	14	9
R8904	8	6
C9890	6	1
L8722	12	8

3. The Louvre Museum is interested in the relation of the age of a painting to public interest in it. The number of people stopping to look at each of 10 randomly selected paintings is observed over a week. (For part f, assume that age is the predictor variable.) The results are as shown:

Painting Title	Approximate Age (Years)		Number of People Stopping to Look	
	X	Z_X	Y	Z_Y
The Entombment	465	1.39	68	−.69
Mys Mar Ste Catherine	515	1.71	71	−.59
The Bathers	240	−.09	123	1.19
The Toilette	107	−.96	112	.82
Portrait of Castiglione	376	.80	48	−1.38
Charles I of England	355	.67	84	−.14
Crispin and Scapin	140	−.75	66	−.76
Nude in the Sun	115	−.91	148	2.05
The Balcony	122	−.86	71	−.59
The Circus	99	−1.01	91	.10

4. A schoolteacher thought that he had observed that students who dressed more neatly were generally better students. To test this idea, the teacher had a friend rate each of the students for neatness of dress. Following are the ratings for neatness, along with each student's score on a standardized school achievement test. (For part f assume that neatness is the predictor variable.)

Child	Neatness Rating		Score on Achievement Test	
	X	Z_X	Y	Z_Y
Janet	18	−.52	60	−.66
Gareth	24	1.43	58	−1.09
Grove	14	−1.82	70	1.47
Kevin	19	−.20	58	−1.09
Joshua	20	.13	66	.62
Nicole	23	1.11	68	1.04
Susan	20	.13	65	.40
Drew	22	.78	68	1.04
Marie	15	−1.50	56	−1.51
Chad	21	.46	62	−.23

5. Solano and Koester (1989) conducted a series of studies about the relationship of loneliness (as measured on the UCLA loneliness scale) with (a) how anxious people are about communicating with other people and (b) a measure of social skills. These tests were given to 321 un-

dergraduates, consisting of 168 males and 153 females. They report their results as follows:

> The correlations between communication anxiety and the UCLA score were similar to those found [in a previous study]. The correlation for the total sample was .35 . . . for males .41 . . . for females .30 . . . . The correlation for the social skill ratings and loneliness for the total sample was −.15, for males −.16 . . . and for females −.10. (p. 130)

Explain the results as if you were writing to a person who has never had a course in statistics. Be sure to comment on possible directions of causality for each result.

6. Deluga (1991) studied the relation of managers' performance to the kinds of influence attempts made by subordinates in a nonprofit community hospital in the northeastern United States. The 80 subordinates studied had completed a standard questionnaire about the ways in which they try to influence their bosses. The questionnaires produced scores in terms of three types of strategies: "hard" (going to higher authorities, making forceful demands, and forming coalitions with other organization members), "soft" (relying on friendliness, ingratiation, flattery), or "rational" (bargaining and using facts and data to support a rational argument). The managers also were rated for their performance in terms of how satisfied the subordinate was with the manager, the manager's overall effectiveness, and the effectiveness of the work unit.

Deluga's main findings are presented in Table 3–8 (p. 130). Explain the results of the analysis for manager effectiveness (the middle row) as if you were writing to a person who understands correlation but has never had any exposure to regression or multiple regression analysis. (Treat the "Adjusted R^2" as if it were an ordinary R^2.)

7. Based on Table 3–8 (from Deluga, 1991), determine the regression equation (for Z scores), and then calculate the predicted manager effectiveness for the manager of each of the following subordinates (figures are Z scores):

Subordinate	Hard	Soft	Rational
A	−1	−1	−1
B	−0	−0	−0
C	−1	−1	−1
D	−1	−0	−0
E	−0	−1	−0
F	−0	−0	−1
G	−3	−1	−1
H	−1	−3	−1
I	−3	−1	−3

TABLE 3–8
Results of Multiple Regression Analysis of Health Care Manager Performance Variables on Subordinate Upward Influence Behavior

Performance Variables	Adjusted R^2	Subordinate-Influencing Behavior		
		Hard β	Soft β	Rational β
Subordinate satisfaction with manager	.25	−.54*	−.04	.04
Manager effectiveness	.23	−.66**	.14	.09
Work unit effectiveness	−.01	−.23	.21	.11

Note: Data from Deluga, R. J. (1991), tab. 1. The relationship of subordinate upward-influencing behavior, health care manager interpersonal stress, and performance. *Journal of Applied Social Psychology, 21*, 78–88. Copyright, 1991, by V. H. Winston & Son, Inc. Reprinted by permission. *$p < .01$. **$p < .001$.

Chapter Appendix: Hypothesis Tests and Power for the Correlation Coefficient

This material is for students who have already completed at least through Chapter 8 and are now returning to this chapter.

Significance of a Correlation Coefficient

Hypothesis testing of a correlation coefficient follows the usual five-step process. However, there are three important points to note. First, usually the null hypothesis can be stated as that the correlation in a population like that observed is no different from a population in which the true correlation is zero. Second, if assumptions (explained in the next paragraph) are met, the comparison distribution is a t distribution with degrees of freedom equal to the number of scores minus 2. Third, the correlation coefficient's score on that t distribution is computed using the formula

$$t = \frac{(r)\,(\sqrt{[N-2]})}{\sqrt{(1-r^2)}}$$

(3–5)

Also, note that the significance tests of a correlation, like a t test, can be either one-tailed or two-tailed. A one-tailed test means that the researcher has predicted the sign (positive or negative) of the correlation.

Assumptions for the significance test of a correlation coefficient are somewhat complex. Ordinarily, both variables should be normally distributed, and the distribution of each variable at each point of the other variable should have about equal variance. However, as with the t test and analysis of variance, moderate violations of these assumptions are not fatal.

An Example

Here is an example using the manager's stress study. We will suppose that the researchers predicted a positive correlation between number of employees supervised and stress, to be tested at the .05 level.

1. Reframe the question into a research hypothesis and a null hypothesis about the populations. The populations of interest are these:

Population 1: Managers like those in this study
Population 2: Managers for whom there is no correlation between number of employees supervised and stress

The null hypothesis is that the two populations have the same correlation. The research hypothesis is that Population 1 has a higher correlation than Population 2. (That is, the prediction is for a population correlation greater than 0.)

2. Determine the characteristics of the comparison distribution. Assuming that we meet the assumptions (in practice, it would be hard to tell with only five cases), the comparison distribution is a t distribution with $df = 3$. (That is, $df = N - 2 = 5 - 2 = 3$.)

3. Determine the cutoff sample score on the comparison distribution at which the null hypothesis should be rejected. The t table (Table A–2 in Appendix A) shows that for a one-tailed test at the .05 level, with 3 degrees of freedom, we need a t of at least 2.353.

4. Determine the score of your sample on the comparison distribution. We computed a correlation of $r = .88$. Applying the formula to find the equivalent t, we get

$$t = \frac{(r)(\sqrt{[N-2]})}{\sqrt{[1-r^2]}} = \frac{(.88)(\sqrt{3})}{\sqrt{(1-.77)}} = \frac{(.88)(1.73)}{\sqrt{.23}} = \frac{1.52}{.48} = 3.17$$

5. Compare the scores obtained in Steps 3 and 4 to decide whether to reject the null hypothesis. The t score of 3.17 for our sample is more extreme than the minimum needed t score of 2.353. Thus, the null hypothesis can be rejected and the research hypothesis is supported.

Effect Size and Power

The correlation coefficient itself is a measure of effect size. Cohen's (1988) conventions for the correlation coefficient are .10 for a small effect size, .30 for a medium effect size, and .50 for a large effect size. Table 3–9 gives approximate power. Table 3–10 gives minimum sample size for 80% power. (More complete tables are provided in Cohen, 1988, pp. 84–95, 101–102.)

TABLE 3–9

Approximate Power of Studies Using the Correlation Coefficient (*r*) for Testing Hypotheses at the .05 Level of Significance

		Effect Size		
		Small (r = .10)	Medium (r = .30)	Large (r = .50)
Two-tailed				
Total N:	10	.06	.13	.33
	20	.07	.25	.64
	30	.08	.37	.83
	40	.09	.48	.92
	50	.11	.57	.97
	100	.17	.86	[a]
One-tailed				
Total N:	10	.08	.22	.46
	20	.11	.37	.75
	30	.13	.50	.90
	40	.15	.60	.96
	50	.17	.69	.98
	100	.26	.92	[a]

[a]Nearly 1.00.

TABLE 3–10

Approximate Number of Participants Needed for 80% Power for a Study Using the Correlation Coefficient (*r*) for Testing a Hypothesis at the .05 Significance Level

	Effect Size		
	Small (r = .10)	Medium (r = .30)	Large (r = .50)
Two-tailed	783	85	28
One-tailed	617	68	22

4 Some Key Ingredients for Inferential Statistics:
The Normal Curve, Probability, and Population Versus Sample

O RDINARILY, social and behavioral scientists do a research study to test some theoretical principle or the effectiveness of some practical procedure. For example, an educational researcher might compare reading speeds of students taught with two different methods to examine a theory of teaching. A sociologist might examine the effectiveness of a program of neighborhood meetings intended to promote water conservation. Such studies are conducted with a particular group of people, but the researchers use inferential statistics to make more general conclusions about the theoretical principle or procedure being studied. These conclusions go beyond the particular group of people studied.

This chapter and Chapters 5, 6, and 7 introduce inferential statistics. In this chapter, we consider three topics: the normal curve, probability, and population versus sample. This is a comparatively short chapter, preparing the way for the next ones, which are more demanding.

The Normal Distribution

We noted in Chapter 1 that the graphs of many of the distributions of variables that social scientists study (as well as many other distributions in nature) follow a unimodal, roughly symmetrical, bell-shaped distribution. These bell-shaped histograms or frequency polygons approximate a precise and important mathematical distribution called the **normal distribution** or, more simply, the **normal curve.** An example of the normal curve is shown in Figure 4–1.

normal distribution
normal curve

FIGURE 4–1
A normal curve.

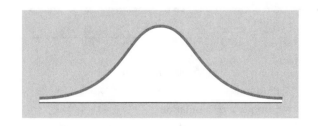

Why the Normal Curve Is So Common in Nature

Take, for example, the number of random letters a particular person can remember accurately on various testings (with different random letters each time). On some testings, the number of letters remembered may be high, on others low, and on most somewhere in between. That is, the number of random letters a person can recall on various testings probably approximately follows a normal curve. Suppose that the person has a basic ability to recall, say, seven letters in this kind of memory task. Nevertheless, on any particular testing, the actual number recalled will be affected by various influences (noisiness of the room, the person's mood at the moment, a combination of random letters unwittingly confused with a familiar name, a sequence of random letters that happens to be all the same letter, and so on).

These various influences add up to make the person do better than seven on some testings and worse than seven on others; however, if the particular combination of such influences that occur at any testing is essentially random, on most testings positive and negative influences should cancel out. The chances of all the negative influences happening to come together on a testing when none of the positive influences show up is not very good. Thus, in general, the person remembers a middle amount, an amount in which all the opposing influences cancel each other out. Very high or very low scores are much less common.

This creates a unimodal distribution (most of the scores near the middle and fewer at the extremes) that is symmetrical (because the number of letters recalled is as likely to be above as below the middle). Being a unimodal symmetrical curve does not guarantee that it will be a normal curve; it could be too flat or too peaked. However, it can be shown mathematically (with some considerable effort) that in the long run, if the influences are truly random and the number of different influences being combined is large, a precise normal curve results. Mathematical statisticians call this principle the *central limit theorem*. We have more to say about this principle in Chapter 6.

The Normal Curve and the Percentage of Scores Between the Mean and 1 and 2 Standard Deviations from the Mean

Because the shape of the normal curve is standard, there is a known percentage of scores below or above any particular point. For example, exactly 50% of the scores is below the mean, because in any symmetrical distribution, half the scores are below the mean. But also, more interestingly, as shown in Figure 4–2, approximately 34% of the scores is always between the mean and 1 standard deviation from the mean. (Notice, incidentally, that in Figure 4–2 the 1 standard deviation (*SD*) point on the normal curve represents the place the curve starts going more out than down.)

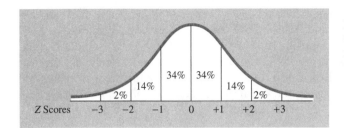

Consider IQ scores. On many widely used intelligence tests, the mean IQ is 100, the standard deviation is 16, and the distribution of IQs is considered to be normal (see Figure 4–3). Knowing about the normal curve and the percentages of scores between the mean and 1 standard deviation above the mean allows us to know that about 34% of people have IQs between 100, the mean, and 116, the IQ score 1 standard deviation above the mean. Similarly, because the normal curve is symmetrical, about 34% of people have IQs between 100 and 84 (the score 1 standard deviation below the mean), and 68% (34% + 34%) have IQs between 84 and 116.

As you can also see from looking at the normal curve, there are many fewer scores between 1 and 2 standard deviations from the mean than there are between the mean and 1 standard deviation from the mean. It turns out that about 14% of the scores fall between 1 and 2 standard deviations above the mean (see Figure 4–2). (Because the normal curve is symmetrical, about 14% of the scores is between 1 and 2 standard deviations below the mean.) Thus, about 14% of people have IQs between 116 (1 standard deviation above the mean) and 132 (2 standard deviations above the mean).

If you can remember the 50%, 34%, and 14% figures, you will have a good sense of the percentage of scores above and below a score if you know its number of standard deviations from the mean.

It also is possible to reverse this approach and figure out a person's number of standard deviations from the mean from a percentage. For example, if you are told a laboratory test showed that a particular archaeological sample of ceramics was in the top 2% of all the samples in the excavation for containing iron (and if you can assume the distribution of iron in such samples is roughly normal), the sample must have a level of iron that is at least 2 standard deviations above the mean level of iron. (This is because of the 50% of

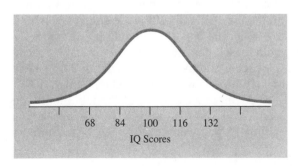

FIGURE 4–3
Distribution of IQ scores on many standard intelligence tests (with *M* = 100 and *SD* = 16).

the scores above the mean. There is 34% between the mean and 1 *SD* and another 14% between 1 and 2 *SD*s above the mean, leaving a remainder of 2% that is 2 *SD*s above the mean.) If you knew the mean and the standard deviation of the iron concentrations in the samples, you could figure out the raw score (the actual level of iron in this sample) that is equivalent to being two SDs above the mean, using the ordinary method for converting *Z* scores (in this case, a *Z* score of +2) to raw scores.

The Normal Curve Table and *Z* Scores

The 50%, 34%, and 14% figures are useful, practical rules for getting a sense of where a particular score stands in relation to others in the group of interest. However, in many research and applied situations, we need more precise information. Because the normal curve is mathematically exact, it is possible to compute the exact percentage of scores between any two points on the normal curve, not just those in which a score happens to be right at 1 or 2 standard deviations from the mean. That is, it is possible to figure the exact percentage of scores between any two *Z* scores. For example, exactly 68.59% of scores have a *Z* score between +.62 and −1.68; exactly 2.81% of scores have a *Z* score between +.79 and +.89, and so forth.

These percentages can be computed using the calculus formula for the normal curve, which you could look up in a mathematical statistics text. However, this can also be accomplished much more simply. Statisticians have worked out tables for the normal curve that give the percentage of scores between the mean (a *Z* score of 0) and any other *Z* score. If you want to know the percentage of scores between the mean and a *Z* score of .62, you simply look up .62 in the table, and it tells you that 23.24% of the scores, in a perfect normal distribution, fall between the mean and this *Z* score.

normal curve table

We have included such a **normal curve table** in Appendix A (Table A–1). As you can see, the first column in the table lists the *Z* score, and the column next to it lists the percentage of scores between the mean and that *Z* score. Notice also that the table repeats these two columns several times on the page, so be sure to look across only one column. Also, notice that the table only lists positive *Z* scores. It is unnecessary to list the negative *Z* scores because the normal curve is perfectly symmetrical; so, the percentage of scores between the mean and, say, a *Z* of +2.38 is exactly the same as the percentage of scores between the mean and a *Z* of −2.38.

In our example, you would find .62 in the "*Z*" column and then, right next to it in the "% Mean to *Z*" column, you would find 23.24.

You also can reverse the process and use the table to find the *Z* score for a particular percentage of scores. For example, suppose you were told that Janice's creativity score was in the top 10% of ninth-grade students. Assuming that creativity scores follow a normal curve, you could figure out her *Z* score as follows: First, you would reason that if she is in the top 10%, 40% of students have scores between her score and the mean. (There are 50% above the mean and she is in the top 10% of scores overall, which leaves 40%.) Then, you would look at the "% Mean to *Z*" column of the table until you found a percentage that was very close to 40%. In this case, the closest you could come would be 39.97%. Finally, you would look at the "*Z*" column to the left of this percentage. In this case, the Z score for 39.97% is 1.28. Thus, Janice's Z score for her level of creativity (as measured on this test) is 1.28. If you know the mean and standard deviation for ninth-grade students' creativity scores, you could figure out Janice's actual raw score on the test by changing this Z score of 1.28 to a raw score using the usual method of changing Z scores to raw scores.

Computing the Percentages of Scores From Raw Scores and Z Scores Using a Normal Curve Table

If you are working with raw scores, change them to Z scores, using the methods from Chapter 2. Proceed as follows.

First, draw a picture of the normal curve and where the Z score falls on it. Shade in the area for which you are trying to find the percentage, and make a rough guess based on the 50%-34%-14% practical rule. When drawing in the Z score, be sure to put it in the right place above or below the mean according to whether it is a positive or negative Z score. Drawing a picture of the problem and making a rough guess is very important to avoid making mistakes in the more precise figuring.

Once you have your picture and your rough guess, go on to find the exact number. The main step is to look up the Z score in the "Z" column of Table A–1 and find the percentage in the "% Mean to Z" column next to it. If you want the percent of scores between the mean and this Z score, this would be your final answer. Often you will need to add 50% to this percentage (if the Z score is positive and you want the total percent below this Z score, or if the Z score is negative and you want the total percent above this Z score). Other times you will have to subtract this percentage from 50% (if the Z score is positive and you want the percent higher than it, or if the Z score is negative and you want the percent lower than it).

Do not try to memorize rules about this. It is much easier to make a picture for the problem and reason out whether the percentage you have from the table is correct as is, or if you need to add or subtract 50%. The reasoning you have to do is about the relation of the area you are trying to figure out (the shaded area in your picture) to the area given by the table, which is the percentage of scores from this Z score to the mean.

Consider a couple of examples using IQ scores. If a person has an IQ of 125, what percentage of people have higher IQs? The Z score for an IQ of 125 is +1.56. (We figured this out based on knowing $M = 100$ and $SD = 16$, and using the usual formula for converting raw scores to Z scores.) In the normal curve table, 1.56 in the "Z" column goes with 44.06 in the "% mean to Z" column. Thus, 44.06% of people have IQ scores between the mean IQ and an IQ of 125 (Z score of +1.56). Because 50% of people are above the mean on any normal curve and 44.06% of the people above the mean are below this person's IQ, that leaves 5.94% above this person's score (that is, $50\% - 44.06\% = 5.94\%$). This is the answer to our problem (and is shown in Figure 4–4). Notice also that with a total of 100%, there are 94.06% with lower IQs than 125.

Consider a person with an IQ of 95. What is the percentage of people with IQs lower than this person? An IQ of 95 has a Z score of –.31. The normal

FIGURE 4–4
Distribution of IQ scores showing percentage of scores above
an IQ score of 125 (the shaded area).

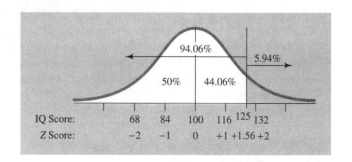

curve table shows that 12.17% of scores are between the mean and a Z score
of .31. The percentage below a Z score of $-.31$ is the total of 50% below the
mean, less the 12.17% between the mean and $-.31$, leaving 37.83% (that is,
$50\% - 12.17\% = 37.83\%$). (This is illustrated in Figure 4–5.) Notice also that
the percentage above a Z score of $-.31$ is 12.17% plus the 50% above the
mean, for a total of 62.17%.

Computing Z Scores and Raw Scores From Percentages Using the Normal Curve Table

Going from a percentage to a Z score is similar to going from a Z score to a
percentage. In both cases, you begin by making a picture of the problem,
shading in the approximate percentage, and making a rough guess of the Z
score using the 50%-34%-14% figures. The rest of the process is almost exactly the reverse of what you did when going from a Z score to a percentage.
Looking at the picture, you figure out the percentage between the mean and
where the shading starts or ends. For example, if your percentage is the top
8%, then the percentage from the mean to where that shading starts is 42%.
If your percentage is the bottom 35%, then the percentage from where the
shading starts is 15%. If your percentage is the top 83%, then the percentage
from the mean to where the shading stops is 33%.

Once you have the percentage from the mean to where the shading starts
or stops, look up the closest number you can find to it in the "% Mean to Z"
column of the normal curve table and find the Z score in the "Z" column next
to it. That Z will be your answer—except it may be negative. The best way to
tell if it is positive or negative is by looking at your picture.

If you need a final answer in raw score terms, you must convert the Z
score to a raw score using the methods you learned in Chapter 2.

FIGURE 4–5
Distribution of IQ scores showing percentage of scores below
an IQ score of 95 (the shaded area).

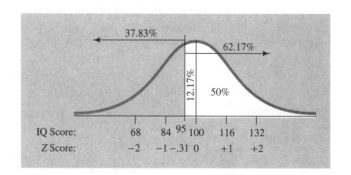

Once again, we will use IQ for our examples. What IQ score would a person need to be in the top 5%? Since 50% of people have IQs above the mean, at least 45% have IQs between this person and the mean (that is, 50% – 5% = 45%). Looking in the "% Mean to Z" column of the normal curve table, the closest figure to 45% is 44.95% (or you could use 45.05%). This goes with a Z score of 1.64 in the "Z" column. We can then use the formula from Chapter 2, $X = M + (Z)(SD)$. With a mean IQ of 100 and a standard deviation of 16, you can conclude that to be in the top 5%, a person would need an IQ of at least 126.24 (see Figure 4–6).

Now consider what IQ would be in the lowest 2.5%. Being in the bottom 2.5% means that at least 47.5% of people have IQs between this IQ and the mean (that is, 50% – 2.5% = 47.5%). In the normal curve table, 47.5% in the "% Mean to Z" column goes with a Z score of 1.96. Because we are below the mean, this becomes –1.96. Converting to a raw score, the IQ for the bottom 2.5% comes out to an IQ of 68.64 (see Figure 4–7).

Probability

The purpose of much social and behavioral science research is to examine the truth of a theory or the effectiveness of a procedure. But scientific research of any kind can only make that truth or effectiveness seem more or less likely; it cannot give us the luxury of knowing for certain. Probability is very important in science. In particular, probability is very important in inferential statistics, the methods social and behavioral scientists use to go from results of research studies to conclusions about theories or applied procedures.

Probability has been studied for centuries by mathematicians and philosophers. Yet even today, the topic is full of controversy. Fortunately, however, you need to know only a few key ideas to understand and carry out the inferential statistical procedures you will be learning in this book.[1] These few key points are not very difficult—indeed, some students find them obvious.

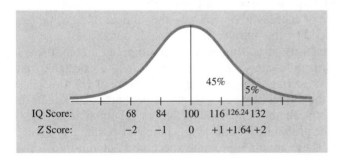

FIGURE 4–6
Z score corresponding to the top 5% of IQ scores (shaded area).

[1]There are, of course, many probability topics that are not related to statistics and other topics related to statistics that are not important for the kinds of statistics used in the social and behavioral sciences. For example, computing joint and conditional probabilities, which is covered in many statistics books, is not covered here because it is rarely seen in published research in the social and behavioral sciences and is not necessary for an intuitive grasp of the logic of the major inferential statistical methods covered in this book.

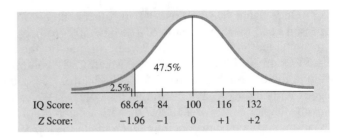

FIGURE 4–7
Z score corresponding to the bottom 2.5% of IQ scores (shaded area).

probability (*p*)
outcome

Expected relative frequency

long-run relative-frequency interpretation of probability

subjective interpretation of probability

Interpretations of Probability

In statistics, we usually define **probability (*p*)** as "the expected relative frequency of a particular outcome." An **outcome** is the result of an experiment (or just about any situation in which the result is not known in advance, such as a coin coming up heads or it raining tomorrow). Frequency is how many times something happens. The relative frequency is the number of times something happens relative to the number of times it could have happened—that is, the proportion of times it happens. (A coin might come up heads 8 times out of 12 flips, for a relative frequency of 8/12, or 2/3.) **Expected relative frequency** is what you expect to get in the long run, if you repeated the experiment many times. (In the case of a coin, in the long run you expect to get 1/2 heads.) This is called the **long-run relative-frequency interpretation of probability.**

We also use probability to indicate how certain we are that a particular thing will happen. This is called the **subjective interpretation of probability.** Suppose you say there is a 95% chance that your favorite restaurant will be open tonight. You could be using a kind of relative frequency interpretation, implying that if you were to check whether this restaurant was open many times on days like today, on 95% of those days you would find it open. However, what you mean is probably more subjective: On a scale of 0% to 100%, you would rate your confidence that the restaurant is open at 95%. To put it another way, you would feel that a bet was fair that had odds based on a 95% chance of the restaurant's being open.

Figuring Probabilities

Regardless of which interpretation one holds, probabilities are usually calculated as the proportion of successful outcomes—the number of possible successful outcomes divided by the number of all possible outcomes.

To figure the probability of getting heads when flipping a coin, there is one possible successful outcome (getting heads) out of two possible outcomes (getting heads or getting tails), making a probability of 1/2, or .5. In a throw of a single die, the probability of a 2 (or any other particular side of the die) is 1/6, or .17, because there is one possible successful outcome out of six possible outcomes. The probability of throwing a die and getting a number 3 or lower is 3/6, or .5. There are three possible successful outcomes (a 1, a 2, or a 3) out of six possible outcomes.

To take a slightly more complicated example, suppose a class has 200 people in it, and 30 are seniors. If you were to pick someone from the class at random, the probability of picking a senior would be 30/200, or .15. This is because there are 30 possible successful outcomes (getting a senior) out of 200 possible outcomes.

Range of Probabilities

Probabilities are proportions (the number of successful outcomes to the total number of possible outcomes). A proportion cannot be less than 0 or greater than 1. In terms of percentages, proportions range from 0% to 100%. Something that has no chance of happening has a probability of 0, and something that is certain to happen has a probability of 1.

Probabilities Expressed as Symbols

Probability usually is symbolized by the letter p. The actual probability number is usually given as a decimal, though sometimes fractions or percentages are used. A 50-50 chance is usually written as $p = .5$, but it could also be written as $p = 1/2$ or $p = 50\%$. It is also common to see a probability written as being "less than" some number using the less than sign. For example, "$p < .05$" means "the probability is less than 5%."

Probability and the Normal Distribution

Until now we have discussed probabilities of specific events that might or might not happen. We also can talk about a range of events that might or might not happen. The throw of a die coming out 3 or lower is an example. Other examples would be the probability of selecting someone on a city street who is between the ages of 30 and 40 and the probability of the temperature tomorrow being lower than 50° F.

If you think of probability in terms of proportion of scores, probability fits in well with frequency distributions (see Chapter 1). In the frequency distribution shown in Figure 4–8, 10 of the total of 50 people scored 7 or higher. If you were selecting people from this group at random, there would be 10 chances (possible successful outcomes) out of 50 (all possible outcomes) of selecting one that was 7 or higher, so $p = 10/50 = .2$.

The normal distribution also can be thought of as a probability distribution. The normal curve is a frequency distribution in which the proportion of scores between any two Z scores is known. As we are seeing, the proportion of scores between any two Z scores is the same as the probability of selecting a score between those two Z scores. For example, the probability of a score falling between the mean and a Z score of +1 (1 standard deviation above the mean) is about 34%; that is, $p = .34$.

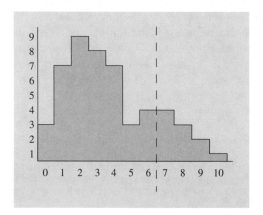

FIGURE 4–8
Frequency distribution (shown as a histogram) of 50 people in which $p = .2$ (10/50) of randomly selecting a person with a score of 7 or higher.

What we are saying may have been obvious all along. In a sense, it is merely a technical point that the normal curve can be seen as either a frequency distribution or a probability distribution. We mention this only so that you will not be confused when we refer later to the probability of a score coming from a particular portion of the normal curve.

Sample and Population

population

sample

We are going to introduce you to some important ideas by thinking of beans. Suppose you are cooking a pot of beans and taste a spoonful to see if they are done. In this example, the pot of beans is a **population,** the entire set of things of interest. The spoonful is a **sample,** the part of the population about which you actually have information. This is illustrated in Figure 4–9.

In social science research, we typically study samples not of beans but of individuals to make inferences about some larger group. A sample might consist of 50 Canadian women who participate in a particular experiment, whereas the population might be intended to be all Canadian women. In an opinion survey, 1,000 people might be selected from the voting-age population and asked for whom they plan to vote. The opinions of these 1,000 people are the sample. The opinions of the larger voting public, to which the pollsters hope to apply their results, is the population (see Figure 4–10).[2]

Why Samples Are Studied Instead of Populations

Obviously, if researchers are going to be drawing conclusions about a population, the results would be most accurate if they could study the entire population, rather than a subgroup from that population. However, in most research situations this is not practical. More important, the whole point of research is usually to be able to make generalizations or predictions about events beyond our reach. We would not call it research if you tested three particular cars to see which gets better gas mileage—unless you hoped to say something about the gas mileage of those models of cars in general. In other words, a researcher might do an experiment on the effect of a particular method of teaching geography using 40 students as participants in the experiment. The purpose of the experiment is not to find out how these particular 40 students respond to the experimental condition but rather to discover something about what works best in general when teaching geography.

The strategy in almost all social and behavioral science research is to study a sample of individuals who are believed to be representative of the general population (or of some particular population of interest). The sample is what is studied, and the population is an unknown that researchers draw conclusions about on the basis of the sample. Most of what you learn in the rest of this book is about the important work of drawing conclusions about populations based on information from samples.

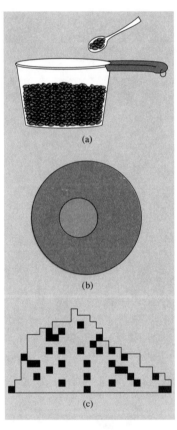

FIGURE 4–9
Populations and samples: In (a), the entire pot of beans is the population, the spoonful is a sample. In (b), the entire larger circle is the population, the circle within it is the sample. In (c), the frequency histogram is of the population and the particular shaded scores together make up the sample.

---

[2]Strictly speaking, population and sample refer to scores (numbers or measurements), not to the people who have those scores. In the first example, the sample is really the *scores* of the 50 Canadian women, not the 50 women themselves, and the population is really what the *scores* would be if all Canadian women were tested.

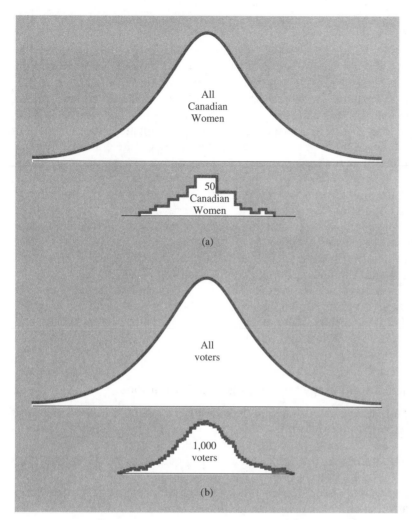

FIGURE 4–10
Additional examples of populations and samples. In (a), the population is the scores of all Canadian women, and a sample consists of the scores of the 50 particular Canadian women studied. In (b), the population is the voting preferences of the entire voting-age population, and sample consists of the voting preferences of the 1,000 voting-age people who were surveyed.

Methods of Sampling

In most cases, the ideal method of picking out a sample to study is called **random selection.** The researcher obtains a complete list of the population and randomly selects some of them to study. An example of a random method of selection would be to put each name on a table-tennis ball, put all the balls into a big hopper, shake it up, and have a blindfolded person select as many as are needed. (In practice, most researchers use a computer-generated list of random numbers.)

It is important not to confuse truly random selection from what might be called **haphazard selection,** such as just taking whoever is available or happens to be first on a list. It is surprisingly easy to accidentally pick a group of people to study that is really quite different from the population as a whole. For example, a survey of attitudes about your statistics instructor taken only among people sitting near you would be affected by all the factors influencing choice of seat, some of which have to do with just what you are studying (how much they like the instructor or the class). Asking people who sit near

random selection

haphazard selection

you would yield opinions more like your own than a truly random sample would.

Unfortunately, it is often impossible to study a truly random sample. One problem is that we do not usually have a complete list of the full population. Another problem is that not everyone a researcher approaches agrees to participate in the study. Yet another problem is the cost and difficulty of tracking down people who live in remote places. For these and other reasons as well, social and behavioral scientists use various approximations to truly random samples that are more practical. However, researchers are consistently careful to rule out, as much as possible in advance, any systematic influence on who gets selected. Once the study has begun researchers are constantly on the alert for any ways in which the sample may be systematically different from the population. For example, in much experimental research in education and psychology, it is common to use volunteer college students as the participants in the study. This is done for practical reasons and because often the topics studied in these experiments (for example, how short-term memory works) are thought to be relatively consistent across different types of people. Even in these cases, researchers avoid, for example, selecting people with a special interest in their research topic. Such researchers are also very aware that their results may not apply beyond college students, volunteers, people from their region, and so forth.

Statistical Terminology for Samples and Populations

population parameters

The mean, variance, and standard deviation of a population are examples of what are called **population parameters.** A population parameter usually is unknown and can only be estimated from what you know about a sample from that population. You do not taste all the beans, just the spoonful. "They are done" is an estimation of the whole pot.

In this book, when referring to the population mean, standard deviation, or variance, even in formulas, we use the word *Population* (or the abbreviated *Pop*)[3] before the *M, SD²*, or *SD*. The mean, variance, and standard deviation you figure for the scores in a sample are called **sample statistics.** A sample statistic is computed from known information. Sample statistics are what we have been calculating all along. Sample statistics use the symbols we have been using all along: M, SD^2 and SD.

sample statistics

Normal Curves, Probabilities, Samples, and Populations in Research Articles

The topics covered in this chapter were basic for understanding what comes next. These topics are rarely mentioned directly in research articles (except articles about methods or statistics). Sometimes you will see the normal

[3]In statistics writing, it is common to use Greek letters to refer to population parameters. For example, the population mean is μ and the population standard deviation is σ. However, we have not used these symbols in this text, wanting to make it easier for students to grasp the formulas without also having to deal with Greek letters.

BOX 4–1

Surveys, Polls, and 1948's Costly "Free Sample"

It is time to make you a more informed reader of poll or survey results in the media. Usually the results of properly done public polls will be accompanied, somewhere in fine print, by a statement like "From a telephone poll of 1,000 American adults taken on June 4 and 5. Sampling error ±3%." What does all this mean?

The Gallup poll is as good an example as any (Gallup, 1972), and there is no better place to begin than 1948, when all three of the major polling organizations—Gallup, Crossley (for Hearst papers), and Roper (for Fortune)—wrongly predicted Thomas Dewey's victory over Harry Truman for the U.S. presidency. Yet Gallup's prediction was based on 50,000 interviews and Roper's on 15,000. By contrast, to predict George Bush's 1988 victory Gallup used only 4,089. Since 1952, the pollsters have never used more than 8,144, but with very small error and no outright mistakes. What has changed?

The method used before 1948, and never repeated since, was called "quota sampling." Interviewers were assigned a fixed number of persons to interview, with strict quotas to fill in all the categories that seemed important, such as residence, sex, age, race, and economic status. Within these specifics, however, they were free to interview whomever they liked. In the United States, Republicans generally tended to be easier to interview: They were more likely to have telephones and permanent addresses and to live in better houses and better neighborhoods. This slight bias had not mattered prior to 1948. Democrats had been winning for years anyway. In 1948, the election was very close, and the Republican bias produced the embarrassing mistake that changed survey methods forever.

Since 1948, Gallup and the other survey organizations have used what is called a "probability method." Simple random sampling is the purest case of the probability method, but simple random sampling for a survey about a U.S. presidential election would require drawing names from a list of all the eligible voters in the nation—a lot of people. Each person selected would have to be found, in diversely scattered locales. So instead, "multistage cluster sampling" is used. To describe it roughly, the United States is divided into seven size-of-community groupings, from large cities to rural open country; these groupings are divided into seven geographic regions (New England, Middle Atlantic, and so on), after which smaller equal-sized groups are zoned, and then city blocks are drawn from the zones, with the probability of selection being proportional to the size of the population or number of dwelling units. Finally, an interviewer is given a randomly selected starting point on the map and is required to follow a given direction, take households in sequence, and ask for the youngest man 18 or older or, if no man is at home, the oldest woman 18 or older. (This has been found to compensate best for the tendencies for young men, and then all men, and then older women, in that order, to be not at home and hence underrepresented.)

Actually, telephoning is often the favored method for polling today. This is because phone surveys cost about one-third of door-to-door polls. Also most persons now own phones, making this method less biased in favor of the rich than in Truman's time. Phoning also allows computers randomly to dial phone numbers through a system called random digit dialing, which, unlike telephone directories, includes unlisted numbers.

Whether the survey is taken by telephone or face to face, there will be about 35% nonrespondents after three attempts to make contact. This creates yet another bias to be reckoned with. Researchers deal with this bias with questions about how much time a person spends at home, so that a slight extra weight can be given to the responses of those who were reached but usually are at home less, to make up for those missed entirely.

Now you know quite a bit about opinion polls, but we have left two important questions unanswered: Why are only about 1,000 included in a poll meant to describe all U.S. adults, and what does the term *sampling error* mean? For these answers, you must wait for Chapter 6 (Box 6–1).

curve mentioned, usually when a researcher is describing the pattern of scores on a particular variable. (We say more about this and give some examples from published articles in Chapter 11, where we consider circumstances in which the scores do not follow a normal curve.)

Probability rarely is discussed directly, except in relation to statistical significance, a topic we mentioned briefly in Chapter 3. In almost any article you look at, the Results section will be strewn with descriptions of various methods associated with statistical significance, followed by something like "$p < .05$" or "$p < .01$." The p refers to probability, but the probability of what? That is the main topic of our discussion of statistical significance in Chapter 5.

Finally, you will occasionally see a brief mention of the method of selecting the sample from the population. For example, Hunsley and Lefebvre (1990) conducted a survey of clinical psychologists in Canada. In the Methods section of their article, they wrote, "The questionnaire was sent . . . to a random sample of 300 members of CRHSPP [Canadian Register of Health Service Providers in Psychology] who were listed in the 1988 membership directory" (p. 351). Hunsley and Lefebvre specified both the listing they used for the population and the method they used (random selection) to obtain their sample.

Summary

The scores on many variables in social science research approximately follow a bell-shaped, symmetrical, unimodal distribution called the normal curve. Because the shape of this curve follows an exact mathematical formula, there is a specific percentage of scores between any two points on a normal curve.

A useful working rule for normal curves is that 50% of the scores fall above the mean, 34% between the mean and 1 standard deviation above the mean, and 14% between 1 and 2 standard deviations above the mean.

A normal curve table gives the percentage of scores between the mean and any particular positive Z score. Using this table, and knowing that the curve is symmetrical and that 50% of the scores fall above the mean, it is possible to determine the percentage of scores above or below any particular Z score and also the Z score corresponding to the point at which a particular percentage of scores begins.

Most social scientists consider the probability of an event to be its expected relative frequency, though some think of probability as the subjective degree of belief that the event will happen. Probability usually is figured as the proportion of successful outcomes to total possible outcomes. It is symbolized by p and has a range from 0 (event is impossible) to 1 (event is certain). The normal distribution can be thought of as providing a way to know the probabilities of scores' being within particular ranges of values.

A sample is an individual or group that is studied—usually as representative of a larger group or population that cannot be studied in its entirety. Ideally, the sample is selected from a population using a strictly random procedure. The mean, variance, and so forth of a sample are called sample statistics; when of a population, they are called population parameters.

Research articles rarely discuss normal curves (except briefly when the variable being studied seems not to follow a normal curve) or probability (except in relation to statistical significance). However, procedures of sampling, particularly when the study is a survey, are usually described, and the representativeness of a sample when random sampling could not be used may be discussed.

Key Terms

expected relative frequency
haphazard selection
long-run relative-frequency interpretation of probability
normal curve
normal curve table

normal distribution
outcome
population
population parameters
probability (p)
random selection

sample
sample statistics
subjective interpretation of probability

Practice Problems

These problems involve computation (with the assistance of a calculator). Most real-life statistics problems are done on a computer. Even if you have a computer, do this by hand to ingrain the method in your mind.

For practice in using a computer to solve statistics problems, refer to the computer section of each chapter of the Student's Study Guide and Computer Workbook *that accompanies this text.*

All data are fictional (unless an actual citation is given).

Answers to selected problems are given at the back of the book.

1. Suppose that the people living in a particular city were found to have a mean score of 40 and a standard deviation of 5 on a measure of concern about the environment and that these attitude scores are normally distributed. Approximately what percentage of people have a score (a) above 40, (b) above 45, (c) above 30, (d) above 35, (e) below 40, (f) below 45, (g) below 30, (h) below 35? What is the minimum score a person has to have to be in the top (i) 2%, (j) 16%, (k) 50%, (l) 84%, (m) 98%? (Use the 50%-34%-14% approximations for this problem.)

2. Suppose that on a test of creativity, the scores of architects are normally distributed. What percentage of architects have Z scores (a) above .10, (b) below .10, (c) above .20, (d) below .20, (e) above 1.10, (f) below 1.10, (g) above −.10, (h) below −.10?

3. Assuming a normal curve, (a) if a person is in the top 10% of the country on mathematics ability, what is that person's Z score? (b) If the person was in the top 1%, what would be the Z score?

4. How high a score would a person need to be in the top 5% on a test of coordination that has a normal distribution with a mean of 50 and a standard deviation of 10? Explain your answer to someone who has never had a course in statistics.

5. The following numbers of individuals in a company received special assistance from the personnel department last year:

Drug/alcohol	10
Family crisis counseling	20
Other	20
Total	50

If you were to select a score at random from the records for last year, what is the probability that it would be (a) drug/alcohol, (b) family, (c) drug/alcohol or family, (d) any category except "Other," (e) any of the three categories?

6. A research article describing the level of self-esteem of Australian high school students emphasizes that it surveyed a "random sample" of high school students. Explain to a person who has never had a course in statistics or research methods what this means and why it is important.

5 Introduction to Hypothesis Testing

I N Chapter 4, you learned about the normal curve, probability, and the distinction between a sample and a population. In this chapter, we introduce the crucial topic of **hypothesis testing.** Hypothesis testing is a systematic procedure for determining whether the results of a research study, which examines a sample, provide support for a particular theory or practical innovation, which applies to a population. Hypothesis testing is the central theme in all the remaining chapters of this book, as it is in most social and behavioral science research.

hypothesis testing

We should warn you at this point that many students find the most difficult part of the course to be mastering the basic logic of this chapter and the next. This chapter in particular requires some mental gymnastics, and even if you follow everything the first time through, you will be wise to review it thoroughly. Hypothesis testing involves a cluster of ideas that make little sense covered in isolation. So in this chapter you will learn a comparatively large number of ideas all at once. On the positive side, once you have a good grasp of the material in this chapter and the two that follow, your mind will be accustomed to this sort of thing, and the rest of the course should seem easier.

At the same time, we have kept this introduction as simple as possible, putting off what we could to later chapters. For example, real-life social science research almost always involves samples of many—sometimes a great many—individuals. To simplify the number of ideas you must learn at the outset, all of the examples in this chapter are about studies in which the sample is a single individual. To accomplish that, we have had to create some rather odd examples. Just remember that we are building a foundation that will, by Chapter 8, prepare you to understand hypothesis testing as it actually is carried out.

A Hypothesis-Testing Example

Here is your first necessarily odd, fictional example. A large research project has been going on for several years. In this project, new babies are given a special vitamin and then their development is monitored during the first 2 years of life. So far, the vitamin has not speeded up the development of babies. The ages at which these and all babies start to walk is shown in Figure 5–1. Notice that the mean is 14 months, the standard deviation is 3 months, and the ages follow a normal curve. For example, it can be seen that less than 2% start walking before 8 months of age. These less than 2% of babies who start walking early fall 2 standard deviations below the mean. (This fictional-for-simplicity's-sake distribution actually is close to the true distribution researchers have found for European babies, although that true distribution is slightly skewed to the right [Hindley, Filliozat, Klackenberg, Nicolet-Meister, & Sand, 1966.])

Based on some new theories, one of the researchers working on the project reasons that if the vitamin the babies are taking could be more highly refined, the effect of the vitamin would be dramatically greater—babies taking the highly purified version should start walking much earlier than other babies. (We will assume that it was absolutely clear that the purification process could not possibly make the vitamin harmful.) However, refining the vitamin in this way is extremely expensive for each dose. So the research team decides to try the procedure with enough doses to serve only one baby. A baby in the project is then randomly selected to take the highly purified version of the vitamin, and its progress is followed along with that of all the other babies in the project. What kind of result should lead the researchers to conclude that the highly purified vitamin allows babies to walk earlier?

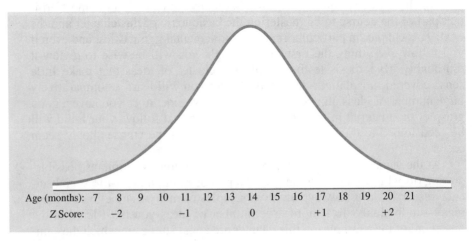

FIGURE 5–1
Distribution of when babies begin to walk (fictional data).

This is an example of a hypothesis-testing problem. The researchers want to draw a general conclusion about the theory that the purified vitamin permits babies to walk earlier, based on information from a sample (in this strange example, a sample of one baby.)

The Core Logic of Hypothesis Testing

There is a standard way to approach a hypothesis-testing problem. The researcher will use the following reasoning. Ordinarily, the chances of a baby's starting to walk at age 8 months or earlier would be less than 2%. Walking at 8 months is highly unlikely. So if the baby in our study starts walking by 8 months, we will be able to *reject* the idea that the specially purified vitamin has *no* effect. If we reject the idea that the specially purified vitamin has no effect, we must *accept* the idea that it *does* have an effect. (You may want to read this paragraph again.)

The researchers first laid out what would have to happen for them to conclude that the special purification procedure makes a difference. Having laid this out in advance, the researchers can then go on to conduct their study. In this case, conducting the study means giving the specially purified vitamin to a particular baby and watching to see how early that baby walks. If the result of the study shows that the baby starts walking before 8 months, they would then conclude that it is unlikely the specially purified vitamin makes no difference and thus conclude that it does make a difference.

This kind of opposite-of-what-you-predict, roundabout reasoning is at the heart of inferential statistics. It is something like a double negative. One reason for this approach is that we can directly determine the probability of getting a particular experimental result if the situation of there being no difference is true. In the case of our purified vitamin example, the researchers know what the probabilities are of babies walking at different ages if the special purification process does not have an effect. It is the probability of a baby's walking at various ages that is already known from examining babies who have not received the specially purified vitamin (the distribution shown in Figure 5–1).

It turns out, in fact, that without such a tortuous way of going at the problem, in most cases the problem simply cannot be solved at all. In almost all cases of research in the social and behavioral sciences, whether involving experiments, surveys, or whatever, we draw conclusions by evaluating the probability of getting our research results if the opposite of what we are predicting were true.

The Hypothesis-Testing Process

We will again examine the solution to our example problem, considering each step in some detail as well as introducing you to the special terminology used. In doing so, we will introduce you to a five-step procedure you will be using for the rest of this book.

Step 1: Restating the Question as a Research Hypothesis and a Null Hypothesis About the Populations

First, note that the researchers are interested in the effects on babies in general (not just this particular baby), so it will be useful to restate the question in terms of populations. That is, for purposes of analyzing the present situation, we can think of babies as falling into two groups:

Population 1: Babies who take the specially purified vitamin
Population 2: Babies who do not take the specially purified vitamin

(Note that although only one real-life baby exists in Population 1, it is a population of an as-yet-unborn future group of many babies to whom the researchers want to apply their results.)

The prediction of the research team, based on a theory of how vitamins of various kinds work, is that Population 1 babies (those who take the specially purified vitamin) will generally walk earlier than Population 2 babies (those who do not take the specially purified vitamin). A statement like this, about the difference between populations predicted by a theory (or based on practical experience) is called a **research hypothesis.**

research hypothesis

If the prediction is wrong, however, an opposite situation holds: Population 1 babies (those who take the specially purified vitamin) will generally not walk earlier than Population 2 babies (those who do not take the specially purified vitamin). This opposite prediction is that there is no difference in when Population 1 and Population 2 babies start walking: They start at the same time. A statement like this, about a lack of difference between populations, is the crucial opposite of the research hypothesis. It is called a **null hypothesis.** The null hypothesis has this name because it states the situation in which there is no difference (the difference is null) between populations.[1,2]

null hypothesis

Step 2: Determining the Characteristics of the Comparison Distribution

Once the question has been restated in terms of a choice between a research hypothesis and a null hypothesis, the next step is to consider how the information we can obtain about a sample might help make this choice. The question we ask is this: Given a particular sample result (in this case, one score), what is the probability of obtaining that result if the null hypothesis is true?

To answer this question, we have to know about the situation if the null hypothesis is true. That is, we need to know the details of the population

---

[1]We have oversimplified a bit here. Because the research hypothesis is that one population will walk earlier than the other, its opposite is that the other group will either walk at the same time or walk later. That is, the opposite of the research hypothesis includes both no difference and a difference in the direction opposite to that predicted. We will discuss this issue in some detail later in the chapter.

[2]The research hypothesis and the null hypothesis are complete opposites. If one is true, the other cannot be true. This oppositeness and the direct focus on the null hypothesis is completely central to the hypothesis-testing logic. For this reason the research hypothesis, which is ultimately our real interest, is sometimes called the "alternative hypothesis."

distribution the sample is coming from if the null hypothesis is true. If we know the distribution of the population our sample comes from, and we know it is a normal curve, we can directly determine the probability of having gotten any particular score from that distribution using the normal curve table.

Knowing the details of the distribution our sample would be coming from if the null hypothesis is true is possible because, if the null hypothesis is true, both populations are the same. Because we usually know about one of the populations (Population 2), in this case we also know about the population from which our sample comes (Population 1), which has to be identical if the null hypothesis is true.

In our purified-vitamin example, if the null hypothesis is true, the baby we test comes from a population that follows a normal curve with a mean of 14 months and a standard deviation of 3 months. (That is, if the null hypothesis is true, the population our baby comes from, Population 1, is the same as Population 2, which has a mean of 14 months and so on.)

In this book, the distribution representing the situation if the null hypothesis is true—the distribution to which you will compare your actual sample—is called the **comparison distribution**.[3] That is, in the hypothesis-testing process, one compares the actual sample score to this distribution in the sense of figuring out the probability of getting a score as extreme as our sample's score on this distribution. In the present example, the comparison distribution is the same as the distribution of scores in Population 2, the population in which the experimental procedure has not been applied.

comparison distribution

Step 3: Determining the Cutoff Sample Score on the Comparison Distribution at Which the Null Hypothesis Should Be Rejected

Ideally, well before conducting the study, researchers consider what score a sample would need to have to be extreme enough that they would decide it is too unlikely that they could get such an extreme score if the null hypothesis were true. This is called the **cutoff sample score.** (The cutoff sample score is also known as the *critical value.*)

cutoff sample score

In the present case, the researchers might decide, for example, that if the null hypothesis were true (meaning that it does not matter whether a baby is fed the specially purified vitamin or not), a baby walking at 8 months or earlier would be very unlikely. That is, being 2 standard deviations below the mean (walking at 8 months) could occur less than 2% of the time. Thus based on the comparison distribution, the researchers can decide, even before doing their study, that *if* the result of their study is a baby who walks before 8 months, they will reject the null hypothesis. If they reject the null hypothesis, they are left with the research hypothesis. We would then say the "research hypothesis is supported."

If the baby whom the researchers study does not start walking until after 8 months, they cannot reject the null hypothesis. They also cannot say the

---

[3]The comparison distribution is also sometimes called a "statistical model." In most cases, it is also called a "sampling distribution," a distribution of a characteristic of samples—an idea we discuss in Chapter 6.

null hypothesis is supported. Not rejecting the null hypothesis leaves a situation that is ambiguous. No conclusions can be drawn except maybe that more research is needed. We have more to say about this later.

When setting in advance how extreme a score has to be to reject the null hypothesis, researchers do not generally use an actual number of units on the direct scale of measurement (in this case, months). Instead, they state how extreme a score should be in terms of a probability and the Z score that goes with that probability. In this case, the researchers might decide that if a result were less likely than 2% (the probability), they would reject the null hypothesis. Being in the bottom 2% on a normal curve is having a Z score of –2 or lower. Thus, the researchers would set –2 as their Z score cutoff point on the comparison distribution for deciding that a result is sufficiently extreme to reject the null hypothesis.

Suppose that the researchers are even more cautious than this and decide that they will reject the null hypothesis only if they get a result that could occur by chance only 1% of the time or less. They could then figure out, using the normal curve table, that to have a score in the lower 1% of a normal curve, you need a Z score of –2.33 or less. (In our example, a Z score of –2.33 means 7 months.) In Figure 5–2, we have shaded the 1% of the comparison distribution in which a score would be so extreme that the possibility that it came from a distribution like this by chance would be rejected.

In general, social science researchers use a cutoff on the comparison distribution with a probability of 5% that a score will be at least that extreme. That is, the null hypothesis is rejected if the probability of getting a result this extreme (if the null hypothesis were true) is less than 5%. This probability is usually written as "$p < .05$." However, in some areas of research, or when researchers want to be especially cautious, they use a cutoff of 1% ($p < .01$) or even .1% ($p < .001$).

conventional levels of significance

These are called **conventional levels of significance.** They are described as the .05 significance level or the .01 significance level. When a sample score is so extreme that the null hypothesis is rejected, the result is said to be

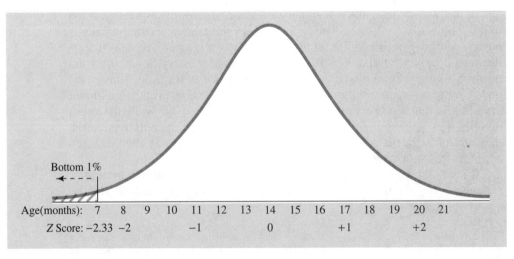

FIGURE 5–2
Distribution of when babies begin to walk, with bottom 1% indicated (fictional data).

statistically significant. We discuss in more detail in Chapter 7 the issues in deciding on the significance level to use.

Step 4: Determining Your Sample's Score on the Comparison Distribution

The next step is to conduct the study and find out the actual result for our sample. The researcher figures out the Z score for the sample's raw score based on the mean and standard deviation of the comparison distribution.

Let us assume that the researchers did the study and the baby who was given the specially purified vitamin started walking at 6 months. The mean of the comparison distribution to which we are comparing these results is 14 months and the standard deviation is 3 months. Thus a baby who walks at 6 months is 8 months below the mean, which is 2 2/3 standard deviations below the mean. The Z score for the sample baby on the comparison distribution is –2.67. Figure 5–3 shows the score of our sample baby on the comparison distribution.

Step 5: Deciding Whether or Not to Reject the Null Hypothesis

This step is entirely straightforward once it is clear (a) what Z score the sample must have on the comparison distribution to reject the null hypothesis (Step 3) and (b) the actual Z score of the sample (Step 4). To determine whether or not to reject the null hypothesis, you compare the needed Z score to the actual Z score. In this case, suppose the researchers determined that the null hypothesis would be rejected if the Z score of the sample were lower than –2. Because the actual result was –2.67, which is lower than –2, they

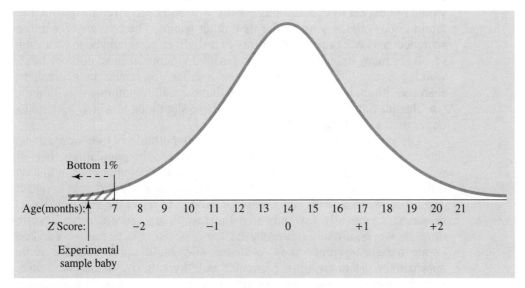

FIGURE 5–3
Distribution of when babies begin to walk, indicating both the bottom 1% and the single baby that is the sample studied (fictional data).

would reject the null hypothesis. (Had they chosen to use the more conservative 1% significance level, the needed Z score would have been –2.33. Because the actual Z was –2.67, even with this more conservative cutoff, they would still have rejected the null hypothesis.)

If a researcher rejects the null hypothesis, what remains is the research hypothesis. In this example, the research team can conclude that the results of the study support the research hypothesis that babies who take the specially purified vitamin walk earlier than other babies.

Implications of Rejecting or Failing to Reject the Null Hypothesis

We want to emphasize two points about the kinds of conclusions you can make from the hypothesis-testing process. First, suppose you reject the null hypothesis, so that your results support the research hypothesis (as in our example). You would still not say that the result "proves" the research hypothesis or that the results show that the research hypothesis is "true." Such conclusions are too strong. They are too strong because the results are always based on probabilities (in this case, they are based on the probability being low of getting your result if the null hypothesis is true). "Proven" and "true" are okay in logic and mathematics, but to use these words in conclusions from scientific research is thoroughly unprofessional. (It is okay to use "true" when speaking hypothetically—for example, "if this hypothesis were true, then . . ."—but not when speaking of an actual result.)

Second, when a result is not extreme enough for us to reject the null hypothesis, we do not say that the result "supports the null hypothesis." A result that is not strong enough for us to reject the null hypothesis means only that the study was inconclusive. Although the results may not be extreme enough to reject the null hypothesis, the null hypothesis might still be false (and the research hypothesis true). Suppose, for example, that in our example the specially purified vitamin had only a slight but still real effect. In that case, we would not expect to find any single baby who had been given the purified vitamin to be walking a lot earlier than other babies. The best way for the researchers to check out this possibility of a slight effect would be to do a study involving many babies receiving the purified vitamin. If most of those began walking even slightly earlier than the average for babies in general, researchers might begin to be convinced that the null hypothesis was unlikely. (In Chapter 6, we examine the logic of these situations in which a sample is larger than a single person.)

The point is that to show that the null hypothesis is true would mean showing that there is really no difference between the populations. It is always possible that there is a difference between the populations, but that the difference is much smaller than what the particular study was able to detect. Therefore, when a result is not extreme enough to reject the null hypothesis, researchers generally say only that the results are "inconclusive." Sometimes, however, if many studies have been done using large numbers and accurate measuring procedures, evidence may build up in support of the approximate accuracy of a particular null hypothesis. Sometimes, when speaking loosely, researchers describe a failure to reject a null hypothesis as a result that "supports the null hypothesis." Technically, however, this is usually much too strong a statement as a result of any one study. (We have more to say on this issue in Chapter 7. Also see Box 5–1.)

Summary of the Steps of Hypothesis Testing

Here is a summary of the five steps of hypothesis testing:

1. Restate the question as a research hypothesis and a null hypothesis about the populations.
2. Determine the characteristics of the comparison distribution.
3. Determine the cutoff sample score on the comparison distribution at which the null hypothesis should be rejected.
4. Determine the score of your sample on the comparison distribution.
5. Compare the scores in Steps 3 and 4 to decide whether to reject the null hypothesis.

One-Tailed and Two-Tailed Hypothesis Tests

In the baby-walking example, the research hypothesis was about a situation in which the researchers were interested in only one direction of the result. The researchers were interested in whether the baby given the specially purified vitamin would walk earlier than other babies. The researchers in this study were really not even imagining the possibility that giving the specially purified vitamins would cause babies to start walking later.

Directional Hypotheses and One-Tailed Tests

The baby-walking study was an example of a **directional hypothesis** because the researchers were interested in a specific direction of the effect. It is important to notice that when a researcher puts forward a directional hypothesis, the appropriate null hypothesis is also, in a sense, directional. If the research hypothesis is that taking the specially purified vitamin will make a baby walk earlier, the null hypothesis is that the specially purified vitamin will either have no effect or make the baby walk later. Thus, as was shown, for example, in Figure 5–2, for the null hypothesis to be rejected, the sample had to have a score in the bottom 1%—the lower extreme or tail of the comparison distribution. (A score at the other tail would be considered the same as a score in the middle for purposes of rejecting the null hypothesis.) For this reason, a test of a directional hypothesis is called a **one-tailed test.**

directional hypothesis

one-tailed test

Nondirectional Hypotheses and Two-Tailed Tests

Sometimes, however, a research hypothesis is simply that one population will differ from the other, without specifying whether it will differ by having lower scores or higher scores. For example, a researcher may be interested in the impact of a new social skills program on worker productivity. It is possible that the program will improve productivity by making the working

BOX 5–1

To Be or Not to Be—But Can Not Being Be? The Problem of Whether and When to Accept the Null Hypothesis

The null hypothesis states that there is no difference between populations represented by different groups or experimental conditions. As we have seen, the usual rule in statistics is that a study cannot find the null hypothesis to be true. A study can only tell you that you cannot reject the null hypothesis. That is, such a study is simply uninformative. Such studies tend not to be published, obviously. In fact, much work could be avoided if people knew what interventions, measures, or experiments had not worked. Indeed, Greenwald (1975) reports that sometimes ideas have been assumed too long to be true just because a few studies found them true, while many more, unreported, had not.

However, Frick (1995) has pointed out a more serious problem with being rigidly uninterested in the null hypothesis. Frick points out that sometimes it may be true that one thing has no effect on another. This does not mean that there would be a zero relationship of no correlation or no difference at all—a result almost impossible to obtain in many situations. It would only mean that it was so small that it probably represented no real or at least no important relationship or difference.

The problem is knowing when to conclude that the null hypothesis (or something close to it) might be true. Frick (1995) gives three criteria. First, the null hypothesis should seem possible. Second, obviously the results in the study should be consistent with the null hypothesis. There

should be no other obvious way to interpret them. Third, and most important, the researcher has to have made a strong effort to find the effect that he or she wants to conclude is not there. Among other things, this means studying a large sample, having very thorough and sensitive measurement, and watching for floor and ceiling effects (which would make the effect impossible to obtain in a study because of the measure). If the study is an experiment, it is important that the experimenter has tried to produce the difference by using a strong manipulation and rigorous conditions of testing.

Frick points out that all of this leaves a subjective element to the acceptance of the null hypothesis: Who decides when a researcher's effort was strong enough? Subjective judgments are a part of science, like it or not. For example, reviewers of articles have to decide if a topic is important enough to be worth the space in their journal. Further, the null hypothesis is being accepted all the time anyway. (For example, many social scientists accept the null hypothesis about the effect of extrasensory perception.) It is better to discuss our basis for accepting the null hypothesis than just to accept it.

What are we to make of all this? It is clear that just failing to reject the null hypothesis is not the same as supporting it. However, Frick reminds us that there are situations in which the evidence ought to convince us that something like the null hypothesis is likely to be the case.

---

environment more pleasant, but it is also possible that it will hurt productivity by encouraging people to socialize instead of work. The research hypothesis would be simply that the skills program changes the level of productivity. The null hypothesis would be that the program does not affect productivity one way or the other.

nondirectional hypothesis

Whenever a hypothesis specifies a difference, without predicting the direction of that difference, it is called a **nondirectional hypothesis.** To test the significance of a nondirectional hypothesis, one must examine whether a score is extreme at either tail of the comparison distribution. This is called a

two-tailed test

two-tailed test.

Determining Cutoff Points With Two-Tailed Tests

There is a special complication in a two-tailed test. Suppose the researcher selects the 5% significance level. With a one-tailed test, a researcher rejects the null hypothesis if the sample score is in a particular extreme 5% of the comparison distribution. With a two-tailed test, you might think the researcher would use the bottom 5% when the score is extreme in the low direction and the top 5% when a score is extreme in the high direction. But if the researcher did that, there would be a total of 10% of the comparison distribution in which the null hypothesis could be rejected. The significance level would really be 10%, which most researchers would find too risky. (That is, with a 10% significance level, one could too easily reject the null hypothesis when, in fact, it was true.)

There is a solution to this problem. When conducting a two-tailed test, you divide the significance percentage between the two tails. For example, with a 5% significance level, you would reject a null hypothesis only if the sample was so extreme that it was in either the top 2 1/2% or the bottom 2 1/2%. In this way, the overall chance of the null hypothesis's being true is kept at a total of 5%. Note that conducting a two-tailed test makes the cutoff Z scores for the 5% level +1.96 and −1.96. For a one-tailed test, the cutoff was not so extreme—only +1.64 or −1.64. With a one-tailed test, only one side of the distribution was considered. These situations are illustrated in Figure 5–4a. Using the 1% significance level, a two-tailed test (.5% at each tail) has cutoffs of +2.58 and −2.58, while a one-tailed test's cutoff is either +2.33 or −2.33 (see Figure 5–4b).

When to Use One-Tailed or Two-Tailed Tests

It is easier to reject the null hypothesis with a one-tailed test than with a two-tailed test, in the sense that a sample's score need not be so extreme before the result is considered significant. However, there is a price: With a one-tailed test, if the result is extreme in the other direction, no matter how extreme, the result cannot be considered significant.

In principle, you plan to use a one-tailed test when you have a clearly directional hypothesis and a two-tailed test when you have a clearly nondirectional hypothesis. In practice, it is not so simple. Even when a theory clearly predicts a particular result, we sometimes find that the result is just the opposite of what we expected. Sometimes this opposite result actually may be more interesting. By using one-tailed tests, we run the risk of having to ignore possibly important results.

Because of these considerations, there is debate as to whether one-tailed tests should be used, even when there is a clearly directional hypothesis. To be safe, many researchers use two-tailed tests for both nondirectional and directional hypotheses. In fact, in most research articles, unless the researcher specifically notes that a one-tailed test was used, it is usually assumed that it was a two-tailed test.

You should remember, however, that usually the final conclusion is not really affected by whether a one- or two-tailed test is used. It is our experience that in general research results are either so extreme that they will be significant by any reasonable standard or so far from extreme that they would not be significant no matter what procedure was used.

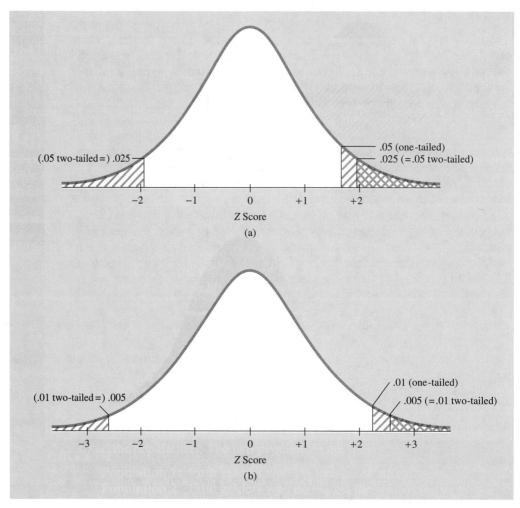

FIGURE 5–4
Comparison of significance level cutoffs for one- and two-tailed tests: (a) .05 significance level; (b) .01 significance level. (The one-tailed tests in these examples assume the prediction was for a high score.)

What happens when a result yields less certain conclusions? The researcher's decision about one- or two-tailed tests takes on added importance. In this situation the researcher attempts to use the approach that will yield the most accurate and noncontroversial conclusion. The idea is to let nature—and not a researcher's decisions—determine the conclusion as much as possible. Furthermore, whenever a result is less than completely clear one way or the other, most researchers will not be comfortable drawing strong conclusions until further research is done.

An Example of Hypothesis Testing Using a Two-Tailed Test

Here is another fictional example, this time using a two-tailed test. A researcher is interested in the effect of going through a natural disaster on the attitude of police chiefs about the goodness of the people in their city. The researchers believe that after a disaster, the police chief is likely to have a more positive attitude about the people of the city (because the chief will have seen many acts of heroism and helping of neighbors after the event). However, it is also possible that a disaster will lead to police chiefs having more negative attitudes, because there may be cases of looting and other dishonest behavior after the disaster. Thus, the researchers will make a nondirectional hypothesis.

Let us assume that there is considerable previous research on the attitudes of police chiefs about the goodness of the people in their cities and that on a standard questionnaire the mean attitude rating is 69.5 with a standard deviation of 14.1, and the attitude scores follow a normal curve. Let us also assume that a major earthquake has just occurred in an isolated city and shortly afterwards the researcher is able to give the standard questionnaire to the police chief of that city.

The hypothesis-testing procedure is then conducted as follows:

1. Restate the question as a research hypothesis and a null hypothesis about the populations. The two populations of interest are these:

Population 1: Police chiefs whose city has just been through a disaster
Population 2: Police chiefs in general

The research hypothesis is that police chiefs whose city has just been through a disaster (Population 1) score differently from police chiefs in general (Population 2) on their attitude toward the goodness of the people of their city. The opposite of the research hypothesis, the null hypothesis, is that police chiefs whose city has just been through a disaster will have the same attitude as police chiefs in general. (That is, the null hypothesis is that the attitudes of Populations 1 and 2 are the same.)

2. Determine the characteristics of the comparison distribution. If the null hypothesis is true, the distributions for Populations 1 and 2 will be the same. We know the distribution of Population 2, so it can serve as our comparison distribution. As noted, it is normally distributed with $M = 69.5$ and $SD = 14.1$.

3. Determine the cutoff sample score on the comparison distribution at which the null hypothesis should be rejected. The researcher selects the 5% significance level. Because the researcher has made a nondirectional hypothesis, a two-tailed test is used. This means that the null hypothesis will be rejected only if the police chief's attitude score is in either the top or bottom 2 1/2% of the comparison distribution. In terms of Z scores, these cutoffs are thus +1.96 and −1.96 (see Figure 5–5).

4. Determine the score of your sample on the comparison distribution. The police chief who went through the earthquake completed the standard attitude questionnaire and had a score of 41. This corresponds to a Z score on the comparison distribution of −2.02.

5. Compare the scores from Steps 3 and 4 to decide whether to reject the null hypothesis. A Z score of −2.02 is just below the Z score of −1.96, which is where the lower 2 1/2% of the comparison distribution begins. This is a result so extreme that it is unlikely to have occurred if this police chief represented a population no different from Population 2. Therefore, the researcher

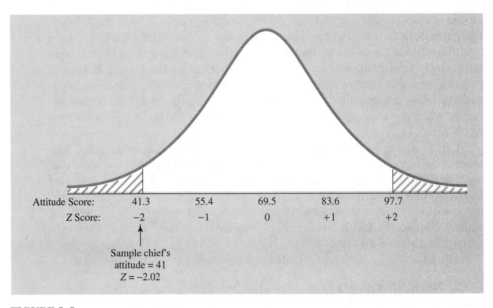

FIGURE 5–5

Distribution of attitudes of police chiefs toward goodness of people in their cities with upper and lower 2 1/2% shaded and showing the sample police chief whose city has just been through a disaster (fictional data).

rejects the null hypothesis. This result supports their research hypothesis that going through a disaster does indeed change police chiefs' attitudes toward their city. In this case, the results would mean that the effect is one of making the chief less positive about the city's people. (Remember, however, that this is a fictional study.)

Hypothesis Tests as Reported in Research Articles

In general, hypothesis testing is reported in research articles as part of one of the specific statistical procedures you learn in later chapters. For each result of interest, the researcher usually first notes whether the result was "statistically significant." Next, the researcher usually gives the name of the specific technique used in determining the probabilities, such as a "*t* test" or an "*F*" computed as part of an "analysis of variance" (these procedures are covered in Chapters 8–12). Finally, there will be an indication of the significance level, such as "$p < .05$" or "$p < .01$." For example, Biner (1991), who conducted a study of the effect of lighting on the evaluation of potentially aversive (unpleasant) events, reported one result as follows: "Subjects exposed to the bright lighting evaluated the potential outcome . . . as much more aversive than those exposed to the dim lighting, $t(18) = 2.38, p < .05$" (p. 222).

When researchers write "$p < .05$," they mean that the probability of their results if the null hypothesis were true is less than .05 (5%). If the result was close but did not reach the significance level chosen, it may be reported anyway as a "near significant trend," with "$p < .10$," for example. If the result is not significant, sometimes the actual p level will be given (for example, "$p = .27$"), or the abbreviation *ns,* for "not significant," will be used. In addition, if a one-tailed test was used, that usually will be noted. Again, when reading research articles, assume a two-tailed test if nothing is said otherwise.

Even though a researcher has chosen a significance level in advance, such as .05, results that meet more rigorous standards may be noted as such. (You are supposed to be impressed.) Thus in the same article you may see results in which some are noted as "$p < .05$," others as "$p < .01$," and still others as "$p < .001$," for example.

Finally, in many cases the results of hypothesis testing are shown simply as asterisks in a table of results, in which a result with an asterisk has attained significance and one without one has not.

Notice that in all of these cases, researchers may not make the research hypothesis or the null hypothesis explicit or describe any of the other steps of the process in any detail. It usually is assumed that the reader understands all of this very well.

Summary

The basic idea of hypothesis testing is to examine the probability that the result of a study could have been obtained even if the actual situation was that the experimental treatment or comparison made no difference. If this probability is low, the scenario is rejected and the theory from which the treatment or comparison was proposed is supported. The expectation of a difference or an effect is the research hypothesis, and the hypothetical situation in which there is no difference or effect is the null hypothesis. When a result would be extremely unlikely if the null hypothesis were true, the null hypothesis is said to be rejected and the research hypothesis supported. If the obtained results are not very extreme, the study is said to be inconclusive.

Social scientists in most fields consider a result too extreme if it is less likely than 5%, though a more stringent 1%, or even .1%, cutoff is sometimes used. These percentages may apply to the probability of the result's being extreme in a predicted direction, a directional or one-tailed test, or to the probability of its being extreme in either direction, a nondirectional or two-tailed test.

The hypothesis-testing process involves five steps:

1. Restate the question as a research hypothesis and a null hypothesis about the populations.
2. Determine the characteristics of the comparison distribution.
3. Determine the cutoff sample score on the comparison distribution at which the null hypothesis should be rejected.
4. Determine the score of your sample on the comparison distribution.
5. Compare the scores from Steps 3 and 4 to decide whether to reject the null hypothesis.

Research articles typically report the results of hypothesis testing by noting that a result was or was not significant and giving the probability level cutoff (usually 5% or 1%) at which the decision was made.

Key Terms

comparison distribution
conventional levels of significance ($p < .05$, $p < .01$)
cutoff sample score

directional hypothesis
hypothesis testing
nondirectional hypothesis
null hypothesis

one-tailed test
research hypothesis
statistically significant
two-tailed test

Practice Problems

These problems involve computation (with the assistance of a calculator). Most real-life statistics problems are done on a computer. Even if you have a computer, do this by hand to ingrain the method in your mind.

For practice in using a computer to solve statistics problems, refer to the computer section of each chapter of the Student's Study Guide and Computer Workbook *that accompanies this text.*

All data are fictional (unless an actual citation is given).

Answers to selected problems are given at the back of the book.

Study	Population M	SD	Sample Score	p	Tails of Test
A	10	2	14	.05	1 (high predicted)
B	10	2	14	.05	2
C	10	2	14	.01	1 (high predicted)
D	10	2	14	.01	2
E	10	4	14	.05	1 (high predicted)
F	10	1	14	.01	2
G	10	2	16	.01	2
H	12	2	16	.01	2
I	12	2	8	.05	1 (low predicted)

1. Define the following terms in your own words: (a) research hypothesis, (b) null hypothesis, (c) hypothesis testing procedure, (d) comparison distribution, (e) .05 significance level, (f) one-tailed test.

2. For each of the following, (a) indicate what two populations are being compared, (b) state the research hypothesis, (c) state the null hypothesis, and (d) say whether you should use a one-tailed or two-tailed test and why.

(i) Do Canadian children whose parents are librarians do better than Canadian children in general on reading ability?

(ii) Is the level of income for residents of a particular city different from the level of income for people in the region?

(iii) Do people who have experienced an earthquake have more or less self-confidence than the general population?

(iv) Based on anthropological reports in which the status of women is scored on a 10-point scale, the mean and standard deviation across many cultures are known. A new culture is found in which there is an unusual family arrangement. The status of women is also rated in this culture. Do cultures with the unusual family arrangement provide higher status to women than cultures in general?

3. Based on the information given for each of the following studies, determine whether or not to reject the null hypothesis. In each case, give the Z-score cutoff on the comparison distribution at which the null hypothesis should be rejected, the Z score on the comparison distribution for the sample score, and the conclusion. (Assume that all populations are normally distributed.)

4. A researcher interested in the senses of taste and smell has conducted an extensive set of studies in which individuals are given each of 20 different foods (apricot, chocolate, cherry, coffee, garlic, and so on), each in the form of a liquid dropped on the tongue. Over the entire student population at her university, the mean number that students can identify correctly is 14, with a standard deviation of 4. (Let us assume that somehow all the students at this college had been tested, perhaps as a part of a medical screening at the start of each year.) The researcher has reason to believe that people's success has more to do with smell than with taste, so she sets up special procedures that keep the person from being able to use the sense of smell during the test. The researcher then tries the procedure on one randomly selected student. This student is able to identify only 5 correctly. Using the .05 significance level, what should the researcher conclude? Explain your answer to someone who has never had a course in statistics.

5. A nursing researcher working with people who have undergone a particular type of major surgery proposed that people will recover from the operation more quickly if friends and family are in the room with them for the first 48 hours after the operation. It is known (in this fictional example) that time to recover is normally distributed with a mean of 12 days and a standard deviation of 5 days. The procedure is tried with a randomly selected patient, and this patient recovers in 18 days. Using the .01 significance level, what should the researcher conclude? Explain your answer to someone who is familiar with mean, standard deviation, Z scores, and the normal curve but doesn't know anything else about statistics or hypothesis testing.

6. Pecukonis (1990), as part of a larger study, measured ego development (a measure of overall maturity) and ability to empathize with others among a group of 24 aggressive adolescent girls in a residential treatment center. The girls were divided into high and low ego development groups, and the empathy ("cognitive empathy") scores of these two groups were compared. In his Results section, Pecukonis reported, "The average score on cognitive empathy for subjects scoring high on ego development was 22.1 as compared with 16.3 for low scorers, . . . $p < .005$" (p. 68). Explain this result to a person who has never had a course in statistics. (Focus on the meaning of this result in terms of the general logic of hypothesis testing and statistical significance.)

6

Hypothesis Tests
With Means of Samples

IN Chapter 5, we introduced the basic logic of hypothesis testing. We used as examples studies in which the sample was a single individual. As we noted, however, in actual practice, social and behavioral science research almost always involves samples of many individuals. In this chapter, we build on what you have learned so far and consider hypothesis testing involving a sample of more than one. Mainly this requires examining in some detail what we call a distribution of means.

The Distribution of Means

Hypothesis testing in the usual research situation, where we are studying a sample of many individuals, is exactly the same as you learned in Chapter 5—with an important exception. When you have more than one person in your sample, there is a special problem with Step 2, determining the characteristics of the comparison distribution. The problem is that the score you care about in your sample is the mean of the group of scores. The comparison distributions we have been considering so far have been distributions of populations of individuals (such as the population of ages when individual babies start walking). Comparing the mean of a sample of, say, 50 people to a distribution of a population of individual scores is a mismatch—like comparing apples to oranges. Instead, when you are interested in the mean of a sample of 50, you need a comparison distribution that is a distribution of all the possible means of samples of 50 scores. Such a comparison distribution we call a **distribution of means.**

distribution of means

Put more formally, a distribution of means is a distribution of the means of each of a very large number of samples of the same size, with each sample randomly drawn from the same population (of individuals).[1] Because the distribution of means is the proper comparison distribution when there is more than one person in a sample, in most research situations determining its characteristics of a distribution of means is necessary for Step 2 of the hypothesis-testing procedure.

Building a Distribution of Means

The idea of a distribution of means can be understood by considering how one could build up such a distribution from an ordinary distribution of individuals. Suppose our population was of the grade levels of the 90,000 elementary and junior high school children in a particular region. Suppose further (to keep the example simple) that there are exactly 10,000 children at each grade level, from first through ninth grade. This population distribution would be rectangular, with a mean of 5, a variance of 6.67, and a standard deviation of 2.58 (see Figure 6–1).

Next, suppose you wrote each child's grade level on a table tennis ball and put all 90,000 plastic balls into a giant tub. The tub would contain 10,000 balls with a 1 on them, 10,000 with a 2 on them, and so forth. Stir up the balls in the tub, and then take two of them out. You have taken a random sample of two balls. Suppose one ball has a 2 on it and the other has a 9 on it. In that case, the mean grade level of your sample of two children's grade level is 5.5, the average of 2 and 9. Now you put the balls back, mix up all the balls, and select two balls again. Maybe this time you get two 4s, making the mean of your second sample 4. Then you try again; this time you get a 2 and a 7, making your mean 4.5. So far you have three means: 5.5, 4, and 4.5.

These three numbers (each a mean of a sample of grade levels of two school children) can be thought of as a small distribution in its own right. The mean of this little distribution of three numbers is 4.67 (the sum of 5.5, 4, and 4.5 divided by 3). The variance of this distribution is .39 (the variance of 5.5, 4, and 4.5). The standard deviation is .62 (the square root of .39). A histogram of this distribution of three means is shown in Figure 6–2.

If you continued the process, the histogram of means would continue to grow. An example after 10 random samples of two balls each is shown in

FIGURE 6–1
Distribution of grade levels among 90,000 school children (fictional data).

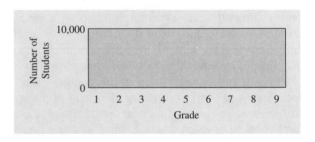

[1]Statisticians also call this distribution of means a "sampling distribution of the mean." In this book, however, we use the term distribution of means to make it clear that we are discussing populations, not samples or distributions of samples.

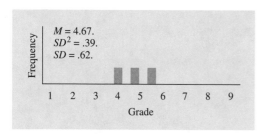

FIGURE 6–2
Distribution of the means of three randomly drawn samples of two school children each from a population of 90,000 school children (fictional data).

Figure 6–3a. Figure 6–3b shows the histogram of the distribution of means after 20 random samples of two each. After 100 random samples, the histogram of the distribution of the means might look like Figure 6–3c; after 1,000, like Figure 6–3d. (We actually constructed the histograms shown in Figure 6–3 by using a computer to make the random selections, instead of using 90,000 table tennis balls and a giant tub.)

In practice, researchers almost never have the opportunity to take many different samples from a population. It is quite a lot of work to come up with a single sample and study the people in that sample. Fortunately, however, as you will soon see, the characteristics of a distribution of means can be figured out directly, using some simple rules, without taking even one sample. The only information you need is the characteristics of the population distribution of individuals and the number of scores in each sample. (Do not worry for now about how you could know the characteristics of the population of individuals.) Although you get the same result, thinking of it in terms of taking a large number of random samples and figuring the mean of each makes it easier to understand what a distribution of means is.

Characteristics of the Distribution of Means

Notice three things about the distribution of means we built up in our example:

1. The mean of the distribution of means came out to be about the same as the mean of the original population of individual grade levels from which the samples were taken (5 in both cases).
2. The spread of the distribution of means came out to be less than the spread of the distribution of the population of individuals from which the samples were taken.
3. The shape of the distribution of means came out to be approximately normal (or at least unimodal and symmetrical).

It turns out that the first two of these three are true for all distributions of means and the third is true for most distributions of means.

These three links of the distribution of means to the population of individuals are the foundation for a set of simple mathematical rules that allow you to determine the mean, variance, and shape of a distribution of means without having to write on plastic balls and take endless samples.

As we noted earlier, to use these rules, all you need to know are the characteristics of the population of individuals (its mean, variance, shape) and the number of scores in each sample in the distribution of means. (In our example, there were two scores in each sample.) (These three rules are based on

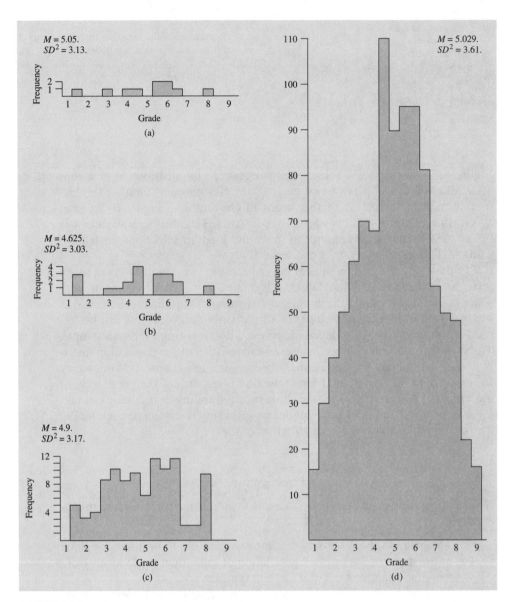

FIGURE 6–3
Distributions of the means of randomly selected samples of two balls each from a population of 90,000 balls, consisting of 10,000 with each of the numbers from 1 through 9. Numbers of sample means in each distribution shown are (a) 10 sample means, (b) 20 sample means, (c) 100 sample means, and (d) 1,000 sample means. (Actual sampling simulated by computer.)

the *central limit theorem,* a fundamental principle in mathematical statistics that we mentioned in Chapter 4.) Let's look more closely at these three rules.

Determining the Mean of a Distribution of Means

mean of a distribution of means

The **mean of a distribution of means** is the same as the mean of the population of individuals from which the samples are taken. Because each sample is based on randomly selected individuals from the population of individuals, sometimes the mean of a sample will be higher and sometimes lower than the mean of the whole population of individuals. However, there is no reason for the means of these samples to tend overall to be consistently higher or consistently lower than the mean of the population. If enough samples are taken, the high means and low means balance each other out.

Determining the Variance of a Distribution of Means

As we said, a distribution of means will be less spread out than the population of individuals from which the samples are taken. The reason for this is as follows: Any one score, even an extreme score, has some chance of being selected in a random sample. The chance is less of two extreme scores being selected in the same random sample, particularly because to create an extreme sample mean, they would have to be two scores that were extreme in the same direction. So there is a moderating effect of increasing numbers. In any one sample, the extremes tend to be balanced out by middle scores or by extremes in the opposite direction, making each sample mean tend toward the middle and away from extreme values. With fewer extreme values for the means, the variance of the means is less.

Consider our example. There were plenty of 1s and 9s in the population, making a fair amount of spread. That is, about a ninth of the time, if you were taking samples of single scores, you would get a 1, and about a ninth of the time you would get a 9. If you are taking samples of two at a time, you would get a sample with a mean of 1 (that is, in which both balls were 1s) or a mean of 9 (both balls being 9s) much less often. The chances of getting two balls that average out to a middle value such as 5 is much more likely (because several combinations could give this result—a 1 and a 9, a 2 and an 8, a 3 and a 7, a 4 and a 6, or two 5s).

The more individuals in each sample, the less spread out the distribution of means of those samples. This is because with a larger number of individuals in each sample, it is even rarer for extremes in that sample not to be balanced out by middle scores or extremes in the other direction in the same sample. In terms of the plastic balls, we saw that it was fairly unlikely to get a mean of 1 when taking samples of two balls at a time. If we were taking three balls at a time, getting a sample with a mean of 1 (all three balls would have to be 1s) is even less likely, and getting middle values for the means becomes more likely.

Using samples of two balls at a time, the variance of the distribution of means came out to about 3.33. This is half of the variance of the population of individuals, which was 6.67. If we had built up a distribution of means using samples of three balls each, the variance of the distribution of means would have been 2.22, which is one-third of the variance of the population of individuals. Had we randomly selected five balls for each sample, the variance of the distribution of means would have been one-fifth of the variance of the population of individuals.

These examples follow a general rule: The **variance of a distribution of means** is the variance of the distribution of the population of individuals divided by the number of individuals in the samples being selected. This rule holds in all situations and can be proven mathematically.

variance of a distribution of means

Formula for the Variance of a Distribution of Means

Stated as a formula, here is the rule for determining the variance of the distribution of means:

$$\text{Population } SD^2_M = \frac{\text{Population } SD^2}{N} \tag{6–1}$$

In this formula, Population SD^2_M is the variance of the distribution of means (based on samples taken from the entire population of individuals). Population SD^2 is the variance of the population of individuals. N is the number of individuals in each sample.

In our example, the variance of the population of individual grade levels was 6.67, and there were two school children's grade levels in each sample. The variance of the distribution of means is figured as follows:

$$\text{Population } SD^2_M = \frac{\text{Population } SD^2}{N} = \frac{6.67}{2} = 3.34$$

To use a different example, suppose a population of individuals had a variance of 400 and you wanted to know the variance of a distribution of means of 25 individuals each:

$$\text{Population } SD^2_M = \frac{\text{Population } SD^2}{N} = \frac{400}{25} = 16$$

Determining the Standard Deviation of a Distribution of Means

standard deviation of a distribution of means

The **standard deviation of a distribution of means**[2] is the square root of the variance of the distribution of means.

Stated as a formula,

$$\text{Population } SD_M = \sqrt{\text{Population } SD^2_M} \tag{6–2}$$

In this formula, Population SD_M is the standard deviation of the distribution of means (based on a population of individuals).

The Shape of a Distribution of Means

shape of the distribution of means

Regardless of the shape of the original distribution of individuals, the distribution of means tends to be unimodal and symmetrical. In the grade-level example, the population distribution of students at individual grade levels was rectangular. (It had an equal number at each grade level.) However, the **shape of the distribution of means** was roughly that of a bell—unimodal and symmetrical. Had we taken many more than 1,000 samples, the shape would have been even more clearly unimodal and symmetrical.

---

[2]Because of its importance in hypothesis testing, the standard deviation of the distribution of means is sometimes called by a special name of its own, the *standard error of the mean,* or the *standard error,* for short. It has this name because it represents the degree to which particular means of samples are typically "in error" as estimates of the mean of the population of individuals. That is, the standard error of the mean tells you how much the particular means in the distribution of means typically deviate from the mean of the population. We will have more to say about this idea in the discussion of confidence intervals at the end of the chapter.

A distribution of means tends to be unimodal due to the same basic process of extremes balancing each other out that we noted in the discussion of the variance: Middle scores for means are more likely, and extreme means are less likely. It tends to be symmetrical because lack of symmetry (skew) is caused by extremes, and with less extremes, there is less skew. In the grade-level example, the distribution of means we created came out so clearly symmetrical because the population distribution of individual grade levels was symmetrical. Had the population distribution of individuals been skewed to one side, the distribution of means would have still been skewed, but not as much.

The more individuals in each sample, the closer the distribution of means is to a normal curve. In fact, with samples of 30 or more individuals, even with a nonnormal population of individuals, the approximation of the distribution of means to a normal curve is very close and the percentages in the normal curve table will be extremely accurate.[3] (This occurs for much the same reason as we discussed in Chapter 4 when considering why things in nature in general tend to follow a normal curve, a logic we said is based on what is called the *central limit theorem*.)

Finally, whenever the population distribution of individuals is normal, the distribution of means will be normal, regardless of the number of individuals in each sample.

Summary of the Rules for Determining the Characteristics of a Distribution of Means

Here are the three rules:

1. The mean of a distribution of means is the same as the mean of the distribution of the population of individuals.
2. The variance of a distribution of means is the variance of the distribution of the population of individuals divided by the number of individuals in each sample. Its standard deviation is the square root of its variance.
3. The shape of a distribution of means is approximately normal if either (a) each sample is of 30 or more individuals, or (b) the distribution of the population of individuals is normal. Otherwise, it will still tend to be unimodal and roughly symmetrical.

These principles are shown graphically in Figure 6–4.

Example of Determining the Characteristics of a Distribution of Means

Consider the population of scores of students who have taken the Graduate Record Examinations (GRE): The distribution is approximately normal with a mean of 500 and a standard deviation of 100. What will be the characteristics

---

[3]We have ignored the fact that a normal curve is a smooth theoretical distribution. In most real-life examples, scores fall at specific intervals. So one difference between the sample distribution of table tennis balls' means and a normal curve is that the normal curve is smooth. However, in social science research, we usually assume that even though our measurements are at specific intervals, the underlying thing being measured is continuous.

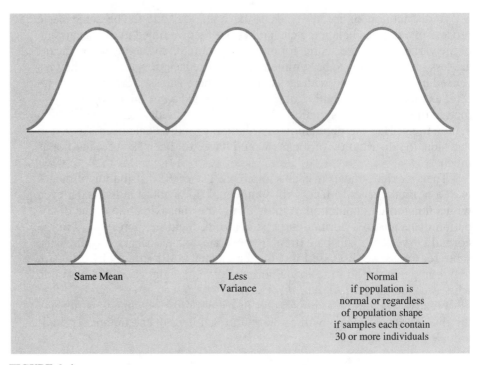

FIGURE 6–4
Illustration of the principles of the relation of the distribution of means (lower curves) to the distribution of the population of individuals (upper curves).

of a distribution of all possible means for samples of 50 students each taken from this population?

1. Because the mean of the population of individuals is 500, the mean of the distribution of means will also be 500.

2. The variance of the distribution of means is the variance of the population of individuals divided by the number of individuals in each sample. Because the standard deviation of the population of individuals is 100, the variance of the population of individuals is 10,000. The variance of the distribution of means is 10,000 divided by 50, which is 200. In terms of the formula,

$$\text{Population } SD^2{}_M = \frac{\text{Population } SD^2}{N} = \frac{10,000}{50} = 200$$

The standard deviation of the distribution of means is the square root of the variance of the distribution of means: $\sqrt{200} = 14.14$.

3. The shape of the distribution of means will be normal because both of our requirements are met. (It would have been enough if only one had been met.) In this case, the population distribution of individuals is normal. And the number of individuals in each sample is 30 or more.

Review of the Three Kinds of Distributions

We have considered three different kinds of distributions: (a) the distribution of a population of individuals, (b) the distribution of a particular sample drawn from that population, and (c) the distribution of means—that is, the distribution of all possible means of samples that could be taken from that population of individuals. Figure 6–5 illustrates these three kinds of distributions and Table 6–1 describes the comparisons.

Hypothesis Testing Involving a Distribution of Means

Now we are ready to turn to hypothesis testing when there is more than one individual in the sample being studied.

The Distribution of Means as the Comparison Distribution in Hypothesis Testing

In this new situation, the distribution of means provides the crucial connection between the sample and the null hypothesis. That is, suppose we are studying a sample of more than one person (the usual situation in research). In this situation, the distribution of means is the comparison distribution. It is the distribution whose characteristics are determined in Step 2 of the hypothesis-testing process. The distribution of means is the distribution to which the sample mean can be compared to see how likely it is that such a sample mean could have been selected if the null hypothesis is true.

Example of Hypothesis Testing With a Sample of More Than One Individual

A (fictional) team of educational researchers are interested in the effects of instructions on timed scholastic achievement tests. They have a theory that if test takers are told to answer each question with the first response that comes into their head, they will do better. To examine this theory, the researchers arrange to have 64 randomly selected fifth-grade school children take a standard school achievement test. The test is given in the usual way, except that the instructions have an additional sentence saying that the students should answer each question with the first response that comes into their head. When given in the usual way, the test has a mean of 200, a standard deviation

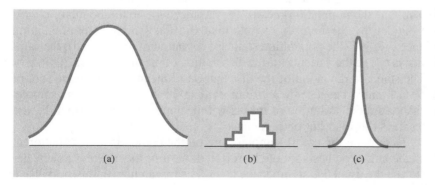

FIGURE 6–5
Three kinds of distributions: (a) the distribution of a population of individuals, (b) the distribution of a particular sample taken from that population, and (c) the distribution of means of all possible samples of a particular size taken from that population.

TABLE 6–1
Comparison of Three Types of Distributions

	Population's Distribution	Particular Sample's Distribution	Distribution of Means
Content	Scores of all individuals in the population	Scores of individuals in a single sample	Means of samples randomly taken from the population
Shape	Could be any shape; often normal	Could be any shape	Normal if population is normal or if samples contain ≥ 30 individuals each
Mean	Population M	$M = \Sigma X/N$ calculated from scores of those in the sample	Pop M_{M} = Pop M
Variance	Population SD^2	$SD = \Sigma\,(X\!-\!M)^2/N$	Pop SD^2_{M} = Pop SD^2/N
Standard Deviation	Population SD	$SD = \sqrt{SD^2}$	Pop $SD_M = \sqrt{\text{Pop } SD^2_{M}}$

of 48, and an approximately normal distribution. This distribution is shown in Figure 6–6a.

Let us follow the steps of hypothesis testing for this example.

1. Restate the question as a research hypothesis and a null hypothesis about the populations. The two populations are these:

Population 1: Fifth graders who get the special instructions
Population 2: Fifth graders who do not get the special instructions

The research hypothesis is that the population of fifth graders who takes the test with the special instructions will have higher scores than the population of fifth graders who takes the test in the normal way. The null hypothesis is that Population 1's scores will not be higher than Population 2's. (Note that these are directional hypotheses.)

2. Determine the characteristics of the comparison distribution. Our study gives us a mean of a sample of 64 individuals (fifth graders in this case). Thus, the comparison distribution has to be the distribution of means for samples of 64 individuals each. This distribution will have a mean of 200 (the same as the population mean). Its variance will be the population variance divided by the number of individuals in the sample. The population variance is 2,304 (the population standard deviation of 48 squared); the sample size is 64; so the variance of the distribution of means will be 2,304/64, or 36. The standard deviation of the distribution of means is the square root of 36, or 6. Finally, because there are more than 30 individuals in the sample, the shape of the distribution of means will be approximately normal. Figure 6–6b shows this distribution of means.

3. Determine the cutoff sample score on the comparison distribution at which the null hypothesis should be rejected. Assume that the researchers decide to use the usual 5% significance level. The researchers in this study have

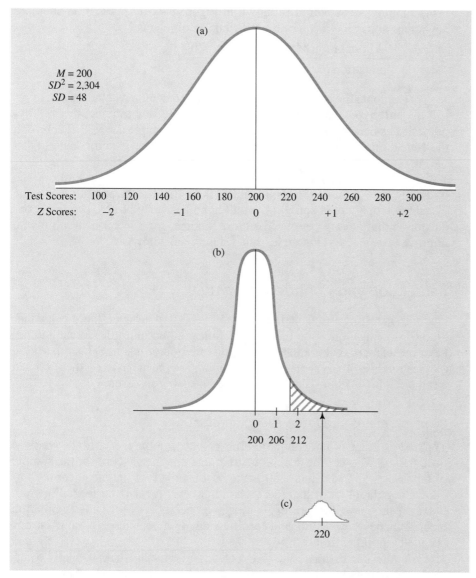

FIGURE 6–6
For the fictional study of performance on a standard school achievement test, (a) the distribution of the population of individuals, (b) the distribution of means (the comparison distribution), and (c) the sample's distribution.

a clear directional prediction and are not really interested in any effect in the opposite direction. (If the special instructions do not improve test scores, they would not be used in the future. Any possible results showing a negative effect are irrelevant.) Hence, the researchers will reject the null hypothesis if the result falls in the top 5% of the comparison distribution. The comparison distribution (the distribution of means) is a normal curve. Thus, the top 5% can be found from the normal curve table to start at a Z score of +1.64. This top 5% is shown as the shaded area in Figure 6–6b.

4. Determine the score of your sample on the comparison distribution. When the researchers tested the 64 fifth graders, they had a mean of 220.

(This sample's distribution is shown in Figure 6–6c.) This is 3.33 standard deviations above the mean of the distribution of means:

$$Z = \frac{M - \text{Population } M}{\text{Population } SD_{\text{M}}} = \frac{220 - 200}{6} = \frac{20}{6} = 3.33$$

5. Compare the scores from Steps 3 and 4 to decide whether or not to reject the null hypothesis. The minimum Z score needed to reject the null hypothesis has been set at +1.64. The Z score of the sample is +3.33. Therefore, the educational researchers can reject the null hypothesis and conclude that the research hypothesis is supported. To put this another way, the result is statistically significant at the $p < .05$ level. This can be seen in Figure 6–6b by noting how extreme the sample mean is on the distribution of means (the distribution that would apply if the null hypothesis were true). The final conclusion is that among people like those studied, the special instructions do improve test scores. (Of course, this is a fictional study.)

Estimation and Confidence Intervals

Hypothesis testing is our main focus in this book. However, there is another kind of statistical question that is sometimes important in the social and behavioral sciences that is related to the distribution of means. This other kind of question is estimating an unknown population mean based on the scores in a sample. This is important, for example, in survey research.

Point Estimates and Interval Estimates

The best estimate of the population mean is the sample mean. In the study of fifth graders who got the special instructions, the mean score for the sample of 64 cases was 220. Thus, 220 is the best estimate of the mean for the unknown population of fifth graders who might ever receive the special instructions. In this case, we are estimating the specific value of the population mean. Whenever we estimate a specific value of a population parameter, this is called a **point estimate.**

point estimate

You also can estimate the range of possible means that are likely to include the population mean. For example, you might estimate that the true population mean for fifth graders who get the special instructions is between 200 and 240. This is called an **interval estimate.**

interval estimate

Principle and Terminology of Confidence Intervals

The wider the interval estimate, the more sure you can be that it will include the true population mean. In our fifth-grader example, you might be quite certain that the true population mean is somewhere between 100 and 340. You would be taking a chance if you estimated that the population mean is somewhere between 219 and 221.

In general, you want an interval that is wide enough to be quite sure it includes the population mean. This is called a **confidence interval.** If you want to be 95% sure, you want the **95% confidence interval.** The 95% confidence interval in the fifth-grader example is from 208.24 to 231.76. That is, based on the sample studied, you can be 95% sure that the true population mean is

confidence interval
95% confidence interval

somewhere between 208.24 and 231.76. (You will learn shortly how to do this yourself.) The upper and lower ends of the confidence interval are called **confidence limits.** In this example, the confidence limits are 208.24 and 231.76

If you want to be even more sure than 95%, you need a wider interval. In our example, the **99% confidence interval** has confidence limits of 204.58 and 235.42.

confidence limits

99% confidence interval

Logic and Computation of Finding Confidence Limits

Confidence limits are based on the distribution of means. What you want to know is the points at which the middle 95% of means begin and end on this distribution. Thus, you need to find the cutoff points for the bottom 2.5% and the top 2.5%. (This leaves a total of 95% in the middle.)

Let's start with the lower limit. As usual, it is easiest to think in terms of Z scores. The Z score for the bottom 2.5% on a normal curve is -1.96. (You would find this from the normal curve table.) The example has a mean of 220 and a standard deviation of the distribution of means of 6. Thus, on this distribution of means, a Z score of -1.96 is 208.24. (That is, we converted the Z score of -1.96 to the raw score of 208.24 using the usual procedure for converting a Z score to a raw score.)

Figuring the upper limit works the same way. The Z score for the top 2.5% is $+1.96$. This comes out to 231.76 on our distribution of means.

For the 99% confidence interval, you would need to figure the scores that go with the top and bottom .5% (leaving 99% in between).

Steps for Figuring Confidence Intervals

Here are three steps for computing confidence intervals. These steps assume that the distribution of means is approximately a normal distribution.

1. Determine the characteristics of the distribution of means.
2. Use the normal curve table to find the Z scores that go with the upper and lower percentage you want. For a 95% confidence interval, this is the Z score that goes with the top and bottom 2.5%. For a 99% confidence interval, this is the Z score for the top and bottom .5%.
3. Convert these Z scores to raw scores on your distribution of means. These are the upper and lower confidence limits.

Confidence Intervals and Hypothesis Testing

You can also use confidence intervals as a way to do hypothesis testing. If the confidence interval does not include the mean of the null hypothesis distribution, the result is significant. This is because the confidence interval says there is a 95% (or 99%) chance that the true population mean falls in a particular range. If this 95% range does not include the Population 2 mean, then there is less than a 5% chance that this sample could have come from Population 2.

Most social science research uses ordinary hypothesis testing. However, sometimes you will see the confidence-interval method used instead. Sometimes you will see both.

BOX 6–1

More About Polls: Sampling Errors and Errors in Thinking About Samples

If you think back to Box 4–1 on surveys and the Gallup poll, you will recall that we left two important questions unanswered about the sort of fine print you find near the results of a poll, saying something like "From a telephone poll of 1,000 American adults taken on June 4 and 5. Sampling error ±3%." First, you might wonder how such small numbers, like 1,000 (but rarely much less), can be used to predict the opinion of the entire U.S. public. Second, after plowing through this chapter, you may wonder what a "sampling error" means when a sample is not randomly sampled but rather selected by the complicated probability method described in Chapter 4.

To begin with the question of sample size, you know from this chapter that when sample sizes are large, like 1,000, the standard deviation of the distribution of means is greatly reduced. That is, the curve becomes very high and narrow, gathered all around the population mean. The mean of any sample of that size is very close to being the population mean.

Still, you might persist in an intuitive feeling that the number required to represent all of the huge U.S. public might need to be larger than just 1,000. However, if you think about it, when a sample is only a small part of a very large population, the sample's absolute size is the only determiner of accuracy. This absolute size determines the impact of the random errors of measurement and selection. What remains important is reducing bias or systematic error, which can be done only by careful planning.

What about the term *sampling error,* in the context of polls, where a simple random sampling is not used. A sampling error in this case is not quite the same as the standard deviation of a distribution of means, or the confidence interval based on it, as described in this chapter. Instead, the sampling error for polls is worked out according to past experience with the sampling procedures used. It is expressed in tables for different sample sizes (usually below 1,000, because that is where error increases dramatically).

So now you understand opinion polls even better. The number of people polled is not very important (provided that it is at least 1,000 or so). What matters very much, however, is the method of sampling and estimating error, which will not be reported even in the fine print in the necessary detail to judge if the results are reliable. The reputation of the organization doing the survey is probably the best criterion. If the sampling and error-estimating approach is not revealed, be cautious.

Hypothesis Tests About Means of Samples and Confidence Intervals as Described in Research Articles

As we have noted several times, research in which there is a known population mean and standard deviation is rare in social and behavioral science research, and we have asked you to learn about this situation mainly as a building block for understanding hypothesis testing in common research situations. In the rare case in which research with a known population distribution is conducted, it is often described as a **Z test,** because it is the Z score that is checked against the normal curve.

Z test

Of the topics we have covered in this chapter, the one you are most likely to see discussed in a research article is the standard deviation of the distribution of means, used as an indication of the amount of variation that might be expected among means of samples of a given size from this population. In

this context, it is usually identified as the **standard error,** abbreviated *SE.*
Often the lines that go above and below the tops of the bars in a bar graph
refer to standard error (instead of standard deviation).

For example, the chart in Figure 6–7 appears in an article by Introini-
Collison and McGaugh (1986). These researchers were evaluating the role of
epinephrine (adrenaline) on retaining material that has just been learned.
This graph shows results of a study in which mice were given either saline
(salt water, a neutral control condition) or low or high dosages of epinephrine
right after learning to identify the correct path in a particular maze.

The bars show the number of errors the mice made 1 day, 1 week, and 1
month later. As can be seen from the graph, at all periods, the mice who had
received the high dose of epinephrine made many fewer errors (indicating retention of learning). Those with the low dose of epinephrine actually did
worse than those given only saline. The fact that the bars represent the means
and the lines the standard error is described cryptically in the figure caption
as "(Means ± *SE*)."

Confidence intervals are sometimes reported in research articles, especially in surveys. A researcher might explain that the average number of
overtime hours worked in a particular industry is 3.7 with a 95% confidence
interval of 2.5 to 4.9. This would tell you that the true average number of
overtime hours is probably somewhere between 2.5 and 4.9, which may be
quite accurate enough for most purposes. For example, Brian Rowe, Krist-
jana Thorsteinson and Gary Bota (1995) conducted a study in which they interviewed bicyclists on the streets of Sudbury, Ontario (Canada). Their focus
was on the proper use of safety helmets. In describing their results, they gave
percentages plus 95% confidence intervals for those percentages. For example, in one part of their Results section they wrote, "Only 66% (95% CI:
57–73%) of helmet owners claimed to wear their helmet 'all the time'" (p.
59). Here "CI" refers to confidence interval.

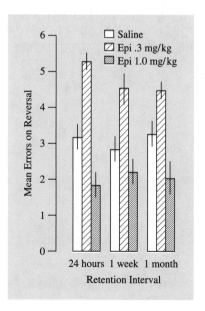

FIGURE 6–7

Effects of posttraining epinephrine (Epi) on discrimination reversal training 1 day, 1
week, and 1 month following original training (Means ± SE). N = 18 per group for 1-day
group, 12 per group for 1-week and 1-month groups. From Introini-Collison, I. B., & Mc-
Gaugh, J. L. (1986). Epinephrine modulates long-term retention of an aversively motivated discrimination. (Behavioral and Neural Biology, 45, 358–365. Copyright, 1986, by
Academic Press, Inc. Reprinted by permission.)

Hypothesis Tests About Means of Samples and Confidence Intervals as Described in Research Articles

Summary

When studying a sample of more than one individual, the comparison distribution in the hypothesis-testing process is a distribution of means of all possible samples of the number of individuals being studied. It can be thought of as like the result of taking a very large number of samples, each of the same number of individuals taken randomly from the population of individuals, and making a distribution of the means of these samples.

The distribution of means has the same mean as the population of individuals. However, it has a smaller variance because the means of samples are less likely to be extreme than individual scores. (Extremes in any one sample are likely to be balanced by middle scores or extremes in the other direction.) Specifically, its variance is the variance of the population of individuals divided by the number of individuals in each sample. (Its standard deviation is the square root of its variance.) The shape of the distribution of means approximates a normal curve if either (a) the population of individuals is normally distributed or (b) the samples are each of 30 or more individuals.

Hypothesis tests involving a single sample of more than one individual and a known population are conducted in exactly the same way as the hypothesis tests of Chapter 5 (where the studies were of a single individual compared to population of individual scores), except that the comparison distribution is now a distribution of means.

The best point estimate for the population mean is the sample mean. You can determine an interval estimate of the population mean based on the distribution of means. The 95% confidence interval will be the middle 95% of the distribution of means.

The kind of hypothesis test described in this chapter is rarely used in research practice. (You have learned it as a stepping stone.) The standard deviation of the distribution of means, often referred to as the "standard error" (*SE*), is occasionally used to describe the expected variability of means, particularly in bar graphs in which the standard error (instead of the more common standard deviation) may be shown as the length of a line above and below the top of each bar.

Confidence intervals are sometimes reported in research articles, particularly when describing results of surveys.

Key Terms

confidence interval
confidence limits
distribution of means
interval estimate
mean of a distribution of means
95% confidence interval

99% confidence interval
point estimate
shape of a distribution of means
standard deviation of a distribution of means (Population SD_M)

standard error (*SE*)
variance of a distribution of means (Population SD^2_M)
Z test

Practice Problems

These problems involve computation (with the assistance of a calculator). Most real-life statistics problems are done on a computer. Even if you have a computer, do this by hand to ingrain the method in your mind.

For practice in using a computer to solve statistics problems, refer to the computer section of each chapter of the Student's Study Guide and Computer Workbook *that accompanies this text.*

All data are fictional (unless an actual citation is given).

Answers to selected problems are given at the back of the book.

1. Explain why the standard deviation of the distribution of means is generally smaller than the standard deviation of the distribution of the population of individuals.

2. For a population of individuals that has a standard deviation of 10, what is the standard deviation of the distribution of means for samples of size (a) 2, (b) 3, (c) 4, (d) 5, (e) 10, (f) 20, (g) 100?

3. For each of the examples in Problem 2, compute the 95% confidence interval (that is, the upper and lower confidence limit). (Assume that in each case it is a normal distribution with mean of 100.)

4. A particular normally distributed population has a mean of 40 and a standard deviation of 6. Which of the following samples would be less likely than 5% to be randomly selected from this population: (a) sample of 10 with a mean of 44, (b) sample of 1 with a mean of 48, (c) sample of 81 with a mean of 42, (d) sample of 16 with a mean of 42? For each part, show how you arrived at your answer, including a diagram of the distributions involved. (When doing this problem assume that we are concerned with a sample being extreme only in its direction from the population mean.)

5. A researcher is interested in whether people are able to identify emotions correctly in people from other cultures. It is known that, using a particular method of measurement, the accuracy ratings of adult North Americans in general are normally distributed with a mean of 82 (out of 100) and a variance of 20. This distribution is based on ratings made of emotions expressed by members of their own culture. In this study, however, the researcher arranges to test 50 adult North Americans rating emotions of individuals from Indonesia. The mean accuracy for these 50 individuals was 78. Using the .05 level, what should the researcher conclude? Explain your answer to a person who understands hypothesis testing with a sample of a single individual but knows nothing about a distribution of means or how to do hypothesis testing involving a sample of more than a single individual.

6. Compute the 95% confidence interval for North Americans' ratings of Indonesians based on the data in Problem 5. Explain what you have done and what your result means to a person who is familiar with the distribution of means, but knows nothing about confidence intervals.

7. A large number of people has seen a particular film of an automobile collision between a moving car and a stopped car. Each person then filled out a questionnaire about how likely it was that the driver of the moving car was at fault, on a scale from *not at fault* = 0 and *completely at fault* = 10. The distribution of ratings under ordinary conditions is known and turns out to be normally distributed with a mean of = 5.5 and a standard deviation of .8. Sixteen randomly selected individuals are tested under conditions in which the wording of the question is changed so that instead of calling them just Car A and Car B, the question asks, "How likely is it that the driver of the car that crashed into the other was at fault?" Using this instruction, these 16 individuals gave a mean at-fault rating of 5.9. Using the 5% significance level, did the changed instructions significantly increase the rating of being at fault? Explain your answer to someone who has never taken statistics.

8. Cut up 100 small slips of paper, and write each number from 0 to 9 on 10 slips each. Put the slips in a large bowl and mix them up. Now take out a slip, write down the number on it, and put it back. Do this 20 times. Make a histogram, and compute the mean and the variance of the result. You should get an approximately rectangular distribution. Then take two slips out, figure out their mean, write it down, and put the slips back. Repeat this process about 20 times. Make a histogram, and compute the mean and the variance of this distribution of means. The variance should be about half of the variance of the distribution of samples of one slip each. Finally, repeat the process again, this time taking three slips at a time. This distribution of means of three slips each should have a variance of about a third of the distribution of samples of one slip each. Also note that as the sample size increases, your distributions are getting closer to normal. (Had you begun with a normally distributed distribution of slips, your distributions of means would have been fairly close to normal regardless of the number in each sample.)

7

Making Sense of Statistical Significance:
Error, Power, and Effect Size

S TATISTICAL significance is extremely important in research. But it can also be misused. Sophisticated researchers and readers of research understand that there is more to the story of a research result than $p < .05$ or *ns*. This chapter helps you become sophisticated about significance.

Gaining this sophistication means learning about three closely interrelated issues: error, power, and effect size.

Type I and Type II Errors

The kind of error we consider here is about how our conclusions from hypothesis testing can be incorrect. It is *not* about making mistakes in calculations or even about using the wrong procedures. It *is* about how, even when we do everything properly, we can still be led to the wrong conclusion. That is, we are talking about error in the sense of getting a wrong result from a correct procedure. There are two kinds of errors of this sort we can make: Type I error and Type II error.

Type I Error

Suppose you conducted a study and set the significance level cutoff at a large probability level, such as 20%. This would mean that the null hypothesis would be rejected very easily. If you conducted many studies like this, you would often (about 20% of the time) be deciding to consider the research hypothesis supported when you should not. This is called a **Type I error.**

Even when we set the probability at .05 or .01, we can still make a Type I error sometimes (5% or 1% of the time). Consider the example from the last

Type I error

chapter on giving special instructions intended to make fifth graders' perform better on a standard achievement test. Suppose the special instructions in reality made no difference. However, in doing the study the researchers just happened to pick some students to receive the new instructions who were unusually good at this test. This would lead to rejecting the null hypothesis and concluding that the special instructions do make a difference. This decision to reject the null hypothesis would be a mistake—a Type I error. (Note that the researchers could not know that they have made an error of this kind.)

Type I errors are of serious concern to social scientists, who might construct entire theories and research programs, not to mention practical applications, based on a conclusion from hypothesis testing that is in fact mistaken. It is because these errors are of such serious concern that they are called Type I.

As we have noted, researchers cannot tell when they have made a Type I error. What they can do is try to conduct studies so that the chance of making a Type I error is as small as possible.

What is the chance of making a Type I error? It is the same as the significance level we set. If we set the significance level at $p < .05$, we are saying we will reject the null hypothesis if there is less than a 5% (.05) chance that we could have gotten our result if the null hypothesis were true. When rejecting the null hypothesis in this way, we are allowing up to 5% chance that we got our results even though the null hypothesis was actually true. That is, we are allowing a 5% chance of a Type I error. (You will sometimes see the significance level, the chance of making a Type I error, referred to as *alpha,* the Greek letter a.) Because the significance level is the same as the chance of making a Type I error, the lower we set the significance level, the smaller the chance of a Type I error. Researchers who do not want to take a lot of risk set the significance level lower than .05, such as $p < .001$. In this way the result of a study has to be very extreme in order for the hypothesis testing process to lead to a conclusion to reject the null hypothesis.

Using a .001 significance level is like buying insurance against making a Type I error. However, as when buying insurance, the better the protection, the higher the cost. There is a cost in setting the significance level at too extreme a level. We turn to that cost next.

Type II Error

If you set a very stringent significance level, such as .001, you run a different kind of risk. In this case you may conduct a study in which in reality the research hypothesis is true, but the result does not come out extreme enough to reject the null hypothesis. Thus, the error you would make is in *not* rejecting the null hypothesis when in fact the reality is that the null hypothesis is false (that the research hypothesis is true). This is called a **Type II error.**

Consider again our example of the fifth graders' standard achievement test. Suppose that, in truth, giving the special instructions does make fifth graders do better on the test. However, in conducting your particular study, the random sample that you selected to try this out on happened to include mainly fifth graders who are unusually poor at this kind of test. Even though your procedure may have helped them do better, their scores may still not be

Type II error

higher than the average of all fifth graders. The results would not be significant. Having decided not to reject the null hypothesis, and thus refusing to draw a conclusion, would be a Type II error.

Type II errors especially concern social scientists interested in practical applications, because a Type II error could mean that a useful theory or practical procedure is not implemented.

As with a Type I error, we cannot know when we have made a Type II error; however, we can try to conduct our studies so as to reduce the probability of making a Type II error. One way of buying insurance against a Type II error is to set a very lenient significance level, such as $p < .10$ or even $p < .20$. In this way, even if a study results in only a very small difference, the results have a good chance of being significant. There is a cost to this insurance policy too.

Relation of Type I and Type II Errors

When it comes to setting significance levels, protecting against one kind of error increases the chance of making the other. The cost of the insurance policy against Type I error (setting a significance level of say .001) is that we increase the chance of making a Type II error. (This is because with an extreme level of significance like .001, even if the research hypothesis is true, the results have to be quite strong to be large enough to reject the null hypothesis.) The cost of the insurance policy against Type II error (by setting a significance level of say .10) is that we increase the chance of making a Type I error. (This is because with a level of significance like .10, even if the null hypothesis is true, it is fairly easy to get a significant result just by accidentally getting a sample that is higher or lower than the general population before the study.)

The trade-off between these two conflicting concerns usually is resolved by compromise, hence the standard 5% and 1% significance levels.

Summary of Possible Outcomes of Hypothesis Testing

The entire issue of possible correct and mistaken conclusions in hypothesis testing can be diagrammed as shown in Table 7–1. Along the top of this table are the two possibilities about whether the research hypothesis is or is not actually true. (You never actually know this.) Along the side is whether, after hypothesis testing, you conclude that the research hypothesis is supported (reject the null hypothesis) or conclude that the results are inconclusive (do not reject the null hypothesis). Table 7–1 shows that there are two ways to be correct and two ways to be in error in any hypothesis-testing situation. We will have more to say about these possibilities after we consider the topic of statistical power.

Statistical Power

Power is the ability to achieve your goals. So a reasonable measure of power in a particular situation is the probability of achieving your goal in that

TABLE 7-1
Possible Correct and Erroneous Decisions in Hypothesis Testing

		Real Status of the Research Hypothesis (in practice, unknown)	
		True	*False*
Conclusion Using Hypothesis-testing Procedure	*Research hypothesis supported (reject null hypothesis)*	Correct decision	Error (Type I)
	Study is inconclusive (do not reject null hypothesis)	Error (Type II)	Correct decision

statistical power

situation. The goal of a researcher conducting a study is to get a significant result—*if* the research hypothesis really is true. The **statistical power** of a research study is the probability that the study will yield a significant result if the research hypothesis is true.

As you learn about statistical power, you will see that it is important for several reasons. For example, computing power when planning a study helps determine how many participants you need. Also, understanding power is extremely important to anyone who reads research articles (for example, in making sense of results that are not significant or results that are statistically but not practically significant).

What Is Statistical Power?

We said that the statistical power of a research study is the probability that the study will give a significant result if the research hypothesis is true. Notice that the power of an experiment is about the situation *if* the research hypothesis is true. If the research hypothesis is false, we do not want to get significant results. (That would be a Type I error.)

Now you may ask, "If the research hypothesis is true won't the experiment necessarily give a significant result?" The answer is no. The particular sample that happens to be selected from the population may not turn out to be extreme enough to reject the null hypothesis.

An Example

Consider again our example of the effects of giving special instructions to fifth graders taking a standard achievement test. In the hypothesis-testing process for this example, we compared two populations:

Population 1: Fifth graders receiving special instructions
Population 2: Fifth graders not receiving special instructions

The research hypothesis was that Population 1 would score higher than Population 2.

The top distribution in Figure 7–1 shows the situation in which this research hypothesis is true. The bottom of the figure shows the distribution for

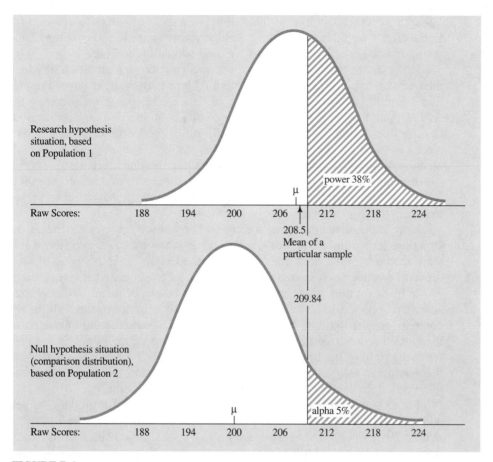

FIGURE 7–1

Distributions of means of 64 individuals from a fictional study of fifth graders receiving special instructions prior to taking a standard achievement test. The lower distribution of means is based on a known distribution of individual test scores of fifth graders who do not receive any special instructions (Population 2). The upper distribution of means is based on a predicted distribution of individual test scores of fifth graders who receive the special instructions for which the researchers predict a mean of 208 (Population 1). Shaded sections of both distributions are the area in which the null hypothesis will be rejected (the area in which a Type I error would occur in the lower distribution, power in the upper). Power = 38%.

Population 2. Because we are interested in means of samples of 64 individuals, both distributions are distributions of means.

The bottom distribution is also the comparison distribution, the distribution of means that you would expect for both populations if the null hypothesis were true. The shaded part of the right tail of this bottom distribution is the area in which you would reject the null hypothesis if, as a result of your study, the mean of your sample was in this area. The shaded rejection area begins at 209.84 (a Z score of 1.64), taking up 5% of this comparison distribution.

The top curve in the figure is the distribution of means for Population 1. This is the distribution of means that the researchers *predict* for the population receiving special instructions. In the last chapter, we never talked about this distribution, partly because this population is quite imaginary unless the research hypothesis is true. If the null hypothesis is true, the distribution for Population 1 would be the same as the distribution based on Population 2 and would not be set off to the right as we have shown in the figure.

However, to learn about power, we now consider the situation in which the research hypothesis is actually true. In this situation, the mean of Population 1 is farther to the right on the scale (has a higher average score on the achievement test) than the mean of the comparison distribution (the distribution for Population 2) shown below it. Specifically, the upper distribution of means is shown with a mean of 208 (whereas the comparison distribution's mean is only 200). This is to show that the population receiving the special instructions is expected to have, on the average, scores that are eight points higher. (We will discuss later how a researcher decides just how much higher to expect this upper distribution's mean to be.)

Now, suppose the researchers carry out the study. They give the special instructions to a group of 64 fifth graders and find their mean score on the test. If the research hypothesis is true, this amounts to saying that the mean of their group of 64 students is from a distribution like the upper distribution of means.

In this example, however, this upper distribution of means (from the researchers' prediction about Population 1) is only slightly to the right of the comparison distribution. That is, the researchers are predicting only a small increase in scores (8 points) so the mean of the upper distribution is not very far to the right of the lower one. What this picture tells us is that chances are that any mean selected from this upper distribution will not be far enough to the right on the lower distribution to reject the null hypothesis.

For example, suppose the particular sample of 64 fifth graders studied had a mean of 208.5, as shown by the arrow in the figure. Because a mean of at least 209.84 is needed to reject the null hypothesis, the result of this experiment would not be significant, even though the research hypothesis under this situation really is true. That is, we would have made a Type II error.

It is possible that the researchers would happen to select a sample from Population 1 with a mean far enough to the right (that is, with a high enough average test score) that it would be in the shaded rejection area in the lower curve. Nevertheless, given the way we have set up the example, there is a better-than-even chance that the study will *not* turn out to be significant *even if the research hypothesis is true.*

When a study like the one in this example has only a small chance of being significant even if the research hypothesis is true, we say the study has low power. If, on the other hand, the situation was one in which the upper curve was expected to be way to the right of the lower curve, so that virtually any sample taken from the upper curve would be in the shaded rejection area in the lower curve, then the study has high power.

Figuring Statistical Power

The power of a study can be calculated. In a situation like the fifth-grader-testing example, calculating power involves figuring out the area of the shaded portion of the upper distribution in Figure 7–1. However, the computations are somewhat laborious and become quite complex once we consider more realistic hypothesis-testing situations starting in the next chapter. Thus, instead of calculating power themselves, researchers usually find the power of a study using special charts called **power tables.** (Such tables have been prepared by Cohen, 1988, and Kraemer & Thiemann, 1987, among others.) In the following chapters, with each method you learn, we will provide basic power tables and discuss how to use them.

power tables

Although you will not be learning to calculate power in this book, it is very important that you understand what power is about, especially understanding the factors that affect the power of a study and how to use power when planning a study and when making sense of a study you read.

What Determines the Power of a Study

The power of a study depends on two main factors: The first is how big an effect the research hypothesis predicts. This first factor of effect size involves both how far apart the means are predicted to be and how much variance is expected within each group. The second main factor is how many participants are in the study (the sample size). Power also is affected by (a) the significance level chosen, (b) whether a one- or two-tailed test is used, and (c) the kind of hypothesis-testing procedure used.

Effect Size

Figure 7–1 shows the situation in which the researchers predicted that those who got the special instructions (Population 1, the top curve) would have a mean score eight points higher than fifth graders in general (Population 2). Figure 7–2 is for the same study but shows the situation in which the researchers predicted that those who got the special instructions would have a mean 16 points higher than fifth graders in general. Comparing the two figures you can see that it is more likely to get a significant result if the situation shown in Figure 7–2 is true. This is because there is more overlap of the top curve with the shaded area on the comparison distribution. In fact, it turns out that the probability of getting a significant result (the power) for the situation in Figure 7–1 is only 38%, but for the situation in Figure 7–2 it is 85%. In any study, the bigger the difference we expect between the means of the two populations, the more power in the study.

Figure 7–3 shows two distributions of means based on the same example but with a smaller variance in the populations, and thus a smaller variance in the distributions of means. (In the example, the standard deviation in the distribution of means is exactly half of what it was in Figure 7–1.) In this example, the predicted mean is the original 208 (from Figure 7–1); however, because both curves are much narrower, there is much less overlap between the upper curve and the shaded rejection area on the lower curve (the comparison distribution). The result is that the power is much higher (85%).

Overall, the general principle is that the less overlap between the two distributions, the more likely that a study will give a significant result. Two distributions might have little overlap either because there is a large difference between their means (as in Figure 7–2) or because they have so little variance that even with a small mean difference they do not overlap much (Figure 7–3). This principle is summarized more generally in Figure 7–4.

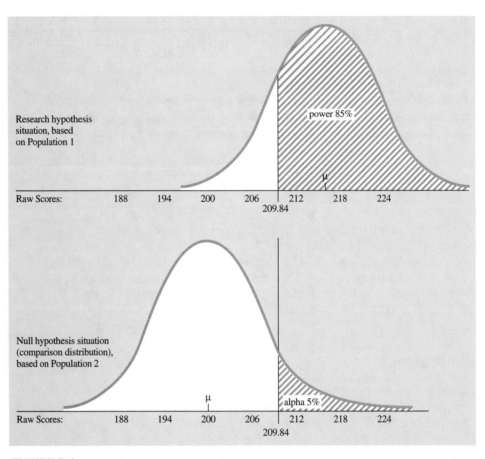

FIGURE 7–2
Distributions of means of 64 individuals based on predicted (upper) and known (lower) distributions of populations of individuals in a fictional study of fifth graders receiving special instructions prior to taking a standard achievement test. Scores are shown on both distributions for the significance cutoff on the lower distribution (significance cutoff based on $p < .05$, one-tailed). But this time the predicted mean (of the upper distribution) is 216. Power = 85%.

effect size

The extent to which the two populations do not overlap is called the **effect size** because it is the extent to which the experimental manipulation has an effect of separating the two populations. That is, the larger the difference expected between the two population means, the greater the effect size; and the smaller the variance within the two populations, the greater the effect size. The greater the effect size, the greater the power.

Calculating Effect Size

When determining power in advance of doing a study, effect size is calculated from (a) the researcher's prediction of the difference between the means of the two populations and (b) the population standard deviation. (The researcher's prediction of the difference between means is based on some precise theory, on previous experience with research of this kind, or on what would be the smallest difference that would be useful.) Here is the rule for calculating effect size: Divide the predicted difference between the means by

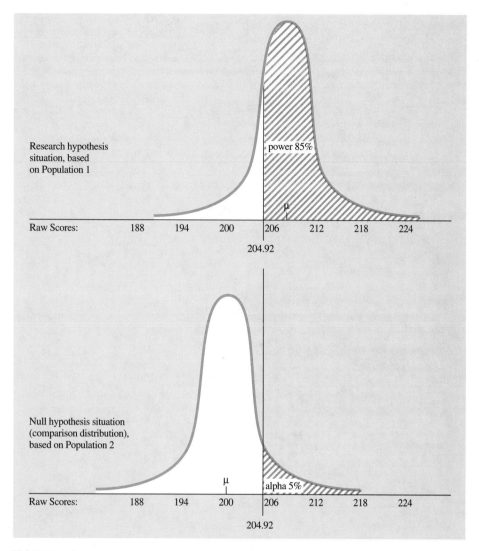

FIGURE 7–3
Distributions of means of 64 individuals based on predicted (upper) and known (lower) distributions of populations of individuals in a fictional study of fifth graders receiving special instructions prior to taking a standard achievement test. Scores are shown on both distributions for the significance cutoff on the lower distribution (significance cutoff based on $p < .05$, one-tailed). But this time the population standard deviation is half as large as that shown in Figure 7–1. Power = 85%.

the population standard deviation (that is, divide by the standard deviation of the population of individuals).[1] Stated as a formula,

$$\text{Effect Size} = \frac{\text{Population 1 } M - \text{Population 2 } M}{\text{Population } SD} \tag{7–1}$$

Notice that when calculating effect size, we do not use the standard deviation of the distribution of means but rather that of the original population of

---

[1]This procedure gives a measure of effect size called "Cohen's d" and is the preferred method for the kind of hypothesis testing you have learned so far. (In later chapters, you learn of other measures of effect size that are appropriate to other hypothesis-testing situations.)

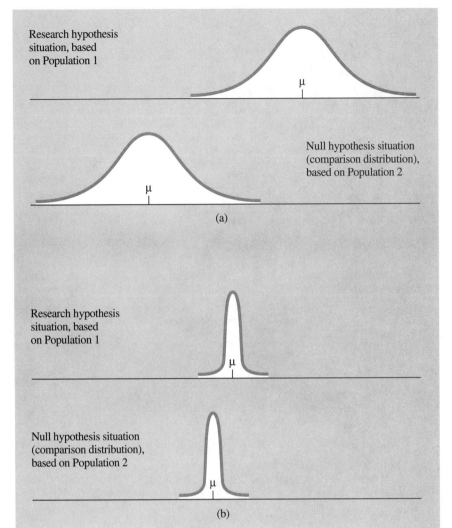

FIGURE 7–4
The predicted and comparison distributions of means might have little overlap (and hence the study has high power) because either (a) the two means are very different or (b) the variance is very small.

Research hypothesis situation, based on Population 1

Null hypothesis situation (comparison distribution), based on Population 2

(a)

Research hypothesis situation, based on Population 1

Null hypothesis situation (comparison distribution), based on Population 2

(b)

individuals. (Also notice that we are only concerned with one population's *SD*. This is because in hypothesis testing we usually assume that both populations have the same standard deviation. We will say more about this in later chapters.)

In the fifth-grader example in Figure 7–1 that we began with, the difference between the two population means is 8 and the standard deviation of the populations of individuals is 48. Thus, the effect size is 8/48, or .17. In terms of the formula,

$$\text{Effect Size} = \frac{\text{Population 1 } M - \text{Population 2 } M}{\text{Population } SD} = \frac{208 - 200}{48} = \frac{8}{48} = .17$$

In the next example, in which the mean difference was 16 test points and the population standard deviation was still 48 (the example in Figure 7–2), the effect size was doubled: 16/48, or .33. When we used a mean difference of 8 with a population standard deviation of 24 (the example of Figure 7–3), the effect size was 8/24, which was also .33.

A More General Importance of Effect Size

When computing effect size, we divide the difference between means by the standard deviation of the population of individuals. This standardizes the difference between means in the same way that a Z score gives a standard for comparison to other scores, even scores on different scales. Especially by using the standard deviation of the population of individuals, we bypass the variation from study to study of different sample sizes, making comparison even easier and effect size even more of a standard.

Knowing the effect size of a study allows us to compare results with effect sizes found in other studies, even those using different sample sizes. Equally important, knowing effect size allows us to compare studies using measures with quite different means and variances. Even within a particular study, our general knowledge of what is a small or a large effect size helps us evaluate the overall importance of a result. For example, a result may be significant but not very large. Or a result that is not significant (perhaps due to a small sample) may have just as large an effect size as was found in another study (perhaps one with a larger sample) in which the result was significant. Knowing the effect sizes of the studies help us make better sense of such results. We examine both of these important implications of effect size in later sections of this chapter.

An important development in statistics in recent years is a procedure called **meta-analysis.** This is a procedure that combines results from different studies, even results using different methods of measurement, to draw general conclusions. When combining results, the crucial thing combined is the effect sizes. As an example, a sociologist might be interested in the effects of cross-race friendships on prejudice, a topic on which there has been a large number of surveys. Using meta-analysis, the sociologist could combine the results of these surveys. This would provide an overall effect size. It also would tell how effect size differs for studies done in different countries or about prejudice towards different ethnic groups. (For an example of such a study, see Pettigrew and Meertens, 1995). For another example of meta-analysis, see Box 7–1, "Effect Sizes for Relaxation and Meditation: A Restful Meta-Analysis."

meta-analysis

Effect Size Conventions

It is difficult to know how big an effect to expect before we do a study. If we knew, we would not need to do the research. Jacob Cohen (1988), a researcher who has done a great deal of work in developing the statistics of power, has helped solve this problem. Cohen has come up with some **effect size conventions** based on the effects observed in many actual studies. These conventions at least tell a researcher what to consider as a small, medium, and large effect. If the researcher believes a particular study should have a medium effect, the researcher now has a specific number that Cohen says is typical of medium effects. The researcher can then use that number to compute power.

effect size conventions

BOX 7–1

Effect Sizes for Relaxation and Meditation: A Restful Meta-Analysis

The results of research on meditation and relaxation have been the subject of considerable controversy. Eppley, Abrams, and Shear (1989) decided to look at the issue systematically and conducted a meta-analysis of the effects of various relaxation techniques on trait anxiety (that is, ongoing anxiety as opposed to a temporary state). Eppley and colleagues chose trait anxiety for their meta-analysis because it is a definite problem related to many other mental health issues, yet in itself is fairly consistent from test to test with the same measure and from one measure to another measure of it.

Following the usual procedure, the researchers culled the scientific literature for studies, reading not only research journals but also books and unpublished doctoral dissertations. Being sure one has found all the relevant research is one of the most difficult parts of meta-analysis.

Once they had found what they hoped were all or most all of the relevant studies, the meta-analysis begin. Eppley and colleagues compared effect sizes for each of the four main methods of mediation and relaxation that have been studied in systematic research. The result was that the average effect size for the 35 Transcendental Mediation (TM) studies was .70. (This means an average difference of .70 standard deviation on the anxiety measure.) This effect size was significantly larger than the average effect sizes for the 44 studies on all other types of meditation (.28), for the 30 progressive relaxation studies (.38), and for the 37 studies on other forms of relaxation (.40).

The meta-analysis had really just begun. People who were screened to be highly anxious contributed more to the effect size, and prison populations and younger subjects seemed to gain more from TM. There was no impact on effect size of the skill of the instructors, expectations of the subjects, whether subjects had volunteered or been randomly assigned to conditions, experimenter bias (the TM results were actually stronger when any apparently pro–TM researchers' data were eliminated), the various measures of anxiety, and the research designs.

One clue to TM's high performance seemed to lie in the fact that techniques involving concentration produced a significantly smaller effect, whereas TM makes a special point of teaching an "effortless, spontaneous" method. Also, TM uses Sanskrit mantras (special sounds) said to come from a very old tradition and selected for each student by the instructor. Results were lower for methods of meditation employing randomly selected Sanskrit sounds or personally selected English words.

Whatever the reasons, the authors conclude that there are "grounds for optimism that at least some current treatment procedures can effectively reduce trait anxiety" (p. 973). So if you are prone to worry about little matters like statistics exams, consider these results.

Recall that we figured effect size as the predicted difference between the means of the two populations, divided by the population standard deviation. Cohen recommends that for the kind of situation we are considering in this chapter, we should think of a "small effect size" as about .2. Cohen notes that with an effect size of .2, the populations of individuals have an overlap of about 85%. This small effect size of .2 is, for example, the difference in height between 15- and 16-year-old girls (see Figure 7–5a), which is about a 1/2-inch difference with a standard deviation of about 2.1 inches. (When we speak of percentage overlap in these examples, we are referring to the overlap of the populations of individuals. The amount of overlap of the distributions of means will be less, depending on the sample size.)

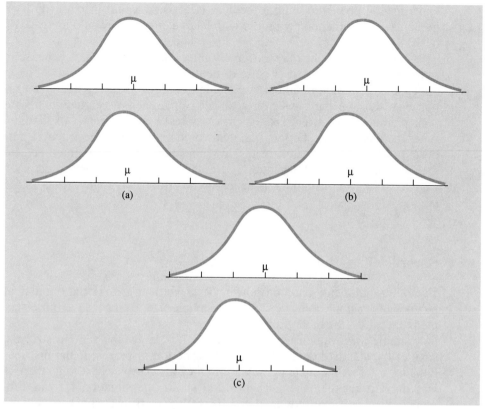

FIGURE 7–5
Comparisons of pairs of population distributions of individuals showing Cohen's conventions for effect size: (a) small effect size (.2), (b) medium effect size (.5), (c) large effect size (.8).

Cohen considers a medium effect size to be .5, which means an overlap of about 67%. This is about the difference in heights between 14- and 18-year-old girls (see Figure 7–5b).

Finally, Cohen defines a large effect size as .8. This is only about 53% overlap. It is about the difference in height between 13- and 18-year-old girls (see Figure 7–5c). These three effect sizes are summarized in Table 7–2.

Consider another example. As we noted earlier in the book, many IQ tests have a standard deviation of 16 points. An experimental procedure that had a small effect size would mean an increase of 3.2 IQ points. (A difference of 3.2 IQ points between the mean of the population who go through the experimental procedure and the population that does not, divided by the population standard deviation of 16; 3.2 divided by 16 comes out to .2.) An

TABLE 7–2
Summary of Cohen's Effect Size Conventions for Mean Differences

Verbal Description	Effect Size
Small	.2
Medium	.5
Large	.8

experimental procedure with a medium effect size would increase IQ by 8 points. An experimental procedure with a large effect size would increase IQ by 12.8 points.

Cohen's conventions are extremely important to researchers because in most research situations it is quite difficult to know in advance how big an effect size to predict. (Without being able to predict an effect size, one cannot even look up the power on a table.) Sometimes researchers can base their predictions of effect size on previous research or theory. Also, sometimes there is a smallest effect size that would matter for some practical purpose. In most cases researchers are studying something for the first time, and they can only make the vaguest guess about the amount of effect they expect. Cohen's conventions help researchers turn that vague guess into a number.

Sample Size

The other major influence on power, besides effect size, is the number of people in the sample that is studied, the sample size. Basically, the more people in the study, the more power.

Sample size influences power because the larger the sample size, the smaller the standard deviation of the distribution of means. If the distributions have a smaller standard deviation, they are narrower and thus there is less overlap between them. Figure 7–6 shows the situation for our fifth grader example if the study included 100 fifth graders instead of the 64 in the original example (Figure 7–1). The power in this case is 51%. (It was 38% with 64 fifth graders.) With 500 participants in the study, power is 98% (see Figure 7–7).

Do not get mixed up. The two distributions of means can be narrow (and thus have less overlap and more power) for two very different reasons. One reason is that the populations of individuals may have small standard deviations. This reason has to do with effect size. The other reason that the two distributions of means can be narrow is that the sample size is large. This reason is completely separate from the first reason. Sample size has nothing to do with effect size, but only with power. Both effect size and sample size influence power. But as we will see shortly, these two different influences on power lead to completely different kinds of practical steps for increasing power when planning a study.

Figuring the Needed Sample Size for a Given Level of Power

When planning a study, the main reason researchers figure power is to help decide how many people they need to include in the study. That is, since sample size is an important influence on power a researcher wants to be sure to have enough people in the study for the study to have fairly high power. If the researchers in our example were planning their study (with their predicted effect size of .17), they would find that they would need 222 fifth graders to have 80% power. To help researchers come up with figures like this, statisticians have prepared special tables that tell you how many participants you need in a study to have a high level of power, given a certain effect

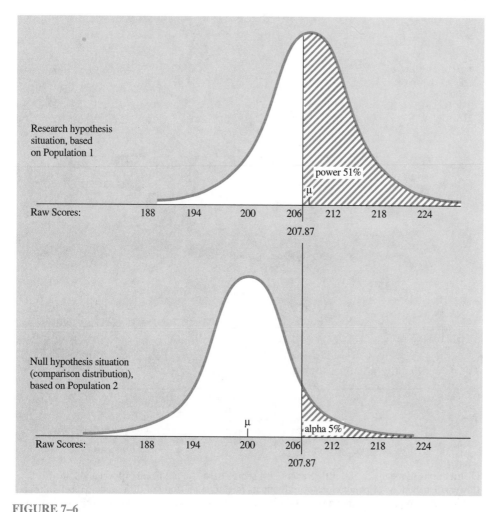

FIGURE 7–6
Distributions of means of 100 (rather than 64, as in Figure 7–1) fifth graders' test scores based on predicted (upper) and known (lower) distributions of populations of individuals in a fictional study of fifth graders receiving special instructions prior to taking a standard achievement test. Scores are shown on both distributions for the significance cutoff on the lower distribution (significance cutoff based on $p < .05$, one-tailed). Power = 51% now.

size. We will provide simplified versions of such tables for each of the main hypothesis testing procedures you will be learning.

Other Influences on Power

Three other factors (besides effect size and sample size) affect power:

1. Significance level (alpha). Less extreme significance levels (such as .10) mean more power, and more extreme significance levels (.01 or .001) mean less power. Less extreme means more power because when the significance level is not very extreme (such as .10), the shaded rejection area on the lower curve is bigger. Thus more of the area in the upper curve is shaded. More extreme means less power because when the significance level is more

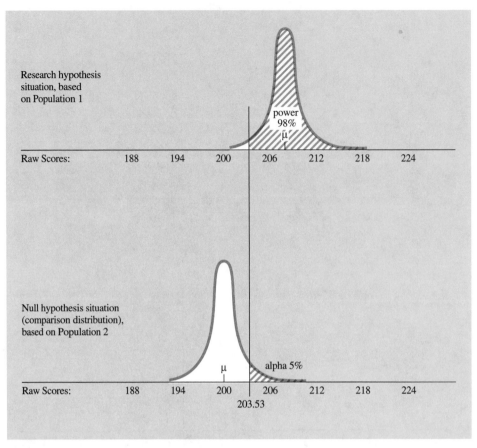

FIGURE 7–7
Distributions of means of 500 fifth graders' test scores based on predicted (upper) and known (lower) distributions of populations of individuals in a fictional study of fifth graders receiving special instructions prior to taking a standard achievement test. Scores are shown on both distributions for the significance cutoff on the lower distribution (significance cutoff based on $p < .05$, one-tailed). Power = 99%.

extreme (such as .01), the shaded rejection region on the lower curve is smaller. Suppose in our original version of the fifth-grader example (Figure 7–1), we had instead used the .01 significance level. The power would have dropped from 38% to only 16% (see Figure 7–8).

2. Number of tails used in testing (one or two). Using a two-tailed test makes it harder to get significance on any one tail. Thus, keeping everything else the same, power is less with a two-tailed test than with a one-tailed test. Suppose we had used a two-tailed test instead of a one-tailed test (but still using the 5% level overall) in our fifth-grade testing example. As shown in Figure 7–9, power would be only 26% (compared to 38% in the original one-tailed version shown in Figure 7–1).

3. Type of hypothesis testing procedure. There are cases where the researcher has a choice of more than one hypothesis testing procedure to use for a particular study. We have not considered any such cases so far in this book but will in Chapter 11.

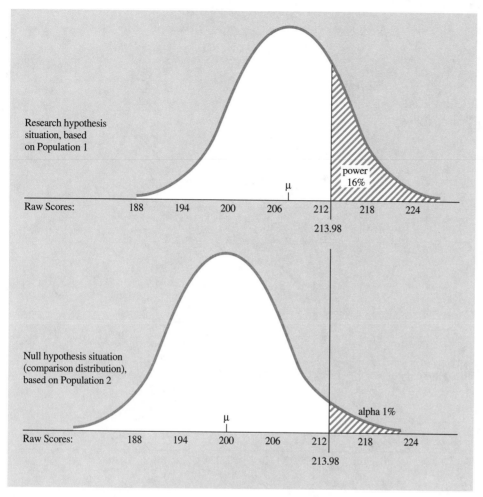

FIGURE 7–8
Distributions of means of 64 fifth graders' test scores based on predicted (upper) and known (lower) distributions of populations of individuals in a fictional study of fifth graders receiving special instructions prior to taking a standard achievement test. Scores are shown on both distributions for the significance cutoff on the lower distribution, now using $p < .01$, one-tailed. Power = 16%.

Summary of Influences on Power

Table 7–3 summarizes the effects of various factors on the power of a study.

Role of Power When Planning a Study

Determining power is very important when planning a study. If the power of a planned study is low, this means that even if the research hypothesis is true, this study is not likely to give significant results in support of it. The time and expense of carrying out the study would probably not be worthwhile. When the power of a planned study is found to be low, researchers attempt to find practical ways to increase the power to an acceptable level.

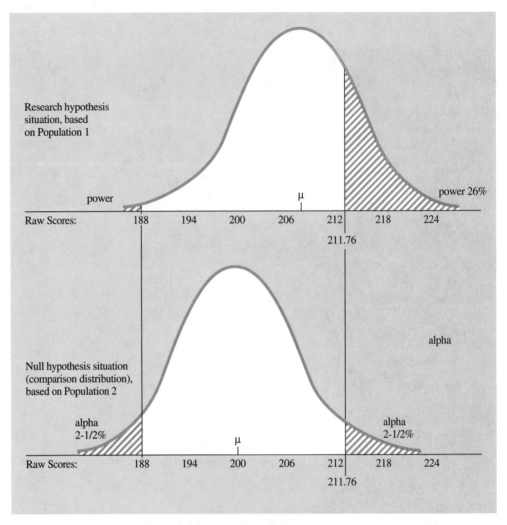

FIGURE 7–9
Distributions of means of 64 fifth graders' test scores based on predicted (upper) and known (lower) distributions of populations of individuals in a fictional study of fifth graders receiving special instructions prior to taking a standard achievement test. Scores are shown on both distributions for the significance cutoffs on the lower distribution, using $p < .05$, but now two-tailed. Power = 26%.

What is an acceptable level of power? Cohen (1988) suggests that ordinarily a study should have 80% power to be worth conducting. Obviously, the more power the better. The costs of greater power, such as studying more people, often make even 80% power beyond one's reach.

How can one increase the level of power of a planned study? The power of a planned study can, in principle, be increased by changing any of the factors summarized in Table 7–3. Let's consider each.

1. Increasing the predicted difference between population means. A researcher cannot just arbitrarily predict a bigger difference. This would increase the power that was calculated but would not in reality make the study more likely to come out significant. In some cases, however, it

TABLE 7–3

Influences on Power

Feature of the Study	Increases Power	Decreases Power
Effect size	Large	Small
Effect size combines the following two features:		
Predicted difference between population means	Large Differences	Small Differences
Population standard deviation	Small Population *SD*	Large Population *SD*
Sample size (*N*)	Large *N*	Small *N*
Significance level (alpha)	Lenient, high alpha (such as .05 or even .10)	Stringent, low alpha (such as .01 or even .001)
One-tailed versus two-tailed test	One-tailed	Two-tailed
Type of hypothesis-testing procedure used	Varies	Varies

is possible to change the way the study is done so the researcher has reason to expect a larger mean difference. Consider again our example of the experiment about the impact of special instructions on fifth graders' test scores. One way to increase the expected mean difference might be to make the instructions more elaborate, spending more time explaining them, perhaps allowing time for practice, and so forth. A disadvantage of this approach is that it can be difficult or costly. Another disadvantage is that it may require using an experimental procedure that is not like the one to which you want the results of your study to apply.

2. Decreasing the population standard deviation. It is possible to decrease the population standard deviation in a planned study in at least two ways. One way is to do the study using a population that is less diverse than the one originally planned. With the fifth-grade testing example, you might only use fifth graders in a particular suburban school system. The disadvantage is that the results apply only to the more limited population.

Another way to decrease the population standard deviation is to use conditions of testing that are more stable and measures that are more precise. For example, testing under a standardized situation or in a controlled laboratory setting usually produces smaller overall variation among scores in results (meaning a smaller standard deviation). Similarly, using tests with clear instructions and clear procedures for marking answers also reduces variation. When practical, this is an excellent way to increase power. But often the study is already as rigorous as it can be.

3. Increasing sample size. The most straightforward way to increase power in a study is to study more people. Of course, if you are studying astronauts who have walked on the moon, there is a limit to how many are available. In most practical cases, sample size is the main way to modify a study to bring it up to sufficient power.

4. Using a less stringent level of significance. Ordinarily, the level of significance used should be the least stringent that reasonably protects against Type I error; normally, this will be .05. It is rare that much can be done to improve power in this way.

5. Using a one-tailed test. Whether you use a one- or a two-tailed test depends on the logic of the hypothesis being studied. As with significance level, it is rare that you have much of a choice about this factor.

6. Using a more sensitive hypothesis-testing procedure. This is fine if alternatives are available. We will consider some options of this kind in Chapter 11. In most cases, however, the researcher begins with the most sensitive method available so little more can be done.

Table 7–4 summarizes some of the practical procedures a researcher can apply to increase the power of a planned experiment.

Importance of Power in Evaluating the Results of a Study

Understanding statistical power and what affects it is of great importance in interpreting the results of research.

Role of Power When a Result Is Significant: Statistical Significance Versus Practical Significance

We have learned that a study with a larger effect size is more likely to come out significant. It also is possible for a study with a very small effect size to come out significant if the study has reasonable power due to other factors, especially a large sample size. Consider a study in which among all students

TABLE 7–4
Summary of Practical Ways of Increasing the Power of a Planned Study

Feature of the Study	Practical Way of Raising Power	Disadvantages
Predicted difference between population means	Increase the intensity of the experimental procedure.	May not be practical or may distort the study's meaning.
Standard deviation	Use a less diverse population.	May not be available; decreases generalizability.
	Use standardized, controlled circumstances of testing or more precise measurement.	Not always practical.
Sample size	Use a larger sample size.	Not always practical; can be costly.
Significance level	Use a more lenient level of significance (such as .10)	Raises alpha, the probability of a Type I error.
One-tailed versus two-tailed test	Use a one-tailed test.	May not be appropriate to the logic of the study.
Type of hypothesis-testing procedure	Use a more sensitive procedure.	None may be available or appropriate.

who take the Scholastic Aptitude Test (SAT) in a particular year, a sample of 10,000 whose first name begins with a particular letter are randomly selected. Suppose that their mean SAT is 504, compared to the mean SAT of 500 (SD = 100) for the entire population. This result would be significant at the .001 level. Its effect size is a minuscule .04. That is, the significance test tells us that we can be quite confident that the population of students whose first name begins with this letter have higher SAT scores than the general population of students. The effect size (or just looking at the mean difference) makes it clear that this difference is not very important. The distributions of the two populations overlap so much that it would be of little use in any individual case to know what letter a person's first name begins with.

The message here is that in evaluating a study, you must consider first whether the result is statistically significant. If it is, and if the study has any potential practical implications, you must then *also* consider whether the effect size is sufficiently large to make the result useful or interesting. If the sample was small, you can assume that a significant result is probably also practically significant. If the sample size is very large, you must consider the effect size directly, as it is quite possible in such a case that it is too small to be useful.

Note that the implications are a bit of a paradox in light of what most people believe about sample size. Most people assume that the more people in the study, the more important the result. In a sense, just the reverse is the case. All other things being equal, if a study with only a few people manages to be significant, that significance must be due to a large effect size. A study with a large number of people in it that is statistically significant may or may not have a large effect size.

Notice that it is not a good idea to compare the significance level of two studies to see which has the more important result. A study with a small number of participants that is significant at the .05 level might well have a larger effect size than a study with a large number of participants that is significant at the .01 level.

Role of Power When a Result Is Not Significant

We saw in Chapter 5 that a result that is not significant is inconclusive. Often, however, we really would like to conclude that there is little or no difference between the populations. Can we ever do that?

Consider the relation of power to a nonsignificant result. If the power of the study was low and we did not get a significant result, the study is entirely inconclusive. Not getting a significant result may have been because the research hypothesis was false or it may have been because the study had too little power (for example, having very few participants).

On the other hand, if the power of a study was high and we did not get a significant result, it seems unlikely that the research hypothesis is true. In this situation (where there is high power), a nonsignificant result is a fairly strong argument against the research hypothesis. This does not mean that all versions of the research hypothesis are false. For example, it is possible that the populations are only very slightly different (and power was computed assuming a large difference).

In sum, a nonsignificant result from a study with low power is truly inconclusive. A nonsignificant result from a study with high power does suggest that either the research hypothesis is false or that there is less of an effect than was predicted when computing power.

Summary of the Role of Significance and Sample Size in Interpreting Research Results

Table 7–5 summarizes the role of significance and sample size in interpreting research results.

Error, Power, and Effect Size as Discussed in Research Articles

Error and power are mainly considered in the planning of research. (Power, for example, is often a major topic in proposals requesting funding for research and in thesis proposals.) As for research articles, power is sometimes mentioned in the final section of an article where the author discusses the meaning of the results. For example, Freund, Russell, and Schweitzer (1991) conducted a study on the effect of the delay between intake and first counseling session on the effectiveness of the counseling. The first paragraph of their Results section addressed the issue of whether their sample was large enough. The paragraph was headed "Power Analyses" and reads as follows:

> Power analyses (Cohen, 1977) were conducted to determine whether the available sample size was adequate to detect medium-sized effects. . . . We projected the median effect size (h^2) for research reported in the *Journal of Counseling Psychology* in 1985 (the year our study was completed) to be .15, which corresponds to Cohen's effect size (d) of .84. Power to detect such an effect size in the comparison of continuers and no-shows was .89, and power for the tests of correlations involving length of delay was .83. ([Footnote:] Power calculations were based on an alpha level of .05 for a directional hypothesis. Directional hypotheses were appropriate here because all previous reported effects of lengthy delays were either nonsignificant or in a negative direction.) These values sig-

TABLE 7-5
Role of Significance and Sample Size in Interpreting Experimental Results

Result Statistically Significant	Sample Size	Conclusion
Yes	Small	Important result
Yes	Large	Might or might not have practical importance
No	Small	Inconclusive
No	Large	Research hypothesis probably false

nify that if a true effect exists in the population from which our sample was drawn, then our statistical tests would yield significant results 89% and 83% of the time, respectively. (p. 5)

Articles also occasionally mention effect size when comparing results of studies or parts of studies. For example, in part of a study of ours (Aron, Aron, Tudor, & Nelson, 1991), people made a series of decisions involving allocating small amounts of money to themselves or another person under anonymous conditions. Based on our theoretical model, we had predicted, and found, that the difference between what people allocate to their best friend versus a stranger is much greater than the difference between what they allocate to a stranger versus the person they know whom they most dislike. (That is, more money is given to the friend than is held back from the enemy.) In commenting on the statistical result, we noted:

The magnitude of the difference is particularly evident if one compares effect sizes. . . . Using the mean difference divided by the standard deviation . . . gives an effect size of 1.31 for the friend-versus-stranger comparison and an effect size of .37 for the disliked-other-versus-stranger comparison. (p. 245)

Summary

In hypothesis testing in general, there are also two kinds of errors. A Type I error is when the null hypothesis is rejected but the research hypothesis is actually false. A Type II error is when the null hypothesis is not rejected but the research hypothesis is actually true. There are also two kinds of correct conclusions: (a) The null hypothesis is rejected and the research hypothesis is actually true, or (b) the null hypothesis is not rejected and the research hypothesis is actually false.

The statistical power of a study is the probability that it will yield a significant result if the research hypothesis is true. Researchers usually look up the power of a study on special tables.

There are two main factors that affect power: effect size and sample size. Effect size consists of both the predicted difference between means (the greater the difference, the larger the effect size) and the population variance (the smaller this is, the larger the effect size). Effect size is calculated as the difference between population means divided by the population standard deviation. Effect size influences power because the greater the effect size the less overlap between the distributions of means of the predicted population and the rejection area of the distribution of means for the comparison population. Cohen's (1988) conventions for effect size consider a small effect to be .2, a medium effect to be .5, and a large effect to be .8. Besides its impact on power and on the planning of studies, effect size is important in its own right in interpreting results of studies. It is also used to compare and combine results of studies, as in meta-analysis, and to compare different results within a study.

The larger the sample, the greater the power. This is because the larger the sample, the smaller the variance of the distribution of means, so that for a given effect size there is less overlap between distributions.

Power also is affected by significance level (the more extreme, such as .01, the lower the power), by whether a one- or two-tailed test is used (with less power for a two-tailed test), and by the type of hypothesis-testing procedure used (in the occasional case where there is a choice of procedure).

The main practical ways to increase the power of a planned experiment are increasing effect size and sample size.

Significant results from a study with high power (such as one with a large sample size) may not have practical importance. Nonsignificant results from a low power study (such as one with a small sample size) make it possible that important, significant results might show up if power were increased. It is not possible to "prove" the null hypothesis, but with sufficient power, a nonsignificant finding may suggest that any true effect is extremely small.

Key Terms

effect size	power tables	Type II error
effect size conventions	statistical power	
meta-analysis	Type I error	

Practice Problems

All data are fictional (unless an actual citation is given).

Answers to selected problems are given at the back of the book.

1. For each of the following studies, make a chart of the four possible correct and incorrect conclusions, and explain what each would mean. (Each chart should be laid out like Table 7–1, but you should put into the boxes the actual result using the names of the variables involved in the study.)

(a) Schoolchildren are studied to see if increasing the amount of recess time improves in-class behavior.

(b) A study is done of whether colorblind individuals can distinguish gray shades better than the population at large.

(c) A study of whether high school students who receive an acquired immune deficiency syndrome (AIDS) prevention program in their school are more likely to practice safe sex than other high school students.

(d) Individuals who have ever been in psychotherapy are compared to the general public to see if they are more tolerant of other people's upsets than the general population is.

2. What is meant by the statistical power of an experiment? (Write your answer for a lay person.)

3. Here is information about several different versions of a planned study, each involving a single sample. (This assumes the researcher can affect the population standard deviation and predicted mean by changing procedures.) Calculate the effect size for each study:

	Population 2		Predicted
	M	*SD*	Population 1 *M*
(a)	90	4	91
(b)	90	4	92
(c)	90	4	94
(d)	90	4	86
(e)	90	2	91
(f)	90	1	91
(g)	90	2	92
(h)	90	2	94
(i)	90	2	86

4. You read a study in which the result is just barely significant at the .05 level. You then look at the size of the sample. If the sample is very large (rather than very small), how should this affect your interpretation of (a) the probability that the null hypothesis is actually true and (b) the practical importance of the result?

5. You read a study that just barely *fails to be significant* at the .05 level. You then look at the size of the sample. If the sample is very large (rather than very small), how should this affect your interpretation of (a) the probability that the null hypothesis is actually true and (b) the probability that the null hypothesis is actually false?

6. What is the effect of each of the following on the power of a study?

(a) A larger predicted difference between the means of the populations

(b) A larger population standard deviation

(c) A larger sample size

(d) Using a more stringent significance level (e.g., .01 instead of .05)

(e) Using a two-tailed test instead of a one-tailed test

7. You are planning a study that you determine from a table as having quite low power. Name six things that you might do to increase power.

8

The *t* Test
for Dependent Means

AT this point, you may think you know all about hypothesis testing. Here's a surprise: What you know so far will not help you much as a researcher. Why? The procedures for testing hypotheses described up to now (which were, of course, absolutely necessary for what you will now learn) involved comparing a group of scores to a known population. In real research practice, you are often comparing two or more groups of scores to each other, without any direct information about populations. For example, you may have two scores for each of several people, such as a score on a test of attitudes toward the courts before and after having gone through a law suit. Or you might have one score per person for two groups of people, such as an experimental group and a control group in a study of the effect of a new method of training teachers. These kinds of research situations are very common in social and behavioral science research, and usually the only information available is from the samples. Nothing is known about the populations that the samples are supposed to come from. In particular, the researcher does not know the variance of the populations involved, which is a crucial ingredient in Step 2 of the hypothesis-testing process (determining the characteristics of the comparison distribution).

In this chapter, we first examine the solution to the problem of not knowing the population variance by focusing on a special situation, the comparison of the mean of a single sample to a population with a known mean but an unknown variance. Then, having seen how this problem of not knowing the population variance is handled, we go on to consider the situation in which there is no known population at all—the situation in which all we have are two scores for each of a number of people.

The hypothesis-testing procedures you learn in this chapter, in which the population variance is unknown, are examples of what are called *t* tests. The *t* test is sometimes called "Student's *t*" because its main principles were originally developed by William S. Gosset, who published his articles under the name "Student" (see Box 8–1).

Introduction to the *t* Test: The *t* Test for a Single Sample

We begin considering the situation in which you have a single sample and a population for which the mean is known but not the variance. This is called carrying out a *t* test for a single sample.

Hypothesis testing in this situation works in basically the same way as you learned in Chapter 6. The five steps are the same. There are only two important new wrinkles, having to do with the details of how you carry out two of the steps.

BOX 8–1

William S. Gosset, Alias "Student": Not a Mathematician, but a "Practical Man"

William S. Gosset graduated from Oxford in 1899 with a degree in mathematics and chemistry. It happened that in the same year the Guinness brewers in Dublin, Ireland, were seeking a few young scientists to take a scientific look at beer-making for the first time. Gosset took one of these jobs and soon had immersed himself in barley, hops, and vats of brew.

The problem was how to make beer less variable, and especially to find the cause of bad batches. A proper scientist would say, "Conduct experiments!" But a business such as a brewery could not afford to waste money on experiments involving large numbers of vats, some of which any brewer worth his hops knew would fail. So Gosset was forced to contemplate the probability of, say, a certain strain of barley producing terrible beer when the experiment could consist of only a few batches of each strain. Adding to the problem was that he had no idea of the variability of a given strain of barley—perhaps some fields of it were better than others. (Does this sound familiar? Poor Gosset, like today's researchers, had no idea of his population's variance.)

Gosset was up to the task. To his colleagues at the brewery, he was a professor of mathematics. To his statistical colleagues, mainly at the Biometric Laboratory at University College in London, he was a mere brewer. In short, Gosset was

the sort of scientist who was not above applying his talents to real life.

In fact, he seemed to revel in real life: raising pears, fishing, golfing, building boats, skiing, cycling, and lawn bowling (after he broke his leg by driving his car, a two-seater Model T Ford that he called "The Flying Bedstead," into a lamppost). He especially reveled in simple tools that could be applied to anything and simple formulas that he could compute in his head. (A friend described him as an expert carpenter but claimed that Gosset did almost all of his finer woodwork with nothing but a penknife!)

Gosset discovered the *t* distribution and invented the *t* test—simplicity itself—for situations when samples are small and the variability of the larger population is unknown. Most of his work was done on the backs of envelopes, with plenty of minor errors in arithmetic that he had to weed out later. Characteristically, he published his paper on his "brewery methods" only when editors of scientific journals demanded it. To this day, most statisticians call the *t* distribution "Student's *t*" because Gosset wrote under the anonymous name "Student" so that the Guinness brewery would not have to admit publicly that it sometimes brewed a bad batch!

References: Peters (1987); Stigler (1986); Tankard (1984).

The first important new wrinkle is in Step 2. Because the population variance is not known, you have to estimate it. The first thing we consider is how to estimate the population variance when it is not known.

The other important new wrinkle affects both Steps 2 and 3. When the population variance has to be estimated, the shape of the comparison distribution is not a normal curve. So the second new wrinkle we consider is what shape the comparison distribution is (for Step 2) and how to use a special table to find the cutoff (Step 3) on this slightly differently shaped distribution.

An Example

Suppose your college newspaper reports an informal survey showing that students at your college spend an average of 2.5 hours studying each day. Suppose also that you think the students in *your* dormitory are studying much more. You randomly pick 16 students from your dormitory and ask them how much they study each day. (We will assume that they are all honest and accurate.) Your result is that these 16 students study an average of 3.2 hours per day. What should you conclude? Do the students in your dormitory study more than the college average? Should you conclude that your results are so close to the college average that the small difference of .7 hours (3.2 hours – 2.5 hours) is merely because you happened to pick 16 of the more studious students in your dormitory?

Step 1 of the hypothesis-testing process is to restate the problem. In this case, the two populations are these:

Population 1: The kind of students who live in your dormitory
Population 2: The kind of students at your college generally

The research hypothesis is that Population 1 students study more than Population 2 students; the null hypothesis is that Population 1 students do not study more than Population 2 students. So far the problem is no different from the ones covered in Chapter 6.

Step 2 is determining the characteristics of the comparison distribution. Its mean will be 2.5, because we are told that is what the survey found for students at your college generally (Population 2).

However, the next part of Step 2 is finding the variance of the distribution of means. With the current example, we face a new kind of problem. In the past, you have always known the variance of the population of individuals. Using that variance, you then computed the variance of the distribution of means. In this example, the variance of number of hours studied for the college as a whole (the Population 2 students) was not reported in the newspaper article. So you phone the paper. Unfortunately, the reporter who did the survey did not calculate the variance, and the original survey results are no longer available, so it cannot be determined. What to do? (Somehow, you have to come up with the variance of the distribution of means as part of Step 2; without it you could not do the rest of the hypothesis-testing steps.)

Basic Principle of the *t* Test: Estimating the Population Variance from the Sample Information

If you do not know the variance of the population of individuals, you can estimate it from what you do know: the scores of the people in your sample.

How is this estimation possible? In the logic of hypothesis testing, the group of people we study is considered to be a random sample from a particular population. The variance of this sample ought to reflect the variance of that population. If the population has a lot of spread (there is a lot of variance in the scores), a sample randomly selected from that population should have a lot of spread; if the population is very compact, with little spread, there should not be much spread in the sample either. It should be possible to use the spread of scores in the sample to make an informed guess about the spread of scores in the population. That is, we could compute the variance of the sample's scores and that should be similar to the variance of the scores in the population. (See Figure 8–1.)

There is, however, one small hitch. The variance of a sample, on the average, will be slightly smaller than the variance of the population from which it is taken. For this reason, the variance of the sample is a **biased estimate** of the population variance. To oversimplify a little, the reason that a sample's variance tends to be smaller than the population's is that it is slightly less likely to include extreme scores.[1]

Fortunately, you can compute an **unbiased estimate of the population variance** by slightly changing the ordinary variance formula. The ordinary way to figure the variance is to take the sum of the squared deviation scores and divide this by the number of scores. In the changed procedure, you still take the sum of the squared deviation scores, but you instead divide it by the number of scores *minus 1*. Dividing by a slightly smaller number makes the result of the dividing (the variance) bigger. It turns out that dividing by the number of scores minus one makes the resulting variance just enough bigger than when you compute it the usual way to make this way of computing the variance an unbiased estimate of the population variance. ("Unbiased" does not mean that your estimate will be exactly correct. It only means that an estimate figured in this way is equally likely to be too high as it is to be too low.)

The symbol for the unbiased estimate of the population variance is S^2. The formula is the usual variance formula, but with the division by $N - 1$ instead of by N:

$$S^2 = \frac{\Sigma(X - M)^2}{N - 1}$$

(8–1)

Let us return to our example of hours spent studying and compute the estimated variance of the population from the sample's 16 scores. First, we compute the sum of squared deviation scores. (Subtract the mean from each of the scores, square those deviation scores, and add them.) Let us presume in our example that this comes out to 9.6. To get the estimated population variance, you divide this sum of squared deviation scores by the number of scores minus 1. The result of 9.6 divided by 15 is .64. In terms of the formula,

biased estimate

unbiased estimate of the population variance

[1]If you are interested, a more precise explanation is as follows: Recall that the variance is based on deviations from the mean, and hence a population's variance is based on deviations from its mean. However, in calculating the variance of a sample, the deviations are figured from the sample's mean. Because the sample's mean is the optimal balance point for its scores, the average squared deviations from it will be less than from any other number, such as the population's mean. Indeed, if you knew the true population mean and used it to compute the deviation scores for each score in the sample, the variance calculated from the sample's scores in this way would not be a biased estimate of the population's variance. One way to think of the correction for bias discussed in the next paragraph is that it exactly accounts for the degree to which a sample's mean tends to vary from the true population mean.

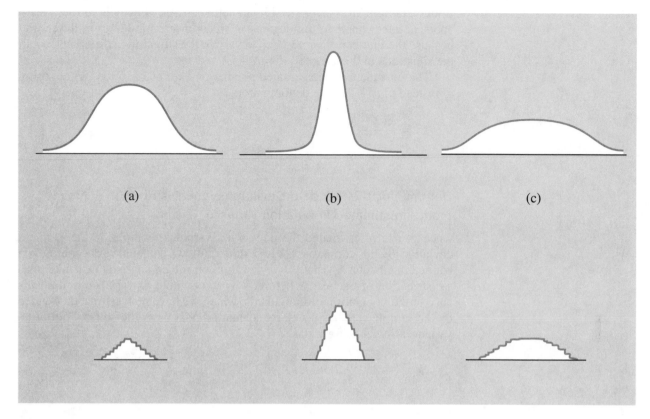

FIGURE 8–1
Variance in samples and the populations they are taken from.

$$S^2 = \frac{\Sigma(X-M)^2}{N-1} = \frac{9.6}{16-1} = \frac{9.6}{15} = .64$$

Degrees of Freedom

The number you divide by to figure the estimated population variance (the number of cases minus 1) has a special name. It is called the **degrees of freedom (df)**. It has this name because it refers to the number of scores in a sample that are "free to vary." This is a somewhat complicated notion. The basic idea is that, when figuring the variance, you first have to know the mean. If you know the mean and all the scores in the sample but one, you can figure out what the last score has to be with a little arithmetic. Once you know the mean, one of the scores in the sample is not free to have any possible value. So the degrees of freedom is the number of scores minus 1. In terms of a formula,

degrees of freedom (*df*)

$$df = N - 1 \qquad\qquad\qquad (8\text{--}2)$$

In our example, $df = 16 - 1 = 15$. (In some situations, which you will learn about in later chapters, the degrees of freedom are figured a bit differently because the number of scores free to vary in the situation is different. For all the situations in this chapter, $df = N - 1$.)

The formula for the estimated population variance is often written using df instead of $N - 1$ in the denominator:

$$S^2 = \frac{\Sigma(X - M)^2}{df}$$

(8–3)

Determining the Standard Deviation of the Distribution of Means From an Estimated Population Variance

Once you have estimated the population variance, computing the standard deviation of the comparison distribution follows the same procedures you learned in Chapter 6. That is, we can think of the comparison distribution as a distribution of means. As before, we can compute its variance as the variance of the population of individuals, which we have now estimated, divided by the sample size. As usual, its standard deviation is the square root of its variance. Stated as formulas,

$$S_{M^2} = \frac{S^2}{N}$$

(8–4)

$$S_M = \sqrt{S_{M^2}}$$

(8–5)

Note that when we are using an estimated population variance, the symbols for the variance and standard deviation of the distribution of means use S instead of Population SD.

In our example, the sample size was 16 and the estimated population variance we just worked out was .64. The variance of the distribution of means based on that estimate will be .64 divided by 16, or .04. The corresponding standard deviation, the square root of .04, is .2. In terms of the formulas,

$$S_{M^2} = \frac{S^2}{N} = \frac{.65}{16} = .04$$

$$S_M = \sqrt{S_{M^2}} = \sqrt{.05} = .2$$

Be careful. To find the variance of a distribution of means, you always divide the population variance by the sample size, regardless of whether the population's variance is known or only estimated. In our example, you divided the population variance, which you had estimated, by 16. It is only when making the estimate of the population variance that you divide by the sample size minus 1.

We have now almost completed Step 2 of the hypothesis-testing process, determining the characteristics of the comparison distribution, for our example in which we have had to estimate the population variance. We have seen that the distribution of means has a mean of 2.5 (the known population mean) and an estimated standard deviation (S_M) of .2. What we still do not know is the shape of the comparison distribution.

The Shape of the Comparison Distribution When Using an Estimated Population Variance: The *t* Distribution

In Chapter 6, where we knew the variance of the population, we saw that so long as it is reasonable to assume that the population distribution follows a normal curve, the shape of the distribution of means that we use as our comparison distribution will also be a normal curve. However, when carrying out the hypothesis-testing process using an estimated population variance (that is, when doing a *t* test), there is less true information and more room for error. The mathematical effect is that when using an estimated population variance, extreme means are slightly more likely to occur than would be found in a normal curve. Further, the smaller your sample size, the bigger this tendency, because you are estimating the population variance on the basis of less information.

The result of all of this is that, when doing hypothesis testing using an estimated variance, instead of your comparison distribution being a normal curve, the comparison distribution is a slightly different curve called a ***t* distribution.** *t* distribution

Actually, there are many *t* distributions. They vary in shape according to the degrees of freedom for the sample used in estimating the population variance. (Given any particular degrees of freedom, there is only one *t* distribution.) Generally, all *t* distributions look to the eye like a normal curve—bell-shaped, completely symmetrical, and unimodal. A *t* distribution differs subtly in having heavier tails (that is, slightly more scores at the extremes). Figure 8–2 shows the shape of a *t* distribution compared to a normal curve. With more area in the tails of the comparison distribution, to reject the null hypothesis (for example, to be in the top 5%), you need a sample with a mean that is farther out on the distribution. That is, it takes a slightly more extreme sample mean to get a significant result when using a *t* distribution than when using a normal curve.

Just how much the *t* distribution differs from the normal curve depends on the degrees of freedom, the amount of information used (the number of scores free to vary) in estimating the population variance. The *t* distribution differs most from a normal curve when the estimate of the population variance is based on a very small sample, so that the degrees of freedom are low. For example, we saw in Chapter 6 that the cutoff for a one-tailed test at the

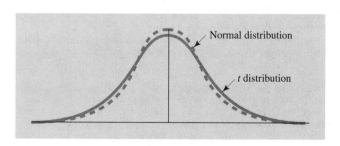

FIGURE 8–2
The *t* distribution compared to the normal curve.

5% level, using the normal curve, is 1.64. On a t distribution based on an estimated variance with 7 degrees of freedom (that is, with a sample size of 8), the cutoff would be 1.895. If the estimate is based on a larger sample, say a sample of 25 (so that $df = 24$), the cutoff is 1.711, a cutoff much closer to that for the normal curve. If your sample size is infinite, the t distribution is the same as the normal curve. (Of course, if your sample size were infinite, it would include the entire population!)

Before going on to learn how you actually find the cutoff using a t distribution, let us first return briefly to our example of the number of hours that students at your dormitory study each night. We finally have everything we need to complete Step 2 about the characteristics of the comparison distribution. In our example, we have already seen that the distribution of means will have a mean of 2.5 hours and a standard deviation of .2. Based on what we have just discussed, we can now add that the shape of the comparison distribution will be a t distribution with 15 degrees of freedom.[2]

Determining the Cutoff Sample Score for Rejecting the Null Hypothesis: Using the t Table

Step 3 of hypothesis testing is determining the cutoff for rejecting the null hypothesis. Because there is a different t distribution according to the degrees of freedom in your sample, there have to be different cutoff points for statistical significance, depending on the degrees of freedom. However, to avoid taking up pages and pages with tables for each possible t distribution, a simplified table is used that gives only the crucial cutoff points. We have included such a **t table** in Appendix A (Table A–2).

In the hours-studied example, you have a one-tailed test. (You are interested in whether students in your dormitory study *more* than students in general at your college.) You will probably want to use the 5% significance level because the cost of a Type I error (mistakenly rejecting the null hypothesis) is not great. You have 16 people, making 15 degrees of freedom on which your estimate of the population variance was based.

Table 8–1 shows a portion of a t table like Table A–2. Find the column for the .05 significance level for one-tailed tests and move down it to the row

t table

---

[2]Statisticians make a subtle distinction in this situation between the comparison distribution and the distribution of means. We have avoided this distinction here and in later chapters in order to greatly simplify the discussion of what is already fairly difficult. If you are interested, the distinction can be understood as follows: The general procedure of hypothesis testing with means of samples as you learned it in Chapter 6 can be described as computing a Z score for your sample's mean, where

$$Z = (\text{Sample } M - \text{Population } M)/\text{Pop } SD_M, \text{ where Pop } SD_M = \sqrt{(\text{Pop } SD^2/N)},$$

and then comparing this Z score to a cutoff Z score from the normal curve table. We described this process as using the distribution of means as your comparison distribution.

Statisticians would say that when doing this, actually you are comparing your computed Z score to a distribution of Z scores, which is simply an ordinary normal curve. Similarly, in the case of a t test, statisticians think of the procedure as computing a t score. We will see shortly that a t score is the same as a Z score, but using estimated values for variances and standard deviations instead of known population variances; that is, $t = (\text{Sample } M - \text{Population } M)/S_M$. The t score is then compared to a cutoff t score from a t distribution table. Thus according to the formal statistical logic, the comparison distribution is a distribution of t scores, not of means, computed for all possible samples (of a given size) taken from the population of individuals.

TABLE 8-1

Cutoff Scores for *t* Distributions with 1 Through 17 Degrees of Freedom

df	One-Tailed Tests			Two-Tailed Tests		
	.10	.05	.01	.10	.05	.01
1	3.078	6.314	31.821	6.314	12.706	63.657
2	1.886	2.920	6.965	2.920	4.303	9.925
3	1.638	2.353	4.541	2.353	3.182	5.841
4	1.533	2.132	3.747	2.132	2.776	4.604
5	1.476	2.015	3.365	2.015	2.571	4.032
6	1.440	1.943	3.143	1.943	2.447	3.708
7	1.415	1.895	2.998	1.895	2.365	3.500
8	1.397	1.860	2.897	1.860	2.306	3.356
9	1.383	1.833	2.822	1.833	2.262	3.250
10	1.372	1.813	2.764	1.813	2.228	3.170
11	1.364	1.796	2.718	1.796	2.201	3.106
12	1.356	1.783	2.681	1.783	2.179	3.055
13	1.350	1.771	2.651	1.771	2.161	3.013
14	1.345	1.762	2.625	1.762	2.145	2.977
15	1.341	**1.753**	2.603	1.753	2.132	2.947
16	1.337	1.746	2.584	1.746	2.120	2.921
17	1.334	1.740	2.567	1.740	2.110	2.898

for 15 degrees of freedom. The crucial cutoff is 1.753. This means that you will reject the null hypothesis if your sample's mean is 1.753 or more standard deviations above the mean on the comparison distribution. (If you were using a known variance, the Z score needed to reject the null hypothesis based on the normal curve would have been 1.645.)

One other point about using the t table. In the full t table in the appendix, there are rows for each degree of freedom from 1 through 30, then for every five degrees of freedom (35, 40, 45, and so on) up to 100. If your study involves degrees of freedom in between two values, to be safe, you use the nearest degrees of freedom *below* yours that is given on the table. For example, if you were doing a study in which there were 43 degrees of freedom, you would use the row in the table for 40 *df.*

Determining the Score of the Sample Mean on the Comparison Distribution: The *t* Score

Step 4 of hypothesis testing is determining the score of your sample's mean on the comparison distribution. In previous chapters, this has meant finding the Z score on the comparison distribution—the number of standard deviations it is from the mean on the comparison distribution. You do exactly the same thing when your comparison distribution is a t distribution. The only difference is that in the past, when the comparison distribution was a normal curve, the score we computed on it was called a Z score. Now, when we are using a t distribution as our comparison distribution, the score we compute on it we call a ***t* score.** In terms of a formula,

t score

$$t = \frac{\text{Sample } M - \text{Pop } M}{S_M}$$

$$(8\text{–}6)$$

In the example, your sample's mean of 3.2 is .7 hours from the mean of the distribution of means, which amounts to 3.5 standard deviations from the mean (.7 hours divided by the standard deviation of .2 hours). That is, the t score in the example is 3.5. In terms of the formula,

$$t = \frac{\text{Sample } M - \text{Population } M}{S_M} = \frac{3.2 - 2.5}{.2} = \frac{.7}{.2} = 3.5$$

Determining Whether to Reject the Null Hypothesis

Step 5 of hypothesis testing is deciding whether or not to reject the null hypothesis. This step is exactly the same with a t test as it was in the situations we considered in previous chapters. You compare the cutoff score from Step 3 with the sample's score on the comparison distribution from Step 4. In our example, the cutoff t score was 1.753 and the actual t score for our sample was 3.5. Conclusion: Reject the null hypothesis; the research hypothesis that students in your dormitory study more than students in the rest of the college is supported.

Figure 8–3 illustrates the various distributions involved in this example.

Summary of Hypothesis Testing When the Population Variance Is Not Known

Table 8–2 compares hypothesis testing when the population's mean and variance are known (the situation you learned about in Chapters 5 and 6) with hypothesis testing when the population's mean, but not its variance, are known (the situation you have just learned about). Table 8–3 summarizes the

FIGURE 8–3
Distributions involved in the hours-studied example.

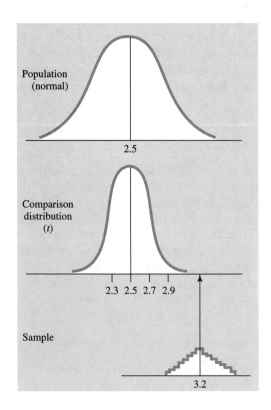

steps of hypothesis testing in this new situation of what is called a *t*-test for a single sample.

The *t* Test for Dependent Means

The type of situation you learned about in the previous section was for when you know the population mean but not its variance and in which you have a single sample of scores. This situation is fairly rare. In most research situations, you know *neither* the population's mean *nor* its variance. Also, as we noted at the start of the chapter, in most research situations a researcher is comparing *two* sets of scores. It turns out that in most research you do not know the population mean *and* you have two sets of scores. These two things, not knowing the population variance and having two sets of scores, almost always go together. This situation is very common. It is in this section that, finally, we start to do the sort of hypothesis testing commonly done by social and behavioral scientists.

Let us begin by considering this issue of having two sets of scores. In particular, in the remainder of this chapter we focus on the situation in which we have two scores from each of a group of participants. This situation of comparing two scores each from a single group of people is called a **repeated-measures design** (also known as a *within-subjects design*). **repeated-measures design** One widely used type of repeated-measures design involves measuring the same people before and after some social or psychological intervention. For

TABLE 8–2

Hypothesis Testing with Single Sample Mean When Population Variance Is Unknown (*t* Test) Compared to When Population Variance Is Known

Step in Hypothesis Testing	Difference From When Population Variance Is Known
1. Restate the question into a research hypothesis and a null hypothesis about the populations.	No difference in method.
2. Determine the characteristics of the comparison distribution:	
Population mean	No difference in method.
Population variance	Estimate from the sample.
Standard deviation of the distribution of sample means	No difference in method (but based on estimated population variance).
Shape of the comparison distribution	Use the *t* distribution with $df = N - 1$.
3. Determine the significance cutoff.	Use the *t* table.
4. Determine score of your sample on the comparison distribution.	No difference in method (but called a *t* score).
5. Compare Steps 3 and 4 to determine whether to reject the null hypothesis.	No difference in method.

TABLE 8–3
Steps for Conducting a *t*-Test for a Single Sample

1. Restate the question into a research hypothesis and a null hypothesis about the populations.

2. Determine the characteristics of the comparison distribution.

   a. The mean is the same as the known population mean.

   b. The standard deviation is computed as follows:

      i. Compute the estimated population variance:
      $S^2 = \sqrt{\Sigma(X - M^2/N - 1)}$.

      ii. Compute the variance of the distribution of means:
      $S_M^2 = S^2/N$.

      iii. Compute the standard deviation: $S_M = \sqrt{S_M^2}$.

   c. The shape will be a *t* distribution with $N - 1$ degrees of freedom.

3. Determine the cutoff sample score on the comparison distribution at which the null hypothesis should be rejected.

   a. Determine the degrees of freedom, desired significance level, and number of tails in the test (one or two).

   b. Look up the appropriate cutoff in a *t* table.

4. Determine the score of your sample on the comparison distribution:
   $t = (\text{Sample } M - \text{Population } M)/S_M$.

5. Compare the scores obtained in Steps 3 and 4 to decide whether or not to reject the null hypothesis.

---

example, an organizational specialist might measure days missed from work for 80 workers before and after a new health promotion program was introduced.

In this common situation of a repeated-measures design, where each person is measured twice, the hypothesis-testing procedure used is called a ***t* test for dependent means.** It has the name "dependent means" because the mean for each group of scores (for example, a group of before scores and a group of after scores) are dependent on each other in that they are both from the same people. (In Chapter 9, we consider the situation in which the research compares scores from two different groups of people, a research design analyzed by a "*t* test for independent means.")

A *t* test for dependent means is conducted exactly the same way as a *t* test for a single sample, except that (a) we use something called difference scores and (b) we assume that the population mean is 0. Let us turn now to each of these new features.

t test for dependent means

Difference Scores

difference scores

With a repeated-measures design, our sample includes two scores for each person instead of just one. The way we handle this in doing a *t* test is to make the two scores per person into one score per person. This magic is done by creating **difference scores:** For each person you subtract one score from the other. In the absence-from-work example, the organizational specialist would subtract the number of days missed after the program from the number of days missed before the program, providing an after-minus-before difference score for each employee. (When the two scores are a before and an after score, we usually take the after score minus the before score, to get a measure of change. In many situations, it really does not matter which you subtract from which, so long as you do it the same way for each person in the sample.)

Once you have the difference score for each person in the study, the entire hypothesis-testing procedure is done using difference scores. That is, you treat the study as if there were a single sample of scores (scores that in this situation happen to be difference scores).[3]

Population of Difference Scores With a Mean of 0

The next problem is that we need to know the mean of the comparison distribution—the mean of the population in which there was no effect, the null hypothesis situation. So far in this book, the population mean was known. For example, in the college dormitory survey of hours studied, the population mean was known to be 2.5 hours. We said that is a rare situation in real life. For example, in this situation using difference scores, the mean of the population of difference scores is usually not known.

The solution is as follows: Ordinarily, the null hypothesis in a repeated-measures design is that there is no difference between the two groups of scores. For example, the null hypothesis in the health promotion study is that absences from work will be the same before and after the health promotion program is introduced. The research hypothesis of a difference is thus compared to a null hypothesis of no difference.

Here is the key point: Saying that in the population there is on the average no difference between the two scores for each person is the same as saying that the mean of the population of the difference scores is 0. (You may want to read that sentence twice.) When working with difference scores, we simply assume, for the purposes of hypothesis testing, an artificial comparison population of difference scores in which there is no difference and which has a population mean of 0.

Example of a *t* Test for Dependent Means

Olthoff (1989) tested the communication quality of engaged couples 3 months before and again 3 months after marriage. To keep the example simple, we will focus on just one of the groups Olthoff studied, a group who received ordinary premarital counseling from their ministers. (We also will consider only the husbands, since the scores for the wives were somewhat more variable, making them a less clear example for learning the *t* test.)

The scores for the 19 husbands are listed in the "Before" and "After" columns in Table 8–4, followed by the entire *t*-test analysis. The mean of the

---

[3]You can also use a *t* test for dependent means when you have scores from pairs of people. You consider each pair as if it were one person and compute a difference score for each pair. For example, suppose you have 30 married couples and you are comparing ages of husbands and wives to see if husbands are consistently older than wives. You could compute for each couple a difference score of husband's age minus wife's age. The rest of the computations would then be exactly the same as for an ordinary *t* test for dependent means. When the *t* test for dependent means is used in this way it is sometimes called a *t test for matched pairs*.

TABLE 8–4

_t_-Test for Communication Quality Scores Before and After Marriage for 19 Husbands Who Received No Special Communication Training

Husband	Communication Quality		Difference (After – Before)	Deviation of Differences From the Mean of Differences	Squared Deviation
	Before	_After_			
A	126	115	– 11	1.05	1.1
B	133	125	– 8	4.05	16.4
C	126	96	– 30	–17.95	322.2
D	115	115	0	12.05	145.2
E	108	119	11	23.05	531.3
F	109	82	– 27	–14.95	233.5
G	124	93	– 31	–18.95	359.1
H	98	109	11	23.05	531.3
I	95	72	– 23	–10.95	119.9
J	120	104	– 16	– 3.95	15.6
K	118	107	– 11	1.05	1.1
L	126	118	– 8	4.05	16.4
M	121	102	– 19	– 6.95	48.3
N	116	115	– 1	11.05	122.1
O	94	83	– 11	1.05	1.1
P	105	87	– 18	– 5.95	35.4
Q	123	121	– 2	10.05	101.0
R	125	100	– 25	–12.95	167.7
S	128	118	– 10	2.05	4.2
Σ:	2,210	1,981	–229	– .05	2,772.9

For difference scores:
 $M = -229/19 = -12.05$.
 Population $M = 0$ (assumed as a no-change baseline of comparison).
 $S^2 = SS/df = 2,772.9/(19 - 1) = 154.05$.
 $S_M^2 = S^2/N = 154.05/19 = 8.11$.
 $S_M = \sqrt{S_M^2} = \sqrt{8.11} = 2.85$.
 t with $df = 18$ needed for 5% level, two-tailed $= \pm 2.101$.
 $t = (M - \text{Pop. } M)/S_M = (-12.05 - 0)/2.85 = -4.23$.

Decision: Reject the null hypothesis.

Note: Data from Olthoff (1989).

before scores was 116.316 and the mean of the after scores was 104.263. More important, however, we also have figured the difference scores. The mean of the difference scores is –12.05. That is, on the average, these husbands' communication quality decreased by about 12 points.

Is this decrease significant? In other words, how unlikely is it that this sample of change scores is a random sample from a population of change scores whose mean is 0?

Let's carry out the hypothesis-testing procedure.

1. Restate the question as a research hypothesis and a null hypothesis about the populations. The two populations in this case are these:

Population 1: Husbands who receive ordinary premarital counseling
Population 2: Husbands whose communication quality does not change from before to after marriage

The research hypothesis is that Population 1 is different from Population 2. That is, the research hypothesis is that husbands who receive ordinary premarital counseling (such as the husbands Olthoff studied) *do* change in communication quality from before to after marriage. The null hypothesis is that the populations are the same. That is, the null hypothesis is that the husbands who receive ordinary premarital counseling do *not* change in their communication quality from before to after marriage.

Notice that we have no actual information about Population 2 husbands. The husbands in the study are a sample of Population 1 husbands. In fact, if the research hypothesis is correct, Population 2 husbands may not even really exist. For the purposes of hypothesis testing, we simply set up Population 2 as a kind of straw man comparison group. That is, we set up a comparison group for purposes of the analysis of husbands who, if measured before and after marriage, would show no change.

2. Determine the characteristics of the comparison distribution. If the null hypothesis is true, the mean of the population of difference scores is 0. The variance of the population of difference scores can be estimated from the sample of difference scores. As shown in Table 8–4, the sum of squared deviations of the difference scores from the mean of the difference scores is 2,772.9. With 19 husbands in the study, there are 18 degrees of freedom. Dividing the sum of squared deviation scores by the degrees of freedom gives an estimated population variance of 154.05.

The distribution of means (from this population of difference scores) will have a mean of 0, the same as the population mean. Its variance will be the estimated population variance (154.05) divided by the sample size (19), which gives 8.11. The standard deviation is the square root of 8.11, which is 2.85. Finally, because Olthoff was using an estimated population variance, the comparison distribution is a t distribution. Because the estimate of the population variance was based on 18 degrees of freedom, this comparison distribution is a t distribution for 18 degrees of freedom.

3. Determine the cutoff sample score on the comparison distribution at which the null hypothesis should be rejected. We use a two-tailed test because there was no clear reason for predicting either an increase or a decrease in communication quality. Using the .05 significance level and 18 degrees of freedom, Table A–2 shows that to reject the null hypothesis you need a t score at or above $+2.101$ or at or below -2.101.

4. Determine the score of your sample on the comparison distribution. Olthoff's sample had a mean difference score of -12.05. That is, the mean was 12.05 points below the mean of 0 on the distribution of means. The standard deviation of the distribution of means that we computed was 2.85. The mean of the difference scores of -12.05 is 4.23 standard deviations below the mean of the distribution of means. So Olthoff's sample of difference scores has a t score of -4.23.

5. Compare the scores from Steps 3 and 4 to decide whether to reject the null hypothesis. The t of -4.23 for the sample of difference scores is more extreme than the needed t of ±2.101. Thus we can reject the null hypothesis. This suggests that Olthoff's husbands are from a population in which

husbands' communication quality is different after marriage from what it was before.

Olthoff's actual study was more complex. You may be interested to know that they found that the wives also showed this decrease in communication quality after marriage. A group of similar engaged couples who were given special communication-skills training had no significant decline in marital communication quality after marriage (see Figure 8–4).

Second Example of a *t* Test for Dependent Means

Suppose a researcher was interested in the theory that people feel more positively toward their government during a war. To test this idea, the researcher surveys a randomly selected group of nine people about their attitudes toward their government while their country is at war and then surveys them again a year after the war is over. (In a real study, the researcher would use a much larger sample. We have made the sample size small to keep the example simple.) The prediction would be that people are more pro-government during the war.

The fictional results, along with all the calculations are shown in Table 8–5. The *t* test is conducted as follows:

1. Restate the question as a research hypothesis and a null hypothesis about the populations. The populations involved are these:

> **Population 1:** People in the country studied
> **Population 2:** People who are not more pro-government during a war than they are one year after a war

The research hypothesis is that Population 1 is different from Population 2. That is, the research hypothesis is that people in the country studied *are* more pro-government during a war than one year after. The null hypothesis is that Population 1 is the same as Population 2. That is, the null hypothesis is that people in the country studied are not more pro-government during a war than they are one year after a war.

2. Determine the characteristics of the comparison distribution. If the null hypothesis is true, the mean of the population of difference scores is 0. What is the variance of this population of difference scores? Estimating from the sample of difference scores, it is the sum of the squared deviations of the

FIGURE 8–4
Communication skills of wives given premarital communications training and wives not given such training. (Based on Olthoff, 1989.)

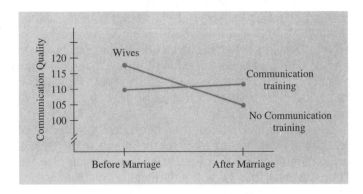

TABLE 8–5
t **Test for a Study of Pro-Government Attitudes During versus One Year After a War. (Fictional Data)**

Survey Respondent	Conditions		Difference	Deviations	Squared Deviations
	During War	*1 Year After*			
1	18	12	6	$6 - 2 = 4$	16
2	21	21	0	-2	4
3	19	16	3	1	1
4	21	16	5	3	9
5	17	19	-2	-4	16
6	20	19	1	-1	1
7	18	16	2	0	0
8	16	17	-1	-3	9
9	20	16	4	2	4
Σ:	170	152	18	0	60

For difference scores:

$M = 18/9 = 2.0$.

Population $M = 0$ (assumed as a no-change baseline of comparison).

$S^2 = SS/df = 60/(9 - 1) = 60/8 = 7.5$.

$S_M^2 = S^2/N = 7.50/9 = .83$.

$S_M = \sqrt{S_M^2} = \sqrt{.83} = .91$.

t for $df = 8$ needed for 5% significance level, one-tailed = 1.860.

$t = (M - \text{Pop. } M)/S_M = (2.00 - 0)/.91 = 2.20$.

Decision: Reject the null hypothesis.

---

difference scores, divided by the degrees of freedom. This is shown in Table 8–5 to be 7.5.

The mean of the comparison distribution will be 0, the same as the null hypothesis population. The standard deviation of the comparison distribution is .91. This is the square root of the estimated population variance divided by the sample size. The comparison distribution will be a *t* distribution for 8 degrees of freedom. It will be a *t* distribution because the variance is known and not estimated. It has 8 degrees of freedom because there were 8 degrees of freedom in the estimate of the population variance.

3. Determine the cutoff sample score on the comparison distribution at which the null hypothesis should be rejected. This is a one-tailed test because there was a reasonable basis for predicting the direction of the difference. Using the .05 significance level with 8 degrees of freedom, Table A–2 shows a cutoff *t* of 1.860.

4. Determine the location of your sample on the comparison distribution. The sample's mean difference of 2 is 2.20 standard deviations (of .91 each) above the mean of 0 on the distribution of means.

5. Compare the scores from Steps 3 and 4 to decide whether to reject the null hypothesis. The sample's *t* score of 2.20 is more extreme than the cutoff *t* of 1.860. Thus we can reject the null hypothesis. People have a more positive attitude toward their government during war time.

You may be interested to know that McLeod, Everland, and Signorielli (1994) conducted an actual study of this kind. They surveyed 167 people in the U.S. by telephone during the Persian Gulf War and then surveyed these same people again one year after the war. Their results, like the fictional example here, showed significantly greater pro-government attitudes during the war than after.

Summary of Steps for Conducting a t Test for Dependent Means

Table 8–6 summarizes the steps in conducting a t test for dependent means.[4]

Assumptions of the t Test

We noted earlier that when using an estimated population variance, the comparison distribution is a t distribution. However, this can be assumed only if

---

TABLE 8–6
Steps for Conducting a t Test for Dependent Means

1. Restate the question as a research hypothesis and a null hypothesis about the populations.

2. Determine the characteristics of the comparison distribution.

(a) Make each person's two scores into a difference score. Do all the rest of the steps using these difference scores.

(b) Figure the mean of the difference scores.

(c) Assume a population mean of 0.

(d) Figure the estimated population variance of difference scores:
$S^2 = [\Sigma(X - M)^2 / (N - 1)]$.

(e) Figure the variance of the distribution of means of difference scores:
$S_M{}^2 = S^2 / N$.

(f) Figure the standard deviation of the distribution of means of difference scores:
$S_M = \sqrt{S_M{}^2}$.

(g) The shape is a t distribution with $df = N - 1$.

3. Determine the cutoff sample score on the comparison distribution at which the null hypothesis should be rejected.

(a) Decide the significance level and whether to use a one-tailed or a two-tailed test.

(b) Look up the appropriate cutoff in a t table.

4. Determine the score of your sample on the comparison distribution:
$t = (\text{Sample } M - \text{Population } M)/S_M$.

5. Compare the scores from Steps 3 and 4 to decide whether to reject the null hypothesis.

---

[4]The usual steps of carrying out a t test for dependent means can be somewhat combined into computational formulas for S and t based on difference scores. For purposes of learning the ideas, we strongly recommend that in doing the practice problems you use the regular procedures as we have discussed them in this chapter. In a real research situation, the computations are usually done by computer. However, if you ever have to do a t test for dependent means for an actual research study by hand (without a computer), you may find these formulas useful. The formulas are as follows (note that D is for difference score):

$$S = \sqrt{\frac{\Sigma D^2 - (\Sigma D)^2 / N}{N - 1}}$$

$$(8\text{–}7)$$

$$t = \frac{\Sigma D / N}{S / \sqrt{N}}$$

$$(8\text{–}8)$$

we think that the distribution of the population of individuals follows a normal curve. Otherwise, the comparison distribution will follow some other shape, which usually cannot be determined.

So strictly speaking, a normal population distribution is a requirement within the logic and mathematics of the *t* test. Such a requirement for a hypothesis-testing procedure is called an **assumption:** A normal population distribution is said to be an assumption of the *t* test. The effect of this assumption is that, technically, if the population distribution is not normal, it is wrong to use the *t* test.

assumption

Unfortunately, you usually cannot tell whether the population is normal because when doing a *t* test usually all you have are the scores in the sample. Fortunately, as we saw in Chapter 4, distributions in the social and behavioral sciences (and in nature generally) quite often do approximate a normal curve. (This also applies to distributions of difference scores.) Also, statisticians have found that in practice, applying the *t* test gives reasonably accurate results even when the population is rather far from normal. The only very common situation in which using a *t* test for dependent means is likely to give a seriously distorted result is when you are using a one-tailed test and the population is highly skewed (is very asymmetrical, with a much longer tail on one side than the other). If the sample of difference scores is highly skewed, this suggests that the population the sample comes from is also highly skewed.

Effect Size and Power for the *t* Test for Dependent Means

In this section we consider effect size, power, and planning sample size.

Effect Size

Effect size for a repeated measures study is figured in the same way as we did in Chapter 7. It is the difference between the population means divided by the population standard deviation. However, when we have a repeated measures study you use the standard deviation of the population of difference scores. If you are computing the effect size after you have conducted a study, you would divide the actual mean of the difference scores in your sample by the estimated variance of the population of difference scores.

The conventions for effect sizes are the same as you learned for the situation we considered in Chapter 7: A small effect size is .20, a medium effect size is .50, and a large effect size is .80.

As an example of computing this kind of effect size, suppose a researcher studying sports competitions plans a study in which she will administer a questionnaire about attitudes toward teammates both before and after winning a championship. She is interested in a minimum meaningful difference from before to after of 4 points on the questionnaire and has reason to think that the standard deviation of difference scores on this attitude questionnaire is 8 points. The effect size is 4 divided by 8, which is .5. In terms of the conventions, her planned study has a predicted medium effect size.

For our first example of a *t* test for dependent means (the Olthoff study of husbands' change in communication quality), the mean of the difference scores was −12.05, and the estimated population standard deviation of the difference scores was 12.41 (that is, since S^2 was 154.05, $\sqrt{S^2} = 12.41$). The effect size is −12.05 divided by 12.41, which is −.97. This is clearly a large effect. (The sign of the effect, in this case negative, only means that the large effect was a decrease.)

Power

Table 8–7 gives the approximate power at the .05 significance level for small, medium, and large effect sizes and one- or two-tailed t tests for dependent means.[5] For example, consider the attitudes-towards-teammates example, where the researcher expected a medium effect size (.50). If she planned to conduct the study using the .05 level, two-tailed, with 20 research participants, the table shows the study would have a power of .59. This means that, if the research hypothesis is in fact true, and has a medium effect size, there is a 59% chance that this study will come out significant.

The power table (Table 8–7) is especially useful when you are reading about a nonsignificant result in a published study. For example, suppose that a study using a t test for dependent means has a nonsignificant result. The study tested significance at the .05 level, two-tailed, and had 10 participants. Should you conclude that there is in fact no difference at all in the populations? Probably not. Even assuming a medium effect size, Table 8–7 shows that there is only a 32% chance of getting a significant result in this study. Consider another study that was not significant. This study also used the .05 significance level, two-tailed. This study had 100 research participants. Table 8–7 tells you that there would be a 63% chance of the study's coming out significant if there were even a true small effect size in the population. If there were a medium effect size in the population, the table indicates that there is almost a 100% chance that this study would have come out significant. In this study with 100 participants, we could conclude from the results of this study that in the population there is probably at most a very small difference.

Planning Sample Size

Table 8–8 gives the approximate number of participants needed to have 80% power for a planned study. (Eighty percent is a common figure used by researchers for the minimum power to make a study worth doing.) The table gives the number of participants needed based on predicted small, medium, and large effect sizes, using one- and two-tailed tests, and for the .05 significance levels.[6] Suppose you plan a study in which you expect a large effect

---

[5]More detailed tables, in terms of numbers of participants, levels of effect size, and significance levels, are provided by Cohen (1988, pp. 28–39). In these tables, effect size, which they label as d, is actually based on a t test for independent means (the situation we consider in Chapter 9). For a t test for dependent means, as you have learned to do in this chapter, first multiply your effect size by 1.4. For example, if your effect size is .30, for purposes of this table, you would consider it to be .42 (that is, $.30 \times 1.4 = .42$). The only other difference from our table is that Cohen uses the letter a (for "alpha level") to indicate significance level, along with a subscript of either 1 or 2, to indicate a one- or two-tailed test.

[6]More detailed tables, giving needed numbers of participants for levels of power other than 80% (and also for effect sizes other than .20, .50, and .80 and for other significance levels) are provided in Cohen (1988, pp. 54–55). However, see footnote 5 in this chapter about using these tables.

TABLE 8–7
Approximate Power for Studies Using the *t* Test for Dependent Means in Testing Hypotheses at the .05 Significance Level

Sample Size (N)	Effect Size		
	Small (.20)	*Medium (.50)*	*Large (.80)*
Two-tailed test			
10	.09	.32	.66
20	.14	.59	.93
30	.19	.77	.99
40	.24	.88	*
50	.29	.94	*
100	.55	*	*
One-tailed test			
10	.15	.46	.78
20	.22	.71	.96
30	.29	.86	*
40	.35	.93	*
50	.40	.97	*
100	.63	*	*

*Nearly 1.

size and will use the .05 significance level, two-tailed. The table shows that for 80% power you would only need 14 participants. On the other hand, for 80% power in a study using the same significance level, also two-tailed, but in which you expect only a small effect size, you would need 196 participants.

The Power of Studies Using *t* Test for Dependent Means

Studies using difference scores (that is, studies using a repeated-measures design) often have much larger effect sizes for the same amount of expected difference between means than other kinds of research designs. That is, testing each of a group of participants twice (once under one condition and once under a different condition) usually gives more power than dividing the participants up into two groups and testing each once (one group tested under one condition and the other tested under the other condition).

The reason repeated-measures designs have so much power is because the standard deviation of difference scores is quite low. (The standard deviation of difference scores is what you divide by to get the effect size when using difference scores.) In a repeated measures design, the only variation is

TABLE 8–8
Approximate Number of Participants Needed for 80% Power for the *t* Test for Dependent Means in Testing Hypotheses at the .05 Significance Level

	Effect Size		
	Small (d = .20)	*Medium (d = .50)*	*Large (d = .80)*
Two-tailed	196	33	14
One-tailed	156	26	12

in the difference scores. Variation among participants on each testing's scores are not part of the variation involved in the analysis because difference scores are all comparing participants to themselves. The effect of all this is that studies using difference scores often have quite large effect sizes (and thus high power) even with a small number of people in the study.

However, although it has advantages from the point of view of power, the kind of repeated-measures study discussed in this chapter often has disadvantages from the point of view of the meaning of the results. The main problem is that when you test a group of people twice, one testing often affects the other testing. For example, consider a study where people are tested before and after some experimental procedure. If you get a significant difference it could be due to the experimental procedure; however, it also could be due to the effect of having been tested before (or even just to time passing). The limitations of this kind of research are discussed in detail in research methods textbooks.

t Tests for Dependent Means as Described in Research Articles

Research articles usually describe *t* tests in a fairly standard format that includes the degrees of freedom, the *t* score, and the significance level. For example, "$t(24) = 2.80, p < .05$" tells you that the researcher used a *t* test with 24 degrees of freedom, obtained a *t* score of 2.80, and the result was significant at the .05 level. Whether a one- or two-tailed test was used may also be noted. (If not, assume that it was two-tailed.) Usually the means, and sometimes the standard deviations, are given for each testing. Rarely is the standard deviation of the difference scores reported.

Olthoff (1989) might have reported his result in the example we used in this way: "There was a significant decline in communication quality, dropping from 116.32 before marriage to 104.26 after marriage, $t(18) = 2.76$, $p < .05$, two-tailed." Here is how McLeod et al. (1994) reported some of their results:

> Confidence in the president declined from 2.57 (out of a possible 3) to 2.17 ($t[165] = 4.32, p < .001$). The decline in confidence in people running Congress was even steeper, falling from 2.23 during the war to 1.74 one year later ($t[165] = 5.26, p < .001$).

Results of *t* tests are sometimes given in tables. For example, Table 8–9 reproduces the table from the McLeod et al. (1994) article. As you can see, the same pattern of pro-government (and also pro-war) attitudes was consistent over almost all the questions asked. Notice, incidentally, the method of using stars to indicate the level of significance. This is a common procedure; in fact, sometimes the *t* value itself is not given, just the stars (with the note at the bottom as to the exact *p* levels to which they refer).

TABLE 8–9
t-Tests for Differences between Time 1 and 2 Responses

	During War Mean	1-Year Later Mean	T-Value
War-related attitude scales (Maximum = 5.0)			
War is justified	3.41	3.11	2.11*
War is correct option	3.61	3.44	2.47**
Institutional confidence variables (Maximum = 3.0)			
Confidence in president	2.57	2.17	4.32***
Confidence in Congress	2.23	1.74	5.26***
Confidence in military	2.83	2.69	1.64*
Confidence in TV	2.16	2.18	–0.24
Confidence in newspapers	2.39	2.34	0.36
Media roles variables (Maximum = 7.0)			
Providing information	6.10	6.42	–2.38**
Explaining significance	5.60	5.71	–0.83
Building solidarity	5.58	5.01	3.26***
Reducing tension	5.07	4.47	3.18***
Restrictive attitude scales (Maximum = 3.0)			
Anti-war gore	2.39	2.12	3.59***
Anti-protest	2.95	2.77	3.38***

$N = 167$
*$p < .05$ **$p < .01$ ***$p < .001$
Note: Data from McLeod, Eveland, & Signorelli (1994).

Summary

The standard five steps of hypothesis testing are used when the variance of the population is not known. However, in this situation you must estimate the population variance from the scores in the sample, using a formula that divides the sum of squared deviation scores by the degrees of freedom ($df = N - 1$). Also, when the variance is not known, the comparison distribution of means is a t distribution (with cutoffs given in a t table). A t distribution has slightly heavier tails than a normal curve (just how much heavier depends on how few degrees of freedom). Finally, in this situation the number of standard deviations from the mean that a sample's mean is on the t distribution is called a t score.

A t test for dependent means is used in studies where each participant has two scores, such as a before score and an after score. In this t test, you first figure a difference score for each participant, then carry out the usual 5 steps of hypothesis testing with the modifications described in the paragraph above and making Population 2 a population of difference scores with a mean of 0 (no difference).

An assumption of the t test is that the population distribution is a normal curve. However, even when it is not, the t test is usually fairly accurate. The main exception involving the t test for dependent means is when the population of difference scores is highly skewed and you are using a one-tailed test.

The effect size of a study using a t test for dependent means is the mean of the difference scores divided by the standard deviation of the difference scores. Power and needed sample size for 80% power can be looked up in special tables. The power of studies using difference scores is usually much higher than that of studies using other designs with the same number of participants, although research of this kind may lead to uncertainty about what the results mean.

t tests are reported in research articles using a standard format. For example, "$t(24) = 2.80$, $p < .05$." They are also reported in tables with the significance level indicated by stars.

Key Terms

assumption
biased estimate
degrees of freedom (df)
difference scores
repeated-measures design

t distribution
t score
t table
t test

t test for a single sample
t test for dependent means
unbiased estimate of the
   population variance (S^2)

Practice Problems

These problems involve computation (with the assistance of a calculator). Most real-life statistics problems are done on a computer. Even if you have a computer, do this by hand to ingrain the method in your mind.

For practice in using a computer to solve statistics problems, refer to the computer section of each chapter of the Student's Study Guide and Computer Workbook *that accompanies this text.*

All data are fictional (unless an actual citation is given).

Answers to selected problems are given at the back of the book.

1. In each of the following studies, a single sample's mean is being compared to a population with a known mean but an unknown variance. For each study, decide whether the result is significant.

	Sample Size (N)	Population Mean	Estimated Population Variance (S^2)	Sample Mean (M)	Tails	Significance Level (α)
(a)	64	12.40	9.00	11.00	1 (low predicted)	.05
(b)	49	1,006.35	317.91	1,009.72	2	.01
(c)	400	52.00	7.02	52.41	1 (high predicted)	.01

2. Suppose a candidate running for sheriff claims that she will reduce the average speed of emergency response to less than 30 minutes, which is thought to be the average response time with the current sheriff. There are no past records, so the actual standard deviation of such response times cannot be determined. Thanks to this campaign, she is elected sheriff, and careful records are now kept. The response times for the first month are 26, 30, 28, 29, 25, 28, 32, 35, 24, and 23 min.

Using the .05 significance level, did she keep her promise? Illustrate your answer with a histogram of the sample's scores and sketches of the population distribution and the distribution of means, showing the t score and cutoff points for significance. Explain your answer to someone who has never taken a course in statistics.

3. For each of the following studies using difference scores, determine if the mean difference is significantly greater than 0. Also compute the effect size.

	Number of Difference Scores in Sample	Mean of Difference Scores in Sample	Estimated Population Variance of Difference Scores	Tails	Significance Level
(a)	20	1.7	8.29	1 (high predicted)	.05
(b)	164	2.3	414.53	2	.05
(c)	15	–2.2	4.00	1 (low predicted)	.01

4. A program to decrease littering was carried out in four cities in California's Central Valley starting in August 1995. The amount of litter in the streets (average pounds of litter collected per block per day) was measured during the July before the program was started and then the next July, after the program had been in effect for a year. The results were as follows:

City	July 1995	July 1996
Fresno	9	2
Merced	10	4
Bakersfield	8	9
Stockton	9	1

Using the 1% level of significance, was there a significant decrease in the amount of litter? Illustrate your answer with a histogram of the sample's difference scores and sketches of the population distribution and distribution of means (both for difference scores), showing the t score and cutoff points for significance. Explain your answer to someone who understands mean, standard deviation, and variance but knows nothing else about statistics.

5. Five people who were convicted of speeding were ordered by the court to attend a workshop. A special device put into their cars kept records of their speeds for 2 weeks before and after the workshop. The maximum speeds for each person during the two weeks before and the two weeks after the workshop follow:

Person	Before	After
L. B.	65	58
J. K.	62	65
R. C.	60	56
R. T.	70	66
J. M.	68	60

Using the .05 significance level, should we conclude that people are likely to drive more slowly after such a workshop? Give the effect size of your result.

6. What is the power of each of the following studies (based on the .05 significance level)?

	Effect Size	N	Tails
(a)	Small	20	1
(b)	Medium	20	1
(c)	Medium	30	1
(d)	Medium	30	2
(e)	Large	30	2

7. For each of the following planned studies, how many participants would you need to have 80% power (based on the .05 significance level)?

	Expected Effect Size	Tails
(a)	Small	1
(b)	Small	2
(c)	Medium	1
(d)	Medium	2
(e)	Large	1
(f)	Large	2

8. A study was done comparing union activity of employees in 10 plants during two different decades. The researchers reported "a significant increase in union activity, $t(9) = 3.28$, $p < .01$." Explain this result to a person who has never had a course in statistics. Be sure to use sketches of the distributions in your answer.

9

The *t* Test
for Independent Means

T HIS chapter examines hypothesis testing in the very common situation of comparing two samples, such as an experimental group and a control group. This is a *t* test situation because the population variances are not known and must be estimated. This time it is called a ***t* test for independent means** because we are comparing the means of two entirely separate groups of people whose scores are independent of each other. This is in contrast to the *t* test for dependent means, considered in the last chapter, in which there were two groups of scores, but both were for the same people (such as the same people measured before and after a health promotion educational program).

t test for independent means

Basic Strategy of the *t* Test for Independent Means: The Distribution of Differences Between Means

The *t* test for independent means works in the same way as the hypothesis testing you have already learned, with one main exception: The key result of the study is a difference between the means of the two samples. Thus the comparison distribution must be a **distribution of differences between means.**

distribution of differences between means

Content of a Distribution of Differences Between Means

This special distribution is, in a sense, two steps removed from the populations of individuals: First there is a distribution of means from each population of individuals; second, a distribution of differences between pairs of means (one of each pair from each of these distributions of means). Think of this distribution of differences between means as being built up as follows: (a) Randomly select one mean from the distribution of means for Population 1, (b) randomly select one mean from the distribution of means for Population 2, and (c) subtract. (That is, take the mean from the first distribution of means minus the mean from the second distribution of means.) This gives a difference score between the two selected means. Then repeat the process. This creates a second difference, a difference between the two newly selected means. Repeating this process a large number of times creates a distribution of differences between means.

Illustration of the Overall Logic of the *t* Test for Independent Means

Figure 9–1 diagrams the entire logical construction involved in a distribution of differences between means. At the top are the two population distributions. We do not know the characteristics of these population distributions, but we do know that if the null hypothesis is true, the two population means are the same. That is, the null hypothesis is that $M_1 = M_2$. We also can estimate the variance of these populations, based on the sample information (these estimated variances will be S^2_1 and S^2_2).

Figure 9–1 shows the two population distributions and, below each, the distribution of means for that population. Using the estimated population variance and knowing the size of each sample, we can figure the variance of each distribution of means in the usual way. (It is the variance of its parent population divided by the size of the samples.)

Below these two distributions of means, and constructed from them, is the crucial distribution of differences between means. Because this distribution's variance is ultimately based on estimated population variances, we can think of it as a *t* distribution. The goal of a *t* test for independent means is to decide whether the difference between the means of our two actual samples is a more extreme difference than the cutoff difference on this distribution of differences. The two actual samples are shown (as histograms) at the bottom. Remember, this whole procedure is really a kind of complicated castle in the

FIGURE 9–1

The steps in creating a distribution of differences between means.

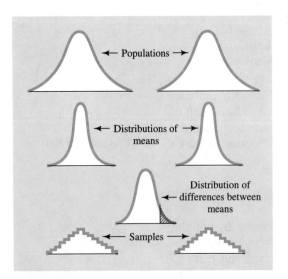

air. It exists only in our minds to help us make decisions based on the results of an actual experiment. The only concrete reality in all of this is the actual scores in the two samples. The population variances are estimated on the basis of these sample scores. The variances of the two distributions of means are based entirely on these estimated population variances (and the sample sizes). As you will see shortly, the characteristics of the distribution of differences between means is based on these two distributions of means.

Still, the procedure is a powerful one. It has the power of mathematics and logic behind it. It helps you develop general knowledge based on the specifics of a particular study.

With this overview of the basic logic, we now turn to five key details: (a) the mean of the distribution of differences between means, (b) the estimated population variance, (c) the variance and standard deviation of the distribution of differences between means, (d) the shape of the distribution of differences between means, and (e) the t score for the difference between the particular two means being compared.

Mean of the Distribution of Differences Between Means

In a t test for independent means, two populations are being considered—one population from which an experimental group is taken and one population from which a control group is taken. In practice, a researcher does not know the mean of either population; but the researcher does know that if the null hypothesis is true, these two populations have the same mean. Also, if these two populations have the same mean, the distribution of means for each of them will have the same mean. Finally, if random samples are taken from two distributions with the same mean, the differences between the means of these random samples, in the long run, should balance out to 0. The result of this logic is that whatever the specifics of the study, the researcher knows that if the null hypothesis is true, the distribution of differences between means has a mean of 0.

Estimating the Population Variance

In Chapter 8, you learned to estimate the population variance by using the scores in your sample. It is the sum of squared deviation scores divided by the degrees of freedom (the number in the sample minus 1).

To carry out a t test for independent means, it has to make sense to assume that the populations that the two samples come from have the same variance. (If the null hypothesis is true, they also have the same mean.) Therefore, when we estimate the variance from the scores in either sample, we are getting two separate estimates of what should be the same number (the variance of each population, which is supposed to be the same for both populations). In practice, the two estimates will almost never be exactly identical. Because they are both supposed to be estimating the same thing, the best solution is to average the two estimates to get the best, single, overall estimate. This is called the **pooled estimate of the population variance (S^2_{Pooled}).**

In making an average, we also have to take into account the fact that if one sample is larger than the other, the estimate it provides is likely to be more accurate (because it is based on more information). If both samples

pooled estimate of the population variance (S^2_{Pooled})

were exactly the same size, we could just take an ordinary average of our two estimates. When they are not the same size, we need to make some adjustment in our averaging to give more weight to the larger sample. We need a **weighted average,** an average weighted by the amount of information each sample provides. To be precise, what matters is not the number of scores in each sample but the number of degrees of freedom in each sample (the number of scores minus 1). When we create a weighted average, it has to be based on the degrees of freedom. The procedure is to figure out what proportion of the total degrees of freedom each sample contributes, and multiply that proportion times the estimate from that sample. Then you add up the two results and that is your weighted estimated. Here is this principle stated as a formula:

$$S^2{}_{\text{Pooled}} = \frac{df_1}{df_{\text{Total}}}(S^2{}_1) + \frac{df_2}{df_{\text{Total}}}(S^2{}_2)$$

(9–1)

In this formula, $S^2{}_{\text{Pooled}}$ is the pooled estimate of the population variance, df_1 is the degrees of freedom for Population 1, and df_2 is the degrees of freedom for Population 2. (Remember each df is the number of scores in its sample minus 1.) df_{Total} is the total degrees of freedom ($df_{\text{Total}} = df_1 + df_2$). $S^2{}_1$ is the estimate of the population variance based on the scores in the sample from Population 1; $S^2{}_2$ is the estimate based on the sample from Population 2.

Consider a study in which the population variance estimate based on an experimental group of 11 participants is 60 and the population variance estimate based on a control group of 31 participants is 80. The estimate from the experimental group is based on 10 degrees of freedom (that is, 11 participants minus 1), and the estimate from the control group is based on 30 degrees of freedom (that is, 31 minus 1). The total information on which the estimate is based is the total degrees of freedom (in this example, 40). The experimental group provides one quarter (10/40 = 1/4) of the information, and the control group provides three quarters (30/40 = 3/4) of the information. The estimate from the experimental group of 60 is then multiplied by 1/4, making 15. The estimate from the control group of 80 is multiplied by 3/4, making 60. Adding the two together gives an overall estimate of 15 plus 60, or 75. Using the formula,

$$S^2{}_{\text{Pooled}} = \frac{df_1}{df_{\text{Total}}}(S^2{}_1) + \frac{df_2}{df_{\text{Total}}}(S^2{}_2) = \frac{10}{40}(60) + \frac{30}{40}(80)$$

$$= \frac{1}{4}(60) + \frac{3}{4}(80) = 15 + 60 = 75$$

Notice this procedure does not give the same result as ordinary averaging (without weighting) of these two estimates would. Ordinary averaging (60 + 80 divided by 2) would give an estimate of 70. This weighted, pooled estimate of 75 is closer to the estimate based on the control group alone than to the estimate based on the experimental group alone. This is as it should be, because the control group estimate was based on more information.

Calculating the Variance of Each of the Two Distributions of Means

The pooled estimate of the population variance is the best estimate for both populations. (Remember, to do a t test for independent means, we have to be able to assume that the two populations have the same variance.) However, even though the two populations have the same variance, the distributions of means taken from them do not usually have the same variance. That is because the variance of a distribution of means is the population variance divided by the sample size. So even if the population variance is the same for two populations, if the sample sizes are different for the two samples, then the two distributions of means will have different variances.

Consider again the example of the study in which there were 11 in the experimental group and 31 in the control group. In that example, we found that the pooled estimate of the population variance is 75. So for the experimental group, the variance of the distribution of means would be 75/11, which is 6.82. For the control group, the variance would be 75/31, which is 2.42. (Remember that when figuring estimated variances, you divide by the degrees of freedom. However, when figuring the variance of a distribution of means, which does not involve any additional estimation, you divide by the actual number in the sample.) In terms of formulas,

$$S_{M1}^2 = \frac{S^2_{\text{Pooled}}}{N_1} = \frac{75}{11} = 6.82$$

$$S_{M2}^2 = \frac{S^2_{\text{Pooled}}}{N_2} = \frac{75}{31} = 2.42$$

Variance and Standard Deviation of the Distribution of Differences Between Means

The **variance of the distribution of differences between means ($S^2_{\text{Difference}}$)** is just the sum of the variance of the distribution of means from Population 1 plus the variance of the distribution of means from Population 2. (This is because when computing a difference between two numbers, the variation in each contributes to the overall variation in the difference. It is like subtracting a moving number from a moving target.) Stated as a formula,

variance of the distribution of differences between means ($S^2_{\text{Difference}}$)

$$S^2_{\text{Difference}} = S_{M1}^2 + S_{M2}^2 \qquad (9\text{--}2)$$

The **standard deviation of the distribution of differences between means ($S_{\text{Difference}}$)** is the square root of the variance:

standard deviation of the distribution of differences between means ($S_{\text{Difference}}$)

$$S_{\text{Difference}} = \sqrt{S^2_{\text{Difference}}} \qquad (9\text{--}3)$$

Consider again the example study with 11 in the experimental group and 31 in the control group. We found that the variance of the distribution of means for the experimental group was 6.82 and the variance of the distribution of means for the control group was 2.42. The variance of the distribution of the difference between means would thus be 6.82 plus 2.42, which is 9.24. This makes the standard deviation of this distribution the square root of 9.24, which is 3.04. In terms of the formulas,

$$S^2_{\text{Difference}} = S_{M1}^2 + S_{M2}^2 = 6.82 + 2.42 = 9.24$$

$$S_{\text{Difference}} = \sqrt{S^2_{\text{Difference}}} = \sqrt{9.24} = 3.04$$

Shape of the Distribution of Differences Between Means

Because our distribution of differences between means is based on using estimated population variances, our comparison distribution is a t distribution. Because it is based on estimates using two samples, the degrees of freedom for this t distribution are the sum of the degrees of freedom of the two samples ($df_{Total} = df_1 + df_2$). What is new in this is that df_{Total}, the total degrees of freedom for both samples taken together, is also the degrees of freedom for our t distribution.

In our example with an experimental group of 11 and a control group of 31, the total degrees of freedom would be 40 ($11 - 1 = 10$; $31 - 1 = 30$; $10 + 30 = 40$). To determine the t score needed for significance, you look up the cutoff point in the t table in the row with 40 degrees of freedom. If you were conducting a one-tailed test using the .05 significance level, the t table shows that with 40 degrees of freedom, the difference between your means must be at least 1.684 standard deviations above the mean difference of 0 on the distribution of differences between means.

The t Score for the Difference Between the Two Actual Means

The t score that you figure in Step 4 of hypothesis testing is found as follows: First, figure the difference between your two means. (That is, subtract one from the other.) Then, figure out where this difference is on the distribution of differences between means. You do this by dividing your difference by the standard deviation of this distribution. In terms of a formula,

$$t = \frac{M_1 - M_2}{S_{Difference}}$$

(9–4)

For example, suppose the mean of the first sample is 198 and the mean of the second sample is 184. The difference between these two means is 198 minus 184, which is 14. Also, suppose in this study the standard deviation of the distribution of differences between means is 7. That would make a t score of 14 divided by 7, which is 2. That is, in this example the difference between the two means is two standard deviations above the mean of the distribution of differences between means. In terms of the formula,

$$t = \frac{M_1 - M_2}{S_{Difference}} = \frac{198 - 184}{7} = \frac{14}{7} = 2$$

Steps of Hypothesis Testing With a t Test for Independent Means

Considering our five steps of hypothesis testing, there are three new wrinkles for a t test for independent means: (a) The comparison distribution is now a distribution of differences between means (which affects Step 2); (b) the degrees of freedom for finding the cutoff on the t table is based on two samples (which affects Step 3); and (c) the score of your sample is based on the difference between your two means (which affects Step 4).

Example of a t Test for Independent Means

Moorehouse and Sanders (1992) studied whether an adolescent boy's sense of how well he is doing in school is related to his mother's work situation. The boys were all in seventh to ninth grade and were all from families in which the mother worked full-time. For purposes of this analysis, the boys were divided into two groups, those in which the mother's work gave her opportunities to solve problems (26 boys) and those in which the mother's work did not give her opportunities to solve problems (17 boys). All 43 boys were given a standard test of perceived academic competence (how successful they see themselves as being at school).

The t-test is illustrated in Figure 9–2; the scores and computations are shown in Table 9–1. Let us go through the full five steps of hypothesis testing.

1. Restate the question as a research hypothesis and a null hypothesis about the populations. The populations are these:

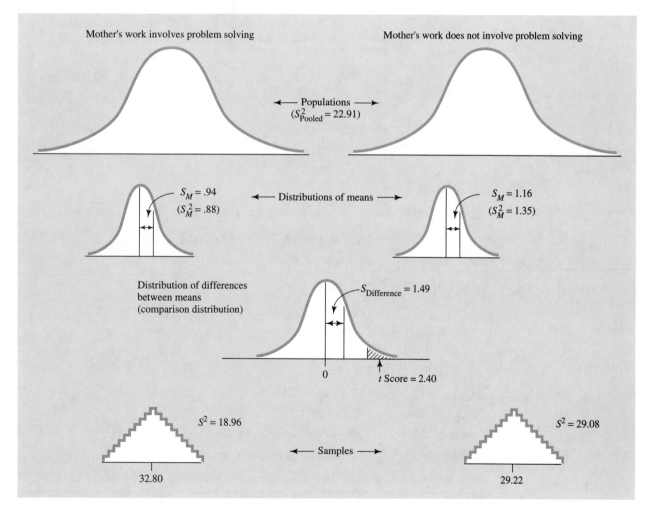

FIGURE 9–2
The distributions involved in the example of a t test for independent means.

TABLE 9–1
t Test for Independent Means for a Study of the Relation of the Work Situation of the Mothers of Adolescent Boys to the Boys' Perceived Academic Competence

Boys Whose Mothers' Work Involves Problem Solving			Boys Whose Mothers' Work Does Not Involve Problem Solving		
Score	Deviation from mean	Squared deviation from mean	Score	Deviation from mean	Squared deviation from mean
36.9	4.1	16.81	23.5	− 5.7	32.49
34.6	1.8	16.81	22.5	− 6.7	44.89
26.4	− 6.4	40.96	36.4	7.2	51.84
33.3	.5	.25	40.0	10.8	116.64
35.4	2.6	6.76	30.6	1.4	1.96
34.8	2.0	4.00	30.5	1.3	1.69
32.3	− .5	.25	34.5	5.3	28.09
34.5	1.7	2.89	31.3	2.1	4.41
36.0	3.2	10.24	19.4	− 9.8	96.04
24.5	− 8.3	68.89	29.6	.4	.16
31.6	− 1.2	1.44	24.8	− 4.4	19.36
36.1	3.3	10.89	25.0	− 4.2	17.64
36.8	4.0	16.00	28.8	− .4	.16
27.9	− 4.9	24.01	32.5	3.3	10.89
34.4	1.6	2.56	33.3	4.1	16.81
33.8	1.0	1.00	29.6	.4	.16
36.9	4.1	16.81	24.5	4.7	22.09
34.4	1.6	2.56			
31.7	− 1.1	1.21			
29.4	− 3.4	11.56			
34.1	1.3	1.69			
18.2	−14.6	213.16			
34.5	1.7	2.89			
35.3	2.5	6.25			
35.5	2.7	7.29			
33.4	.6	.36			
Σ: 852.7	0.0	473.97	496.8	0.0	465.32

$M_1 = 32.80$; $S_1^2 = 473.97/25 = 18.96$; $M_2 = 29.22$; $S_2^2 = 465.32/16 = 29.08$

$N_1 = 26$; $df_1 = N_1 - 1 = 25$; $N_2 = 17$; $df_2 = N_2 - 1 = 16$

$df_{Total} = df_1 + df_2 = 25 + 16 = 41$

$$S_{Pooled}^2 = \frac{df_1}{df_{Total}}(S_1^2) + \frac{df_2}{df_{Total}}(S_2^2) = \frac{25}{41}(18.96) + \frac{16}{41}(29.08) = .61(18.96) + .39(29.08) = 11.57 + 11.34 = 22.91$$

$S_{M1}^2 = S_P^2/N_1 = 22.91/26 = .88$

$S_{M2}^2 = S_P^2/N_2 = 22.91/17 = 1.35$

$S_{Difference}^2 = S_{M1}^2 + S_{M2}^2 = .88 + 1.35 = 2.23$

$S_{Difference} = \sqrt{S_{Difference}^2} = \sqrt{2.23} = 1.49$

Needed *t* with $df = 41$ (using $df = 40$ in table), 5% level, one-tailed = 1.684

$t = (M_1 - M_2)/S_{Difference} = (32.80 - 29.22)/1.49 = 3.58/1.49 = 2.40$

Conclusion: Reject the null hypothesis; the research hypothesis is supported.

Note: Data from Moorehouse & Sanders (1992).

Population 1: Boys whose mothers' work involves solving problems

Population 2: Boys whose mothers' work does not involve solving problems

Based on theory and previous research, Moorehouse and Sanders expected that boys whose mothers' work involved solving problems to have higher scores on the test of perceived academic competence. The research hypothesis was that Population 1 boys would score higher than Population 2 boys. (That is, this was a directional hypothesis.) The null hypothesis was that the Population 1 boys would not score higher than the Population 2 boys.

2. Determine the characteristics of the comparison distribution. The comparison distribution is a distribution of differences between means. Its mean is 0 (as it almost always is in a t test for independent means, because we are interested in whether there is more than 0 difference between the two populations). The population variance estimated from the two samples comes out to 18.96 and 29.08. The pooled estimate of the population variance is the weighted average of these two: 25/41 times 18.96 and 16/41 times 29.08. This comes out to 22.91. The variance for each distribution of means, this pooled estimate divided by its sample size (22.91/26 and 22.91/17), comes out to .88 and 1.35. Summing the variance of these two gives the variance of the distribution of differences between means, 2.23. The square root of this variance, the standard deviation of the distribution of differences between means, is 1.49. The shape of this comparison distribution will be a t distribution with a total of 41 degrees of freedom.

3. Determine the cutoff sample score on the comparison distribution at which the null hypothesis should be rejected. This requires a one-tailed test because a particular direction of difference between the two populations was predicted. Since the t table in Appendix A (Table A–2) does not have exactly 41 degrees of freedom, the next lowest (40) is used. At the .05 level, a t of at least 1.684 is needed.

4. Determine the score of the sample on the comparison distribution. The t score is the difference between the two sample means (32.80 – 29.22, which is 3.58) divided by the standard deviation of the distribution of differences between means (which is 1.49). This comes out to 2.40.

5. Compare the scores in Steps 3 and 4 to decide whether to reject the null hypothesis. Our t score of 2.40 for the difference between our two actual means is larger than the needed t score of 1.684. The null hypothesis should be rejected. The research hypothesis is supported: Boys whose mothers' work involves solving problems see themselves as better at schoolwork than boys whose mothers' work does not involve solving problems.

A Second Example of a t Test for Independent Means

Suppose a researcher wants to study the effectiveness of a new job skills training program for people who have not been able to hold a job. Fourteen people who have not been able to hold a job agree to be in the study. The researcher randomly picks seven of these volunteers to be an experimental group that will go through the special training program. The other seven volunteers are put in a control group that will go through an ordinary job skills training program. After finishing their training program (of whichever type), all 14 are placed in similar jobs.

A month later, each volunteer's employer is asked to rate how well the new employee is doing using a 9-point scale. The fictional results and the full *t* test analysis are shown in Table 9–2. The analysis is illustrated in Figure 9–3. Let us also conduct the analysis, following the hypothesis-testing procedure step by step.

1. Restate the question as a research hypothesis and a null hypothesis about the populations. The populations are these:

Population 1: Individuals who could not hold a job who then participate in the special job skills program

Population 2: Individuals who could not hold a job who then participate in an ordinary job skills program

It is possible for the special program to have either a positive or a negative effect compared to the ordinary program, and either result would be of interest. The research hypothesis is that the means of the two populations are different. This is a nondirectional hypothesis. The null hypothesis is that the means of the two populations are the same.

TABLE 9–2
Computations for a *t* Test for Independent Means for an Experiment Examining the Effectiveness (Using Employers' Ratings) of a New Job Skills Program for People Who Have Previously Not Been Able to Hold Jobs

	Experimental Group (Receiving Special Program)			Control Group (Receiving Standard Program)		
	Score	*Deviation from mean*	*Squared deviation from mean*	*Score*	*Deviation from mean*	*Squared deviation from mean*
	6	0	0	6	3	9
	4	−2	4	1	−2	4
	9	3	9	5	2	4
	7	1	1	3	0	0
	7	1	1	1	−2	4
	3	−3	9	1	−2	4
	6	0	0	4	1	1
Σ:	42	0	24	21	0	26

$M_1 = 6; S_1^2 = 24/6 = 4; M_2 = 3; S_2^2 = 26/6 = 4.33$

$N_1 = 7; df_1 = N_1 - 1 = 6; N_2 = 7; df_2 = N_2 - 1 = 6$

$df_T = df_1 + df_2 = 6 + 6 = 12$

$S_{Pooled}^2 = \dfrac{df_1}{df_{Total}}(S_1^2) + \dfrac{df_2}{df_{Total}}(S_2^2) = \dfrac{6}{12}(4) + \dfrac{6}{12}(4.33) = .5(4) + .5(4.33) = 2.00 + 2.17 = 4.17$

$S_{M1}^2 = S_P^2/N_1 = 4.17/7 = .60$

$S_{M2}^2 = S_P^2/N_2 = 4.17/7 = .60$

$S_{Difference}^2 = S_{M1}^2 + S_{M2}^2 = .60 + .60 = 1.20$

$S_{Difference} = \sqrt{S_{Difference}^2} = \sqrt{1.20} = 1.10$

Needed *t* with *df* = 12, 5% level, two-tailed = ±2.179

$t = (M_1 - M_2)/S_{Difference} = (6.00 - 3.00)/1.10 = 3.00/1.10 = 2.73$

Conclusion: Reject the null hypothesis; the research hypothesis is supported.

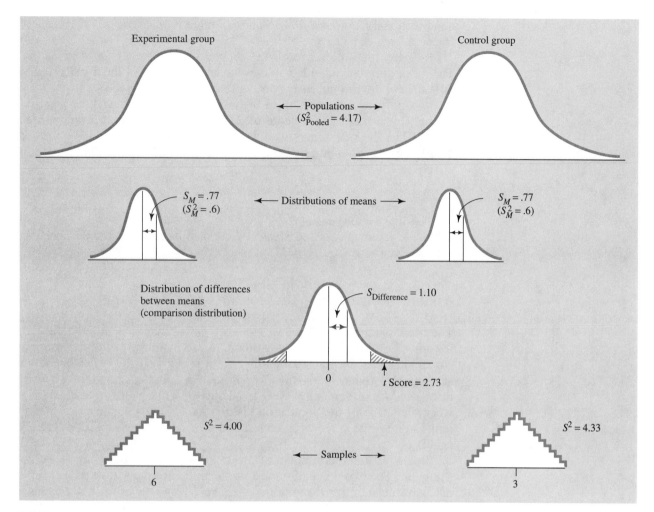

FIGURE 9–3
The distributions involved in the second example of a *t* test for independent means.

2. Determine the characteristics of the comparison distribution. The distribution of differences between means will have a mean of 0, as usual. We compute its standard deviation by (a) finding the estimated population variance based on each sample; (b) finding the pooled estimate by taking a weighted average of these two estimates (because we have equal numbers in the two samples a weighted average comes out the same as an ordinary average); (c) for each population, dividing the pooled estimate by the sample size to get the variance of each distribution of means; (d) adding together the variances of the two distributions of means to get the variance of the distribution of differences between means; and (e) taking the square root of this variance. As shown in Table 9–2, this standard deviation is 1.10. The shape of the comparison distribution is a *t* distribution with a total of 12 degrees of freedom.

3. Determine the cutoff sample score on the comparison distribution at which the null hypothesis should be rejected. The researchers use the ordinary .05 significance level and a two-tailed test (because the hypothesis is

nondirectional). Looking this up on the t table in the row for 12 degrees of freedom, we need a t score of at least ± 2.179.

4. Determine the score of the sample on the comparison distribution. The mean difference divided by the standard deviation of the distribution of differences between means comes out to a t score of 2.73.

5. Compare the scores from Steps 3 and 4 to decide whether to reject the null hypothesis. Our t score of 2.73 is more extreme than the needed 2.179. Thus the researchers would reject the null hypothesis and conclude that the research hypothesis is supported, that the new job skills program is effective.

Summary of Steps for Conducting a t Test for Independent Means

Table 9–3 summarizes the steps for conducting a t test for independent means.[1]

Assumptions of the t Test for Independent Means

The first assumption for a t test for independent means is the same as that for any t test: The population distributions are assumed to follow a normal curve. However, in practice, this is only a problem if the two populations are thought to have dramatically skewed distributions, and in opposite directions. More generally, the t test holds up quite well in practice even when the shape of the population distributions is fairly far from normal so long as one is using a two-tailed test and the sample sizes are not extremely small.

In a t test for independent means, there is also a second important assumption: The two populations are assumed to have the same variance. (We take advantage of this assumption when we average the estimates from each of our two samples.) Once again, however, it turns out that in practice the t test gives pretty accurate results even when there are fairly large differences in the population variances, particularly when there are equal numbers of scores in the two samples.

However, the t test can give quite misleading results if (a) the scores in the sample suggest that the populations are very far from normal, (b) the variances are very different, or (c) both problems are there. In these situations, there are alternatives to the ordinary t test procedure, some of which we will consider in Chapter 11.

---

[1]The steps of figuring the standard deviation of the distribution of differences between means can be combined into a single overall computational formula:

$$S_{\text{Difference}} = \sqrt{\frac{(N_1 - 1)(S_1^2) + (N_2 - 1)(S_2^2)}{N_1 + N_2 - 2} \left(\frac{1}{N_1} + \frac{1}{N_2} \right)} \qquad (9\text{--}5)$$

As usual, we urge you to use the full set of steps in your computations when doing the exercises in this book because those steps help you learn the basic principles. However, this computational formula will be useful if a computer is not available and you have to compute by hand a t test for independent means on actual data from a study with many participants in each group.

TABLE 9–3
Steps for Conducting a *t* Test for Independent Means

1. Restate the question into a research hypothesis and a null hypothesis about the populations.
2. Determine the characteristics of the comparison distribution.
   a. Its mean will be 0.
   b. Compute its standard deviation.
      i. Compute estimated population variances based on each sample (that is, compute two estimates).
      ii. Compute a pooled estimate of population variance:

$$S^2_{Pooled} = \frac{df_1}{df_{Total}}(S^2_1) + \frac{df_2}{df_{Total}}(S^2_2)$$

$(df_1 = N_1 - 1 \text{ and } df_2 = N_2 - 1; df_{Total} = df_1 + df_2)$

   iii. Compute the variance of each distribution of means: $S^2_{M1} = S^2_{Pooled}/N_1$ and $S^2_{M2} = S^2_{Pooled}/N_2$
   iv. Compute the variance of the distribution of differences between means:
   $$S^2_{Difference} = S^2_{M1} + S^2_{M2}$$
   v. Compute the standard deviation of the distribution of differences between means:
   $$S_{Difference} = \sqrt{S^2_{Difference}}$$
   c. Determine its shape: It will be a *t* distribution with df_{Total} degrees of freedom.
3. Determine the cutoff sample score on the comparison distribution at which the null hypothesis should be rejected.
   a. Determine the degrees of freedom (df_{Total}), desired significance level, and tails in the test (one or two).
   b. Look up the appropriate cutoff in a *t* table. If the exact *df* is not given, use the *df* below.
4. Determine the score of the sample on the comparison distribution: $t = (M_1 - M_2)/S_{Difference}$
5. Compare the scores obtained in Steps 3 and 4 to decide whether to reject the null hypothesis.

Effect Size and Power for the *t* Test for Independent Means

Effect Size

Effect size for the *t* test for independent means is the difference between the population means divided by the standard deviation of the population of individuals. When using data from a completed study, the effect size is estimated as the difference between the sample means divided by the pooled estimate of the population standard deviation (the square root of the pooled estimate of the population variance). Stated as formulas:

$$\text{Effect Size} = \frac{\text{Population } 1\, M - \text{Population } 2\, M}{\text{Population } SD} \qquad (9\text{–}6)$$

$$\text{Estimated Effect Size} = \frac{M_1 - M_2}{S_{Pooled}} \qquad (9\text{–}7)$$

Cohen's (1988) conventions for the *t* test for independent means are the same as in all the situations we have considered so far: .20 for a small effect size, .50 for a medium effect size, and .80 for a large effect size.

BOX 9–1

Two Women Make a Point About Gender and Statistics

One of the most useful advanced statistics books written so far is *Using Multivariate Statistics* by Barbara Tabachnick and Linda Fidell (1996), two experimental psychologists at California State University at Northridge. These two met at a faculty luncheon soon after Tabachnick was hired. Fidell recalls that, "I had this enormous data set to analyze, and out came lots of pretty numbers in nice neat little columns, but I was not sure what all of it meant, or even whether my data had violated any critical assumptions. That was in 1975. I had been trained at the University of Michigan; I knew statistics up through the analysis of variance. But none of us were taught the multivariate analysis of variance at that time. Then along came these statistical packages to do it. But how to comprehend them?" (You will be introduced to the multivariate analysis of variance in Chapter 12.)

Both Fidell and Tabachnick had gone out and learned on their own, taking the necessary courses, reading, asking others who knew the programs better, trying out what would happen if they did this with the data, what would happen if they did that. Now the two women asked each other, why must this be so hard? Were others reinventing this same wheel at the very same time? They decided to put their wheel into a book.

"And so began fifteen years of conflict-free collaboration," reports Fidell. (That is something to compare to the feuds recounted in other boxes in this book.) The authors had no trouble finding a publisher, and the book, now in its second edition, has sold "nicely." In Fidell's opinion, statistics is a field in which women seem particularly to excel and feel comfortable. It is a branch of mathematics that, according to Fidell, women often come to find "perfectly logical, perfectly reasonable—and then, with time, something they can truly enjoy."

In teaching new students, the math-shy ones in particular, she finds that once she can "get them to relax," they often find that they thoroughly enjoy statistics. She tells them, "I intend to win you over. And if you will give me half a chance, I will do it."

Reference: Personal interview with Linda Fidell.

Power

Table 9–4 gives the approximate power for the .05 significance level for small, medium, and large effect sizes and one- or two-tailed tests.

For example, suppose you have read a study using a *t* test for independent means that had a nonsignificant result using the .05 significance level, two-tailed, with 50 people in each group. Should you conclude that there is in fact no difference at all in the populations? This conclusion seems quite unjustified. Table 9–4 shows a power of only .17 for a small effect size. This suggests that if such a small effect does indeed exist in the populations, this study would not show it. On the other hand, we can also conclude that if there is a true difference in the populations, it is probably not large. Table 9–4 shows a power of .98 for a large effect size. This suggests that if a large effect exists, it almost surely would have shown up in this study.

Power When Sample Sizes Are Not Equal

Power is greatest when the participants in a study are divided into two equal groups. For example, an experiment with 10 people in the control group and 30 in the experimental group is much less powerful than one with 20 in both groups.

There is a practical problem in figuring power from tables when sample sizes are not equal. Like most power tables, Table 9–4 assumes equal num-

TABLE 9–4
Approximate Power for Studies Using the *t* Test for Independent Means Testing Hypotheses at the .05 Significance Level

Number of Participants in Each Group	Effect Size		
	Small (.20)	*Medium (.50)*	*Large (.80)*
One-tailed test			
10	.11	.29	.53
20	.15	.46	.80
30	.19	.61	.92
40	.22	.72	.97
50	.26	.80	.99
100	.41	.97	*
Two-tailed test			
10	.07	.18	.39
20	.09	.33	.69
30	.12	.47	.86
40	.14	.60	.94
50	.17	.70	.98
100	.29	.94	*

*Nearly 1.
Note: Based on Cohen (1988), pp. 28–39.

bers in each of the two groups. What do you do when your two samples have different numbers of people in them? It turns out that in terms of power, the **harmonic mean** of the two unequal sample sizes gives the equivalent sample size for what you would have with two equal samples. The harmonic mean sample size is given by this formula:

harmonic mean

$$\text{Harmonic Mean} = \frac{(2)(N_1)(N_2)}{N_1 + N_2} \tag{9–8}$$

Consider an extreme example in which there are 6 people in one group and 34 in the other. The harmonic mean comes out to about 10:

$$\text{Harmonic Mean} = \frac{(2)(N_1)(N_2)}{N_1 + N_2} = \frac{(2)(6)(34)}{6 + 34} = \frac{408}{40} = 10.2$$

So even though you have a total of 40 participants, the study has the power of a study with equal sample sizes of only about 10 in each group. (This means that a study with a total of 20 participants divided equally would have had just as much power.) If the researcher is using the .05 level, two-tailed, and expects a large effect size, Table 9–4 indicates that this study would have a power of less than .39 (the figure for using 10 participants in each group). Suppose the researcher had been able to set up the study by dividing the 40 participants into 20 per group. That would have given the study a power of .69.

Planning Sample Size

Table 9–5 gives the approximate number of participants needed for 80% power for estimated small, medium, and large effect sizes using one- and two-tailed tests, all using the .05 significance level. Suppose you plan a study in which you expect a medium effect size and will use the .05 significance level, one-tailed. Based on Table 9–5, you need 50 people in each group (100

TABLE 9–5
Approximate Number of Participants Needed in Each Group (Assuming Equal Sample Sizes) for 80% Power for the *t* Test for Independent Means, Testing Hypotheses at the .05 Significance Level

	Effect Size		
	Small *(.20)*	*Medium* *(.50)*	*Large* *(.80)*
One-tailed	310	50	20
Two-tailed	393	64	26

total) to have 80% power. But if you did a study using the same significance level but could expect a large effect size, you would need only 20 people in each group (40 total).

The *t* Test for Independent Means as Described in Research Articles

A *t* test for independent means usually is described in research articles by giving the means (and sometimes also the standard deviations) of the two samples, plus the standard way of giving the *t* numbers—for example, "t(38) = 4.72, p < .01".

The result of the Moorehouse and Sanders (1992) example might be written up as follows: "The mean perceived academic competence for the boys whose mothers' work involved problem solving was 32.8 (*SD* = 4.27), and the mean for the boys whose mothers' work did not involve problem solving was 29.2 (*SD* = 5.23); $t(41) = 2.42$, p < .05, one-tailed."

Often results of *t* tests for independent means are given in tables. Table 9–6 shows the results of several *t* tests for independent means in a study con-

TABLE 9–6
T-tests for Means on Passive Smoking Knowledge, Attitude and Efforts According to Smoking Status, for Total Group and Men and Women

	Brother Smoker	Brother Nonsmoker	T-Value	Sig.
Total Group	*N =*	*N =*		
Knowledge	2.03 (96)	1.88 (140)	2.61	.01
Attitude	1.95 (94)	1.70 (137)	3.29	.001
Efforts	2.36 (92)	2.23 (133)	1.88	.061
Phys. Resp.*	1.78 (95)	1.61 (142)	2.02	.04
Men				
Knowledge	2.15 (54)	1.92 (69)	2.97	.004
Attitude	2.08 (54)	1.83 (67)	2.12	.036
Efforts	2.50 (52)	2.31 (66)	1.87	.064
Phys. Resp.*	1.81 (54)	1.65 (69)	1.27	.207
Women				
Knowledge	1.87 (42)	1.85 (71)	.30	.767
Attitude	1.77 (40)	1.57 (70)	2.43	.018
Efforts	2.17 (40)	2.15 (67)	.26	.797
Phys. Resp.*	1.76 (41)	1.58 (73)	1.51	.136

*Physician's Responsibility.
Note: Data from Frisch, Shamsuddin, & Kurtz (1995).

ducted by Ann Frisch, Khadijah Shamsuddin, and Margot Kurtz (1995). (Our table is reproduced from their Table 2.) In this study, 293 medical students in Malaysia were surveyed on their views about smoking and on whether their family members and friends smoked. This table compares those students who have a brother who is a smoker to those who have a brother who is a nonsmoker. (The article did not explain what the researchers did if a person had two brothers, one who smokes and one who does not.) The measures were Knowledge (of the health risks of being around smokers), Attitude (toward being around smokers), Efforts (to avoid being around smokers), and Physicians' Responsibility (to inform patients of health risks of being around smokers). All scales were scored so that higher scores were pro-smoking. Lower scores meant more concern about the health risks.

The first line of the table shows that those with a brother who was a smoker scored higher on the Knowledge scale. This means that such students have less knowledge about the health risks of being around smokers. The second line shows those with a brother smoker have a more positive attitude toward being around smokers. (That is, they do not see it as being as much of a health risk.)

Note that some of these results were not significant. What should be concluded about these? Consider the women medical students' beliefs about physician's responsibility. In this comparison, there were 41 with smoker brothers and 73 with nonsmoker brothers. The formula for the harmonic mean indicates that for purposes of computing power, there are 52.5 participants per group. That is,

$$\text{Harmonic Mean} = \frac{(2)(N_1)(N_2)}{N_1 + N_2} = \frac{(2)(41)(73)}{41 + 73} = \frac{5{,}986}{114} = 52.5$$

We can look up power in Table 9–4 using 50 participants (the nearest number of participants in the table to 52.5) and a two-tailed test. We find that the power of this study to find significance for a small effect size is only .17. On the other hand, the power of the study to find a medium effect size is .70 and for a large effect size, .98. If, in fact, there is a small effect for having a brother who is a smoker, this would probably not have shown up in this study. However, suppose there was in fact a medium effect of this kind. In that case, the result of this study probably would have been significant. Almost certainly if there was a large effect the study would have come out significant. We can fairly confidently take from this study that having a brother who is a smoker probably does not make a large difference for Malaysian women medical students' beliefs about a physician's responsibility to inform their patients about the risks of being around smokers. We cannot conclude that there might not be a small effect of this kind.

Summary

A *t* test for independent means is used for hypothesis testing with two samples of scores. The main difference from a *t* test for a single sample is that the comparison distribution is a distribution of differences between means of samples. This distribution can be thought of as being built up in two steps: Each population of individuals produces a distribution of means, and then a new distribution is created of differences between pairs of means selected from these two distributions of means.

The distribution of differences between means has a mean of 0 and is a t distribution with the total of the degrees of freedom from the two samples. Its standard deviation is figured in several steps: (a) Each sample is used to estimate the population variance; (b) because the populations are assumed to have the same variance, a pooled estimate is figured by a weighted average of the two estimates (multiplying each estimate by the proportion of the total degrees of freedom its sample contributes and adding up the products); (c) the pooled estimate is divided by each sample's number of scores to give the variances of its populations's distribution of means; (d) these two variances are added together to give the variance of the distribution of differences between means; and (e) the square root is taken.

The assumptions of the t test for independent means are that the two populations are normally distributed and have the same variance. However, the t test gives fairly accurate results when the true situation is moderately different from the assumptions.

Effect size for a t test for independent means is the difference between the means divided by the standard deviation. Power is greatest when sample sizes of the two groups are equal. When they are not equal, when looking up power on a table, use the harmonic mean of the two sample sizes.

t tests for independent means are usually reported in research articles with the means of the two groups plus the degrees of freedom, t score, and significance level. Results may also be reported in a table where each significant difference is shown by a star.

Key Terms

distribution of differences between means
harmonic mean
pooled estimate of the population variance (S^2_{Pooled})

standard deviation of the distribution of differences between means ($S_{Difference}$)
t test for independent means

variance of the distribution of differences between means ($S^2_{Difference}$)
weighted average

Practice Problems

These problems involve computation (with the assistance of a calculator). Most real-life statistics problems are done on a computer. Even if you have a computer, do these by hand to ingrain the method in your mind.

For practice in using a computer to solve statistics problems, refer to the computer section of each chapter of the Student's Study Guide and Computer Workbook *that accompanies this text.*

All data are fictional (unless an actual citation is given).

Answers to selected problems are given at the back of the book.

1. (a) Explain when you would use a t test for dependent means and when you would use a t test for independent means.

(b) Make up an example not in the book or your lectures of a study of each kind.

2. For each of the following experiments, decide if the difference between conditions is statistically significant at the .05 level (two-tailed). Also determine the effect size and approximate power (from Table 9–4).

	Experimental Group			Control Group		
	N	M	S^2	N	M	S^2
(a)	30	12.0	2.4	30	11.1	2.8
(b)	20	12.0	2.4	40	11.1	2.8
(c)	30	12.0	2.2	30	11.1	3.0

3. A communication researcher randomly assigned 82 volunteers to one of two experimental groups. Sixty-one were instructed to get their news for a month only from television and 21 were instructed to get their news for a month only from the radio. (Why the researcher did not assign equal numbers to the two conditions is a mystery!) In any case, after the month was up, all participants were tested on their knowledge of several political issues. The researcher did not have a prediction as to which news source would make people more knowledgeable. That is, the researcher simply predicted that there is some kind of difference. These were the results of the study. TV group: $M = 24$, $S^2 = 4$; radio group: $M = 26$, $S^2 = 6$. Using the .01 level, what should the researcher conclude? Also, based on the results, what is the approximate effect size of this study? Explain your answers to someone who has never had a course in statistics.

4. A teacher was interested in whether using a student's own name in a story affected children's attention span while reading. Six children were randomly assigned to read a story under normal conditions (using names like Dick and Jane). Five other children read versions of the same story, but with each child's own name substituted for one of the children in the story. The researcher kept a careful measure of how long it took each child to read the story. The results follow. Using the .05 level, does including the child's name make any difference? (Give the approximate effect size and power based on the results.) Explain your answer to a person who understands the t test for dependent means but does not know anything about the t test for independent means.

Normal Story		Own-Name Story	
Student	**Reading Time**	**Student**	**Reading Time**
A	2	G	4
B	5	H	16
C	7	I	11
D	9	J	9
E	6	K	8
F	6		

5. What are the approximate number of participants needed for each of the following planned studies to have 80% power, assuming equal numbers in the two groups and all using the .05 significance level. (Be sure to give the total number of participants needed, not just the number needed for each group.)

	Expected Means		**Expected**	
Study	M_1	M_2	**Pop SD**	**Tails**
a	107	149	84	1
b	22.5	16.2	31.5	2
c	14	12	2.5	1
d	480	520	50	2

6. Frodi, Grolnick, Bridges, and Berko (1990) studied the play behavior of 63 infants that were 13 months old, 33 of them born to adult mothers and 30 to teenage mothers. (The adult mothers, in addition to being older, were also more likely to be middle-class.) The infants were video-taped playing with a set of toys that involved problem solving under structured and unstructured play conditions. The tapes were later rated for the degree to which the infant showed persistence, competence at solving the problems the toys presented, and positive mood. The results presented here apply to the structured-play situation. Explain what these results mean to a person who has never had a course in statistics. (You need not try actually to compute the effect size; just discuss the issues of power and such in general, considering the sample sizes.)

	Infants of Teenage Mothers	**Infants of Adult Mothers**	t	p
Persistence	231	171	2.78	.007
Affect	173.0	173.3	3.21	.002
Competence	158	753	.81	n.s.

7. Do men or women have longer first names? Take out a phone book and use the random numbers given here to select a page. (If your phone book has closer to 100 pages, use just the first two digits.) On the first page, look for the first clearly female name, and write down how many letters it has. Do the same thing (find the page for the numbers, and so on) 16 times. Then continue, getting lengths for 16 male names. (You will have to exclude names for which you cannot tell the gender.) Compute a t test for independent means using these two samples.

121, 798, 107, 971, 534, 740, 156, 55, 741, 128, 571, 939, 946, 731, 682, 516, 609, 569, 72, 932, 435, 912, 573, 581, 381, 120, 514, 338, 571, 743, 982, 471, 385, 663, 201, 323, 609, 430, 788, 296, 398, 174, 314, 120, 612, 100, 801, 352, 312, 993, 226

10 Introduction to the Analysis of Variance

CINDY Hazan and Philip Shaver (1987) arranged to have the *Rocky Mountain News,* a large Denver area newspaper, print a mail-in survey. In this survey, readers answered questions that allowed the researchers to compare the amount of jealousy reported by people with three different attachment styles: secure, anxious, and avoidant. (These attachment styles are thought to be different ways of behaving and thinking in close relationships that develop from a person's experience with caretakers in infancy.)

With a *t* test, Hazan and Shaver could have compared the mean jealousy scores of any two of the attachment styles; but they were interested in differences among all three attachment styles. The statistical procedure for testing variation among the means of several groups is called the **analysis of variance,** sometimes abbreviated as **ANOVA.** (You could use the analysis of variance for a study with only two groups, but the *t* test, which gives the same result in that situation, is simpler. When you have more than two groups, it does not work to use a series of *t* tests to compare the various pairs of means with each other. This does not work because the series of *t* tests would not tell you whether there is an overall difference among the means of all the groups.)

In this chapter, we introduce the analysis of variance, focusing on the fundamental logic, how to carry out an analysis of variance in the most basic situation, and how to make sense of more complicated forms of the analysis of variance when reading about them in research articles.

Basic Logic of the Analysis of Variance

The null hypothesis in an analysis of variance is that the several populations being compared all have the same mean. For example, in the Hazan and

analysis of variance

ANOVA

Shaver study, the null hypothesis would be that the populations of secure, anxious, and avoidant people all have the same degree of jealousy—that the mean jealousy is the same in these three populations. The research hypothesis would be that the degree of jealousy differs among these three populations—that their means are not all the same.

Hypothesis testing in analysis of variance is about whether the means of the samples differ more than you would expect if the null hypothesis were true. This question about *means* is answered, surprisingly, by analyzing *variances* (hence the name *analysis of variance*). (To oversimplify something you will understand much better shortly, we focus on variances because when you are interested in how several means differ, you are studying the variation among those means.) To understand the logic of analysis of variance, we turn to considering variances. In particular, we begin by considering two different ways of estimating population variances. As you will see, the analysis of variance is about a comparison of the results of these two different ways of estimating population variances.

Estimating Population Variance From Variation Within Each Sample

In the analysis of variance, as in the *t* test, we do not know the true population variances. As with the *t* test, the variance of each of the populations can be estimated in the usual way from the samples. Also as with the *t* test, we assume in the analysis of variance that all populations have the *same* variance. Because they are all assumed to have the same variance, the estimates from each sample can be pooled or averaged into a single best estimate. The resulting pooled estimate is called the **within-group estimate of the population variance.** It has this name because it is an average of estimates figured entirely from the scores *within* each of the samples.

within-group estimate of the population variance

The most important thing to remember about this within-group estimate is that it is not affected by whether or not the null hypothesis is true. That is, this estimate comes out the same whether the means of the populations are all the same (as would be the case if the null hypothesis were true) or whether the means of the populations are very different (as would be the case if the null hypothesis were not true). This estimate comes out the same, because it only focuses on the variation inside of each population, so it does not matter how far apart the means of different populations are.

Estimating the Population Variance From Variation Between the Means of the Samples

There is also a second way of estimating the population variance. This section explains this second method.

Each sample's mean is a number in its own right. If there are several samples, there are several such numbers, and these numbers will have some variation among them. It turns out that the variation among these means gives another way to estimate the variance in the populations that the samples come from. Just how this works is a bit tricky, so follow the next two paragraphs closely.

When the Null Hypothesis Is True. First, we will consider the situation in which the null hypothesis is true, so that all samples come from populations that have the same mean. Remember that we are assuming that all populations have the same variance (and also that they are all normal curves). If the null hypothesis is true, all populations are identical. (They have the same mean, variance, and shape.)

If you have samples from several identical populations, even though the populations are identical, the samples will each be a little different, and their means will each be a little different. How different can the means be? That depends on how much variation there is within each population. If a population has very little variation in the scores within it, then any sample from that population will be very similar to any other sample from that population and the means of any samples from that population will be very similar. If several identical populations each have a great deal of variation in the scores within each, then if you take one sample from each population, those samples can be very different from each other, and their means can thus be very different. Being very different, they will have a great deal of variance. The point of all this is that the more variance within each of several identical populations, the more variance there will be between the means of samples when you take a random sample from each population.

Here is an example. Suppose you were studying samples of six children from each of three large classrooms (the populations in this example). If each classroom had children who were all either 9 or 10 years old, the means of your three samples would all be between 9 and 10. This would mean not much variance among those means. If each classroom had children ranging from 5 to 15 years old, the means of the three samples would probably vary quite a bit. Therefore, the variation among the means of the samples is related directly to the amount of variation within each of the populations from which the samples are taken. The more variation in each population, the more variation among the means of samples taken from those populations.

Look also at our example of the populations of secure, anxious, and avoidant attachment types studied by Hazan and Shaver. There will, of course, be some variance in the degree of jealousy of different people within each of these populations. Let us suppose for the moment that these three populations all have the same mean degree of jealousy (as would be the case if the null hypothesis is true). Even in this case of all having the same mean, a sample drawn from one population will probably not have exactly the same mean as a sample drawn from the second. Similarly, a sample drawn from the third likely will be a little different from the other two, and so forth. Further, the more each of these populations varies within itself, the more the means of samples taken from these populations will vary, even if, in fact, the populations' means were identical.

This principle we have been considering is illustrated in Figure 10–1. The three identical populations on the left have small variances and the three identical populations on the right have large variances. In each set of three identical populations, even though the means of three populations are the same, the variation among the means of the samples from those populations are not the same. Most important to notice, the means from the populations with less variance are closer together (have less variance among them). The means from the populations with more variance are more spread out (have more variance among them).

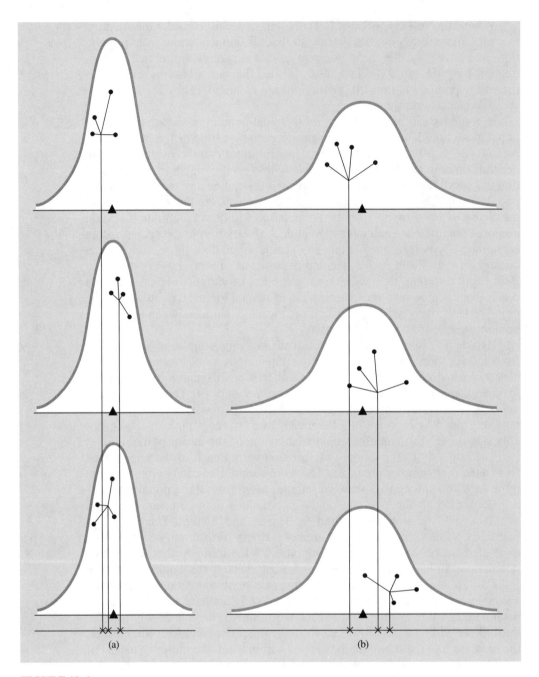

FIGURE 10–1
Means of samples from identical populations will not be identical. (a) Sample means from populations with less variation will vary less. (b) Sample means from populations with more variation will vary more. Population means are indicated by a triangle, sample means by an X.

We have now seen that the variation among the means of samples taken from identical populations is related directly to the variation of the scores within each of those populations. This has a very important implication: It should be possible to estimate the variance within each population from the variation among the means of our samples. That is, we should be able to use the variation in the means of our samples to figure out how much variation there is in the populations from which these samples come.

Such an estimate is called a **between-group estimate of the population variance.** (It has this name because it is based on the variation between the means of the samples, the "groups." Grammatically, it ought to be *among* groups; but *between* groups is traditional.) We will turn to how one actually calculates this estimate later in the chapter.

between-group estimate of the population variance

Remember that all of this logic has been assuming that the null hypothesis is true, in which case there is no variation among the means of the populations. Let us now consider what happens when the null hypothesis is not true and instead the research hypothesis is true.

When the Null Hypothesis Is Not True. If the null hypothesis is not true and the research hypothesis is true, the populations themselves have different means. In this situation, the variation among means of samples taken from these populations still is caused by the variation within the populations. In this situation in which the research hypothesis is true, the variation among the means of the samples also is caused by the variation between the population means. That is, in this situation the means of the samples are spread out both because of variation within each of the populations and also because of variation between the populations. Figure 10–2a shows three populations with the same means and the means of samples taken from them. (This is the same situation as in Figure 10–1, a and b). Figure 10–2b shows three populations with different means and the means of samples taken from them. (This is the situation we have just been discussing.) Notice that the means of the

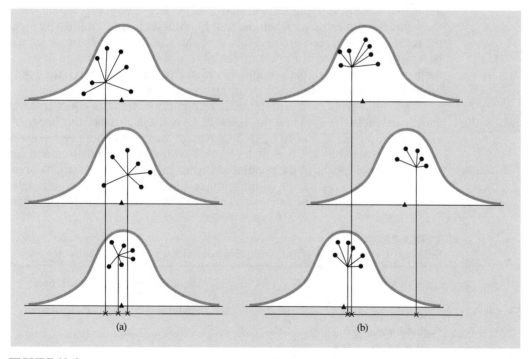

FIGURE 10–2
Means of samples from populations whose means differ (b) will vary more than sample means taken from populations whose means are the same (a). Population means are indicated by a triangle, sample means by an *X*.

samples are more spread out in Figure 10–2b than in Figure 10–2a, even though the variations within the populations are the same in Figure 10–2b as in Figure 10–2a. This additional spread (variance) is due to the populations having different means.

In sum, the between-group estimate of the population variance is figured based on the variation among the means of the samples. If the null hypothesis is true, this estimate is an accurate indication of the variation within the populations. If the null hypothesis is false, this method of estimating the population variance is influenced both by the variation within the populations and the variation between them. It will not give an accurate estimate of the variation within the populations because it also will be affected by the variation between the populations. This difference has important implications. It is what makes the analysis of variance a method of testing hypotheses about whether there is a difference among means of groups.

Comparing the Within-Group and Between-Group Estimates of Population Variance

Table 10–1 summarizes what we have seen so far about the within-group and between-group estimates of population variance when the null hypothesis is true versus when the research hypothesis is true. When the null hypothesis is true, the within-group and between-group estimates are based on the same thing. Literally, they are estimates of the same population variance. When the null hypothesis is true, both estimates should be about the same. (Only *about* the same: These are estimates and they are not perfectly accurate.) Here is another way of describing this similarity of the between-group estimate and the within-group estimate when the null hypothesis is true. In this situation, the ratio of the between-group estimate to the within-group estimate should be approximately 1 to 1. For example, if the within-group estimate is 107.5, the between-group estimate should be around 107.5, so that the ratio would be about 1. (A ratio is found by dividing one number by the other.)

The situation is quite different when the null hypothesis is not true. As shown in Table 10–1, when the research hypothesis is true, the between-group estimate is influenced by two sources of variation. These two sources of variation are the variation of the scores within each population and the variation of the means of the populations from each other. Even when the research hypothesis is true, the within-group estimate still only is influenced by the variation within the populations. Therefore, when the research hypothesis

TABLE 10–1
Sources of Variation in Within- and Between-Group Variance Estimates

	Variation Within Populations	Variation Between Populations
Null hypothesis is true		
Within-group estimate reflects	X	
Between-group estimate reflects	X	
Research hypothesis is true		
Within-group estimate reflects	X	
Between-group estimate reflects	X	X

is true, the between-group estimate should be larger than the within-group estimate. In this situation, the ratio of the between-group estimate to the within-group estimate should be greater than 1 to 1. For example, the between-group estimate might be 638.9 and the within-group estimate 107.5, making a ratio of 638.9 to 107.5 or 5.94. That is, if we divide the larger, the between-group estimate, by the smaller, the within-group estimate, we get not 1 but more than 1.

This is the central principle of the analysis of variance: When the null hypothesis is true, the ratio of the between-group variance estimate to the within-group variance estimate should be about 1. When the research hypothesis is true, this ratio should be greater than 1. If we compute this ratio and it comes out much bigger than 1, we can reject the null hypothesis. That is, it is unlikely that the null hypothesis could be true and the between-group estimate be much bigger than the within-group estimate.

The *F* Ratio

This crucial ratio of the between-group to the within-group variance estimate is called an ***F* ratio.** (The *F* is for Sir Ronald Fisher, an eminent statistician who developed the analysis of variance; see Box 10–1.)

F ratio

The *F* Distribution and the *F* Table

We have said that if the crucial ratio of between-group estimate to within-group estimate (the *F* ratio) is much larger than 1, we can reject the null hypothesis. The next question is, just how much bigger than 1 does it need to be before we can reject the null hypothesis with confidence?

As you might have guessed by now, statisticians have developed the mathematics of an ***F* distribution** and have prepared tables of *F* ratios. For any given situation, you merely look up in an ***F* table** how extreme an *F* ratio is needed to reject the null hypothesis at, say, the .05 level. (You will learn to use the *F* table later in the chapter.)

F distribution
F table

For an example of an *F* ratio, return to the Hazan and Shaver (1987) attachment style study. The results of that study, for jealousy, were as follows: The between-group population variance estimate was 23.19. (This number is figured based on the means of the three attachment style samples, which were 2.17, 2.88, and 2.57; you will learn to do such computations yourself shortly.) The within-group population variance estimate was .53. (This number was figured by pooling the estimates of the variance of each population based on the scores within each sample.) The ratio of the between-group to the within-group variance estimates (23.19/.53) came out to 43.91; that is $F = 43.91$. This *F* ratio is considerably larger than 1. In fact, in this case the *F* ratio needed to reject the null hypothesis at the .05 level is only 3.01. Hazan and Shaver confidently rejected the null hypothesis and concluded that amount of jealousy varies according to attachment style.

An Analogy

Some students find an analogy helpful in understanding the analysis of variance. The analogy is to what engineers call the signal-to-noise ratio. For

BOX 10–1

Sir Ronald Fisher: Caustic Genius of Statistics

Ronald A. Fisher, a contemporary of William Gosset (see Box 8–1) and Karl Pearson (see Box 11–1), was probably the brightest and certainly the most productive of this close-knit group of British statisticians. In the process of writing 300 papers and 7 books, he developed many of the modern field's key concepts: variance, analysis of variance, statistics (in the sense of describing a sample, as opposed to parameters of a population), significance levels, the null hypothesis, and almost all of our basic ideas of research design, including the fundamental importance of randomization.

It is one of those family legends that little Ronald, born in 1890 in East Finchley, a northern suburb of London, was so fascinated by math that one day, at age 3, when put into his high chair for breakfast, he asked his nurse, "What is a half of a half?" Told it was a quarter, he asked, "What's half of a quarter?" To that answer he wanted to know what was half of an eighth. At the next answer he purportedly thought a moment and said, "Then I suppose that a half of a sixteenth must be a thirty-toof." Ah, baby stories.

As a grown man, however, Fisher seems to have been anything but darling. Some observers ascribe this to a cold and unemotional mother, but whatever the reason, throughout his life the man was embroiled in bitter feuds, even with scholars who had previously been his closest allies and who certainly ought to have been comrades in research. When he was teased, apparently he responded with deadly seriousness; when others were anxious, he joked. William G. Cochran (a well-known statistician in his own right) reported a tale of their crossing a street together at a moment that was obviously unsafe. When Cochran hesitated, Fisher supposedly chided him: "Oh come on, a spot of natural selection won't hurt us." Cochran sheepishly risked his neck.

Fisher's thin ration of compassion extended to his readers as well—not only was his writing hopelessly obscure, but it often simply failed to supply important assumptions and proofs. Gosset said that when Fisher began a sentence with "Evidently," it meant two hours of hard work before one could hope to see why the point was evident. Another statistician sought to excuse him, however, saying that, "Fisher was talk-

example, your ability to make out the words in a shortwave radio broadcast depends on the strength of the signal versus the amount of random noise. In the case of the F ratio in the analysis of variance, the difference among the means of the samples is like the signal; it is the information of interest. The variation within the samples is like the noise. When the variation among the samples is sufficiently great in comparison to the variation within the samples, you conclude that there is a significant effect.

Carrying Out an Analysis of Variance

Having considered the basic logic of the analysis of variance, we will go through an example to illustrate the details. (We use a fictional study to keep the numbers simple.)

Suppose a researcher is interested in the influence of knowledge of previous criminal record on juries' perception of the guilt or innocence of a defendant. The researcher recruits 15 volunteers who have been selected for jury duty (but have not yet served at a trial) and shows them a videotape of a 4-hour trial. In the trial, a woman is accused of passing bad checks. Prior to ing on a plane barely understood by the rest of humanity." It is true that he was invariably admired and respected for his work, if not for his manners.

Indeed, his lack of empathy extended to all of humankind. Like Galton, Fisher was fond of eugenics, favoring anything that might increase the birthrate of the upper and professional classes and skilled artisans. Not only did he see contraception as a poor idea—fearing that the least desirable persons would use it least, but he defended infanticide as serving an evolutionary function. It may be just as well that his opportunities to experiment with breeding never extended beyond the raising of his own children and some crops of potatoes and wheat.

The greatest influence on Fisher was probably his 14 years working at an agricultural experimental station called Rothamsted, in Hertfordshire, 25 miles north of London. At Rothamsted, Fisher, like Gosset at his brewery in Dublin, faced all sorts of practical problems, such as whether yearly applications of manure improved the yield of a field in the long run or was the cause of mysterious declines in production after many decades. Perhaps it was even this isolation

from the personality disputes among London academics and this closeness to real issues that helped Fisher concentrate on developing statistics as a powerful research tool.

Although Fisher eventually became the Galton Professor of Eugenics at University College, his most influential appointment probably came when he was invited to Iowa State College in Ames for the summers of 1931 and 1936 (where he was said to be so put out with the terrible heat that he stored his sheets in the refrigerator all day). At Ames, Fisher greatly impressed George Snedecor, an American professor of mathematics also working on agricultural problems. Consequently, Snedecor wrote a textbook of statistics for agriculture that borrowed heavily from Fisher's work at Rothamsted. The book so popularized Fisher's ideas about statistics and research design that its second edition sold 100,000 copies.

While Fisher was at Ames, he also won over E. F. Lindquist, professor of education at the University of Iowa in Iowa City. Lindquist filled his next textbook with Fisher's ideas, introducing them to the fields of education and psychology, where they have played a major role to this day.

viewing the tape, however, all of the research participants are given a "background sheet" with age, marital status, education, and other such information about the accused woman. The sheet is the same for all 15 participants, with one difference. For five of the participants, the last section of the sheet says that the woman has been convicted several times before for passing bad checks. (The participants who get this version of the background sheet we will call the "criminal record group.") For five other participants, the last section of the sheet says the woman has a completely clean criminal record. (We will call these participants the "clean record group."). Finally, for the remaining five participants the sheet does not mention anything about criminal record one way or the other. (We will call these participants the "no information group.")

The participants are randomly assigned to the version of the background sheet they read. After viewing the tape of the trial, all 15 participants make a rating on a 10-point scale, which runs from completely sure she is innocent (1) to completely sure she is guilty (10). The results of this fictional study are shown in Table 10–2. The table shows that the means of the three groups are different (8, 4, and 5). There is also quite a bit of variation within each of the three groups. (Population variance estimates from the score of these three groups are 4.5, 5.0, and 6.5.)

We need to do three computations to test the hypothesis that the three populations are different: (a) a population variance estimate based on the variation of the scores within each of the samples, (b) a population variance estimate based on the differences among the group means, and (c) the ratio of the two, the F ratio. (In addition, we need the significance cutoff from an F table.) Let us consider each of these calculations in turn.

Estimating Population Variance on the Basis of Variation of Scores Within Each Group

The population variance can be estimated from any one group (that is, sample) by using the usual method for estimating a population variance from a sample. First, compute the sum of the squared deviation scores. That is, take the deviation of each score from its group's mean, square that deviation score, and sum all the squared deviation scores. Second, divide that sum of squared deviation scores by that group's degrees of freedom. (The degrees of freedom for a group are the number of scores in the group minus 1.) For the example, as shown in Table 10–2, this gives an estimated population variance of 4.5 based on the criminal record group, an estimate of 5.0 based on the clean record group, and an estimate of 6.5 based on the no-information group.

Recall that in analysis of variance, as with the t test, we always assume that the populations have the same variance. Because these estimates are all of populations assumed to have the same variance, the estimates based on each sample's scores are all estimating the same number (the true population variance). Because the sample sizes are equal in this example, each group represents an estimate based on an equal amount of information. We can pool these variance estimates by straight averaging. This yields an overall estimate of the population variance based on the variation within groups of the sum of 4.5, 5.0, and 6.5 (which is 16), divided by the number of groups (3), which comes out to 5.33.

The estimated variance based on the variation of the scores within each of the groups is the within-group variance estimate (S^2_{Within}). The formula for the within-group variance estimate when sample sizes are equal follows:

$$S^2_{Within} = \frac{S^2_1 + S^2_2 + \cdots + S^2_{Last}}{N_{Groups}}$$

(10–1)

TABLE 10–2
Results of the Criminal Record Study (Fictional Data)

	Criminal Record Group			Clean Record Group			No Information Group		
	Rating	Deviation from Mean	Squared Deviation from Mean	Rating	Deviation from Mean	Squared Deviation from Mean	Rating	Deviation from Mean	Squared Deviation from Mean
	10	2	4	5	1	1	4	−1	1
	7	−1	1	1	−3	9	6	1	1
	5	−3	9	3	−1	1	9	4	16
	10	2	4	7	3	9	3	−2	4
	8	0	0	4	0	0	3	−2	4
Σ:	40	0	18	20	0	20	25	0	26

$M = 40/5 = 8$ $M = 20/5 = 4$ $M = 25/5 = 5$
$S^2 = 18/4 = 4.5$ $S^2 = 20/4 = 5.0$ $S^2 = 26/4 = 6.5$

In this formula, S^2_1 is the estimated population variance based on the scores in the first group (the one associated with Population 1), S^2_2 is the estimated population variance based on the scores in the second group, S^2_{Last} is the estimated population variance based on the scores in the last group. (The dots, or ellipses, in the formula show that you are to fill in the population variance estimate for as many other groups as there are in the analysis). N_{Groups} is the number of groups.

Using this formula for our computations, we get

$$S^2_{Within} = \frac{S^2_1 + S^2_2 + \cdots + S^2_{Last}}{N_{Groups}} = \frac{4.5 + 5.0 + 6.5}{3} = \frac{16.3}{3} = 5.33$$

Estimating Population Variance on the Basis of Differences Between Group Means

Determining the between-group estimate of the population variance involves two steps. First, you estimate from a few means (the means of your samples) the variance of a distribution means (the distribution of all possible means of samples the size of your samples). Second, based on the variance of this distribution of means, you calculate the variance of the population of individuals.

Estimating the Variance of the Distribution of Means. You can think of the means of your samples as taken from a distribution of means of samples. Use the usual procedure of using the scores in a sample to estimate the variance of the population from which these scores are taken. In this case, think of the means of your samples as the scores and the distribution of means as the population from which these scores come. What this all means is that you first figure the sum of squared deviations. (This means you find the mean of your samples' means, figure the deviation of each sample mean from this mean of means, square each of these deviations, and then sum these squared deviations.) Then, divide this sum of squared deviations by the degrees of freedom, which is the number of means minus 1. In terms of a formula (when sample sizes are all equal),

$$S^2_M = \frac{\Sigma(M - GM)^2}{df_{Between}}$$

(10-2)

In this formula, S^2_M is the estimated variance of the distribution of means (estimated based on the means of the samples in your study). M is the mean of each of your samples. GM is the **grand mean,** the overall mean of all your scores, which is also the mean of your means. $df_{Between}$ is the degrees of freedom in the between-group estimate, the number of groups minus 1 (that is, $df_{Between} = N_{Groups} - 1$).

grand mean

In our jury example, the three means are 8, 4, and 5. The computations of S^2_M are shown in Table 10–3.

From the Estimated Variance of the Distribution of Means to an Estimated Variance of the Population of Individual Scores. What we have just calculated from a sample of a few means is the estimated variance of a distribution of means. From this we want to make an estimation of the variance of the population (the distribution of individuals) that the distribution of means is based on. We saw in Chapter 6 that the variance of a distribution of means is smaller than the variance of the population (the distribution of

TABLE 10–3
Estimated Variance of the Distribution of Means Based on Means of the Three Experimental Groups in the Criminal Record Study (Fictional Data)

Sample Means	Deviation from Grand Mean	Squared Deviation from Grand Mean
(M)	$(M - GM)$	$(M - GM)^2$
4	−1.67	2.79
8	2.33	5.43
5	− .67	.45
Σ: 17	−0.01	8.67

$GM = \Sigma M/N_{\text{Groups}} = 17/3 = 5.67; S_M^2 = \Sigma(M - GM)^2/df_{\text{Between}} = 8.67/2 = 4.34.$

individuals) that it is based on. This is because means are less likely to be extreme than individual scores are (because several scores that are extreme in the same direction are unlikely to be included in any one sample). Specifically, you learned in Chapter 6 that the variance of a distribution of means is the variance of the distribution of individual scores divided by the number of scores in each sample.

Now, however, we are going to do reverse what we did in Chapter 6. In Chapter 6 you figured the variance of the distribution of means by *dividing* the variance of the distribution of individuals by the sample size. Now you are going to figure the variance of the distribution of individuals by *multiplying* the variance of the distribution of means times the sample size. That is, to come up with the variance of the population of individuals, we multiply our estimate of the variance of the distribution of means times the sample size. The result of this process is the between-group variance estimate. Stated as a formula (for when sample sizes are equal),

$$S^2_{\text{Between}} = (S^2_M)(n) \tag{10–3}$$

In this formula, S^2_{Between} is the estimate of the population variance based on the variation between the means (the between-group variance estimate). n is the number of scores in each sample.

Let us return to our example in which there were 5 in each sample and an estimated variance of the distribution of means of 4.34. In this example, multiplying 4.34 times 5 gives a between-group population variance estimate of 21.7. In terms of the formula,

$$S^2_{\text{Between}} = (S^2_M)(n) = (4.34)(5) = 21.7$$

To summarize, the procedure of estimating the population variance based on the differences between group means is (a) to calculate the estimated variance of the distribution of means and then (b) to multiply that estimated variance times the number of scores in each group.

Figuring the *F* Ratio

The *F* ratio is the ratio of the between-group estimate of the population variance to the within-group estimate of the population variance. Stated as a formula,

$$F = \frac{S^2_{\text{Between}}}{S^2_{\text{Within}}} \tag{10–4}$$

In the example, our ratio of between to within is 21.7 to 5.33. Carrying out the division gives an F ratio of 4.07. In terms of the formula,

$$F = \frac{S^2_{\text{Between}}}{S^2_{\text{Within}}} = \frac{21.7}{5.33} = 4.07$$

The F Distribution

The next step is to determine the cutoff for the F being large enough to reject the null hypothesis. This requires there being a distribution of F ratios that you can use to figure out what is an extreme F ratio.

In practice, you simply look up the needed cutoff on a table. To understand from where that number on the table comes, you need to understand the F distribution. The easiest way to understand this distribution is to think about how you would go about making one.

Start with three identical populations. Next, randomly select five scores from each. On the basis of these three samples (of five scores each), you calculate to get an F ratio. (That is, you use these scores to make a between-group estimate and a within-group estimate and divide the first by the second.) Let us say that you do this and the F ratio you come up with is 1.36. Now, select three new random samples of five scores each and figure the F ratio using these three samples. Perhaps this time you get an F of .93. If you do this whole process many times, you will eventually get many F ratios. The distribution of all possible F ratios figured in this way (from random samples from identical populations) is called the F distribution. Figure 10–3 shows an example of an F distribution. (There are many different F distributions and each has a slightly different shape. The exact shape depends on how many samples you take each time and how many scores are in each sample. The general shape is like that shown in the figure.)

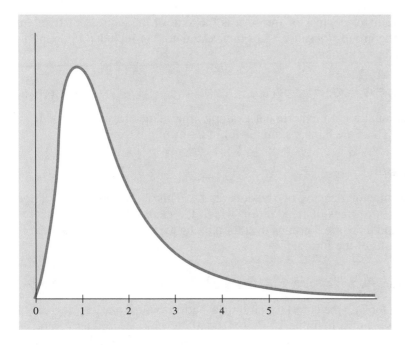

FIGURE 10–3
An F distribution.

Of course, in practice no one actually goes about making their own F distributions in this way. It is a mathematical distribution whose exact characteristics can be found from a formula. Mathematics can also prove that if you had the patience to follow this procedure of taking random samples and figuring the F ratio of each for a very long time, you would get the same result.

As you can see in Figure 10–3, the F distribution is not symmetrical but has a long tail on the right. The reason for the positive skew is that an F distribution is a distribution of ratios of variances. Variances are always positive numbers. (A variance is an average of squared deviations, and anything squared is a positive number.) A ratio of a positive number to positive number can never be less than 0. There is nothing to stop a ratio from being a very high number. The F ratios' distribution cannot be lower than 0 and can rise quite high. (Most F ratios pile up just on the two sides of 1, but do spread out more on the positive side, where they have more room to spread out.)

The F Table

The F table is a little more complicated than the t table. This is because there is a different F distribution according to both the degrees of freedom used in the between-group variance estimate and the degrees of freedom used in the within-group variance estimate. That is, you must consider two different degrees of freedom to look up the needed cutoff. One is the **numerator degrees of freedom.** This is the degrees of freedom used in the between-group variance estimate, the numerator of the F ratio. The other is the **denominator degrees of freedom.** This is the total degrees of freedom that go into figuring the within-group variance estimate, the denominator of the F ratio.

The numerator degrees of freedom is the number of groups minus 1 (because that is the degrees of freedom used in computing the between-groups variance estimate). Stated as a formula,

$$df_{\text{Between}} = N_{\text{Groups}} - 1 \tag{10–5}$$

The denominator degrees of freedom is the sum of the degrees of freedom for all of the groups (because all of their estimates are included in the pooling). Stated as a formula,

$$df_{\text{Within}} = df_1 + df_2 + \cdots + df_{\text{Last}} \tag{10–6}$$

In the criminal record experiment example, the numerator degrees of freedom is 2. (There are 3 means, minus 1.) In terms of the formula,

$$df_{\text{Between}} = N_{\text{Groups}} - 1 = 3 - 1 = 2$$

The denominator degrees of freedom is 12. This is because each of the groups has 4 degrees of freedom on which the estimate is based (5 scores minus 1) and there are 3 groups overall, making a total of 12 degrees of freedom. In terms of the formula,

$$df_{\text{Within}} = df_1 + df_2 + \cdots + df_{\text{Last}} = (5-1) + (5-1) + (5-1) = 4 + 4 + 4 = 12$$

You would look up the cutoff for an F distribution "with 2 and 12" degrees of freedom. As shown in Table 10–4, for the .05 level, you need an F ratio of

TABLE 10–4
Cutoffs for the _F_ Distribution (Portion)

Denominator Degrees of Freedom	Significance Level	Numerator Degrees of Freedom					
		_1_	_2_	_3_	_4_	_5_	_6_
10	.01	10.05	7.56	6.55	6.00	5.64	5.39
	.05	4.97	4.10	3.71	3.48	3.33	3.22
	.10	3.29	2.93	2.73	2.61	2.52	2.46
11	.01	9.65	7.21	6.22	5.67	5.32	5.07
	.05	4.85	3.98	3.59	3.36	3.20	3.10
	.10	3.23	2.86	2.66	2.54	2.45	2.39
12	.01	9.33	6.93	5.95	5.41	5.07	4.82
	.05	4.75	**3.89**	3.49	3.26	3.11	3.00
	.10	3.18	2.81	2.61	2.48	2.40	2.33
13	.01	9.07	6.70	5.74	5.21	4.86	4.62
	.05	4.67	3.81	3.41	3.18	3.03	2.92
	.10	3.14	2.76	2.56	2.43	2.35	2.28

3.89 to reject the null hypothesis. (At the .01 level, you would need an _F_ of 6.93.) The full _F_ table appears as Table A–3 in Appendix A.

Hypothesis Testing with the Analysis of Variance

Let us consider how these steps work in the criminal record experiment.

1. Restate the question as a research hypothesis and a null hypothesis about the populations. The populations are these:

Population 1: Jurors told that the defendant has a criminal record
Population 2: Jurors told that the defendant has a clean record
Population 3: Jurors given no information on the defendant's record

The null hypothesis is that these three populations have the same mean. The research hypothesis is that the populations' means differ.

2. Determine the characteristics of the comparison distribution. The comparison distribution is an _F_ distribution with 2 and 12 degrees of freedom.

3. Determine the cutoff sample score on the comparison distribution at which the null hypothesis should be rejected. Using the _F_ table for the .05 significance level, the needed _F_ ratio is 3.89.

4. Determine the score of the sample on the comparison distribution. In the analysis of variance, the comparison distribution is an _F_ distribution, and the sample's score on that distribution is thus its _F_ ratio. In the example, the _F_ ratio we computed was 4.07.

5. Compare the scores from Steps 3 and 4 to decide whether to reject the null hypothesis. In the example, the computed _F_ ratio is more extreme than the .05 significance level cutoff. The researcher would reject the null hypothesis that the three groups come from populations with the same mean. This suggests that they come from populations with different means: that people exposed to different kinds of information (or no information) about the criminal record of a defendant in a situation of this kind will differ in their ratings of the defendant's guilt.[1]

Summary of Steps for Hypothesis Testing using the Analysis of Variance

Table 10–5 summarizes the steps involved in an analysis of variance of the kind we have been considering in this chapter.[2]

Assumptions in the Analysis of Variance

The assumptions for the analysis of variance are basically the same as for the *t* test for independent means. That is, you get strictly accurate results only when the populations follow a normal curve and have equal variances. As with the *t* test, in practice you obtain quite acceptable results even when your populations are moderately far from normal and have moderately different variances. In Chapter 11, we consider what to do when you have reason to think that your populations are a long way from meeting these assumptions.

Comparing Each Group to Each Other Group

The result of an analysis of variance is about whether the means of three or more populations are, overall, different from each other. This is not quite the same thing as the populations all having different means. It could be that two of the populations have about the same mean but both of these are different from the mean of a third population. In this case, if the populations that have different means have very different means, then the overall analysis of variance might turn out significant (even though some groups have about the same mean). Even when we find a significant analysis of variance, we still do

---

[1] Several real studies have looked at whether knowing a defendant's prior criminal record affects the likelihood of conviction. The overall conclusion seems to be reasonably consistent with that of the fictional study described here. For a review of such studies, see Dane and Wrightsman (1982).

[2] There are some computational formulas that are helpful if you have to do an analysis of variance without a computer. Also, the procedure you have learned to do in the chapter only works (without modification) if you have equal numbers of scores in each group. These computational formulas also work when there are unequal numbers of scores in each group. These formulas require that you first figure an intermediary for the two variance estimates, called "sum of squares" or SS for short. For the between-group estimate, $S^2_{\text{Between}} = SS_{\text{Between}} / df_{\text{Between}}$. The formula for SS_{Between} is as follows,

$$SS_{\text{Between}} = \frac{(\Sigma X_1)^2}{n_1} + \frac{(\Sigma X_2)^2}{n_2} + \cdots + \frac{(\Sigma X_{\text{Last}})^2}{n_{\text{Last}}} - \frac{(\Sigma X)^2}{N}$$

(10-7)

For the within-group estimate, $S^2_{\text{Within}} = SS_{\text{Within}} / df_{\text{Within}}$. The formula for SS_{Within} is as follows,

$$SS_{\text{Within}} = \Sigma X^2 - \frac{(\Sigma X)^2}{N} - SS_{\text{Between}}$$

(10-8)

However, as usual, we urge you to use the definitional formulas as we have presented in the chapter to work out the practice problems. The definitional formulas are closely related to the meaning of the procedures. Using the definitional formulas to work out the problems helps you learn the meaning of the analysis of variance.

TABLE 10–5
Steps for Conducting an Analysis of Variance (When Sample Sizes Are Equal)

1. Restate the question as a research hypothesis and a null hypothesis about the populations.
2. Determine the characteristics of the comparison distribution.
   (a) The comparison distribution is an F distribution.
   (b) The numerator degrees of freedom is the number of groups minus 1: $df_{Between} = N_{Groups} - 1$.
   (c) The denominator degrees of freedom is the sum of the degrees of freedom in each group (the number in the group minus 1): $df_{Within} = df_1 + df_2 + \ldots + df_{Last}$.
3. Determine the cutoff sample score on the comparison distribution at which the null hypothesis should be rejected.
   (a) Determine the desired significance level.
   (b) Look up the appropriate cutoff in an F table, using the degrees of freedom from Step 2.
4. Determine the score of the sample on the comparison distribution. (This will be an F ratio.)
   (a) Calculate the between-group population variance estimate ($S^2_{Between}$).
      (i) Calculate the means of each group.
      (ii) Calculate a variance estimate based on the means of the groups: $S^2_M = \Sigma(M - GM)^2/df_{Between}$.
      (iii) Convert this estimate of the variance of a distribution of means to an estimate of the variance of a population of individual scores by multiplying it times the number of scores in each group: $S^2_{Between} = (S^2_M)(n)$.
   (b) Calculate the within-group population variance estimate S^2_{Within}.
      (i) Calculate population variance estimates based on each group's scores: For each group, $S^2 = \Sigma(X - M)^2/(n - 1)$.
      (ii) Average these variance estimates: $S^2_{Within} = (S^2_1 + S^2_2 + \ldots + S^2_{Last})/NGroups$.
   (c) Calculate the F ratio: $F = S^2_{Between}/S^2_{Within}$.
5. Compare the scores from Steps 3 and 4 to decide whether to reject the null hypothesis.

not know which population means are different from which other population means.

For this reason, we often do not stop after getting a significant result with an analysis of variance. Instead, we may go on to compare each population to each other population. For example, with three groups, we would compare group 1 to group 2, group 1 to group 3, and group 2 to group 3. We could do each of these comparisons using ordinary t tests for independent means. However, there is a problem with using ordinary t tests like this. The problem is that we are making three comparisons, each at the .05 level. The overall chance of at least one of them being significant just by chance is more like .15.

Some statisticians argue that it is all right to do three t tests in this situation because we have first checked that the overall analysis of variance is significant. These are called **protected t tests.** We are protected from making too big an error by the overall analysis of variance being significant. Other statisticians believe that the protected t test is not enough protection. Advanced statistics texts give procedures that provide even more protection.

protected t tests

Effect Size and Power for the Analysis of Variance

Effect Size

Effect size for the analysis of variance is a little more complex than for a t test. With the t test, we took the difference between the two means and divided by the standard deviation. In the analysis of variance, we still can divide by the standard deviation. In analysis of variance, we have more than two means, so it is not obvious just what is the equivalent to the difference between the means, the numerator in figuring effect size. Cohen (1988) suggests that in the analysis of variance, we should think of the effect size as the variation among the means. Specifically, Cohen recommends using the standard deviation of the distribution of means. He defines the **effect size for the analysis of variance** as the standard deviation of the distribution of means divided by the standard deviation of the individuals. Stated as a formula in terms of estimated variances,

effect size for the analysis of variance

$$\text{Estimated Effect Size} = \frac{S_M}{S_{\text{Within}}}$$

(10–9)

Cohen's conventions for effect size for analysis of variance are .10 for a small effect, .25 for a medium effect, and .40 for a large effect size.

Consider our fictional criminal-record experiment. In that study we computed S^2_M, the estimated variance of the distribution of means based on the means of our three samples, to be 4.34. S_M, the square root of S^2_M, is 2.08. We computed S^2_{Within}, the estimate of the variance of each population of individuals, based on the variance estimates using each group's scores, to be 5.33. S_w, the square root of S^2_{Within}, is 2.31. Applying the formula for effect size,

$$\text{Estimated Effect Size} = \frac{S_M}{S_{\text{Within}}} = \frac{2.08}{2.31} = .90$$

This is a very large effect size (thanks to our fictional data).

With a bit of algebraic manipulation, it turns out that the effect size using estimated variances can be computed directly from knowing the F and the number of scores in each group. The formula is,

$$\text{Estimated Effect Size} = \frac{\sqrt{F}}{\sqrt{n}}$$

(10–10)

For example, in the criminal record study we had calculated F to be 4.07 and there were five people in each group. Using the formula,

$$\text{Estimated Effect Size} = \frac{\sqrt{F}}{\sqrt{n}} = \frac{\sqrt{4.07}}{\sqrt{5}} = \frac{2.02}{2.24} = .90$$

This formula is very helpful when evaluating the effect size of a completed study reported in a published research article.

Power

Table 10–6 shows the approximate power for the .05 significance level for small, medium, and large effect sizes; sample size of 10, 20, 30, 40, 50, and 100 per group; and three, four, and five groups. These are the most common values of the various influences on power.[3]

[3]More detailed tables are provided in Cohen (1988, pp. 289–354). When using these tables, note that the value of u at the top of each table refers to df_{Between}, which in the case of a one-way analysis of variance is the number of groups minus 1, not the number of groups directly as used in our Table 10–6.

TABLE 10–6
Approximate Power for Studies Using the Analysis of Variance Testing Hypotheses at the .05 Significance Level

Participants per Group (n)	Small (.10)	Effect Size Medium (.25)	Large (.40)
Three groups ($df_{Between} = 2$)			
10	.07	.20	.45
20	.09	.38	.78
30	.12	.55	.93
40	.15	.68	.98
50	.18	.79	.99
100	.32	.98	*
Four groups ($df_{Between} = 3$)			
10	.07	.21	.51
20	.10	.43	.85
30	.13	.61	.96
40	.16	.76	.99
50	.19	.85	*
100	.36	.99	*
Five groups ($df_{Between} = 4$)			
10	.07	.23	.56
20	.10	.47	.90
30	.13	.67	.98
40	.17	.81	*
50	.21	.90	*
100	.40	*	*

*Nearly 1.

For example, a planned study comparing five groups of 10 participants each, with an expected large effect size (.40) and using the .05 significance level, would have power of .56. This means that even if the research hypothesis is in fact true and has a large effect size, there is only a little greater than even chance (56%) that the study will come out significant.

As we have noted in previous chapters, determining power is especially useful when interpreting the practical implication of a nonsignificant result. For example, suppose you have read a study using an analysis of variance for four groups of 30 participants each in which the researcher reports a nonsignificant result at the .05 level. Table 10–6 shows a power of only .13 for a small effect size. This suggests that even if such a small effect exists in the population, this study would be very unlikely to have come out significant. The table shows a power of .96 for a large effect size. This suggests that if a large effect existed in the population, it almost surely would have shown up in this study.

Planning Sample Size

Table 10–7 gives the approximate number of participants needed in each group for 80% power at the .05 significance level for estimated small, medium, and large effect sizes for studies with three, four, and five groups.[4]

[4]More detailed tables are provided in Cohen (1988, pp. 381–389). If you use these, see footnote 3 in this chapter.

TABLE 10–7

Approximate Number of Participants Needed in Each Group (Assuming Equal Sample Sizes) for 80% Power for the One-Way Analysis of Variance Testing Hypotheses at the .05 Significance Level

	Effect Size		
	Small (.10)	Medium (.25)	Large (.40)
Three groups ($df_{Between} = 2$)	322	52	21
Four groups ($df_{Between} = 3$)	274	45	18
Five groups ($df_{Between} = 4$)	240	39	16

For example, suppose you are planning a study involving four groups and you expect a small effect size (and will use the .05 significance level). For 80% power you would need 274 participants in each group, a total of 1,096 in all. However, suppose you could adjust the research plan so that it was now reasonable to predict a large effect size (perhaps by using more accurate measures and a more powerful experimental manipulation). Now you would need only 18 in each of the four groups, for a total of 72.

Factorial Analysis of Variance

Factorial analysis of variance

Factorial analysis of variance is an extension of the procedures you have just learned. Factorial analysis of variance is a wonderfully flexible and efficient approach that handles many types of studies used in experimental research. The actual computation of a factorial analysis of variance is beyond what we can cover in an introductory book. Our goal in this section is to help you understand the basic approach and the terminology so you can make sense of research articles that use this common method.

We will introduce factorial analysis of variance with an example. Hobfoll and Leiberman (1987), two Israeli researchers, were interested in how married women cope with the outcome of pregnancy (normal births, miscarriages). In one of their studies, they measured depression following the end of a pregnancy, comparing women with high and low self-esteem. They were also interested in whether depression was different for women who had high or low intimacy with their husbands. Hobfoll and Leiberman could have conducted two studies, one comparing women with high versus low self-esteem, another comparing women with high versus low intimacy with their husband.

Instead, they looked at both self-esteem and intimacy in a single study. That is, they considered four groups of women (see Table 10–8): (a) with high self-esteem and high intimacy, (b) with high self-esteem and low intimacy, (c) with low self-esteem and high intimacy, and (d) with low self-esteem and low intimacy.

Factorial Research Design Defined

factorial research design

The Hobfoll and Leiberman study is an example of a **factorial research design.** A factorial research design is a study in which the effect of two variables is studied at once by making groupings of every combination of the two

TABLE 10–8
Factorial Design Employed by Hobfoll and Leiberman (1987)

	Self-Esteem	
	High	*Low*
Intimacy *High*	a	c
Intimacy *Low*	b	d

variables. In our example, there were two levels of self-esteem (high and low) and two levels of intimacy (high and low). This allows four possible combinations. Hobfoll and Leiberman used all four of these combinations in the study.

A factorial research design has a major advantage over conducting separate studies of each variable. With the factorial design, you can study both variables at once, without needing twice as many participants. In the example, Hobfoll and Leiberman were able to use all the women to study self-esteem and also to use all the women to study intimacy. This way they were able to do both studies with a single group of women.

Interaction Effects

There is another, even more important advantage of a factorial research design. With a factorial research design you can study the effects of the combination of your two variables. In the example, self-esteem and intimacy might affect depression in a simple additive way. Their combined influence is just the sum of their separate influences; or, it could be that only one, or neither, has an influence. In all these cases, looking at them in combination does not add any interesting information. However, it is also possible that the combination of the two changes the result. Perhaps high self-esteem and high intimacy combine so that the whole is more than the sum of the parts, and together they create a much bigger drop in depression than the sum of their effects separately. Perhaps they cancel each other out somehow when both occur together. Perhaps self-esteem makes a difference only in the low-intimacy group or only in the high-intimacy group.

These situations in which the *combination* of variables has a special effect is called an **interaction effect.** It is an interaction effect when the effect of one variable depends on the presence or absence of the other variable. In the Hobfoll and Leiberman study, there was an interaction effect. Look at Table 10–9. The result was that the women in three of the four combinations

interaction effect

TABLE 10–9
Mean Depression Scores in the Hobfoll and Leiberman (1987) Study

	Self-Esteem	
	High	*Low*
Intimacy *High*	18.33	20.67
Intimacy *Low*	17.57	32.00

had very little depression. Only the low-intimacy and low-self-esteem group had high depression. The women managed well enough without intimacy or without self-esteem, but not without both.

Suppose the researchers had looked at self-esteem and intimacy in two separate studies. They would have concluded that each has a moderate effect. That conclusion is technically correct but in fact misleading. For example, the average depression for the low self-esteem women overall was greater than the average for all high self-esteem women overall. However, most of that difference was due to those low on intimacy.

Some Terminology

two-way analysis of variance

one-way analysis of variance

main effect

cell
cell mean

marginal means

The Hobfoll and Leiberman study is an example of what is called a **two-way analysis of variance** (or a *two-way factorial research design*). By contrast, the situations we considered earlier in the chapter (such as the attachment style study or the criminal record experiment) were examples of a **one-way analysis of variance.** Such studies are called one-way because they study the effect of only one variable (such as a person's attachment style or information about a defendant's criminal record).

In a two-way analysis, each variable or "way" (each dimension in the diagram) is a possible **main effect.** If the result for a variable, averaging across the other variable or variables, is significant, it is said to be a main effect. This is in contrast to the possibility of an interaction effect of the combination of variables. In the Hobfoll and Leiberman study, there was a possibility of two main effects (one for self-esteem and one for intimacy) and one interaction effect (the combination of intimacy and self-esteem). In a two-way analysis of variance, you are always testing two main effects and one two-way interaction.

Each grouping combination in a factorial design is called a **cell.** The mean of the scores in each grouping is called a **cell mean.** For example, in the Hobfoll and Leiberman study, there are four cells and four cell means, one for each combination of the self-esteem and intimacy levels. That is, one cell is high self-esteem, high intimacy (as shown in Table 10–9, its mean is 18.33); one cell is low self-esteem, high intimacy (20.67); one cell is high self-esteem, low intimacy (17.57); and one cell is low self-esteem, low intimacy (32.00).

The means just considering one variable at a time are called **marginal means.** For example, in the Hobfoll and Leiberman study there are four marginal means, one mean for all the high self-esteem women, one for all low self-esteem women, one for all high intimacy women, and one for all low intimacy women. (Because we were mainly interested in the interaction, these means were not shown in the tables.)

To look at a main effect, you focus on the marginal means. To look at the interaction effect, you focus on the pattern of individual cell means.

Recognizing and Interpreting Interaction Effects

It is very important to understand interaction effects. Not only are they an important part of understanding the results of any factorial study, but in many experiments the interaction effect is the main point of the research.

As we have seen, an interaction effect is when the effect of one variable depends on the level of another variable. In the Hobfoll and Leiberman

(1987) study results (Table 10–9), there was an interaction effect because the effect of self-esteem was different with high intimacy than with low intimacy.

An interaction effect can be made clear in three ways: in words, in numbers, or in a graph. You can think out an interaction effect in words by saying that an interaction effect occurs when the effect of one variable changes according to the level of another variable. In our Hobfoll and Leiberman example, you can say that the effect of self-esteem depends on the level of intimacy. (You can also say that the effect of intimacy depends on the level of self-esteem. Interaction effects are completely symmetrical, in that you can state them in either direction.)

You can see an interaction effect numerically by looking at the pattern of cell means. If there is an interaction effect, the differences in cell means across one row will not be the same as the differences in cell means across another row. In the Hobfoll and Leiberman example, the difference in the cell means across the high-intimacy row is such that the high self-esteemers (18.33) scored about the same as the low self-esteemers (20.67). The difference for high versus low self-esteem for those with high intimacy was only 2.34 points on the depression scale. Looking at the low-intimacy row, the cell means differ quite a bit—17.57 versus 32.00, making a difference of 14.43.

Table 10–10 gives cell and marginal means for six possible results of a fictional two-way factorial study looking at the effects of age and education on income. Age has two levels (younger, such as 25 to 29, versus older, such as 30 to 34) and education has two levels (high school versus college). These fictional results are exaggerated, to make clear when there are interactions and main effects. In real life, we often find small mean differences in the direction of an interaction or main effect that are not large enough to be statistically significant.

In Outcome A, there is an interaction because in the "Younger" row, education makes no difference, but in the "Older" row, the college cell mean is much higher than the high school cell mean. One way to express this verbally would be to say that these results indicate that education is not related to

TABLE 10–10
Possible Means for Results of a Study of the Relation of Age and Education to Income

	Outcome A				Outcome B				Outcome C		
	High School	*College*	*Overall*		*High School*	*College*	*Overall*		*High School*	*College*	*Overall*
Younger	20	20	20		30	20	25		10	30	20
Older	20	30	25		20	30	25		20	40	30
Overall	20	25			25	25			15	35	

	Outcome D				Outcome E				Outcome F		
	High School	*College*	*Overall*		*High School*	*College*	*Overall*		*High School*	*College*	*Overall*
Younger	10	10	10		20	30	25		20	30	25
Older	60	60	60		20	40	30		30	50	40
Overall	35	35			20	35			25	40	

income for the younger group, but for the older group, people with a college education earn much more than those with less education.

Fictional Outcome B is also an interaction, because in the "Younger" row the high school mean income is higher than the college mean income, but in the "Older" row the high school mean income is lower. Expressed verbally, this pattern indicates that among younger people, those with only a high school education make more money (perhaps because they entered the workplace earlier or the kinds of jobs they have start out at a higher level), but among older people those with a college education make more money.

Fictional Outcome C, interestingly, is not an interaction effect. In the "Younger" row, the high school mean is 20 lower than the college mean, and the same is true in the "Older" row. In words, whether young or old, people with college educations earn $20,000 more.

In fictional Outcome D, there is also no interaction—in neither row is there any difference. Regardless of education, older people earn $50,000 more.

Fictional Outcome E is an interaction because in the "Younger" row, the college mean is 10 higher, but in the "Older" row, the college mean is 20 higher. So among young people, college-educated people earn a little more, but among older people, those with a college education earn much more.

Finally, Outcome F is also an interaction effect because there is a smaller difference in the "Younger" row than in the "Older" row. As with Outcome E, this pattern indicates that for people with a college education, income increases more with age than it does for those with only a high school education.[5]

Identifying Interaction Effects Graphically

Another common way of making sense of interaction effects is graphing them. The way to graph an interaction effect is easiest to show with an example. Figure 10–4a is taken from the results graph that Hobfoll and Leiberman included in their article. The two self-esteem levels are across the bottom, and there is a line for each level of intimacy.

The graphs in Figure 10–5 are for the same fictional outcomes we considered earlier involving the relation of age and education to income.

One thing to notice about such graphs is this: Whenever there is an interaction, the lines in the graph will not be parallel. Being nonparallel is just a graphic way of saying that the pattern of differences between the cell means from row to row is not the same. Notice that Outcomes C and D in Figure 10–5 have lines that are parallel. These were the examples that did not have interactions. All the other outcomes, which did have interactions, have lines that are not completely parallel.

[5]Based on 1990 statistics from the U.S. Department of Education, the actual situation in the United States is closest to Outcome F, though not as extreme. People with a college education earn more than those with only a high school education in both age groups, but the difference is somewhat greater for the older group. However, it is important to keep in mind that whether or not people receive a college education is also related to the social class of their parents and other factors that may affect income more than education does.

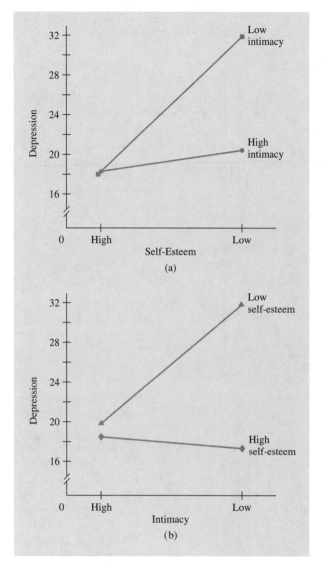

FIGURE 10–4
(a) Graph of Table 10–9 results as presented in the Hobfoll and Leiberman (1987) study. (b) Alternative version. ([a] From Hobfoll, S. E., & Leiberman, J. R. [1987]. Personality and social resources in immediate and continued stress resistance among women. *Journal of Personality and Social Psychology,* 52, 18–26. Copyright, 1987, by the American Psychological Association. Used by permission of the author.)

Relation of Interaction and Main Effects

It is possible for any combination of main and interaction effects to be significant. For example, they may all be significant, as in the Hobfoll and Leiberman study. Or there can be an interaction effect with no main effects (a perfect crossover of effects), as in Outcome B in the age and education example. See how many possibilities you can identify in the two sets of fictional outcomes in Table 10–10. (When examining the corresponding graphs in Figure 10–5, notice that a main effect for the variable across the bottom will appear as the lines averaging out to be not flat, and that a main effect for the variable whose levels represent the different lines appears as one of the lines being placed higher, overall, than the other.)

When there is no interaction, a main effect has a straightforward meaning. However, when there is an interaction along with a main effect, you have to be cautious in drawing conclusions about the main effect. In the Hobfoll

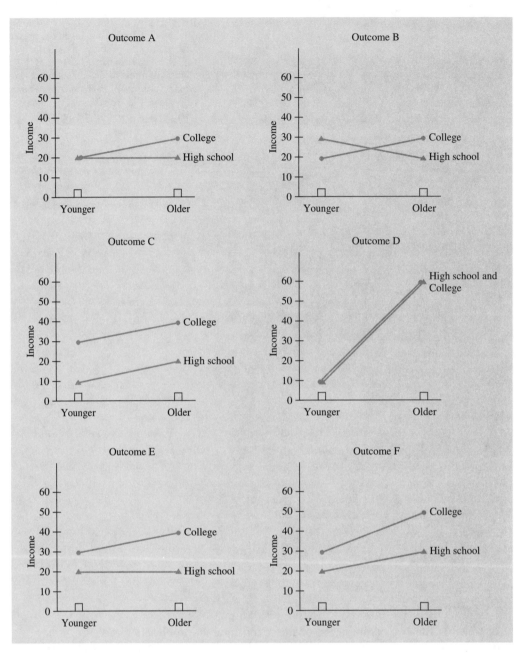

FIGURE 10–5
Graphs for the outcomes of the fictional data shown in Table 10–10.

and Leiberman study, there were two main effects, along with the interaction. But the pattern of cell means (and the graph) make it clear that the main effects are entirely due to the low self-esteem, low intimacy cell. It would be misleading to make any statement about intimacy or self-esteem in general without noting that the effect of either of these really depends on the other.

Sometimes the main effect clearly holds up over and above any interaction. For example, in Outcome F in the age and education example (Table 10–10), it seems clear that the main effect for age holds up over and above the interaction. That is, it is true for both people with and without a college education that older people earn more. (There is still an interaction, of course, because the extent to which older people earn more differs according to education.)

Extensions and Special Cases of the Factorial Analysis of Variance

Analysis of variance is very versatile. Factorial designs can be extended into three-way and higher designs. There are also procedures to handle situations in which the same participants are tested more than once. This is like the *t* test for dependent means but works with more than two testings. It is called a *repeated measures analysis of variance.* Yet another special extension of the analysis of variance are procedures for figuring out just which groups or combinations of groups in analysis of variance are responsible for an overall significant difference. For example, in the criminal record study, we found an overall difference among the three experimental conditions. Ordinarily a researcher would next want to know which particular conditions were significantly different from each other. The procedures for doing these kinds of tests are called *multiple comparisons.*

Analyses of Variance as Described in Research Articles

A one-way analysis of variance is usually described in a research article by giving the *F*, the degrees of freedom, and the significance level. For example, "$F(3, 67) = 5.21, p < .01$." The means for the groups usually are given in a table, although if there are only a few groups and only one or a few measures, the means may be given in the text. Returning to the criminal record experiment example, we could describe the analysis of variance results this way: "The means for the criminal record, clean record, and no information groups were 7.0, 4.0, and 5.0, respectively, $F(2, 12) = 4.07, p < .05$."

In a factorial analysis of variance, results are usually presented with a description in the text plus a table. The text gives the *F* ratio and the information that goes with it for each main and interaction effect. The table gives the cell means and sometimes also the marginal means. If there is an interaction effect, there may also be a graph. For example, Hobfoll and Leiberman (1987) described their primary result as follows:

> Mean depression scores for this analysis are presented in Table [10–9] and depicted in Figure [10–4a]. Self-Esteem, $F(1, 85) = 12.73, p < .001$, and Spouse Intimacy, $F(1, 85) = 5.06, p < .05$, and their interaction, $F(1, 85) = 6.63, p < .01$, were significant. Both high Self-Esteem and Spouse Intimacy resulted in lower depression at event occurrence. However, the interaction indicated that women possessing either one or both resources did equally well, whereas women having neither resource were significantly more depressed than those possessing either one or both. (p. 22)

Summary

The analysis of variance (ANOVA) is used to test hypotheses involving differences among means of several samples. The procedure compares two estimates of population variance. One, called the "within-group estimate," is determined by averaging the variance estimates from each of the samples. The other, called the "between-group estimate," is based on the variation among the means of the samples.

The F ratio is the between-group estimate divided by the within-group estimate. The null hypothesis is that all the samples come from populations with the same mean. If the null hypothesis is true, the F ratio should be about 1, because the two population variance estimates are based on the same element, the variation within each of the populations. If the research hypothesis is true, and the samples come from populations with different means, the F ratio should be larger than 1. This is because the between-group estimate is now influenced by the variation both within the populations and between them. The within-group estimate is still affected only by the variation within each of the populations.

When the samples are of equal size, the within-group population variance estimate is the average of the estimates of the population variance computed from each sample. The between-group population variance estimate is done in two steps. First, you estimate the variance of the distribution of means based on the means of your actual samples. (This is figured with the usual formula for estimating population variance from sample scores.) Second, you multiply this estimate times the sample size. This step takes you from the variance of the distribution of means to the variance of the distribution of individual scores.

The distribution of F ratios when the null hypothesis is true is a mathematically defined distribution that is skewed to the right. Significance cutoffs are given on an F table according to the degrees of freedom for each population variance estimate, the between-group (numerator) estimate being based on the number of groups minus 1 and the within-group (denominator) estimate being based on the sum of the degrees of freedom in each sample.

The assumptions for the analysis of variance are the same as for the t test: the populations must be normally distributed, with equal variances. Like the t test, the analysis of variance is considered robust to moderate violations of these assumptions.

Researchers may follow up an analysis of variance with a comparison of each group to each other group with a series of t tests. If the overall analysis of variance was significant, the researcher is protected somewhat from the several t tests giving a few significant results by chance. These are called *protected t tests.*

Effect size in the analysis of variance can be computed for a completed study as the square root of F divided by the square root of the number of participants in each group. Power depends on effect size, number of people in the study, significance level, and number of groups.

In a factorial research design, participants are put into groupings according to the combinations of the variables whose effects are being studied. Such designs mean that you can study the effects of two variables without needing twice as many participants and also that you can study the effects of combinations of the two variables (interaction effects). An interaction effect is when the effect of one variable depends on the presence or absence of the other variable. A main effect is the effect of one variable, ignoring the effect of the other variable.

Key Terms

analysis of variance (ANOVA)
between-group estimate of the population variance ($S^2_{Between}$)
cell
cell mean
denominator degrees of freedom (df_{Within})
effect size for the analysis of variance

factorial analysis of variance
factorial research design
F distribution
F ratio
F table
grand mean (GM)
interaction effect
main effect
marginal mean

numerator degrees of freedom ($df_{Between}$)
one-way analysis of variance
protected t tests
two-way analysis of variance
within-group estimate of the population variance (S^2_{Within})

Practice Problems

These problems involve computation (with the assistance of a calculator). Most real-life statistics problems are done on a computer. Even if you have a computer, do this by hand to ingrain the method in your mind.

For practice in using a computer to solve statistics problems, refer to the computer section of each chapter of the Student's Study Guide and Computer Workbook *that accompanies this text.*

All data are fictional (unless an actual citation is given).

Answers to selected problems are given at the back of the book.

1. For each of the following studies, decide if the null hypothesis (that the groups come from identical populations) can be rejected at the .05 level. Also compute the effect size and approximate power.

(a)

	Group 1	Group 2	Group 3
n	10	10	10
M	7.4	6.8	6.8
S^2	.82	.90	.80

(b)

	Group 1	Group 2	Group 3	Group 4
n	25	25	25	25
M	94	101	124	105
S	24	28	31	25

(c)

	Group 1	Group 2	Group 3	Group 4	Group 5
n	25	25	25	25	25
M	94	101	124	105	106
S	24	28	31	25	27

2. For each of the following studies, decide if the null hypothesis (that the groups come from identical populations) can be rejected at the .01 level. Also, compute the effect size.

(a)

Group 1	Group 2	Group 3
8	6	4
8	6	4
7	5	3
9	7	5

(b)

Group 1	Group 2	Group 3
12	10	8
04	02	0
12	10	8
04	02	0

3. Do students at various colleges differ in how sociable they are? Twenty-five students were randomly selected from each of three colleges in a particular city and were asked to report on the amount of time they spent socializing each day with other students. The results for College X was a mean of 5 and an estimated population variance of 2; for College Y, $M = 4$, $S^2 = 1.5$; and for College Z, $M = 6$, $S^2 = 2.5$. What should you conclude? Use the .05 level. Explain your answer to someone who understands everything involved in conducting a t test for independent means but who has never heard of the analysis of variance.

4. A social worker at a small mental hospital was asked to determine whether there was any clear difference in the length of stay of patients with different categories of diagnosis. Looking at the last four clients in each of the three major categories, the results (in terms of weeks of stay) were as follows:

Diagnosis Category

Affective Disorders	Cognitive Disorders	Drug-related Conditions
7	12	08
6	08	10
5	09	12
6	11	10

Using the .05 level, is there a significant difference in length of stay among diagnosis categories? Explain your answer to someone who understands everything involved in conducting a t test for independent means but who has never heard of the analysis of variance.

5. A researcher was interested in whether individuals working in different sectors of the company differed in their attitudes toward the company. The results for the three people surveyed in engineering were 10, 12, and 11; for the three in the marketing department, 6, 6, and 8; for the three in accounting, 7, 4, and 4; and for the three in production, 14, 16, and 13 (higher numbers mean more positive attitudes). Was there a significant difference in attitude toward the company among employees working in different sectors of the company at the .05 level? Explain your answer to a person who knows about hypothesis testing using the t test for independent means but is unfamiliar with the analysis of variance.

6. A researcher is concerned that the level of need for health care among prisoners is different in different types of prison facilities. The researcher randomly selects 40 prisoners from each of the three main types of prisons in a particular U.S. state and conducts exams to determine their need for health care, using a standard health assessment method. In the article describing the results, the researcher reported the means for each group and then added: "The need for health care among prisoners in the three types of prison systems appeared to be clearly different, $F(2, 117) = 5.62$, $p < .01$." Explain what this means to a person who has never had a course in statistics. As part of your discussion, compute the effect size (using Formula 10.8) and discuss its meaning.

7. Each of the following represents a table of means in a factorial design. Assuming that any differences are statistically significant, for each table, (a) make two graphs showing the results; (b) indicate which effects (main and interaction), if any, are found; and (c) describe the meaning of the pattern of means and any main or interaction effects (or the lack thereof) in words. (All data are fictional.)

(i) Dependent variable: Income (thousands of dollars)

Age	Young	Old
Lower	20	35
Upper	25	100

(ii) Dependent variable: Grade point average

Major	Science	Arts
Community	2.1	2.8
Liberal Arts	2.8	2.1

(iii) Dependent variable: Days sick per month

Gender	Females	Males
Exercisers	2.0	2.5
Controls	3.1	3.6

(iv) Dependent variable: Rated restaurant quality (10 = high)

City	New York	Chicago	Vancouver
Expensive	9	5	7
Moderate	6	4	6
Inexpensive	4	3	5

8. In a study by Baron, Burgess, and Kao (1991), male and female participants read accounts that included a description of a sexist act perpetrated by either a male or a female against a female. The 193 participants described the perpetrator in a way that could be scored for intensity of sexist behavior. Part of their Results section reads:

Perpetrator gender and subject gender main effects were both significant. Female subjects, compared with male subjects, gave more intense ratings to both male and female perpetrators . . . : $F(1, 189) = 5.06$, $p < .03$. . . . Furthermore, male perpetrators were seen as displaying more intense gender bias than female perpetrators: $F(1, 189) = 15.97$, $p < .0001$. The interaction between subject gender and perpetrator gender was nonsignificant in both analyses: $p < .34$. . . . These results can be seen in [the figure]. (p. 119).

Briefly describe the meaning of these results to a person who has never had a course in statistics. (Do not go into the computational details, just the basic logic of the pattern of means, the significant results, effect sizes, and issues of interpreting nonsignificant results.)

9. Cut up 100 little pieces of paper of about the same size and write a 1 on 16, a 2 on 34, a 3 on 34, and a 4 on 16 of them. (You are creating an approximately normal distribution.) Put the slips into a bowl or hat, mix them up, draw out two, write the numbers on them down, and put them back. Then draw out another two, write down their numbers, and put them back, and finally another two, write down their numbers, and put them back. (Strictly speaking, you should sample "with replacement"—that means putting each one, not two, back after writing its number down—but we want to save you a little time, and it should not make very much difference in this case.) Then, compute an analysis of variance for these three randomly selected groups of two each. Write down the F ratio, and repeat the entire drawing process and analysis of variance again. Do this entire process at least 20 times, and make a frequency polygon of your results. You are creating an F distribution for 2 (3 groups − 1) and 3 (2 − 1 in each of three groups) degrees of freedom. At what point do the top 5% of your F scores begin? Compare that to the 5% cutoff given on the F table in the Appendix for 2 and 3 degrees of freedom.

11

Chi-Square and Strategies When Population Distributions Are Not Normal

T HE hypothesis testing procedures you have learned in the last few chapters (the t test and the analysis of variance) are very versatile, but there are many research situations in which these methods cannot be used. One such situation is when the variable measured uses categories (such as a person's region of the country or religion). The t test and the analysis of variance all require that the variable have scores that are quantitative, such as rating on a 7-point scale or number of years served as mayor. Another research situation in which the ordinary t test and analysis of variance do not apply is when the populations clearly do not follow a normal curve.

This chapter examines hypothesis testing in these two situations in which the ordinary hypothesis testing procedures cannot be used properly. The first half of the chapter focuses on chi-square tests.[1] **Chi-square tests** are used when the scores are on a nominal variable. The second half of the chapter focuses on strategies for hypothesis testing when you cannot assume that the population distributions are even roughly normal.

Chi-square tests

Chi-Square Tests

Let us begin with an example. Stasser, Taylor, and Hanna (1989) conducted a study comparing how different kinds of small groups share information. The group discussions were about three fictional candidates running for student body office. As part of setting up the study, the researchers tried to write

---

[1]Chi is the Greek letter X; it is pronounced *ki,* rhyming with high and pie.

descriptions of the three candidates that they hoped would be equally appealing. That is, they wanted to describe the candidates so that just from reading about them, they would be about equally preferred. (Then it was hoped that different kinds of group discussion would create a greater preference for one or the other.) So when the study was completed, one of the first things the researchers did was to check whether the three candidates were, in fact, equally preferred on ratings made before the group discussion.

Here is what Stasser et al. found. Of the 531 people in the study, 197 (37%) initially preferred Candidate A, 120 (23%) preferred Candidate B, and 214 (40%) preferred Candidate C. If the three candidates had been equally preferred, then about 177 (33 1/3%) of the subjects should have preferred each. This information is laid out in the second and third columns of Table 11–1. That is, the second column shows the breakdown of preferences the researchers actually observed and the third column shows the breakdown you would expect if the candidates had been exactly equally preferred. Clearly, there is a discrepancy. The question is this: Should we assume that this discrepancy is no more than we would expect just by chance for a sample of this size? That is, even if among people in general (the population) these three candidates would be equally preferred, in a particular sample of individuals from that population we would not expect a perfectly equal breakdown of preferences. If the breakdown in the sample is a long way from equal, we would have reason to doubt that the preferences in the population really are equal. In other words, we are in a hypothesis-testing situation, much like the ones we have been considering all along; but with a big difference too.

In the previous situations, the scores have all been numerical values on some dimension, such as score on a standard achievement test, length of time in a relationship, employer's ratings of an employee's job effectiveness on a 9-point scale, response in a reaction time test, or number of people in a family. Preference for a particular candidate, by contrast, is an example of what in Chapter 1 we called a **nominal variable** (or a *categorical variable*). A nominal variable is one in which the information is the number of people in each category. (These are called nominal variables because the different categories or levels of the variable have names instead of numbers.)

nominal variable

Hypothesis testing with nominal variables use what are called chi-square tests. The chi square tests were originally developed by Karl Pearson (see Box 11–1).

TABLE 11–1
Observed and Expected Frequencies of Preferences for Three Candidates

Candidate Preferred	Observed Frequency[a] (O)	Expected Frequency (E)	Difference $(O - E)$	Difference Squared $(O - E)^2$	Difference Squared Weighted by Expected Frequency $(O - E)^2/E$
A	197	177	20	400	2.26
B	120	177	–57	3,249	18.36
C	214	177	37	1,369	7.73

[a]Data from Stasser, Taylor, and Hanna (1989).

BOX 11–1

Karl Pearson: Inventor of Chi-Square and Center of Controversy

Karl Pearson, sometimes hailed as the founder of the science of statistics, was born in 1857, the son of a Yorkshire barrister. Most of both his virtues and his vices are revealed in what he reported to his colleague Julia Bell as his earliest memory: He was sitting in his high chair, sucking his thumb, when he was told to stop or his thumb would wither away. Pearson looked at his two thumbs and silently concluded, "I can't see that the thumb I suck is any smaller than the other. I wonder if she could be lying to me." Here we see Pearson's faith in himself and in observational evidence and his rejection of authority. We also see his tendency to doubt the character of people with whom he disagreed.

Pearson studied mathematics on a scholarship at Cambridge. Soon after he arrived, he requested to be excused from compulsory divinity lectures and chapel. As soon as his request was granted, however, he appeared in chapel. The dean summoned him for an explanation, and Pearson declared that he had asked to be excused not from chapel "but from compulsory chapel."

After graduation, Pearson traveled and studied in Germany, becoming a socialist and a self-described "free-thinker." Returning to England, he wrote an attack on Christianity under a pen name and in 1885 founded a "Men and Women's Club" to promote discussion of the relations between the sexes. The club died out, but through it he met his wife, Maria Sharp.

Pearson eventually turned to statistics out of his interest in proving the theory of evolution, being especially influenced by Sir Francis Galton's work (see Box 3–1). Most of Pearson's research from 1893 to 1901 was on the laws of heredity and evolution, but he needed better sta-

tistical methods for his work, leading to his most famous contribution, the chi-square test. Pearson also invented the method of computing correlation used today and coined the terms histogram, skew, and spurious correlation. When he felt that biology journals failed to appreciate his work properly, he founded the famous journal of statistics called *Biometrika*. In short, he led statistics from its early position as a matter largely ignored to one central to the scientific method, especially in the natural sciences.

Unfortunately, Pearson was a great fan of eugenics, the "improvement" of the human race through selective breeding, and his work was later used by the Nazis as justification for their treatment of Jews and other ethnic minorities. As Pearson aged, his opinions met strong resistance and much discrediting evidence from other, younger statisticians, which only turned Pearson against more and more of his colleagues.

Indeed, throughout his life, Pearson was a man who evoked either devoted friendship or deep dislike. William S. Gosset (see Box 8–1), inventor of the *t* test, was one of his friends. Sir Ronald Fisher, inventor of the analysis of variance and a man associated with even more extreme attitudes (he is described in Box 10–1), was one of Pearson's worst enemies. The kindly, peaceable Gosset, friends of both, was always trying to smooth matters between them. In 1933, Pearson finally retired, and Fisher, of all persons, took over his chair, the Galton Professorship of Eugenics at University College in London. In 1936, the two entered into their bitterest argument yet; Pearson died the same year.

References: Peters (1987); Stigler (1986); Tankard (1984).

The Chi-Square Statistic and the Chi-Square Test for Goodness of Fit

The basic idea of any chi-square test is that you compare how well an observed breakdown of people over various categories fits the breakdown you expected. In terms of the candidate example, you are comparing the observed breakdown of 197, 120, and 214 to the expected breakdown of 177, 177, and 177. A breakdown of numbers of people expected in each category is actually a frequency distribution, as you learned in Chapter 1. A chi-square test is more formally described as comparing an observed frequency distribution to an expected frequency distribution. Overall, what the hypothesis testing involves is first calculating a number for the amount of mismatch between the **observed frequency** and the **expected frequency** and then seeing whether that number is a greater mismatch than you would expect by chance.

Let us begin with considering how you would come up with that number for the amount of mismatch between the observed and expected frequencies. The degree of mismatch between observed and expected for any one category is simply the observed frequency minus the expected frequency. For example, in the Stasser et al. (1989) study, for Candidate A the observed frequency of 197 is 20 more than the expected frequency of 177 (1/3 of 571). For the second category, the difference is –57. For the third, 37.

We do not use these differences directly. One reason is that because some are positive and some negative, they would cancel each other out. We solve that problem by squaring each difference. (This is the same strategy we saw in Chapter 2 when dealing with difference scores in figuring the variance.) In the example, the squared difference for Candidate A is 20 squared, or 400. For Candidate B it is 3,249. For C, 1,369.

In the Stasser et al. example, the expected frequencies are the same in each category. In many other research situations, expected frequencies for the different categories may not be the same. A particular amount of difference between observed and expected has a different importance according to what the expected frequency is. For example, a difference of 8 between observed and expected is a much bigger mismatch if the expected frequency is 10 than if the expected frequency is 1,000. If the expected frequency is 10, a difference of 8 would mean that the observed frequency was 18 or 2, frequencies that are dramatically different from 10. If the expected frequency is 1,000, a difference of 8 is only a slight mismatch. (It would mean that the observed frequency was 1,008 or 992, frequencies that are only slightly different from 1,000.)

To come up with a good number to show the degree of mismatch between observed and expected, we need to adjust this difference taking into account the expected frequency for its category. This is done by dividing your squared difference for a category by the expected frequency for that category. If the expected frequency for a particular category is 10, you divide the squared difference by 10. If the expected frequency for the category was 1,000, you would divide the observed frequency by 1,000. In this way, we put the squared difference onto a more appropriate scale of comparison.

In our example, for Candidate A you would do this adjustment by dividing the squared difference of 400 by 177, giving 2.26. For Candidate B, 3,249 divided by 177 gives 18.36. For Candidate C, 1,369 divided by 177 gives 7.73.

What remains is to get an overall indication of the mismatch between observed and expected frequencies. This final step is done by adding up the results for all the categories. That is, you take the result of the squared difference divided by the expected frequency for the first category, plus the result of the squared difference divided by the expected frequency for the second category, and so on. In the example, this would be 2.26 plus 18.36 plus 7.73, for a total of 28.35.

This final number (the sum of the weighted squared differences) is an overall indication of the amount of mismatch between the expected and observed frequencies. It is called the **chi-square statistic.** In terms of a formula,

$$X^2 = \Sigma \frac{(O-E)^2}{E}$$

$$(11\text{–}1)$$

In this formula, X^2 is the chi-square statistic. Σ is the summation sign, telling you to sum over all the different categories. O is the observed frequency for a category (the number of people actually found in that category in the study). E is the expected frequency for a category.

Applying the formula to the Stasser example,

$$X^2 = \Sigma \frac{(O-E)^2}{E} = \frac{(197-177)^2}{177} + \frac{(120-177)^2}{177} + \frac{(214-177)^2}{177} = 28.35$$

Summary of Steps for Calculating the Chi-Square Statistic

1. Determine the actual, observed frequencies in each category.
2. Determine the expected frequencies in each category.
3. In each category, compute observed minus expected frequencies.
4. Square these differences in each category.
5. Divide each squared difference by the expected frequency for its category.
6. Add up the results of Step 5 for all the categories.

The Chi-Square Distribution

The next question is whether the chi-square statistic you have figured is a bigger mismatch than you would expect by chance. To answer that, you need to know how likely it is to get chi-square statistics of various sizes by chance. That is, you need the distribution of chi-square statistics that would arise by chance. Fortunately, it turns out that so long as we have a reasonable number of people in the study, the distribution of the chi-square statistic follows a known mathematical distribution quite closely. This distribution is called, not surprisingly, the **chi-square distribution.**

The exact shape of the chi-square distribution depends on the degrees of freedom. For a chi-square test, the degrees of freedom are the number of categories that are free to vary, given the totals. In our candidate example, there are three categories. If you know the total number of people and you know the number in any two categories, then you automatically can figure out the number in the third category—its number is fixed. In a study like this example, if there are three categories, there are two degrees of freedom.

The chi-square distributions for several different degrees of freedom are shown in Figure 11–1. Note that the distributions are all skewed to the right. This is because the chi-square statistic cannot be less than 0 but can have very high values. (Chi-square must be positive because it is figured by adding a group of fractions in which the numerator is a squared term and thus must be positive and the denominator is an expected frequency which also has to be a positive number.)

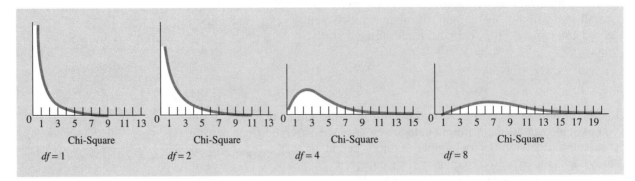

FIGURE 11–1
Examples of chi-square distributions for different degrees of freedom.

The Chi-Square Table

What matters most about the chi-square distribution for hypothesis testing is the cutoff for a chi-square to be extreme enough to reject the null hypothesis. For example, if you want to use the .05 significance level, then you want to know the point on the chi-square distribution where 5% of the cases are more extreme. A **chi-square table** provides the cutoff chi-square values for different significance levels for chi-square distributions of various degrees of freedom. For example, Table 11–2 shows a portion of a chi-square table like the one in Appendix A (Table A–4). Consider the candidate example, where there were two degrees of freedom. The table shows that the cutoff chi-square for the .05 level using a chi-square distribution with 2 degrees of freedom is 5.992.

chi-square table

The Chi-Square Test for Goodness of Fit

We now have all the information needed for hypothesis testing in the Stasser et al. example. Recall that the chi-square statistic we figured for this example was 28.35. We also just found that the chi-square cutoff for this example (using the .05 significance level) is 5.992. Putting these two together, the chi-square for the study is clearly more extreme than the cutoff. The researchers in this study rejected the null hypothesis. That is, they rejected as too unlikely that the mismatch they observed could have occurred if in fact in the population there were equal preferences for the three candidates. It seemed more reasonable to hold that the preferences for the candidates were truly different.

TABLE 11–2
Portion of a Chi-Square Table

	Significance Level		
df	.10	.05	.01
1	2.706	3.841	6.635
2	4.605	**5.992**	9.211
3	6.252	7.815	11.345
4	7.780	9.488	13.277
5	9.237	11.071	15.087

What we have just done is to complete a full hypothesis-testing procedure for the Stasser et al. example. This example involved a differing number of people in different levels of single nominal variable (in this case, which candidate the participants preferred). This kind of chi-square test is called a **chi-square test for goodness of fit.**

It will be useful to review the process of conducting a chi-square test for goodness of fit. We will use the same example, but this time following systematically our standard five steps. In the process we also consider some fine points.

1. Restate the question as a research hypothesis and a null hypothesis about the populations. These are the two populations:

Population 1: People like those in the experiment
Population 2: People who initially prefer each candidate equally

The research hypothesis is that the distribution of people over categories in the two populations are different; the null hypothesis is that they are the same.

2. Determine the characteristics of the comparison distribution.

The comparison distribution in this case is a chi-square distribution with 2 degrees of freedom. (Once you know the total, there are only two categories worth of information that are free to vary. That is, if you know the total and the numbers of people in two of the categories, the number in the third is fixed.)

It is important not to be confused by the terminology here. The comparison distribution is the distribution to which we compare the number that summarizes the whole pattern of the result. With a t test, this number is the t score and we use a t distribution. With an analysis of variance, it is the F and we use an F distribution. Accordingly, with a chi-square test, our comparison distribution is a distribution of the chi-square statistic.

What can be confusing is that in the process of preparing to use the chi-square distribution we compared a distribution of observed frequencies to a distribution of expected frequencies. The distribution of expected frequencies is not a comparison distribution in the sense that we use this term in Step 2 of hypothesis testing.

3. Determine the cutoff on the comparison distribution at which the null hypothesis should be rejected. You do this by looking up the cutoff on the chi-square table for the appropriate significance level and the appropriate degrees of freedom. In this case, we assumed that we wanted the .05 significance level, and we determined in Step 2 that there were 2 degrees of freedom. This gives a cutoff chi-square of 5.992.

4. Determine the score of your sample on the comparison distribution. The score of your sample means the chi-square statistic you compute from the sample. In other words, this is the step where you do all the chi-square computation, including figuring out the expected frequencies for each category. For each category, you need to find the squared difference between the observed and expected frequencies and then divide that result by the expected value. Summing this figure over all the categories gives the chi-square statistic for your study—in the example, 28.35.

5. Compare the scores from Steps 3 and 4 to decide whether to reject the null hypothesis. Because the chi-square needed to reject the null hypothesis is 5.992 and the chi-square of our sample is 28.35, the null hypothesis is rejected. The research hypothesis that the two populations are different is supported. That is, the researchers conclude that the distribution of preferences is probably not equal.

The Chi-Square Test for Independence

So far, we have looked at the distribution of one nominal variable with several categories, such as preferences for one candidate or the other. In fact, this kind of situation is fairly rare in research. We began with an example of this kind because it provides a good stepping stone to get to the more common actual research situation, to which we turn now.

The most common use of chi-square is where there are two nominal variables, each with several categories. For example, in the Stasser et al. study they might have been interested in whether the breakdown of preferences for the three candidates was the same for women and men. If that was their purpose, we would have had two nominal variables, preference for a particular candidate would be the first nominal variable and gender (women vs. men) would be the second nominal variable. Hypothesis testing in this situation is called a **chi-square test for independence.** You will learn shortly why it has this name.

Consider the following fictional study. Researchers at a large university conduct a survey of 200 staff members who commute to work. The staff members are asked about the kind of transportation they use and whether they prefer to go to bed early and awaken early (these are "morning people") or go to bed late and awaken late ("night people"). The results are shown in Table 11–3. Notice the two nominal variables: type of transportation (with three levels) and sleep tendency (with two levels).

Contingency Tables

A table like Table 11–3, in which the distributions of two nominal variables are laid out so that you have the frequencies of their combinations as well as the totals, is called a **contingency table.** A contingency table is similar to tables used in factorial experiments (see Chapter 10). However, in a contingency table, the numbers are frequencies (not means), the number of people in each category or combination of categories. A contingency table like Table 11–3 is called a 3×2 contingency table because it has three levels of one variable crossed with two levels of the other. (Which dimension is named first does not matter.) It is also possible to have larger contingency tables,

chi-square test for independence (margin note)

contingency table (margin note)

TABLE 11–3
Contingency Table of Observed Frequencies of Morning and Night People Using Different Types of Transportation (Fictional Data)

		Transportation			Total
		Bus	*Carpool*	*Own Car*	
Sleep Tendency	*Morning*	60	30	30	120 (60%)
	Night	20	20	40	80 (40%)
	Total	80	50	70	200 (100%)

such as a 4 × 7 or a 6 × 18 table, or to have a smaller table, a 2 × 2 contingency table.

Independence

The question in this example is whether there is any relation between the type of transportation people use and whether they are morning or night people. If there is no relation, then whether a person is a night or a morning person has no connection to the type of transportation that person uses. Or to put it the other way, if there is no relation, the proportion of morning and night people is the same among bus riders, carpoolers, and drivers of their own car. This situation of no relation between the variables in a contingency table is called **independence.**

Independence usually is used to talk about a lack of relation between two nominal variables. But the meaning of independence is roughly the same as the situation of no correlation or a 0 correlation coefficient (see Chapter 3). (You may also be sensing that there is something here like an interaction in a two-way analysis of variance, and you are right. Think it through if you like, or be content that your intuition is correct.)

Sample and Population

In the example survey, the proportions of night and morning people vary with different types of transportation. For example, the bus riders are split 60-20, so three-fourths of the bus riders are morning people. Among people who drive their own car, the split is 30-40, so a slight majority are night people. Still, the sample is only of 200. It is possible that in the larger population, the type of transportation a person uses is independent of the person's being a morning or a night person. The question is whether the lack of independence in the sample is large enough to reject the null hypothesis of independence in the population.

Applying Chi-Square to a Test of Independence

To test whether the lack of independence in a sample is large enough to reject the null hypothesis of independence in the population, two things are required. First, we need a number for the amount of mismatch between the sample's lack of independence and what we would expect of the sample if there were perfect independence in the sample. This is a chi-square statistic. Second, we need to know the distribution of that statistic if the null hypothesis were true. That is the chi-square distribution. Just as we did in the three candidates example, we have to figure a chi-square statistic and compare it to a chi-square cutoff from a table. What is new are the details of how we figure the chi-square and on how we figure the degrees of freedom to look up the cutoff on the chi-square table.

Determining Expected Frequencies

Just as we did before, to figure the chi-square statistic, we have to compare observed frequencies to expected frequencies. One thing that is new is that you now base your chi-square on differences between observed and expected for each combination of categories (each cell of the contingency table). The more important new part of the procedure has to do with figuring out what the expected frequencies should be.

Table 11–4 is the contingency table for our example survey, but this time with the expected frequencies put in parentheses next to the observed frequencies. Follow the logic of the next two paragraphs while looking at these numbers.

Suppose the two variables, transportation and sleep tendency, are independent. If they are independent, then the breakdowns up and down each of the transportation columns should be the same. For example, if there is a particular proportional breakdown of morning to night people for those who take the bus, their should be the same proportional breakdown of morning to night people for those who carpool or use their own car. In fact, all of these proportional breakdowns should be the same as the overall proportional breakdown of morning to night people for all the people in the survey. Put another way, the distribution of morning and night people in each column should be the same as the overall distribution. This would mean that transportation method is not affecting the proportion of morning to night people, that transportation method is independent of the proportion of morning and night people. What we expect when the two variables are independent is the expected frequency.

In terms of the actual numbers involved in our example survey, overall there are 60% morning people and 40% night people. If transportation method is independent of being a morning or night person, this 60%-40% split should hold for each column (each transportation type). First, the 60%-40% overall split should hold for the bus group. This would make an expected frequency in the bus cell for morning people of 60% of 80, which is 48. The expected frequency for the bus riders who are night people is 32 (that is, 40% of 80). Similarly, the expected frequencies in the carpool column should break down its total of 50 people into a 60%-40% split of 30 (that is, 60% of 50) for morning people and 20 (that is, 40% of 50) for night people. Stated as a formula,

$$E = \left(\frac{R}{N}\right)(C)$$

(11–2)

In this formula, E is the expected frequency for a particular cell (combination of categories), R is the number of cases observed in this cell's row, N is the

TABLE 11-4

Contingency Table of Observed (and Expected) Frequencies of Morning and Night People Using Different Types of Transportation (Fictional Data)

		Transportation			Total
		Bus	Carpool	Own Car	
Sleep Tendency	Morning	60 (48)[a]	30 (30)	30 (42)	120 (60%)
	Night	20 (32)	20 (20)	40 (28)	80 (40%)
	Total	80	50	70	200 (100%)

[a]Expected frequencies are in parentheses.

number of cases total, and C is the number of cases observed in this cell's column. (If you mix up rows and columns, the result still comes out the same.)

Applying the formula to morning persons who ride the bus,

$$E = \left(\frac{R}{N}\right)(C) = \left(\frac{120}{200}\right)(80) = (.60)(80) = 48$$

Looking at the entire Table 11–4, notice that the expected frequencies add up to the same totals across columns and rows as the observed frequencies. For example, in the first column (Bus), the expected frequencies of 32 and 48 add up to 80, just as the observed frequencies in that column of 60 and 20 do. Similarly, in the top row (Morning), the expected frequencies of 48, 30, and 42 add up to 120, just as the observed frequencies of 60, 30, and 30 do. As a check on your arithmetic, it is always a good idea to make sure that the expected frequencies do add up to the same row and column totals.

Computing Chi-Square

Once the observed and expected frequencies are known, computing chi-square follows the same procedures as in the chi-square test for goodness of fit. Add up the results for each cell. We use the same formula as before, but now to compute the chi-square for our two-variable survey example:

$$X^2 = \Sigma \frac{(O-E)^2}{E} = \frac{(60-48)^2}{48} + \frac{(30-30)^2}{30} + \frac{(30-42)^2}{42} + \frac{(20-32)^2}{32}$$
$$+ \frac{(20-20)^2}{20} + \frac{(40-28)^2}{28}$$
$$= 3 + 0 + 3.43 + 4.5 + 0 + 5.14 = 16.07$$

Degrees of Freedom

As you have come to expect, before you can test for significance with most statistics, you must know the degrees of freedom. A rule for degrees of freedom in a chi-square contingency table is that it is the number of columns minus 1 times the number of rows minus 1. Put as a formula,

$$df = (N_{Columns} - 1)(N_{Rows} - 1) \tag{11–3}$$

In this formula $N_{Columns}$ is the number of columns and N_{Rows} is the number of rows. Using this formula for our survey example,

$$df = (N_{Columns} - 1)(N_{Rows} - 1) = (3-1)(2-1) = (2)(1) = 2$$

A contingency table with many cells may have relatively few degrees of freedom. In our example, there are six cells and 2 degrees of freedom. This is because in a chi-square test the degrees of freedom are the number of categories free to vary once the totals are known. In the case of a chi-square test of independence, the number of categories refers to the number of cells (that is, the number of combinations of categories) and the totals refer to the row and column totals as well as the overall total. If you know the row and column totals, this gives a great deal of information.

Consider our sleep tendency and transportation example. If you know the first two cell frequencies across the top, for example, and all the row and column totals, you could compute all the other cell frequencies. Table 11–5 shows the contingency table for this example with just the row and column totals (and the overall total) and these two cell frequencies. You can complete the rest of the top row by figuring that if there is a total of 120 (that row's total) and the other two cells have 90 in them (60 + 30), then only 30 remain. These must go in the own car cell. If you know the frequencies for all the morning people cells and the column totals for each type of transportation, then each cell frequency for the night people is its column's total minus the morning people in that column. (For example, if there are 80 bus riders and 60 are morning people, the remaining 20 must be night people.) In this example, although there are six cells, there are only 2 degrees of freedom, only two cells whose frequencies are really free to vary once we have all the row and column totals.

Hypothesis Testing

With 2 degrees of freedom, Table 11–2 (or Table A–4) shows that the chi-square needed for significance at the .01 level is 9.211. The chi-square of 16.07 for our example is more extreme than this cutoff point. We can reject the null hypothesis that the two variables are independent in the population.

Steps of Hypothesis Testing and the Chi-Square Test for Independence: An Example

We have just conducted a complete hypothesis test using the chi-square test for independence (that is, for two variables). However, once again it will be useful to review the process, using the same example, but this time following systematically the five steps of hypothesis testing.

1. Restate the question as a research hypothesis and a null hypothesis about the populations. These are the two populations:

TABLE 11–5
Contingency Table Showing Marginal and Two Cells' Observed Frequencies to Illustrate Computation of Degrees of Freedom

		Transportation			Total
		Bus	*Carpool*	*Own Car*	
Sleep Tendency	*Morning*	60	30	——	120 (60%)
	Night	——	——	——	80 (40%)
	Total	80	50	70	200 (100%)

Population 1: People like those surveyed
Population 2: People for whom being a night or a morning person is independent of the kind of transportation used to commute to work

The null hypothesis is that the two populations are the same, that in general the breakdown of transportation types used is the same for morning and night people. The research hypothesis is that the two populations are different, that among people in general the breakdowns over types of transportation are different for night and morning people.

Put another way, the null hypothesis is that the two variables are independent (that they are unrelated to each other). The research hypothesis is that they are not independent (that they are related to each other).

2. Determine the characteristics of the comparison distribution. The comparison distribution is a chi-square distribution with 2 degrees of freedom. If you know the number of cases in two cells and the row and column totals, all the others are fixed. Or, using the rule for contingency tables, the number of cells free to vary is the number of columns minus 1 times number of rows minus 1.

3. Determine the cutoff on the comparison distribution at which the null hypothesis should be rejected. You use the same table as for any chi-square test. In the example, setting a .01 significance level with 2 degrees of freedom, you need a chi-square of 9.211.

4. Determine the score of your sample on the comparison distribution. In the example, the total chi-square statistic was 16.07.

5. Compare the scores from Steps 3 and 4 to determine whether to reject the null hypothesis. Because the chi-square needed to reject the null hypothesis is 9.211 and the chi-square for our sample is 16.07, the null hypothesis can be rejected (see Figure 11–2). The research hypothesis that the two variables are not independent in the population is supported.

Another Example

Richard Riehl (1994) conducted a survey at Indiana State University to examine the college experience of first-year students who were the first generation in their family to attend college. They were compared to other students who were not the first generation in their family to go to college. One of the variables Riehl measured was whether or not students dropped out during their first semester.

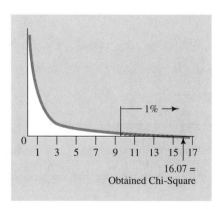

FIGURE 11–2
For the sleep tendency and transportation example, chi-square distribution ($df = 2$) showing the cutoff for rejecting the null hypothesis at the .01 level.

Table 11–6 shows the results along with the percentages in the Dropout and Not-Dropout groups plus the expected frequencies (shown in parenthesis) based on these percentages. The computations for the chi-square test of independence follow the contingency table.

1. Restate the question as a null hypothesis and a research hypothesis about the populations. There are two populations:

Population 1: Students like those surveyed

Population 2: Students whose dropping out or staying at college their first semester is independent of whether or not they are the first generation in their family to go to college

The null hypothesis is that the two populations are the same, that in general whether or not students drop out in their first semester is independent of whether or not they are the first generation to go to college. The research hypothesis is that the populations are not the same, that students like those surveyed are unlike the hypothetical population in which dropping out is unrelated to whether or not you are first generation.

2. Determine the characteristics of the comparison distribution. This is a chi-square distribution with 1 degree of freedom.

TABLE 11–6
Results and Computation of the Chi-Square Test for Independence Comparing Whether First Generation College Students Differ from Others in First Semester Dropouts

| | Generation to Go to College | | | | |
	First		Other		Total	
Dropped Out	73	(57.7)	89	(103.9)	162	(7.9%)
Did Not Drop Out	657	(672.3)	1,226	(1,211.1)	1,883	(92.1%)
	730		1,315		2,045	

$$df = (N_{\text{Columns}} - 1)(N_{\text{Rows}} - 1) = (2-1)(2-1) = (1)(1) = 1$$

Chi-square needed, $df = 1$, .01 level: 6.635.

$$X^2 = \Sigma \frac{(O-E)^2}{E} = \frac{(73-57.7)^2}{57.7} + \frac{(89-103.9)^2}{103.9} + \frac{(657-672.3)^2}{672.3}$$
$$+ \frac{(1,226-1,211.1)^2}{1,211.1}$$
$$= \frac{15.3^2}{57.7} + \frac{-14.9^2}{103.9} + \frac{-15.3^2}{672.3} + \frac{14.9^2}{1,211.1}$$
$$= \frac{234.1}{57.7} + \frac{222}{103.9} + \frac{234.1}{672.3} + \frac{222}{1,211.1}$$
$$= 4.06 + 2.14 + .3 + .2$$
$$= 6.7$$

Conclusion: Reject the null hypothesis.

Notes:
1. With a 2×2 analysis, differences and squared differences (numerators) for each cell are identical. In this example, the differences are due to rounding error.
2. Data from Riehl (1994). The exact chi-square (6.7) is slightly different from that reported in the article (7.2), due to rounding error.

3. Determine the cutoff on the comparison distribution at which the null hypothesis should be rejected. Using the .01 level and 1 degrees of freedom, the needed chi-square for significance is 6.635. This is illustrated in Figure 11–3.

4. Determine the score of your sample on the comparison distribution. To figure the chi-square, you first have to calculate the expected frequencies for each cell. This is done by multiplying the expected percentages times the number in the sample. For example, consider the first-generation dropouts. Dropouts overall are 7.9% of the students. So, if the null hypothesis were true, they should be 7.9% of the 730 first-generation students. Thus, the expected frequency for the first-generation dropouts is 7.9% times 730 is 57.7. Once you have figured the expected frequencies for each cell, the rest of the chi-square analysis is the usual procedure of finding the difference for each cell, squaring it, dividing it by the expected frequencies, and adding these results up for all the cells. As shown in Table 11–6, this gives a chi-square of 6.7.

5. Compare the scores from Steps 3 and 4 to determine whether to reject the null hypothesis. Because our value of 6.7 is more extreme than the cutoff chi-square of 6.635, the conclusion is to reject the null hypothesis (see Figure 11–3). Thus, judging from a sample of Indiana University students, first generation students are somewhat more likely to drop out during their first semester than are other students. (Remember, of course, that there could be many reasons for this result.)

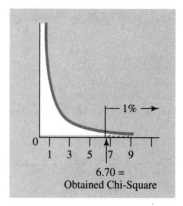

FIGURE 11–3
For the example from Riehl (1994), chi-square distribution (*df* = 1) showing the cutoff for rejecting the null hypothesis at the .01 level.

Assumptions for the Chi-Square Test of Independence

The chi-square test does not require the usual assumptions of normal population variances and such. There is, however, one key assumption: Each score must not have any special relation to any other scores. Basically, this means that you can't use chi-square if the scores are based on the same people being tested more than once. For example, a study in which 20 people were tested to see if the distribution of their preferred brand of breakfast cereal changed from before to after a recent nutritional campaign would not be able to be tested with the usual chi-square.

Effect Size for Chi-Square Tests for Independence

In chi-square tests of independence, it is possible to use the chi-square statistic you calculate to figure a number that indicates the degree of association of your two nominal variables. In the case of a 2×2 contingency table, the measure of association is called the **phi coefficient (Φ).** It is the square root of chi-square divided by the number of cases in the entire sample. In terms of a formula,

phi coefficient (Φ)

$$\Phi = \sqrt{\frac{X^2}{N}}$$

(11–4)

The phi coefficient has a minimum of 0 and a maximum of 1 and can be thought of as like a correlation coefficient.[2]

---

[2]In fact, it is really identical to a correlation coefficient. Suppose you were to take the two variables in a 2×2 contingency table and arbitrarily make one of the values of each equal to 1 and the other equal to 2 (or any other two numbers). If you then calculated a correlation coefficient between the two variables, the result would be exactly the same as the phi coefficient. (Whether it was a positive or negative correlation, however, would depend on which categories in each variable got the 1 and which the 2.)

Cohen's (1988) conventions for the phi coefficient are that .10 is a small effect size, .30 is a medium effect size, and .50 is a large effect size. (These are exactly the same conventions as for a correlation coefficient.)

For example, in the Riehl (1994) study of first generation college students, the chi square we calculated was 6.7 and there were 2,045 people in the study. Applying the formula for the phi coefficient,

$$\Phi = \sqrt{\frac{X^2}{N}} = \sqrt{\frac{6.7}{2,045}} = \sqrt{.00328} = .06$$

This phi coefficient is equivalent to a correlation of .06 between being a first-generation college student and dropping out in your first semester. This is a very small effect size. The significance results tell us that the greater likelihood of first-generation students dropping out is probably not due to chance. The phi coefficient tells us that this nonchance difference may not be a very important factor in practice. (See Chapter 7 for a discussion of the situation when a result is statistically significant but has a very small effect size.)

Cramer's phi statistic

The phi statistic only applies when you have a 2×2 situation. **Cramer's phi statistic** can be thought of as an extension of the ordinary phi coefficient so that it can be applied to contingency tables that are larger than 2×2. (Cramer's phi is also known as Cramer's V and is sometimes written Φ_C or V_C.) It is calculated in the same way as the ordinary phi coefficient, except that instead of dividing by N, you divide by N times the degrees of freedom of the smaller side of the table ($df_{Smaller}$). Here it is stated as a formula:

$$\text{Cramer's } \Phi = \sqrt{\frac{X^2}{(N)(df_{Smaller})}} \tag{11–5}$$

In the transportation preference example, the chi-square statistic was 16.07, the total number of subjects was 200, and the degrees of freedom for the smaller side of the table (the rows) was 1. Cramer's phi is the square root of what you get when you divide 16.07 by 200 times 1, which comes out to .28. In terms of the formula,

$$\text{Cramer's } \Phi = \sqrt{\frac{X^2}{(N)(df_{Smaller})}} = \sqrt{\frac{16.07}{(200)(1)}} = \sqrt{.08} = .28$$

Cohen's conventions for effect size for Cramer's phi depend on the degrees of freedom for the smaller side of the table. Table 11–7 shows Cohen's

TABLE 11–7
Cohen's Conventions for Cramer's Phi

Smallest Dimension of Contingency Table	Effect Size		
	Small	*Medium*	*Large*
2 ($df_{Smaller} = 1$)	.10	.30	.50
3 ($df_{Smaller} = 2$)	.07	.21	.35
4 ($df_{Smaller} = 3$)	.06	.17	.29

(1988) effect size conventions for Cramer's phi for tables in which the smallest side of the table is 2, 3, and 4. Note that when the smallest side of the table is 2, and thus degrees of freedom is 1, the effect sizes given in the table for this situation are the same as for the ordinary phi coefficient. (The computation also gives the same result, since multiplying by 1 does not change anything. That was the situation in the transportation example we just considered.)

Based on the table, you can see that in this fictional example there is an approximately medium effect size, a medium amount of relationship between type of transportation one uses and whether one is a morning or a night person.

Power and Needed Sample Size for Chi-Square Test for Independence

Table 11–8 shows the approximate power at the .05 significance level for small, medium, and large effect sizes and total sample sizes of 25, 50, 100, and 200. Values are given for tables with 1, 2, 3, and 4 degrees of freedom.[3]

For example, consider the power of a planned 2×4 study ($df = 3$) of 50 people with an expected medium effect size (Cramer's $\Phi = .30$), to be carried

TABLE 11–8
Approximate Power for the Chi-Square Test for Independence for Testing Hypotheses at the .05 Significance Level

Total df	Total N	Effect Size		
		Small ($\phi = .10$)	Medium ($\phi = .30$)	Large ($\phi = .50$)
1	25	.08	.32	.70
	50	.11	.56	.94
	100	.17	.85	*
	200	.29	.99	*
2	25	.07	.25	.60
	50	.09	.46	.90
	100	.13	.77	*
	200	.23	.97	*
3	25	.07	.21	.54
	50	.08	.40	.86
	100	.12	.71	.99
	200	.19	.96	*
4	25	.06	.19	.50
	50	.08	.36	.82
	100	.11	.66	.99
	200	.17	.94	*

*Nearly 1.

[3]More detailed tables are provided in Cohen (1988, pp. 228–248). Cohen's tables are based on an effect size called w, which is equivalent to phi but not to Cramer's phi. He provides a helpful conversion table of Cramer's phi to w on page 222.

out using the .05 level. Using Table 11–8, this study would have a power of .40. This means that if the research hypothesis is in fact true, and there is a true medium effect size, there is about a 40% chance that the study will come out significant.

Table 11–9 gives the approximate total number of participants needed for 80% power with small, medium, and large effect sizes at the .05 significance level for chi-square tests of independence of 2, 3, 4, and 5 degrees of freedom.[4] For example, suppose you are planning a study with a 3×3 ($df = 4$) contingency table. You expect a large effect size and will use the .05 significance level. According to the table, you would only need 48 participants.

Strategies for Hypothesis Testing When Population Distributions Are Not Normal

The second main topic of this chapter is hypothesis-testing procedures when you cannot assume that the population distributions are even roughly normal (or in which you fail to meet other requirements for ordinary hypothesis-testing procedures, such as having equal population variances).

This second main part of the chapter examines some strategies researchers use when analyzing the results of a study in which the variables are quantitative, but the assumption of a normal population distribution is clearly violated. (This assumption underlies most ordinary hypothesis-testing procedures, such as the t test and the analysis of variance.) First, we briefly review the role of assumptions in the standard hypothesis-testing procedures. Then we examine two approaches researchers use when the assumptions have not been met: data transformations and rank-order tests.

Assumptions in the Standard Hypothesis-Testing Procedures

As we saw in Chapters 8 through 10, you have to make certain assumptions to carry out a t test or an analysis of variance. In these hypothesis-testing procedures, we treat the data in our experiment as if they came from some larger,

TABLE 11–9
Approximate Total Number of Participants Needed for 80% Power for the Chi-Square Test for Independence for Testing Hypotheses at the .05 Significance Level

Total *df*	Effect Size		
	Small ($\phi = .10$)	*Medium* ($\phi = .30$)	*Large* ($\phi = .50$)
1	785	87	26
2	964	107	39
3	1,090	121	44
4	1,194	133	48

[4]More detailed tables are provided in Cohen (1988, pp. 253–267).

though unknown, population or populations. One assumption we make is that the population or populations involved have a normal (bell-shaped) distribution. The other main assumption we make is that the populations have equal variances.

You also learned that when the study even comes close to meeting these assumptions, we get fairly accurate results. Our concern here, however, is with the situation where it is clear that the populations are nowhere near normal (or nowhere near having equal variances). In such situations, if you use the ordinary *t* test or analysis of variance you can get quite incorrect results. For example, you could do all the figuring correctly and based on your results decide to reject the null hypothesis. Yet, if your populations do not meet the standard assumptions, this result could be wrong in the sense that instead of there actually being only a 5% chance of getting your results if the null hypothesis is true, in fact there might be a 15% or 20% chance! You would be rejecting the null hypothesis when you should not be.

It is important to keep in mind that assumptions are about populations and not about samples. It is quite possible for a sample not to be normally distributed even though it comes from a population that is normal. Figure 11–4

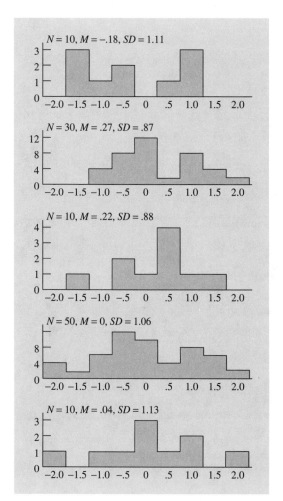

FIGURE 11–4
Histograms for several random samples, each drawn from a normal population with a mean of 0 and a standard deviation of 1.

shows histograms for several random samples, each of which is taken randomly from a normal population. (Notice that the smaller the sample, the harder it is to see that it came from a normal population.) Of course, it is quite possible for nonnormal populations to produce any of these samples as well. Unfortunately, the sample is all we have when doing a study. What researchers do is make a histogram for the sample; and if it is not drastically different from normal, the researcher assumes that the population it came from is normal. When it comes to normality, most researchers consider a distribution innocent until proven guilty.

One common situation in which a researcher might doubt the assumption that the population follows a normal distribution is when there is a ceiling or floor effect (see Chapter 1). Another common situation that raises such doubts is when the sample has outliers, extreme cases at one or both ends of the sample distribution. Figure 11–5 shows some examples of distributions with outliers. Outliers are a big problem in the statistical methods we ordinarily use because these methods rely, ultimately, on squared deviations from the mean. An outlier, because it is so far from the mean, has a huge influence when its deviation is squared. The result is that a single outlier, if it is extreme enough, can cause a statistical test to give a significant result even when all the other scores would not. An outlier can also make a result not significant that without the outlier would be significant.

FIGURE 11–5
Distributions with outliers at one or both ends.

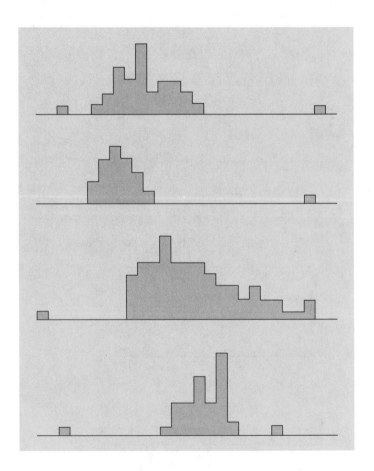

Data Transformations

One widely used procedure when the scores in the sample do not appear to come from a normal population is to change the data! Not by fudging—although at first it may sound that way, until we explain. The researcher simply takes each of the scores and applies some mathematical procedure to it, such as taking the square root. The goal is to make a nonnormal distribution closer to normal. (Sometimes this can also make the variances of two or more groups more similar as well.) This is called a **data transformation.** Once you have made a data transformation, if the other assumptions are met, you can then go ahead with a usual *t* test or analysis of variance, and you will get accurate results.

data transformation

Data transformation has an advantage over other procedures of coping with nonnormal populations that you will learn about in that it permits the use of familiar and sophisticated hypothesis-testing procedures.

Consider an example. Measures of reaction time are usually highly skewed to the right. There are many short (quick) responses and a few, but sometimes quite extreme, long (slow) ones. It is hard to imagine that the reaction times shown in Figure 11–6 come from a normally distributed population. The population of reaction-time scores itself is probably skewed.

However, consider what happens if you take the square root of each reaction time. Most reaction times are affected only a little. A reaction time of 1 second stays 1 second; a reaction time of 1.5 seconds reduces to 1.22. But very long reaction times, the ones that create the long tail to the right, are substantially reduced. For example, a reaction time of 9 seconds is reduced

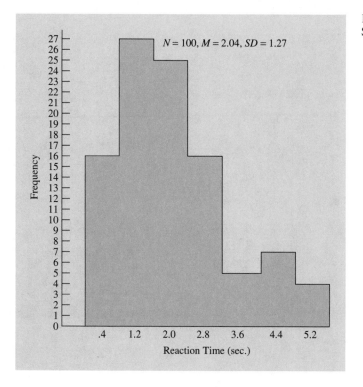

FIGURE 11–6
Skewed distribution of reaction times (fictional data).

to 3, and a reaction time of 16 seconds (the person was really distracted and forgot about the task) reduces to 4 seconds. Figure 11–7 shows the result of taking the square root of each score in the skewed distribution shown in Figure 11–6. As you can see, after a *square-root transformation,* this distribution of scores seems much more likely to have come from a population with a normal distribution (of transformed scores).

Legitimacy of Data Transformations

Do you feel that this is somehow cheating? It would be if it were done to only some scores or done in any other way to make the result more favorable to the researcher's predictions. However, in actual research practice, the first step after the data are collected and recorded is to check that they meet assumptions and then to carry out transformations if they do not. Hypothesis testing is done only after this checking and any transformations.

Also it is important to remember that any transformation of scores has to be done for all the people in the study, not just those in a particular subgroup. Most important, no matter what transformation procedure we use, the order of the scores always stays the same. A raw score that is the second highest in a group of scores will still be second highest in the group of transformed scores.

The procedure may seem somehow to distort reality to fit the statistics. In some cases, this is a legitimate concern. If you are looking at the difference in income between two groups, you are probably interested not in how much the two groups differ in the square root of their income but in how much the actual dollar earnings differ.

FIGURE 11–7
Data from Figure 11–6 after square-root transformation.

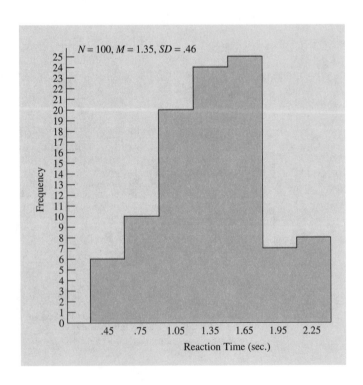

On the other hand, consider a survey question in which the person indicates their agreement with the statement "I am satisfied with local law enforcement" on a 7-point rating from 1, strongly disagree, to 7, strongly agree. Higher scores on this scale certainly mean more agreement; lower scores, less agreement. However, each unit of increase on the scale is not necessarily related to an equal amount of increase in an agreement. It is just as likely that the square root of each unit's increase is directly related to the person's agreement. In many research situations, there may be no strong reason to think that the transformed version is any less accurate a reflection of the reality than the original version. Also, the transformed version may meet the normality assumption.

Kinds of Data Transformations

There are several types of data transformations. We already have illustrated a square-root transformation: Instead of using each score, you use the square root of each score. We gave an example in Figures 11–6 and 11–7. The general effect is shown in Figure 11–8a. As you can see, a distribution skewed to the right becomes less skewed to the right after square-root transformation. To put it numerically, moderate numbers become only slightly lower and high numbers become much lower; as a result, the right-hand side is pulled in toward the middle. (If the distribution is skewed the other way, you may want to *reflect* all the scores, that is subtract them all from some high number so that they are now all reversed. Then using the square root will have the correct effect. However, you then have to remember when looking at the final results that you have reversed the direction of scoring.)

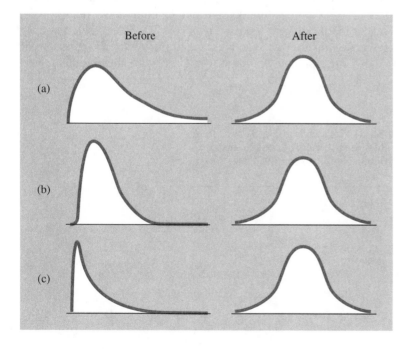

FIGURE 11–8
Distributions to which transformations are applied (a) Moderately skewed to the right and a square-root transformation has been applied; (b) strongly skewed to the right and a log transformation has been applied; and (c) extremely skewed to the right and an inverse transformation has been applied.

There are many other kinds of transformations you will see in social and behavioral science research articles. One common type is called a *log transformation.* (In a log transformation, instead of the square root, the researcher takes the logarithm of each score.) Some other transformations you might see are *inverse transformations* and *arcsine transformations.* We will not go into examples of all these kinds of transformations here. Just learning the square root transformation will help you learn the principle. The main thing to remember about other kinds of transformations is that they all use this same principle of taking each score and applying some arithmetic to it, usually to make the set of scores come out more like a normal curve. Once again, whatever transformation you use, a score that is between two other scores always stays between those two other scores.

An Example of a Data Transformation

Consider a fictional study in which four children who score high on a test of being "highly sensitive" are compared on the number of books read in the preceding year to four children who score low on the test. On the basis of theory, the researcher predicts that more books will be read by the highly sensitives. Table 11–10 shows the results.

Ordinarily in a study like this, involving a comparison of two independent groups, we would use a *t* test for independent means. But the *t* test for independent means, like all of the procedures you have learned for hypothesis testing (except chi-square), requires that the parent populations of scores for each group be normally distributed. In this study, the distribution of the sample is clearly skewed to the right. That is, the scores tend to bunch up at the left, leaving a long tail to the right. It seems likely that the population of scores of number of books read (for both sensitives and nonsensitives) is also skewed to the right. In fact, this seems reasonable, considering that a child cannot read less than zero books, but once a child starts reading, it is not hard to read a lot of books in a year. Also note that the estimated population variances based on the two samples are dramatically different, 95.58 versus 584, another reason one would not want to just go ahead with an ordinary *t* test.

TABLE 11–10
Results of a Study Comparing Highly Sensitive and Not Highly Sensitive Children on the Number of Books Read in the Past Year (Fictional Data)

	Highly Sensitive	
	No	*Yes*
	0	17
	3	36
	10	45
	22	75
Σ:	35	173
$M =$	8.75	43.25
$S^2 =$	95.58	584.00

Suppose we carry out a square root transformation on the scores (Table 11–11). The result is that both samples are much more like a normal curve. In this case, the transformation also seems appropriate in terms of the meaning of the numbers. Number of books read is meant as a measure of interest in things literary. The difference between 0 and 1 book is a much greater difference than the difference between 20 and 21 books. We could then go ahead and do the *t* test using the transformed scores.

Table 11–12 shows the *t* test analysis using the transformed scores.

Rank-Order Tests

Another way of coping with nonnormal distributions is to use a special kind of transformation in which you change the scores to ranks. Suppose you have a sample with scores 4, 8, 12, and 64. This would be a rather surprising sample if the population was really normal. A **rank-order transformation** would change the scores to 1, 2, 3, and 4, the 1 referring to the lowest number in the group, the 2 to the second lowest, and so forth.

rank-order transformation

The only complication with a rank-order transformation is when you have two or more scores that are tied. The usual solution to ties is to give them each the average rank. For example, the scores 12, 81, 81, 107, and 154 would be ranked 1, 2.5, 2.5, 4, and 5.

Converting the scores to ranks is a kind of data transformation. Unlike the transformation we have considered so far, a rank-order transformation is not used to produce a normal distribution. It does, however, produce a particular distribution. The distribution you get from a rank-order transformation is rectangular, with equal numbers of cases (one) at each value. (The only exception is for ties.) Ranks have the effect of spreading the scores out evenly.

There are several special hypothesis-testing procedures that make use of rank-ordered data. These are called **rank-order tests.** They also have two other common names. Because data from a population with any shaped distribution can be transformed into ranks, these tests are sometimes called *distribution-free tests*. Because the distribution of rank-order data is known exactly rather than estimated, rank-order tests do not require estimating any parameters (population values). (For example, there is no need to estimate a population variance because you can determine exactly what it will be if you know that ranks are involved.) Hence, hypothesis-testing procedures based

rank-order tests

TABLE 11–11
Square-Root Transformation of the Data in Table 11–10

Highly Sensitive			
No		Yes	
X	$\sqrt{X}$	X	$\sqrt{X}$
0	0.00	17	4.12
3	1.73	36	6.00
10	3.16	45	6.71
22	4.69	75	8.66

TABLE 11–12
Computations for a _t_ Test for Independent Means Using Square-Root-Transformed Scores for the Study of Books Read by Highly Sensitive Versus Not Highly Sensitive Children (Fictional Data)

t needed for .05 significance level, $df = (4 - 1) + (4 - 1) = 6$, one tailed = 1.943.

Highly Sensitive

	_No_	_Yes_
	0.00	4.12
	1.73	6.00
	3.16	6.71
	4.69	8.66
Σ:	9.58	25.49
$M =$	9.58/4 = 2.40	25.49/4 = 6.37
$S^2 =$	12.03/3 = 4.01	10.56/3 = 3.52

$$S^2_{Pooled} = 3.77$$

$S^2_M =$	3.77/4 = .94	3.77/4 = .94

$S^2_{Difference} = .94 + .94 = 1.88$
$S_{Difference} = \sqrt{1.88} = 1.37$
$t = (6.37 - 2.40)/1.37 = 2.90$

Conclusion: Reject the null hypothesis.

---

on ranks are also called *nonparametric tests.* The ordinary hypothesis-testing procedures you have learned (*t* test and analysis of variance) are examples of *parametric tests.* Chi-square, like the rank-order tests, is considered a nonparametric test, but it is distribution-free only in the sense that no assumptions are made about the shape of the population distributions. However, the terms *distribution-free* and *nonparametric* are typically used interchangeably; the subtleties of differences between them are a matter of ongoing debate among statisticians.

Rank-order tests also have the advantage that they can be used where the actual scores in the study are themselves ranks—if the study is comparing class standing of two types of graduates. Also, sometimes researchers feel that although their measures are intended to be numeric in the usual sense, the exact meaning of the numbers are questionable and that it would be more sensible to use ranks which do not imply such an exact linkage of the number to the underlying meaning.

Overview of Rank-Order Tests

Table 11–13 shows the name of the rank-order test that you would substitute for each of the parametric hypothesis-testing procedures you have learned. Where more than one possible test is listed, the procedures are approximately equivalent.

Next, we will describe how such tests are done in a general way, including an example. However, we do not actually provide all the needed information for you to carry them out in practice. We introduce you to these techniques because you will see them used in articles you read and be-

TABLE 11–13
Major Rank-Order Tests Corresponding to Major Parametric Tests

Parametric Test	Corresponding Rank-Order Test
t test for dependent means	Wilcoxon signed-rank test
t test for independent means	Wilcoxon rank-sum test or Mann-Whitney U test
Analysis of variance	Kruskal-Wallis H test
t test for correlation	Spearman rho or Kendall's tau

cause their logic is the foundation of an alternative procedure that we do teach you to use (shortly). This alternative procedure does roughly the same thing as these rank-order tests and is closer to what you have already learned.

Basic Logic of Rank-Order Tests

Consider a study involving an experimental group and a control group. (This is the kind of situation for which researchers would use a t test for independent means if all the assumptions were met.) If you wanted to use a rank-order test, you would first transform all the scores into ranks, ranking all the scores from lowest to highest, regardless of whether a score was in the experimental or the control group. If the two groups were scores randomly taken from a single population, there should be about equal amounts of high ranks and low ranks in each group. (That is, if the null hypothesis is true, the ranks in the two groups should not differ.) Because the distribution of ranks can be worked out exactly, statisticians can figure the exact probability of getting any particular division of ranks into two groups if in fact the two groups were randomly drawn.

The way this actually works is that the researcher converts all the scores to ranks, adds up the total of the ranks in the group with the lower scores, and then compares this total to a cutoff from a special table of significance cutoffs for totals of ranks in this kind of situation.

An Example of a Rank-Order Test

Table 11–14 shows a computation of the Wilcoxon rank-sum test for the kind of situation we have just described, using the same data as for our first data transformation example (the fictional study of number of books read by highly sensitive versus not highly sensitive children). The logic is a little different, so be patient until we explain it.

Notice that the significance cutoff was first established, as would be the case in any hypothesis-testing procedure. (This cutoff is based on a table you don't have but is available in most intermediate statistics texts.) The next step was to rank all the scores from lowest to highest. Then you total the ranks within each group. Finally, you compare the smaller total to the cutoff to see if it is lower than the cutoff. In the example, the total of the ranks for the group with the smaller total was in fact lower than the cutoff. The null hypothesis was rejected.

TABLE 11–14

Computations for a Wilcoxon Rank-Sum Test for the Study of Books Read by Highly Sensitive Versus Not Highly Sensitive Children (Fictional Data)

Cutoff for significance: Maximum sum of ranks in the not highly sensitive group for significance at the .05 level, one-tailed (from a standard table) = 11.

Highly Sensitive

No			Yes	
X	*Rank*		*X*	*Rank*
0	1		17	4
3	2		36	6
10	3		45	7
22	5		75	8
Σ:	11			

Comparison to cutoff: Sum of ranks of group predicted to have lower scores, 11, equals but does not exceed cutoff for significance.

Conclusion: Reject the null hypothesis.

Using Parametric Tests with Rank-Transformed Data

Two statisticians (Conover & Iman, 1981) have shown that instead of using the special procedures for rank-order tests, you get approximately the same results if you transform the data into ranks and then apply all the usual arithmetic for calculating an ordinary parametric statistic, such as a *t* test.

The result of using a parametric test with data transformed into ranks will not be quite as accurate as either the ordinary parametric test or the rank-order test. It will not be as accurate as the ordinary parametric test because the assumption of normal distributions is clearly violated: The distribution is, in fact, rectangular when ranks are involved. It will not be as accurate as the rank-order test because the parametric test uses the *t* or *F* distribution instead of the special tables that rank-order tests use, which are based on exact probabilities of getting certain divisions of ranks. However, the approximation seems to be quite close.[5]

Table 11–15 shows the computations of an ordinary *t* test for independent means for the fictional sensitive children data, using each subject's rank instead of actual number of books read. Again we get a significant result.

Chi-Square Tests, Data Transformations, and Rank-Order Tests as Reported in Research Articles

Chi-Square Tests

The reporting of chi-square tests usually includes the frequencies in each category or cell as well as the degrees of freedom, number of subjects, com-

---

[5]A researcher who is particularly concerned about accuracy could calculate t or F using the rank-transformed scores, convert the result to the rank-order statistic result (using one of the conversion formulas given by Conover & Iman), and then look up that number in the appropriate rank-order test's table.

TABLE 11–15

Computations for a *t* test for Independent Means Using Ranks Instead of Raw Scores for the Study of Books Read by Highly Sensitive Versus Not Highly Sensitive Children (Fictional Data)

t needed for .05 significance level, $df = (4 - 1) + (4 - 1) = 6$, one-tailed $= -1.943$

	Highly Sensitive	
	No	*Yes*
	1	4
	2	6
	3	7
	5	8
Σ	11	25
$M =$	11/4 = 2.75	25/4 = 6.25
$S^2 =$	8.75/3 = 2.92	8.75/3 = 2.92

$$S^2_{Pooled} = 2.92$$

$S^2_M =$	2.92/4 = .73	2.92/4 = .73

$S^2_{Difference} = .73 + .73 = 1.46$

$S_{Difference} = \sqrt{1.46} = 1.21$

$t = (2.75 - 6.25)/1.21 = -2.89$

Conclusion: Reject the null hypothesis.

---

puted chi-square, and significance level. Sandra Moriarty and Shu-Ling Everett (1994) conducted a study of television viewing. In their study, graduate students actually went to 55 different homes and observed people watching television for 45-minute sessions. In one part of their results, they compared the number of people they observed who fell into one of four distinct categories, using a chi-square test of goodness of fit:

> Flipping [very rapid channel changing], the category dominated by the most active type of behavior, occurred most frequently, in 33% of the sessions ($n = 18$). The grazing category [periods of browsing thought channels] dominated 24% of the sessions ($n = 13$), and 22% were found to be in each of the continuous and stretch viewing categories ($n = 12$). These differences were not statistically significant ($X^2 = 1.79$, $df = 3$, $p > .05$).

Here is an example of a chi-square test for independence. As part of a study about attitudes of heterosexuals toward homosexuality, Whitley (1990) asked 366 heterosexual students on an anonymous questionnaire whether or not they knew anyone who was a homosexual. Whitley reports, "Female (61.9%) and male (59.5%) respondents were equally likely to report knowing a gay person, $X^2(1, N = 366) < 1$." Whitley continues, "However, among the respondents knowing a gay person, women were more likely to report knowing a lesbian (63.4%) than men were to report knowing a gay man (14.4%), $X^2(1, N = 223) = 12.602$, $p < .001$" (p. 374).

Although Whitley does not give the effect size for the significant result, we can compute it from the information provided. The appropriate effect size statistic is a phi coefficient, because this is a 2×2 chi-square table (women-men × knowing lesbian vs. not knowing lesbian). Using the formula,

$$\Phi = \sqrt{\frac{X^2}{(N)}} = \sqrt{\frac{12.602}{223}} = \sqrt{.00565} = .24$$

This suggests that there is a moderate effect size.

Data Transformations

Data transformations usually are mentioned in the Results section, just prior to the description of the analysis using the data that were transformed. For example, Dixon, Heppner, and Anderson (1991) conducted a study in which they were looking at the relation of problem-solving skills to thoughts about suicide. Nearly 1,300 students completed measures of these and related variables, and a multiple regression analysis was planned. However, prior to describing the statistical analysis, Dixon and colleagues noted,

> As scores on the SSI [Scale for Suicide Ideation] range from 0 to 38, the mean of 1.5 suggests that the majority of students appraised themselves as very low suicide ideators. . . . Because of the statistical difficulties inherent in the positive skewness of the suicide scores, a square root transformation . . . was conducted to help normalize the SSI scores. (p. 53)

Rank-Order Tests

A study by Manning, Hall, and Gold (1990) on the effects of sugar on memory in older people provides an example of rank-order tests reported in a research article. In this case, just prior to presenting the results, the authors wrote a short paragraph headed "Statistical Analysis":

> Reliabilities of the tests, relationships between increases in glucose levels and performance, and relationships across neuropsychological tests were assessed using Spearman rank-order correlations. Comparisons of performance on treatment and control days used Wilcoxon rank comparisons of two samples . . . (two-tailed). (p. 308)

The specific tests were not mentioned again in their Results section. Nevertheless, when reporting significant differences, the Z score was given (as opposed to a t or an F score, which would ordinarily be expected in such comparisons), reminding the reader that a normal curve approximation for a rank-order test is being used: "Performance on the Logical Memory Test at both recalls and Long-Term Word Memory on the SRT [Selective Reminding Test] was significantly enhanced after glucose ingestion ($z = 2.98, p < .005; z = 2.81, p < .005; z = 1.99, p < .05$, respectively)" (p. 308).

Summary

Chi-square tests are used for hypothesis tests involving nominal variables. The chi-square statistic measures the amount of mismatch between expected and observed frequencies over several levels or categories. It is computed by finding for each category or combination of categories the difference between observed frequency and expected frequency, squaring this difference (to eliminate positive and negative signs), and dividing by the expected frequency (to help make the squared differences more proportionate to the numbers involved). The results are then added up for all the categories or combinations of categories. The distribution of the chi-square statistic is known and the cutoffs can be looked up in standard tables.

The chi-square test of independence is used to test hypotheses about the relation between two nominal variables, that is, about whether the breakdown over the categories of one variable has the same proportional pattern within each of the categories of the other variable. The data are set up in a contingency table, in which the two variables are crossed and the numbers in each combination are placed in each of the resulting cells. The frequency expected for a cell if the two variables are independent is the percentage of all the scores in that cell's row times the total number of cases in that cell's column. The degrees of freedom for the test of independence are the number of columns minus 1 times the number of rows minus 1.

The estimated effect size for a chi-square test of independence (that is, the degree of association) for a 2×2 contingency table is the phi coefficient, and for larger tables, Cramer's phi. Phi is the square root of the result of dividing the computed chi-square by the number of cases. Cramer's phi is the square root of the result of dividing the computed chi-square by the product of the number of cases times the degrees of freedom in the smaller dimension of the contingency table. These coefficients range from 0 to 1 and can be interpreted in approximately the same way as a correlation coefficient. A phi of .10 is considered a small effect, .30 a medium effect, and .50 a large effect.

Ordinary hypothesis testing procedures assume that populations follow a normal curve. When samples suggest that the populations are very far from normal (for example, due to outliers), using the ordinary procedures gives incorrect results.

One approach when the populations appear to be nonnormal is to transform the scores, such as taking the square root of each score so that the distribution of the transformed scores appears to represent a normally distributed population. The ordinary hypothesis-testing procedures can then be applied.

Another approach is to rank all of the scores in a study. Special rank-order tests (sometimes called nonparametric or distribution-free tests) use basic principles of probability to determine the chance of the ranks being unevenly distributed across experimental groups. However, in many cases, using the rank-transformed data in an ordinary parametric test produces a good approximation.

Key Terms

chi-square distribution	contingency table	observed frequency
chi-square statistic (X^2)	Cramer's phi statistic	phi coefficient (Φ)
chi-square table	data transformation	rank-order tests
chi-square test	expected frequency	rank-order transformation
chi-square test for goodness of fit	independence	
chi-square test for independence	nominal variable	

Practice Problems

These problems involve computation (with the assistance of a calculator). Most real-life statistics problems are done on a computer. Even if you have a computer, do these by hand to ingrain the method in your mind.

For practice in using a computer to solve statistics problems, refer to the computer section of each chapter of the Student's Study Guide and Computer Workbook *that accompanies this text.*

All data are fictional (unless an actual citation is given).

Answers to selected problems are given at the back of the book.

1. Compute a chi-square test for each of the following, using the .05 level for each. In each case, the expected distribution is equal frequencies in each category. (These are problems like the Stasser et al. example in which you are doing a chi-square for a single nominal variable. They are not chi-square tests for independence and do not involve any contingency tables.)

(a) 5 10 5
(b) 10 15 10
(c) 10 20 10
(d) 5 15 5

2. A director of a social service agency is trying to plan hiring of temporary staff to assist with intake and is wondering if there is any difference in the use of the agency at different seasons of the year. Last year there were 28 new clients in the winter, 33 in the spring, 16 in the summer, and 51 in the fall. On the basis of last year's data, should the director conclude that season makes a difference? (Use the .05 level.) Explain your answer to a person who has never taken a course in statistics. (This problem is like the Stasser et al. example in which you are doing a chi-square for a single nominal variable. It is not a chi-square tests for independence and does not involve any contingency tables.)

3. Carry out a chi-square test for independence for each of the following contingency tables. (Use the .01 level, and compute phi or Cramer's phi for each.)

(a)	10	16	(b)	100	106	(c)	100	160	
	16	10		106	100		160	100	
(d)	10	16	10	(e)	10	16	16	(f)	10	16	10
	16	10	10		16	10	16		16	10	16

4. An educational researcher is interested in whether students who use a typewriter or a word processor (or neither) when writing in their private room tend to use a pen or a pencil when they are taking notes in class. The researcher surveys 200 students. The results are shown in the accompanying table. Is there a significant relationship between these two variables? (Use the .05 level, and compute

Cramer's phi.) Explain your answer to a person who has never taken a course in statistics.

	Device Used in Their Room		
	Typewriter	**Word Processor**	**Neither**
Pen	42	62	26
Pencil	18	38	14

5. A political analyst is interested in whether the community a person lives in is related to that person's opinion on an upcoming water conservation ballot initiative. The analyst surveys 90 people by phone with the results shown here. Is opinion related to community at the .05 level? Also compute Cramer's phi. Explain your answer to a person who has never taken a course in statistics.

	Community A	Community B	Community C
For	12	6	3
Against	18	3	15
No opinion	12	9	12

6. Blass (1991), as part of a discussion of studies of obedience to authority, considered a possible cross-cultural difference. In obedience-to-authority studies, individuals are led to believe that they will be giving a series of increasingly strong and painful electric shocks to another subject. In one version of these studies, the subject meets the person who will receive the shocks and then goes into the next room where the subject can hear what the subject believes is the person screaming and complaining. The issue in these studies (which have raised considerable ethical debate) is how many subjects under these conditions will obey the experimenter and continue to give the shocks.

In his article, Blass compares the results of the original version of these studies conducted by Milgram (1974) in the United States to some Australian studies done shortly thereafter:

In Australia, Kilham and Mann (1974) found a significantly lower rate of obedience (28% [14 of 50]) than Milgram (1974) did in a comparable voice-feedback condition (Experiment 2; 62.5% [25 of 40]) with his American subjects, X^2 (1, $N = 90$) = 10.77, $p < .01$). (p. 407)

A footnote at this point in Blass's article says, "Chisquare was computed by me."

Explain this result to a person who has never had a course in statistics.

7. A researcher compares the typical family size in 10 cultures, 5 from Language Group A and 5 from Language Group B. The figures for the Group A cultures are 1.2, 2.5,

4.3, 3.8, and 7.2. The figures for the Group B cultures are 2.1, 9.2, 5.7, 6.7, and 4.8. Based on these 10 cultures, does typical family size differ in cultures with different language groups? Use the .05 level, and conduct a square-root transformation. (To keep things simple, round off the transformed scores to one decimal place.) Explain what you have done and why to someone who is familiar with the t test but not with data transformation.

8. A researcher randomly assigns subjects to watch one of three kinds of films: one that tends to make people sad, one that tends to make people exuberant, and one that tends to make people angry. They are then asked to rate a series of photos of individuals of the opposite sex on their attractiveness. The ratings for the sad-film group were 201, 523, and 614; the ratings for the angry-film group were 136, 340, and 301; and the ratings for the exuberant-film group were 838, 911, and 1,007. First, make a rank transform of the data, and then conduct a one-way analysis of variance. Explain what you have done and why to a person who understands the analysis of variance but not rank transformations or nonparametric tests.

9. June, Curry, and Gear (1990) surveyed black students at a midwestern university about problems in their use of college services. Surveys were conducted of about 250 students each time, at the end of the spring quarter in 1976, 1978, 1980, 1982, and 1987. The researchers ranked the nine main problem areas for each of the years. One of their analyses then proceeded as follows: "A major question of interest was whether the ranking of most serious problems and use of services varied by years. Thus, a Kruskal-Wallis one-way analysis of variance (ANOVA) was performed on the rankings but was not significant . . ." (p. 180). Explain why the researchers used the Kruskal-Wallis test instead of an ordinary analysis of variance and what conclusions can be drawn from this result.

12 Making Sense of Advanced Statistical Procedures in Research Articles

MOST research you will read uses one or more of the procedures you have learned in this book, but sometimes you will see procedures that you will not learn to do yourself until you take more advanced courses in statistics. Fortunately, these more advanced procedures are often straightforward extensions of what you have learned. These advanced procedures are not straightforward enough that you will understand all their subtleties or limitations, but they are straightforward enough that you will be able to make sense of the general idea.

We can divide these advanced statistical techniques into those that focus on associations among variables and those that focus on differences among groups. The procedures we cover first focus on associations among variables. They are all basically extensions and elaborations of what you learned in Chapter 3 on correlation and regression. After a brief review of multiple regression as a foundation, we introduce hierarchical and stepwise multiple regression, partial correlation, reliability, factor analysis, and causal modeling. We then turn to techniques that focus on differences between groups. These are basically extensions or elaborations of what you learned in Chapter 10 on the analysis of variance. These procedures include the analysis of covariance, multivariate analysis of variance, and multivariate analysis of covariance. We conclude the chapter with a discussion of what to do when you read a research article that uses a statistical technique you have never heard of.

Brief Review of Multiple Regression and Correlation

As you learned in Chapter 3, multiple correlation is about the association of one dependent variable with the combination of two or more predictor variables. In a fictional example we used in that chapter, there was a multiple correlation (R) of .96 between the amount of stress that managers experienced and the combination of the number of employees they supervise, the amount of noise in the workplace, and the number of decisions they must make each month.

As you also learned, multiple regression is about predicting a dependent variable on the basis of two or more predictor variables. (Regression, if you recall, is just the prediction aspect of correlation.) A multiple regression prediction rule has a regression coefficient for each predictor variable. If you know a person's scores on the predictor variables, you multiply each predictor variable's score times that variable's regression coefficient. The sum of these multiplications is the person's predicted score on the dependent variable. When working with Z scores, the regression coefficients are standardized regression coefficients, called beta weights (β).[1] For example, with three independent variables, the form of the prediction rule is as follows:

$$\text{Predicted } Z_Y = (\beta_1)(Z_{X_1}) + (\beta_2)(Z_{X_2}) + (\beta_3)(Z_{X_3})$$

(12–1)

In the managers' stress example, the Z-score multiple regression prediction rule was as follows:

$$\text{Predicted } Z_{\text{Stress}} = (.51)(Z_{\text{Employees}}) + (.11)(Z_{\text{Noise}}) + (.33)(Z_{\text{Decisions}})$$

In multiple correlation and regression, researchers can determine the statistical significance of both the overall multiple correlation coefficient, R, as well as for each beta individually. In most cases, however, if the overall R is not significant, the individual betas will not be tested for their significance. Yet, it is quite possible for the overall R to be significant but for some of the individual betas not to be significant. For example, the overall significant correlation might be due to the strong influence of only one predictor variable, with the others having only a slight contribution.

Hierarchical and Stepwise Multiple Regression

Hierarchical Multiple Regression

Sometimes researchers are interested in looking at the influence of several predictor variables in a sequential way. That is, they want to know what the correlation will be of the first predictor variable with the dependent variable, and then how much is added to the overall multiple correlation by including a second predictor variable, and then perhaps how much more is added by including a third predictor variable, and so on. This is known as **hierarchical multiple regression.**

hierarchical multiple regression

[1]When working with raw scores, the raw score regression coefficient (b) is multiplied by the raw score of each predictor variable. A particular number, the raw score regression constant (a) is also added in. Here is the standard form of the formula:

$$\text{Predicted } Y = a + (b_1)(X_1) + (b_2)(X_2) + (b_3)(X_3)$$

In the managers' stress example, the raw-score multiple-regression prediction rule was as follows:

$$\text{Predicted } Y = -4.70 + (.56)(X_1) + (.06)(X_2) + (.86)(X_3)$$

In research using hierarchical multiple regression, the amount that each successive variable adds to the overall prediction usually is described in terms of an increase in R^2, the proportion of variance accounted for or explained.

For example, Barocas and his colleagues (1991) conducted a study of 159 four-year-old children and their mothers to investigate various possible predictors of a child's IQ. Three main categories of predictors were measured: (a) the "contextual risk," the extent to which the family situations put the child at risk for problems, such as poverty, many children in the family, or mental illness of the mother; (b) "maternal teaching style" (MTS), the way the mother instructed the child to carry out a standard task as observed in the researcher's laboratory (variables included mother's positive, negative, or flattened emotional tone; how involved she was with her child; and how much thinking she demanded of the child, called "mental operational demand," or MOD; and (c) the child's ability to direct attention and willfully control his or her own actions as measured by two laboratory tasks ("Luria errors" and delayed-match-to-sample task, or DMS). A hierarchical regression analysis was carried out to see whether each group of predictors, when added to the preceding, contributed any significant additional variance accounted for. The researchers described their results as follows:

> Table [12–1] shows the hierarchical multiple-regression analysis in which maternal- and family-risk factors are entered in the prediction equation first, followed by the maternal teaching measures and by the child's laboratory-attention measures. . . . When maternal teaching is added, a significant increase of 9% in variance explained is achieved; when the attention measures are entered, an additional significant increase of 7% is obtained. Taken together, these measures of maternal and family risk, MTS, . . . and the child's attention and self-regulation as assessed in the DMS and Luria situations account for more than half the variance in IQ. (p. 483)

TABLE 12–1
Summary of Hierarchical Multiple Regression Analysis With Verbal IQ as Criterion

Predictor Variables	R^2	R^2 Change	F (Change)
Step 1			
Contextual risk	.376	.376	94.43*
Step 2			
MTS positive			
MTS negative			
MTS flattened			
MTS involved			
MTS low MOD			
MTS medium MOD	.468	.092	4.35*
Step 3			
Luria errors			
DMS group	.538	.071	11.38*

Note: MTS = maternal teaching style. MOD = mental operational demand. DMS = delayed-match-to-sample task. IQ = intelligence quotient.

From Barocas, R., Seifer, R., Sameroff, A. J., Andrews, T. A., Croft, R. T., & Ostrow, E. (1991), tab. 2. Social and interpersonal determinants of developmental risk. *Developmental Psychology*, 27, 479–488. Copyright, 1991, by the American Psychological Association. Reprinted by permission of the author.

Stepwise Multiple Regression

Often, especially in an exploratory study, a researcher may have measured many potential predictor variables and wants to pick out which ones make a useful contribution to the overall prediction. In the most common form of **stepwise multiple regression,** a computer program goes through a step-by-step procedure in which it first picks out the variable that has the highest correlation with the dependent variable. If this correlation is not significant, the process stops, since even the best predictor is not of any use. If this correlation is significant, the process goes on to the next step. The next step is to pick out the predictor variable which, in combination with this first one, has the highest multiple R. The computer then checks this to see whether this combination is a significant improvement over the best single predictor variable alone. If it is not, the process stops. If it is a significant improvement, the program goes on to the next step. The next step is to pick out which of the remaining predictor variables, when taken in combination with these first two, creates the highest multiple R. Then this combination is checked to see if it is a significant improvement in prediction over and above just the first two predictors. The process continues until either all the predictor variables are included or adding any of the remaining ones does not give a significant improvement. Because this procedure proceeds one step at a time, it is called "stepwise." It is diagrammed in Table 12–2.

Here is an example. Mooney, Sherman, and Lo Presto (1991) examined predictors of adjustment to college (the dependent variable) among 82 women in their fourth week of their first semester at college. The women in the study were all living away from home. The predictor variables were distance from home (in miles), perceived distance from home (a scale from *just right* to *too far*), a self-esteem scale, and an "academic locus of control" scale that measures how much a person feels in control over being successful at school. One purpose of the study was to find out whether all of these variables made their own unique contributions to predicting college adjustment,

stepwise multiple regression

TABLE 12–2
The Process of a Stepwise Multiple Regression

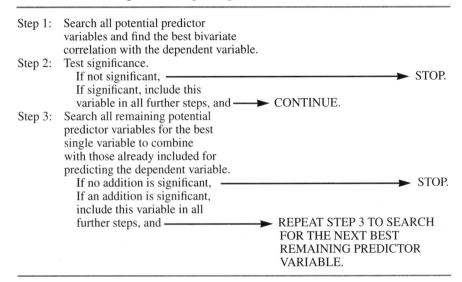

Step 1:   Search all potential predictor variables and find the best bivariate correlation with the dependent variable.

Step 2:   Test significance.
   If not significant, ——————————————————————→ STOP.
   If significant, include this variable in all further steps, and ——→ CONTINUE.

Step 3:   Search all remaining potential predictor variables for the best single variable to combine with those already included for predicting the dependent variable.
   If no addition is significant, ——————————————→ STOP.
   If an addition is significant, include this variable in all further steps, and ——————→ REPEAT STEP 3 TO SEARCH FOR THE NEXT BEST REMAINING PREDICTOR VARIABLE.

and if not all of them, which ones? The authors describe the procedure they used as follows:

> For this analysis, a stepwise procedure was employed, with forward entry of predictor variables continuing until significant relationships with remaining partialed variables were exhausted. Three predictors were retained: academic locus of control, perceived distance from home, and self-esteem. . . . With these variables in the equation, 59% of the variance in the dependent variable was accounted for ($R = .77$, $R^2 = .59$ . . .). The standardized beta coefficients [of the regression equation including these three predictor variables] indicated that academic locus of control was weighted the most, followed by self-esteem and perceived distance. . . . (p. 447)

What the authors are telling us is that of the four potential predictors, the proportion of variance accounted for by three of these variables was not improved upon by also including the fourth (actual distance from home). Actual distance from home was left out of the final regression equation because it did not add anything to include it.

One caution about stepwise regression. The prediction formula that results is the best group of variables for predicting the dependent variable, *based on the sample studied*. However, it often happens that when the same variables are studied with a new sample, a somewhat different combination of variables turns out to be best.

Hierarchical and Stepwise Regression Compared

Hierarchical and stepwise regression are similar in an important way. In both methods you are adding one variable at a time and checking whether the addition makes a significant improvement in the prediction. There is also a very important difference. In hierarchical regression, the order of adding the predictor variables is based on some theory or plan, decided in advance by the researcher. In stepwise regression, there is no initial plan. The computer simply figures out the best variables to add until adding more makes no additional contribution.

Hierarchical regression is used in research that is based on theory or some substantial previous knowledge. Stepwise regression is useful in exploratory research where we do not know what to expect or in applied research where we are looking for the best prediction formula without caring about its theoretical meaning.

Partial Correlation

Partial correlation is another technique that is widely used in the social and behavioral sciences. Partial correlation is the amount of association between two variables, over and above the influence of one or more other variables. Suppose a sociologist wants to know how much the stress people experience in married life is related to how long they have been married. However, the researcher is aware that part of what might make marital stress go together with marriage length is that people who have been married longer are likely to have children, and having children could create marital stress. Simply figuring the correlation between marital stress and marriage length would be

Partial correlation

misleading. The researcher wants to know the relation between stress and length that would occur if everyone had the same number of children. To put it another way, the researcher wants somehow to subtract the information provided by number of children from the information provided by marital stress and length. Partial correlation accomplishes this.

In this case, the researcher would compute a partial correlation between marital stress and length of marriage, **holding constant** number of children. This is also described as **partialing out** or **controlling for** number of children. ("Holding constant," "partialing out," and "controlling for" all mean the same thing and are used interchangeably.) The actual statistic for partial correlation is called the **partial correlation coefficient,** which has values from −1 to +1 and is thought of like an ordinary correlation between two variables, except for remembering that some third variable is being controlled for.

Here is another way of thinking of partial correlations. In the example, the researcher could compute a correlation between stress and marriage length using only people who have no children, then compute the same correlation for only those with one child, and so on. Each of these correlations considered by itself is not affected by differences in number of children. (This is because, of the people considered in each of these correlations, there are no differences in the number of children.) The researcher could figure a kind of average of these various correlations, each of which is not affected by number of children. This average of these correlations is the partial correlation. It is literally a correlation that holds constant the number of children.

In fact, the calculations for a partial correlation are fairly straightforward and do not require figuring all these individual correlations and averaging them. However, the result of the process amounts to doing this.

Partial correlation often is used to help sort out alternative theoretical explanations for the relations among variables. Suppose the sociologist found an ordinary correlation between marital stress and marriage length. The sociologist might want to use this result as support for a theory that the effect of time is to make people feel more stress in their marriage because their partners take them for granted. The sociologist would also be aware that another possible explanation for what is going on is that when people are married longer, they are likely to have more children, and having children might create stress in the marriage. If the correlation between stress and length is found, even after controlling for number of children, this alternate explanation about children is made unlikely.

Here is an actual research example. Baer (1991) was interested in verbal creativity (storytelling, poetry, and so on). Specifically, his study focused on whether verbal creativity is a single, general trait or whether it is a group of individual abilities. In the past, researchers had found that creativity tests tend to correlate to a moderate degree with each other, and this was taken as evidence for the general, single trait idea. Baer, however, reasoned that the correlations among these tests may be due to factors, such as IQ, that may make people do better on any kind of test. In one of his studies, Baer gave 50 eighth graders several creativity tests along with IQ and scholastic achievement tests. As was found in the previous studies, Baer also found that there were low to moderate correlations among the creativity tests. Then, Baer figured these correlations again, this time as partial correlations, holding constant scores on verbal IQ, reading achievement, math IQ, math achievement, and gender. (That is, all of these variables were partialed out at once.) In most cases, the partial correlations were clearly lower than the ordinary correlations. For example, the correlation between the story-task creativity test and the poetry-task creativity test went from an ordinary correlation of .23 to a partial correlation of −.01. Similarly, the correlation between poetry-task creativity and word-problem creativity went from .31 to .19.

Reliability

Measures such as questionnaires or systematic observations of what people do, are rarely perfectly stable or consistent. The degree of consistency is called **reliability.** Roughly speaking, reliability is the extent to which you would obtain the same result if you were to administer the same measure again to the same person under the same circumstances. Computing the reliability of a measurement is central to almost all areas of research, and you will often see reliability statistics in articles.

    One way to evaluate a measure's reliability is to use the measure with the same group of people twice. The correlation between the two testings is called **test-retest reliability.** However, this approach often is not practical or appropriate. For example, you cannot use this approach if taking a test once would influence the second taking (such as with an intelligence test).

    For many measures, such as most questionnaires, you also can evaluate its reliability by correlating the responses of half the items with the other half. For example, you could correlate the average score on all the odd-numbered items with the average score on all the even-numbered items. If the person is answering consistently, this should be a high correlation. This is called **split-half reliability.**

    A problem with the split-half method is which way to split the halves. Odd versus even items makes sense in most cases, but by chance it could give too low or too high a correlation. A more general solution is to divide the test up into halves in all possible ways and figure the correlation using each division. The average of these correlations is called **Cronbach's alpha (α).** Cronbach's alpha is the most widely used measure of reliability. Cronbach's alpha also can be thought of as describing how much each item is associated with each other item. It describes the overall consistency of the test, the extent to which high responses go with highs and lows with lows over all the test items.

    In general, in the social and behavioral sciences, a measure should have a reliability of at least .7 and preferably closer to .9 to be considered useful.

    One context in which reliabilities are nearly always discussed is when a research article is mainly about the development of a new measure. For example, Berscheid, Snyder, and Omoto (1989) developed a questionnaire to assess interpersonal closeness. They asked students to answer their questionnaires with regard to the person with whom they have the "closest, deepest, most involved, and most intimate relationship" (p. 793). (Some indicated family members, others close friends, others romantic partners.) The researchers reported on the reliability of their Strength subscale (34 questions about the extent to which this close other influenced the student). "We found high internal-consistency reliability for this measure across all relationship types (α = .90), as well as within the three main relationship types" (p. 795).

reliability

test-retest reliability

split-half reliability

Cronbach's alpha (α)

The Greek letter "alpha" (α) refers to Cronbach's alpha. (This should not to be confused with alpha as the probability of a Type I error in hypothesis testing.) They tested a subgroup of 75 of their subjects a second time, 3 to 5 weeks later, and reported that "the correlation between . . . scores at Time 1 and Time 2 [for the entire questionnaire] was $r(75) = .82$, $p < .001$" (p. 797). They also reported the "test-retest coefficient" for specific subscales, which for strength was ".81 ($p < .001$)" (p. 797).

Factor Analysis

Factor analysis

factor

factor loading

Factor analysis is used when a researcher has measured people on a large number of variables. Factor analysis tells the researcher which variables tend to clump together—which ones tend to be correlated with each other and not with other variables. Each such clump (group of variables) is called a **factor.** The relative connection of each of the original variables to a factor is called that variable's **factor loading** on that factor. (Variables have loadings on each factor but usually will have high loadings on only one.) Factor loadings can be thought of as the correlation of the variable with the factor, and like correlations, they range from –1, a perfect negative association with the factor, through 0, no relation to the factor, to +1, a perfect positive correlation with the factor. Normally, a variable is considered to contribute meaningfully to a factor only if it has a loading of at least about .3 (or below –.3). Some researchers use .35, .40, or even higher levels as the cutoff.

Which variables end up in which factor is calculated using standard formulas. The researcher does have some leeway and can select from a variety of methods of factor analysis, each of which may give slightly different results. The only really subjective part of the process is in the name given to a factor. (When reading a research article reporting a factor analysis, you should think closely as to whether the name the researcher gives to a factor really does a good job of describing the variables that make up that factor.)

Consider an example of factor analysis. Hendrick and Hendrick (1989) gave 19 different love scales to 391 students. These researchers then conducted a factor analysis of the scores to "determine commonalities among the scales" (p. 791). Table 12–3 presents the results of this analysis. (On the Love Attitudes Scale, Eros refers to passionate, romantic love; Ludus, to game-playing love; Storge to friendship-based love; Pragma to practical love; Mania to possessive, dependent love; and Agape to altruistic love.)

This particular table leaves blank factor loadings below .35 to make it easy to see which variables go with what factor. Also note that the last line of this table tells you the percentage of variance that the factor as a whole accounts for (that is, what the R^2 would be of this factor with all the variables). Notice that the five factors, even taken together, do not account for all the variance in the 19 variables. Accounting for a total of 69% (32% + 14% + 8% + 8% + 7%) of the variance in 19 variables with only five factors is an impressive simplification. It is this kind of simplification that is the goal of factor analysis.

Hendrick and Hendrick interpret each of the factors in some detail. For example, with regard to the first factor:

> The first factor that emerged included the love styles of Eros, Mania, and Agape; Sternberg's Intimacy, Passion, and Commitment; the Passionate Love Scale; and Davis's Viability, Intimacy, Passion, Care, and Satisfaction. The highest

TABLE 12–3
Factor Analysis of All Love Scales Combined

Individual Measures	Factor Structure and Loadings				
	1	*2*	*3*	*4*	*5*
Attachment Styles					
Avoidant	—	—	—	-.81	—
Anxious-Ambivalent	—	—	.80	—	—
Secure	—	—	—	.83	—
Love Attitudes Scale					
Eros	.76	—	—	—	—
Ludus	—	-.65	—	—	—
Storge	—	—	—	—	.80
Pragma	—	-.39	—	—	.73
Mania	.39	—	.68	—	—
Agape	.54	—	—	—	—
Triangular Theory of Love Scale					
Intimacy	.72	.44	—	—	—
Passion	.85	—	—	—	—
Commitment	.82	—	—	—	—
Passionate Love Scale					
Passionate Love	.80	—	—	—	—
Relationship Rating Form					
Viability	.51	.67	—	—	—
Intimacy	.58	.52	—	—	—
Passion	.82	—	—	—	—
Care	.72	.43	—	—	—
Satisfaction	.78	.38	—	—	—
Conflict	—	-.70	—	—	—
% variance	32	14	8	8	7

Note: Only factor loadings of .35 or larger are shown. $N = 391$.

From Hendrick, C., & Hendrick, S. S. (1989), tab. 4. Research on love: Does it measure up? *Journal of Personality and Social Psychology*, *56*, 784–794. Copyright, 1989, by the American Psychological Association. Reprinted by permission of the author.

loadings on the factor were those of Commitment and the three measures of Passion, although the other variables also had substantial loadings. Passionate love was certainly a major component of the factor, but intimacy, commitment, satisfaction, and aspects of caring love also appeared to be important. (p. 791)

After describing each factor in this way, they concluded:

In summary, the various love scales primarily tap passionate love (Factor 1); however, two types of bipolar closeness-distance dimensions (Factors 2 and 4) are also important, as well as ambivalence-mania (Factor 3) and practicality-friendship (Factor 5). (p. 791)

Causal Modeling

In causal modeling techniques, as in factor analysis, the researcher has tested a number of people on a number of variables. Unlike factor analysis, the goal of causal modeling techniques is to examine whether the pattern of correlations among the variables fits with the researcher's underlying theory of which variables are causing which.

Causal modeling techniques are used widely in the social sciences. We first introduce the older method of path analysis, then proceed to the newer, more elaborate, structural equation modeling approach.

Path Analysis

path analysis

In **path analysis,** the researcher makes a diagram with arrows connecting the variables. The arrows, or paths, show the cause-and-effect connections between variables based on the researcher's theory. Then the researcher calculates path coefficients for each path. The **path coefficient** is like a beta in multiple regression: It tells you how much a change in the variable at the start of the arrow is associated with a change in the variable at the end of the arrow. (This coefficient is figured so that it partials out the influence of any other variables that have arrows to the variable at the end of the arrow.)

path coefficient

Here is an example. Bierman and Smoot (1991) interviewed parents of 75 grade school boys about parental discipline practices, parental hostility, marital satisfaction, and the boys' "home conduct problems." The researchers also gave questionnaires to the boys' teachers about "school conduct problems" and collected ratings from schoolmates of how much they liked these boys as a measure of "peer social performance." Based on their theory, Bierman and Smoot had, in advance, predicted a specific pattern of causal connections among the variables measured. Figure 12–1 reproduces Bierman and Smoot's path diagram. This diagram shows their predicted pattern of causal connections, as well as the path coefficients figured based on their results. (This path diagram is somewhat complicated in that the variables on the left and home conduct problems were measured for both mothers and fathers. The path coefficients based on the fathers' correlations are shown in parentheses. On the other hand, the overall model is considerably simpler than most path models.)

For some reason, Bierman and Smoot do not actually put in the arrowheads. (Usually they are shown.) Nevertheless, it is clear that the causality is intended to go from left to right. In interpreting this path diagram, be sure to notice that some of the signs of the paths are negative. For example, the path

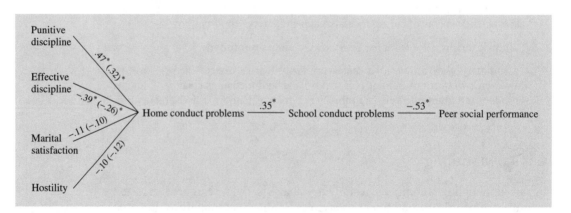

FIGURE 12–1
A path analysis. (Figure 1 from Bierman, K. L., and Smoot, D. L. [1991]. Linking family characteristics with poor peer relations: The mediating role of conduct problems. *Journal of Abnormal Child Psychology, 19,* 341–356. Copyright, 1991, by Plenum Publishing Corporation. Reprinted by permission.)

from home conduct problems to school conduct problems has a positive path coefficient. This means that the more of one, the more of the other. The coefficient for the final path, from school conduct problems to peer social performance, is negative. This means that the more school conduct problems, the less the peer social performance.

In this path diagram, the most important paths had significant coefficients in the predicted directions. Bierman and Smoot consider the results to be encouraging support for their theory.

Structural Equation Modeling

Structural equation modeling is also known as *latent variable modeling* and other names as well. Often it is referred to as **LISREL,** after the name of a specific computer program that can be used to calculate an analysis of this kind. Basically, structural equation modeling is just a special extension of path analysis. It also involves a path diagram with arrows between variables and path coefficients for each arrow.

However, structural equation modeling has several important advantages over the older path analysis method. One major advantage is that the procedure gives an overall indication of the fit between the data and the theory (as described in the path model). This indication of overall fit is called a **fit index** or an index of *goodness of fit.* There are several different fit indexes used, but in general, a fit of .9 or higher is considered a good fit. (The maximum is usually 1.)

In structural equation modeling, one also can compute a kind of significance test for whether the data fit the theory. We say a "kind of significance test" because the null hypothesis in this case is that the theory fits. This means that a significant result is saying that the theory does not fit. In other words, a researcher trying to demonstrate a theory hopes for a nonsignificant result in this significance test!

A second major advantage of structural equation modeling over ordinary path analysis is that it uses what are called latent variables. A **latent variable** is a variable that is not actually measured but stands for the true variable that the researcher would like to measure but can only approximate with real-life measures. For example, a latent variable might be social class, which the researcher tries to approximate with several measured variables, such as level of income, years of education, prestige of occupation, and home square footage. None of these measured variables by itself is a very good stand-in for social class (though some are better than others). What is needed is some kind of weighted average that also takes into account that as a whole, the group of measured variables still does not perfectly get at the true latent variable.

In structural equation modeling, the mathematics is set up so that a latent variable is a combination of the measured variables, combined in such a way as to use only what they have in common with each other. The idea is that what they have in common is the true score on the thing they are all getting at parts of. (A latent variable is actually like a factor in factor analysis, in that the factor is not directly measured itself, but it stands for a weighted combination of several variables that make it up.)

In a structural equation modeling path diagram, the variables that actually are measured usually are shown in squares; the latent variables are shown in circles. This is illustrated in the example in Figure 12–2. Notice in the figure that the arrows from the latent variables (the ones in circles) go to the measured variables (the ones in boxes). The idea is that the latent variable is the underlying cause of the measured variables, the measured variables being the best we can do to measure the true latent variable.

Also notice that all of the other arrows are between latent variables. In most cases, structural equation modeling works in this way: The measured variables are used to make up latent variables and the main focus of the analysis is on the causal relations (the paths) between the latent variables.

An Example of Structural Equation Modeling

This example is about a similar topic to the one we considered in the path analysis example. In this research, Capaldi and Patterson (1991) studied 169 boys in fourth grade and then the same boys again in sixth grade. A large number of measures were used so that there were several measured variables for each of their latent variables. For example, the latent variable Maternal Antisocial Behavior was indicated by four measured variables: mother's arrests and license suspensions, mother's drug use, mother's score on a personality test measuring deviancy, and how young the mother was when she had her first child.

Capaldi and Patterson's diagram (Figure 12–3) shows only the latent variables and the paths between them. (This is often done in research articles to keep the diagram simple.) The researchers also give fit indexes and a kind of significance test. The fit indexes were all in the range of .9, which is a good fit. The significance test was reported as "X^2 (61, $N = 169$) = 76.13, $p = .09$." This nonsignificant result is considered good. That is, the path diagram, which represents the researchers theory, is not a significantly bad fit to the data. (This diagram also shows a statistic called D, which is not usually included in such diagrams. Roughly speaking, D is the variation in the latent variable *not* accounted for by the variables with arrows leading to that latent variable.)

FIGURE 12–2
A structural equation model path diagram.

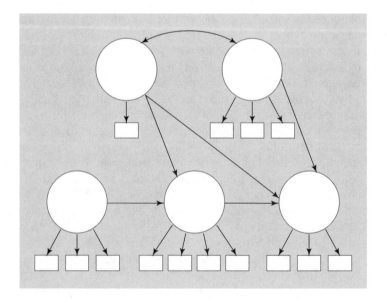

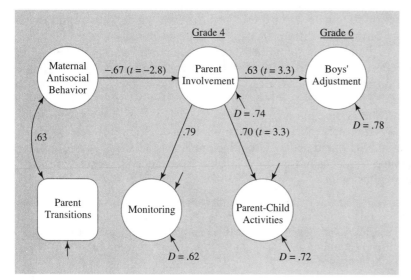

FIGURE 12–3
Mediated model. (X^2 (61, N = 169) = 76.13, p = .09. Bentler-Bonett normed fit index = .84; Bentler-Bonett nonnormed fit index = .95; comparative fit index = .96.) (Example of structural equation model from Capaldi, D. M., & Patterson, G. R. [1991]. Relation of parental transitions to boys' adjustment problems: I. A linear hypothesis. II. Mothers at risk for transitions and unskilled parenting. *Developmental Psychology,* 27, 489–504. Copyright, 1991, by the American Psychological Association. Reprinted by permission of the author.)

A Key Limitation of Causal Modeling

It is important to realize how little magic there is behind these wonderful methods. They still rely entirely on a researcher's deep thinking. All the predicted paths in a path analysis diagram can be significant and a structural equation model can have an excellent fit and yet it is still quite possible that other patterns of causality could work equally well or better.

Alternatives could have arrows that go in the opposite direction or make different connections, or the pattern could include additional variables not in the original diagram. Any kind of causal modeling shows at best that the data are consistent with the theory. The same data could also be consistent with quite different theories. Ideally, a researcher tries out alternative theories and finds that the data do not fit them well. Nevertheless, there can always be alternative theories the researcher did not think of at all.

Analysis of Covariance (ANCOVA)

So far in this chapter, we have been exploring statistical procedures that emphasize associations among variables and are basically fancy elaborations of correlation and regression. Next, we turn to procedures that focus on differences between group means, procedures that are basically elaborations of the analysis of variance.

One of the most widely used of these elaborations is called the **analysis of covariance (ANCOVA).** In this procedure, the researcher does an ordinary analysis of variance, but only after first adjusting the variables to get rid of the effect of some unwanted additional variable. The analysis of covariance does for the analysis of variance what partial correlation does for ordinary correlation. The variable controlled for or partialed out is called the **covariate.** The rest of the results are interpreted like any other analysis of variance.

For example, in another part of the article by Capaldi and Patterson (1991) on boys' adjustment in grades 4 and 6, these researchers compared the

analysis of covariance (ANCOVA)

covariate

adjustment of boys who had experienced different levels of parental transitions since birth. (The different levels of parental transition were no transition, loss of father, new stepfather, and two or more new stepfathers.) The authors report, "An ANOVA showed that there were significant differences among the transition groups, $F(3, 170) = 7.53$, $p < .001$." (The pattern of means for the four levels was in the predicted direction of the more parental transitions, the poorer the adjustment of the boy.) The authors were aware that the boys' families in the four transition levels were of different socioeconomic status (SES) and had different income levels. Could these differences, and not the differences in transition level, be the underlying cause of the difference in adjustment?

> Next, we tested the hypothesis that the differences among transition groups were primarily a function of the differences in SES and income. To test this assumption, an ANOVA was run with SES and per capita income as covariates. The difference among the transition groups remained significant, $F(5, 167) = 4.0$, $p < .01$. (pp. 492–493)

(The pattern of means was also the same in this analysis as in the original.) Although they did not use the term, an ANOVA with covariates is an analysis of covariance.

Multivariate Analysis of Variance (MANOVA) and Multivariate Analysis of Covariance (MANCOVA)

In all of the procedures we have discussed so far in this book, including in this chapter, there is only one dependent variable. There may be two or even many independent or predictor variables, as in multiple regression or in the factorial analysis of variance. In all cases, there has been only one dependent variable.

multivariate statistics

In this section we consider **multivariate statistics,** which are procedures used when you have two or more dependent variables. Specifically, we focus on the two most widely used multivariate procedures. These are multivariate elaborations of the analysis of variance and the analysis of covariance; that is, these are versions of the analysis of variance and covariance that are able to handle more than one dependent variable.

Multivariate analysis of variance (MANOVA)

Multivariate analysis of variance (MANOVA) is an analysis of variance in which there can be several dependent variables. Usually, these dependent variables are different measures of approximately the same thing, such as three different political involvement scales or three different reading ability tests. The results of the MANOVA are interpreted basically the same as an ordinary analysis of variance. Suppose there are three groups studied and each subject is measured on four dependent variables. The MANOVA would give an overall F and significance level for the difference among the three groups, in terms of how much they differ on the combination of the four variables.

When researchers do find an overall significant difference among groups with MANOVA, this says that the groups differ on the combination of dependent variables. The researcher will then usually also want to know whether the groups differ on any or all of the dependent variables considered individually. It is common to follow up a MANOVA with a series of ordinary analyses of variance, one for each of the dependent variables. These individual analyses of variance are sometimes referred to as "univariate" analyses of variance (as opposed to the multivariate analyses), because each has only one dependent variable.

Consider an example. Lynn and his colleagues (1991) carried out a 2×2 factorial design study of hypnosis. In this study, there were two independent variables. One was "Context," whether the hypnotist did or did not create a strong rapport with the subject. Context was manipulated by the researchers as part of the experiment. The other independent variable was high versus low "Hypnotizability." Hypnotizability was measured using a personality test. There were three dependent variables, each a questionnaire scale completed after the hypnotic session. The three scales were all part of the "AIM" test. They focused on the participant's relationship with the hypnotist. These three scales were hypnotist power, emotional bond, and fear of negative appraisal.

Lynn and co-workers described their analysis as follows:

> A 2 (context) $\times$ 2 (hypnotizability) MANOVA performed on the three scales of the AIM revealed a significant multivariate effect for hypnotizability, $F(3, 39) = 4.08$, $p = .01$. For this factor, significant univariate effects were obtained for the measures of hypnotist power, $F(1, 41) = 4.49$, $p < .05$ (M high hypnotizable = 29.54, $SD = 7.82$ vs. M low hypnotizable = 24.29, $SD = 7.82$), and emotional bond with the hypnotist, $F(1, 41) = 8.35$, $p < .01$ (M high hypnotizable = 32.46, $SD = 9.29$ vs. M low hypnotizable = 24.76, $SD = 9.33$). Neither the multivariate Context effect nor the multivariate Context $\times$ Hypnotizability interaction achieved significance. (p. 741)

(This analysis, incidentally, was a secondary aspect of the study, which was mainly about hypnotic performance. In that analysis, which was not a MANOVA, their predicted effect was found: The highly hypnotizable subjects were about equally responsive to hypnosis regardless of the degree of rapport with the hypnotist. Low-hypnotizable subjects were much more responsive to hypnosis when there was a strong sense of rapport.)

An analysis of covariance in which there is more than one dependent variable is called a **multivariate analysis of covariance (MANCOVA).** The difference between it and an ordinary analysis of covariance is precisely parallel to the difference between a MANOVA and an ordinary analysis of variance. That is, a MANCOVA is a MANOVA in which there are one or more covariates (variables controlled for).

multivariate analysis of covariance (MANCOVA)

Overview of Statistical Techniques

Table 12–4 shows in a systematic way the various techniques we have considered in this chapter, along with the other parametric procedures covered throughout the book. Just to prove to yourself how much you have learned, you might cover the right-hand column and play "Name That Statistic."

How to Read Results Involving Unfamiliar Statistical Techniques

Based on this chapter and what you have learned throughout this book, you should be well prepared to read and understand, at least in a general way, the

TABLE 12–4
Major Statistical Techniques

Association or Difference	Number of Independent Variables	Number of Dependent Variables	Any Variables Controlled?	Name of Technique
Association	1	1	No	Bivariate correlation/regression
Association	Any number	1	No	Multiple regression (including hierarchical and stepwise regression)
Association	1	1	Yes	Partial correlation
Association	Many, not differentiated		No	Reliability coefficients Factor analysis
Association	Many, with specified causal patterns			Path analysis Structural equation modeling
Difference	1	1	No	One-way analysis of variance; t test
Difference	Any number	1	No	Analysis of variance
Difference	Any number	1	Yes	Analysis of covariance
Difference	Any number	Any number	No	Multivariate analysis of variance
Difference	Any number	Any number	Yes	Multivariate analysis of covariance

results in most research articles. However, you will still now and then come up against new techniques (and sometimes unfamiliar names for old techniques). This happens even to well-seasoned researchers. So what do you do when you run into something you have never heard of before?

First, do not panic. In most cases, you can figure out the basic idea. Almost always a p level will be given and it should be clear just what pattern of results is being considered significant or not. In addition, there will usually be some indication of the size of the effect—of the degree of association or the size of the difference. If the statistic is about the association among some variables, it is probably stronger as the result gets closer to 1 and weaker as the result gets closer to 0. Do not expect to understand every word in a situation like this. Try to grasp as much as you can about the meaning of the result.

An Example of Dealing with an Unfamiliar Statistical Technique

Biernat and Wortman (1991) conducted a study of the home lives of women professionals. Near the beginning of their Results section, the researchers mention that in some of their analyses, they will be comparing women academics to businesswomen. Therefore, they explain, they checked whether

BOX 12–1

The Golden Age of Statistics: Four Guys Around London

In the last chapter of his little book *The Statistical Pioneers,* James Tankard (1984) discusses the interesting fact that the four most common statistical techniques were created by four Englishmen born within 68 years of each other, three of whom worked in the vicinity of London (and the fourth, Gosset, stuck at his brewery in Dublin, nevertheless visited London to study and kept in good touch with all that was happening in that city). What were the reasons?

First, Tankard feels that their closeness and communication were important for creating the "critical mass" of minds sometimes associated with a golden age of discovery or creativity. Second, as is often the case with important discoveries, each man faced difficult practical problems or "anomalies" that pushed him to the solution he arrived at. (None simply set out to invent a statistical method in itself.)

Tankard also discusses three important social factors specific to this "golden age of statistics." First, there was the role of biometrics, which was attempting to test the theory of evolution mathematically. Biometrics had its influence through Galton's reading of Darwin and his subsequent influence on Pearson. Second, this period saw the beginning of mass hiring by industry and agriculture of university graduates with "high-powered" mathematical training. Third, since the time of Newton, Cambridge University had been a particular, centralized source for England of brilliant mathematicians. They could spread out through British industry and still, through their common alma mater, remain in contact with students and each other and conversant with the most recent breakthroughs—an interesting time.

Today is also an interesting time for statistics. In particular, the computer has made possible all kinds of new statistical methods. The fundamentals developed in the Golden Age are mainly what you have learned in this book. They probably will remain the fundamentals for a long time to come. What can be done beyond the fundamentals is changing incredibly rapidly. If you go on to take an advanced statistics course, much of what you learn will be procedures developed in the last decade or two. Ideas currently being worked on are especially exciting and could well revolutionize the research possibilities open to social scientists in the years to come.

---

the variables to be compared seemed to meet the assumption of equal population variances. Regarding one variable they comment, "Variability in education was higher for businesswomen ($SD = 1.26$) than for academic women ($SD = 0.12$), Cochran's $C(2, 136) = .99$, $p < .0001$" (p. 848).

You have probably never heard of "Cochran's C." However, from the context you can figure out that it is a significance test comparing the variability of two groups. You probably cannot figure out what the numbers in parentheses after the C mean exactly or what the .99 refers to at all. You can make sense of the "$p < .0001$." This tells you that the difference in variabilities of the two groups is significant. You could even go further and look directly at the two standard deviations, which give a quite clear idea of how very different the variabilities in the two groups are.

Suppose you really cannot figure out anything about a statistical technique used in a research article. In that case, you can try to look up the procedure in a statistics book. Intermediate and advanced statistics textbooks are sometimes a good bet. We should warn you that trying to make sense of an intermediate text on your own can be quite difficult. Many such texts are heavily mathematically oriented. Even quite accessible textbooks will each use their own set of symbols. It can be hard to make sense of their description of a particular method without having read the whole book. Perhaps a better solution in this case is to ask for help from a professor or graduate student in your field. If you know the basics as you have learned them in this book, you should be able to understand the essentials of their explanations.

If this happens often, the best solution is to take more statistics courses. Usually, the next course after this one would be an intermediate statistics course in your particular major. In fact, some people find statistics so fascinating that they choose to make a career of it. You might too.

New statistical methods are being invented constantly. Social and behavioral scientists all encounter unfamiliar numbers and symbols in the research articles they read. They puzzle them out, and so will you. We say that with confidence because you have arrived, safe and knowledgeable, at the back pages of this book. You have mastered a thorough introduction to a complex topic. That should give you complete confidence that with a little time and attention you can understand anything further in statistics. Congratulations on your accomplishment.

Summary

In hierarchical multiple regression, predictor variables are included in the prediction rule in a planned sequential fashion. This allows the researcher to determine the relative contribution of each successive variable over and above those already included. Stepwise multiple regression is an exploratory procedure in which potential predictor variables are searched in order to find the best predictor, then the remaining variables are searched for the predictor which in combination with the first produces the best prediction. This process continues until adding the best remaining variable does not provide a significant improvement.

Partial correlation describes the degree of correlation between two variables while holding one or more other variables constant.

Reliability coefficients indicate the extent to which scores on a test are internally consistent (usually with Cronbach's alpha) or consistent over time (test-retest reliability).

Factor analysis identifies groupings of variables that correlate maximally with each other and minimally with other variables.

Causal analysis examines whether the correlations among several variables is consistent with a systematic, hypothesized pattern of causal relationships among them. Path analysis describes these relationships with arrows each pointing from cause to effect and each with a path coefficient indicating the influence of the hypothesized causal variable on the hypothesized effect variable. Structural equation modeling is an advanced version of path analysis that includes latent, unmeasured theoretical variables (each of which consists of the common elements of several measured variables). It also provides measures of the overall fit of the data to the hypothesized causal pattern.

The analysis of covariance is an analysis of variance that controls for one or more variables. The multivariate analysis of variance is an analysis of variance with two or more dependent variables. The multivariate analysis of covariance is an analysis of covariance with more two or more dependent variables.

Key Terms

analysis of covariance
    (ANCOVA)
controlling for
covariate
Cronbach's alpha (α)
factor
factor analysis
factor loading
fit index
hierarchical multiple regression

holding constant
latent variable
LISREL
multivariate analysis of covari-
    ance (MANCOVA)
multivariate analysis of variance
    (MANOVA)
multivariate statistics
partial correlation
partial correlation coefficient

partialing out
path analysis
path coefficient
reliability
split-half reliability
stepwise multiple regression
structural equation modeling
test-retest reliability

Practice Problems

*For Problems 1 through 6, you are expected only to ex-
plain the general meaning of the results at the level at
which the various methods were described in the chapter.
You are not, of course, expected to describe the logic of the
statistical procedures covered here in the way that you
have been doing in previous chapters.*

*Answers to selected problems are given at the back of
the book.*

1. Meier (1991) studied the relationship of stress and
related variables to the number of physical symptoms
(stomachaches, sleeplessness, headaches, and so on) during the past 2 weeks. Meier also measured social desirability (SD), the tendency to give the responses on a test that
make you look good. SD and gender were included in the
study so that they could be controlled when analyzing the
relationship of stress to symptoms. Meier explains one
analysis as follows:

> A hierarchical regression analysis was calculated with
> gender, social desirability, and the [other] measures as in-
> dependent variables. Gender . . . alone accounted for 15%
> of the symptoms variance. Next SD was entered, but failed
> to contribute further to explained variance. The MBA
> [Meir Burnout Assessment] was entered, accounting for
> only 2% additional variance. However, when the MBI
> [Maslach Burnout Inventory] was entered, it contributed
> 10% more of the symptom variance. State anxiety was en-
> tered next and accounted for 3% additional variance,
> bringing the [R^2 to .30]. The final variable, depression, did
> not add to the proportion of variance explained. (p. 94)

Explain this result to a person who is familiar in a general way with ordinary multiple regression but has never
heard of hierarchical multiple regression.

2. Rusbult et al. (1991) reported a series of studies
about the way people deal with a relationship partner doing
something destructive to the relationship. The start of their
Results section for their first two studies in this article has

a section headed "Reliability of Measures." In this section,
they explain that they calculated "reliability coefficients"
for their major measures and that "these analyses revealed
sizable alphas for the measures of destructive reactions
(. . . .91 for Study 1 and .86 for Study 2) and constructive
reactions (. . . .61 and .67)." Explain these results to someone who is familiar with correlation but has never heard of
reliability or the statistics associated with it.

3. Kirby and Das (1988) report a study in which participants did nine different mental tasks related to intelligence. A table (Table 12–5) in their study gives the results
of a factor analysis of the scores on these tasks. Explain
these results to a person who is familiar with correlation
but knows nothing about factor analysis.

4. Bandura and Jourden (1991) did a study in which
business-school graduate students took part in a laboratory
simulation of a business organization. In their study, they
focused on how performance on this task was related to
self-efficacy (belief that one can be effective) and other
variables. Figure 12–4 is reproduced from the Results section of their article. It shows a path diagram for the major
variables they studied. Note that participants were tested
three times in succession. The left half of the diagram is
about the situation prior to the second testing, the middle
"Performance" refers to the second testing, and the far-
right "Performance" to their third testing.

Using this diagram as an example, explain the general
principles of interpreting a path diagram (including the
limitations) to a person who understands multiple regression in a general way but knows nothing about path diagrams. (You may ignore the figures in parentheses, which
are ordinary correlations.)

5. Carlin and Saniga (1990) compared a group of special education children (mentally retarded or emotionally
disturbed) to a group of regular education students. They
compared the two groups on their teachers' and their
own ratings of voice problems. For the special education

TABLE 12–5
Varimax Factor Loadings of Tasks

Task	Factor		
	I	*II*	*III*
Tokens	−16	42*	20
Figure recognition	−14	40*	13
Matrices	−14	51*	15
Hand movements	− 8	15	44*
Successive ordering	−28	18	44*
Word recall	− 3	11	43*
Matching numbers	51*	−18	−19
Visual search	54*	−11	− 4
Trails	53*	−21	−12

Note: $N = 430$. Decimal points are omitted. Loadings > .30 are noted [with asterisks]. Factor I is defined by the three marker tests of planning, Factor II by the three marker tests of simultaneous coding, and Factor III by the three marker tests of successive coding.

From Kirby, J. R., & Das, J. P. (1990), tab. 1. A cognitive approach to intelligence: Attention, coding, and planning. *Canadian Psychology, 31,* 320–333. Copyright, 1990, by the Canadian Psychological Association. Reprinted by permission.

students, the mean teachers' rating was 53.2 and the mean self rating was 53.8. For the regular education students, the corresponding ratings were 56.8 and 53.2. (In these ratings, high scores mean fewer voice problems.) The researchers reported:

A two-way analysis of covariance with . . . age as the covariate yielded an *F* of 4.17 (*df:* 1, 129, $p < 0.04$) for the main effect of placement [special versus regular education]. . . . The main effect of the teachers' versus the children's ratings was nonsignificant ($F_{1,130} = 0.37$). . . . The interaction of placement and rater was significant at the .001 level ($F_{1,130} = 11.19$). (pp. 301–302)

Explain these results to someone who understands the analysis of variance and correlation but not the analysis of covariance.

6. Yukl and Falbe (1991) asked workers in several companies to answer questions about how their managers exert power. Four main measures were used. There were two measures of personal power (expertise, persuasiveness, and so forth). One of these two measures focused on personal power "downward" over subordinates; the other focused on personal power over workers at the same level. The other two measures were of "position power" (formal status, ability to give rewards and punishments, and so

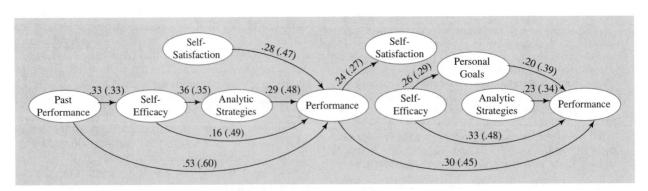

FIGURE 12–4
Path analysis of causal structures in the second and third phase of the experiment. (The initial numbers in the paths of influence are the significant standardized path coefficients, $p < .05$; the numbers in parentheses are the first-order correlations. The network of relations on the left half of the figure are for the second phase, and those for the right are those for the third phase.) (Figure 3 from Bandura, A., & Jourden, F. J. [1991]. Self-regulatory mechanisms governing the impact of social comparison on complex decision making. *Journal of Personality and Social Psychology, 60,* 941–951. Copyright, 1991, by the American Psychological Association. Reprinted by permission of the author.)

forth). One of these latter two measures focused on position power downward and one on position power with regard to workers at the same level. In one of their analyses, the researchers compared middle managers with supervisors (lower-level managers) on these four measures of power:

> The MANOVA . . . on the four composite measures of position and personal power indicated significant power differences between middle managers and supervisors, $F(4, 181) = 2.8$, $p < .05$. Univariate F tests showed that the differences occurred only for the scales measuring position power, $F(1, 184) = 8.0$. . . . Middle managers had more downward position power ($M = 3.7$) than did supervisors ($M = 3.4$). (p. 420)

Explain this result to someone who understands the ordinary analysis of variance but knows nothing about MANOVA.

7. For each of the following fictional studies, what would be the most appropriate statistical technique?

(a) A study in which the researcher has a complex theory of the pattern of cause and effect among several variables

(b) A study of the degree of association between two variables

(c) A study to determine whether a questionnaire scale is consistent internally (that is, that the items correlate with each other) and consistent over time in giving the same result

(d) A 3×2 factorial design with three dependent measures

(e) A study in which seven variables have been measured that are thought to predict a particular dependent variable, and the researcher wants to determine which variables contribute significantly to the prediction (but has no theory about which ones might be the most likely)

(f) A study in which a researcher measures 16 variables in a large number of subjects and wants to explore whether there is any simpler, underlying structure among them

(g) A study in which an experimental group and a control group are being compared on a single dependent variable

(h) A study comparing five groups of individuals on a single dependent variable

(i) A study in which the researcher is studying the effect of several predictor variables on a single dependent variable, has a specific theory about their relative importance, and wants to check whether each successive additional predictor adds anything to what the preceding variables predict

8. At the library find an article in a recent issue of a journal in your major that uses one of the statistical procedures described in this chapter. Write a brief summary of the study you found, referring specifically to the statistics.

9. At the library, find an article in a recent issue of a scientific journal in your major that uses a statistical procedure not covered anywhere in this book. Write a brief summary of the study you found, referring specifically to the statistics.

APPENDIX

Tables

TABLE A-1
Normal Curve Areas: Percentage of the Normal Curve Between the Mean and the Z Scores Shown

Z	% Mean to Z	Z	% Mean to Z	Z	% Mean to Z
.00	.00	.24	9.48	.48	18.44
.01	.40	.25	9.87	.49	18.79
.02	.80	.26	10.26	.50	19.15
.03	1.20	.27	10.64	.51	19.50
.04	1.60	.28	11.03	.52	19.85
.05	1.99	.29	11.41	.53	20.19
.06	2.39	.30	11.79	.54	20.54
.07	2.79	.31	12.17	.55	20.88
.08	3.19	.32	12.55	.56	21.23
.09	3.59	.33	12.93	.57	21.57
.10	3.98	.34	13.31	.58	21.90
.11	4.38	.35	13.68	.59	22.24
.12	4.78	.36	14.06	.60	22.57
.13	5.17	.37	14.43	.61	22.91
.14	5.57	.38	14.80	.62	23.24
.15	5.96	.39	15.17	.63	23.57
.16	6.36	.40	15.54	.64	23.89
.17	6.75	.41	15.91	.65	24.22
.18	7.14	.42	16.28	.66	24.54
.19	7.53	.43	16.64	.67	24.86
.20	7.93	.44	17.00	.68	25.17
.21	8.32	.45	17.36	.69	25.49
.22	8.71	.46	17.72	.70	25.80
.23	9.10	.47	18.08	.71	26.11

TABLE A-1 (cont.)

Z	% Mean to Z	Z	% Mean to Z	Z	% Mean to Z
.72	26.42	1.29	40.15	1.86	46.86
.73	26.73	1.30	40.32	1.87	46.93
.74	27.04	1.31	40.49	1.88	46.99
.75	27.34	1.32	40.66	1.89	47.06
.76	27.64	1.33	40.82	1.90	47.13
.77	27.94	1.34	40.99	1.91	47.19
.78	28.23	1.35	41.15	1.92	47.26
.79	28.52	1.36	41.31	1.93	47.32
.80	28.81	1.37	41.47	1.94	47.38
.81	29.10	1.38	41.62	1.95	47.44
.82	29.39	1.39	41.77	1.96	47.50
.83	29.67	1.40	41.92	1.97	47.56
.84	29.95	1.41	42.07	1.98	47.61
.85	30.23	1.42	42.22	1.99	47.67
.86	30.51	1.43	42.36	2.00	47.72
.87	30.78	1.44	42.51	2.01	47.78
.88	31.06	1.45	42.65	2.02	47.83
.89	31.33	1.46	42.79	2.03	47.88
.90	31.59	1.47	42.92	2.04	47.93
.91	31.86	1.48	43.06	2.05	47.98
.92	32.12	1.49	43.19	2.06	48.03
.93	32.38	1.50	43.32	2.07	48.08
.94	32.64	1.51	43.45	2.08	48.12
.95	32.89	1.52	43.57	2.09	48.17
.96	33.15	1.53	43.70	2.10	48.21
.97	33.40	1.54	43.82	2.11	48.26
.98	33.65	1.55	43.94	2.12	48.30
.99	33.89	1.56	44.06	2.13	48.34
1.00	34.13	1.57	44.18	2.14	48.38
1.01	34.38	1.58	44.29	2.15	48.42
1.02	34.61	1.59	44.41	2.16	48.46
1.03	34.85	1.60	44.52	2.17	48.50
1.04	35.08	1.61	44.63	2.18	48.54
1.05	35.31	1.62	44.74	2.19	48.57
1.06	35.54	1.63	44.84	2.20	48.61
1.07	35.77	1.64	44.95	2.21	48.64
1.08	35.99	1.65	45.05	2.22	48.68
1.09	36.21	1.66	45.15	2.23	48.71
1.10	36.43	1.67	45.25	2.24	48.75
1.11	36.65	1.68	45.35	2.25	48.78
1.12	36.86	1.69	45.45	2.26	48.81
1.13	37.08	1.70	45.54	2.27	48.84
1.14	37.29	1.71	45.64	2.28	48.87
1.15	37.49	1.72	45.73	2.29	48.90
1.16	37.70	1.73	45.82	2.30	48.93
1.17	37.90	1.74	45.91	2.31	48.96
1.18	38.10	1.75	45.99	2.32	48.98
1.19	38.30	1.76	46.08	2.33	49.01
1.20	38.49	1.77	46.16	2.34	49.04
1.21	38.69	1.78	46.25	2.35	49.06
1.22	38.88	1.79	46.33	2.36	49.09
1.23	39.07	1.80	46.41	2.37	49.11
1.24	39.25	1.81	46.49	2.38	49.13
1.25	39.44	1.82	46.56	2.39	49.16
1.26	39.62	1.83	46.64	2.40	49.18
1.27	39.80	1.84	46.71	2.41	49.20
1.28	39.97	1.85	46.78	2.42	49.22

TABLE A-1 (cont.)

Z	% Mean to Z	Z	% Mean to Z	Z	% Mean to Z
2.43	49.25	2.64	49.59	2.85	49.78
2.44	49.27	2.65	49.60	2.86	49.79
2.45	49.29	2.66	49.61	2.87	49.79
2.46	49.31	2.67	49.62	2.88	49.80
2.47	49.32	2.68	49.63	2.89	49.81
2.48	49.34	2.69	49.64	2.90	49.81
2.49	49.36	2.70	49.65	2.91	49.82
2.50	49.38	2.71	49.66	2.92	49.82
2.51	49.40	2.72	49.67	2.93	49.83
2.52	49.41	2.73	49.68	2.94	49.84
2.53	49.43	2.74	49.69	2.95	49.84
2.54	49.45	2.75	49.70	2.96	49.85
2.55	49.46	2.76	49.71	2.97	49.85
2.56	49.48	2.77	49.72	2.98	49.86
2.57	49.49	2.78	49.73	2.99	49.86
2.58	49.51	2.79	49.74	3.00	49.87
2.59	49.52	2.80	49.74	3.50	49.98
2.60	49.53	2.81	49.75	4.00	50.00
2.61	49.55	2.82	49.76	4.50	50.00
2.62	49.56	2.83	49.77		
2.63	49.57	2.84	49.77		

TABLE A-2
Cutoff Scores for the t Distribution

	One-Tailed Tests			Two-Tailed Tests		
df	*.10*	*.05*	*.01*	*.10*	*.05*	*.01*
1	3.078	6.314	31.821	6.314	12.706	63.657
2	1.886	2.920	6.965	2.920	4.303	9.925
3	1.638	2.353	4.541	2.353	3.182	5.841
4	1.533	2.132	3.747	2.132	2.776	4.604
5	1.476	2.015	3.365	2.015	2.571	4.032
6	1.440	1.943	3.143	1.943	2.447	3.708
7	1.415	1.895	2.998	1.895	2.365	3.500
8	1.397	1.860	2.897	1.860	2.306	3.356
9	1.383	1.833	2.822	1.833	2.262	3.250
10	1.372	1.813	2.764	1.813	2.228	3.170
11	1.364	1.796	2.718	1.796	2.201	3.106
12	1.356	1.783	2.681	1.783	2.179	3.055
13	1.350	1.771	2.651	1.771	2.161	3.013
14	1.345	1.762	2.625	1.762	2.145	2.977
15	1.341	1.753	2.603	1.753	2.132	2.947
16	1.337	1.746	2.584	1.746	2.120	2.921
17	1.334	1.740	2.567	1.740	2.110	2.898
18	1.331	1.734	2.553	1.734	2.101	2.879
19	1.328	1.729	2.540	1.729	2.093	2.861
20	1.326	1.725	2.528	1.725	2.086	2.846
21	1.323	1.721	2.518	1.721	2.080	2.832
22	1.321	1.717	2.509	1.717	2.074	2.819
23	1.320	1.714	2.500	1.714	2.069	2.808
24	1.318	1.711	2.492	1.711	2.064	2.797
25	1.317	1.708	2.485	1.708	2.060	2.788
26	1.315	1.706	2.479	1.706	2.056	2.779
27	1.314	1.704	2.473	1.704	2.052	2.771
28	1.313	1.701	2.467	1.701	2.049	2.764
29	1.312	1.699	2.462	1.699	2.045	2.757
30	1.311	1.698	2.458	1.698	2.043	2.750
35	1.306	1.690	2.438	1.690	2.030	2.724
40	1.303	1.684	2.424	1.684	2.021	2.705
45	1.301	1.680	2.412	1.680	2.014	2.690
50	1.299	1.676	2.404	1.676	2.009	2.678
55	1.297	1.673	2.396	1.673	2.004	2.668
60	1.296	1.671	2.390	1.671	2.001	2.661
65	1.295	1.669	2.385	1.669	1.997	2.654
70	1.294	1.667	2.381	1.667	1.995	2.648
75	1.293	1.666	2.377	1.666	1.992	2.643
80	1.292	1.664	2.374	1.664	1.990	2.639
85	1.292	1.663	2.371	1.663	1.989	2.635
90	1.291	1.662	2.369	1.662	1.987	2.632
95	1.291	1.661	2.366	1.661	1.986	2.629
100	1.290	1.660	2.364	1.660	1.984	2.626
∞	1.282	1.645	2.327	1.645	1.960	2.576

TABLE A-3
Cutoff Scores for the *F* Distribution

Denom-inator *df*	Signi-ficance Level	Numerator Degrees of Freedom					
		1	*2*	*3*	*4*	*5*	*6*
1	.01	4,052	5,000	5,404	5,625	5,764	5,859
	.05	162	200	216	225	230	234
	.10	39.9	49.5	53.6	55.8	57.2	58.2
2	.01	98.50	99.00	99.17	99.25	99.30	99.33
	.05	18.51	19.00	19.17	19.25	19.30	19.33
	.10	8.53	9.00	9.16	9.24	9.29	9.33
3	.01	34.12	30.82	29.46	28.71	28.24	27.91
	.05	10.13	9.55	9.28	9.12	9.01	8.94
	.10	5.54	5.46	5.39	5.34	5.31	5.28
4	.01	21.20	18.00	16.70	15.98	15.52	15.21
	.05	7.71	6.95	6.59	6.39	6.26	6.16
	.10	4.55	4.33	4.19	4.11	4.05	4.01
5	.01	16.26	13.27	12.06	11.39	10.97	10.67
	.05	6.61	5.79	5.41	5.19	5.05	4.95
	.10	4.06	3.78	3.62	3.52	3.45	3.41
6	.01	13.75	10.93	9.78	9.15	8.75	8.47
	.05	5.99	5.14	4.76	4.53	4.39	4.28
	.10	3.78	3.46	3.29	3.18	3.11	3.06
7	.01	12.25	9.55	8.45	7.85	7.46	7.19
	.05	5.59	4.74	4.35	4.12	3.97	3.87
	.10	3.59	3.26	3.08	2.96	2.88	2.83
8	.01	11.26	8.65	7.59	7.01	6.63	6.37
	.05	5.32	4.46	4.07	3.84	3.69	3.58
	.10	3.46	3.11	2.92	2.81	2.73	2.67
9	.01	10.56	8.02	6.99	6.42	6.06	5.80
	.05	5.12	4.26	3.86	3.63	3.48	3.37
	.10	3.36	3.01	2.81	2.69	2.61	2.55
10	.01	10.05	7.56	6.55	6.00	5.64	5.39
	.05	4.97	4.10	3.71	3.48	3.33	3.22
	.10	3.29	2.93	2.73	2.61	2.52	2.46
11	.01	9.65	7.21	6.22	5.67	5.32	5.07
	.05	4.85	3.98	3.59	3.36	3.20	3.10
	.10	3.23	2.86	2.66	2.54	2.45	2.39
12	.01	9.33	6.93	5.95	5.41	5.07	4.82
	.05	4.75	3.89	3.49	3.26	3.11	3.00
	.10	3.18	2.81	2.61	2.48	2.40	2.33
13	.01	9.07	6.70	5.74	5.21	4.86	4.62
	.05	4.67	3.81	3.41	3.18	3.03	2.92
	.10	3.14	2.76	2.56	2.43	2.35	2.28
14	.01	8.86	6.52	5.56	5.04	4.70	4.46
	.05	4.60	3.74	3.34	3.11	2.96	2.85
	.10	3.10	2.73	2.52	2.40	2.31	2.24

Denom- inator df	Signi- ficance Level	Numerator Degrees of Freedom					
		1	2	3	4	5	6
15	.01	8.68	6.36	5.42	4.89	4.56	4.32
	.05	4.54	3.68	3.29	3.06	2.90	2.79
	.10	3.07	2.70	2.49	2.36	2.27	2.21
16	.01	8.53	6.23	5.29	4.77	4.44	4.20
	.05	4.49	3.63	3.24	3.01	2.85	2.74
	.10	3.05	2.67	2.46	2.33	2.24	2.18
17	.01	8.40	6.11	5.19	4.67	4.34	4.10
	.05	4.45	3.59	3.20	2.97	2.81	2.70
	.10	3.03	2.65	2.44	2.31	2.22	2.15
18	.01	8.29	6.01	5.09	4.58	4.25	4.02
	.05	4.41	3.56	3.16	2.93	2.77	2.66
	.10	3.01	2.62	2.42	2.29	2.20	2.13
19	.01	8.19	5.93	5.01	4.50	4.17	3.94
	.05	4.38	3.52	3.13	2.90	2.74	2.63
	.10	2.99	2.61	2.40	2.27	2.18	2.11
20	.01	8.10	5.85	4.94	4.43	4.10	3.87
	.05	4.35	3.49	3.10	2.87	2.71	2.60
	.10	2.98	2.59	2.38	2.25	2.16	2.09
21	.01	8.02	5.78	4.88	4.37	4.04	3.81
	.05	4.33	3.47	3.07	2.84	2.69	2.57
	.10	2.96	2.58	2.37	2.23	2.14	2.08
22	.01	7.95	5.72	4.82	4.31	3.99	3.76
	.05	4.30	3.44	3.05	2.82	2.66	2.55
	.10	2.95	2.56	2.35	2.22	2.13	2.06
23	.01	7.88	5.66	4.77	4.26	3.94	3.71
	.05	4.28	3.42	3.03	2.80	2.64	2.53
	.10	2.94	2.55	2.34	2.21	2.12	2.05
24	.01	7.82	5.61	4.72	4.22	3.90	3.67
	.05	4.26	3.40	3.01	2.78	2.62	2.51
	.10	2.93	2.54	2.33	2.20	2.10	2.04
25	.01	7.77	5.57	4.68	4.18	3.86	3.63
	.05	4.24	3.39	2.99	2.76	2.60	2.49
	.10	2.92	2.53	2.32	2.19	2.09	2.03
26	.01	7.72	5.53	4.64	4.14	3.82	3.59
	.05	4.23	3.37	2.98	2.74	2.59	2.48
	.10	2.91	2.52	2.31	2.18	2.08	2.01
27	.01	7.68	5.49	4.60	4.11	3.79	3.56
	.05	4.21	3.36	2.96	2.73	2.57	2.46
	.10	2.90	2.51	2.30	2.17	2.07	2.01
28	.01	7.64	5.45	4.57	4.08	3.75	3.53
	.05	4.20	3.34	2.95	2.72	2.56	2.45
	.10	2.89	2.50	2.29	2.16	2.07	2.00

Denominator df	Significance Level	Numerator Degrees of Freedom					
		1	2	3	4	5	6
29	.01	7.60	5.42	4.54	4.05	3.73	3.50
	.05	4.18	3.33	2.94	2.70	2.55	2.43
	.10	2.89	2.50	2.28	2.15	2.06	1.99
30	.01	7.56	5.39	4.51	4.02	3.70	3.47
	.05	4.17	3.32	2.92	2.69	2.53	2.42
	.10	2.88	2.49	2.28	2.14	2.05	1.98
35	.01	7.42	5.27	4.40	3.91	3.59	3.37
	.05	4.12	3.27	2.88	2.64	2.49	2.37
	.10	2.86	2.46	2.25	2.11	2.02	1.95
40	.01	7.32	5.18	4.31	3.83	3.51	3.29
	.05	4.09	3.23	2.84	2.61	2.45	2.34
	.10	2.84	2.44	2.23	2.09	2.00	1.93
45	.01	7.23	5.11	4.25	3.77	3.46	3.23
	.05	4.06	3.21	2.81	2.58	2.42	2.31
	.10	2.82	2.43	2.21	2.08	1.98	1.91
50	.01	7.17	5.06	4.20	3.72	3.41	3.19
	.05	4.04	3.18	2.79	2.56	2.40	2.29
	.10	2.81	2.41	2.20	2.06	1.97	1.90
55	.01	7.12	5.01	4.16	3.68	3.37	3.15
	.05	4.02	3.17	2.77	2.54	2.38	2.27
	.10	2.80	2.40	2.19	2.05	1.96	1.89
60	.01	7.08	4.98	4.13	3.65	3.34	3.12
	.05	4.00	3.15	2.76	2.53	2.37	2.26
	.10	2.79	2.39	2.18	2.04	1.95	1.88
65	.01	7.04	4.95	4.10	3.62	3.31	3.09
	.05	3.99	3.14	2.75	2.51	2.36	2.24
	.10	2.79	2.39	2.17	2.03	1.94	1.87
70	.01	7.01	4.92	4.08	3.60	3.29	3.07
	.05	3.98	3.13	2.74	2.50	2.35	2.23
	.10	2.78	2.38	2.16	2.03	1.93	1.86
75	.01	6.99	4.90	4.06	3.58	3.27	3.05
	.05	3.97	3.12	2.73	2.49	2.34	2.22
	.10	2.77	2.38	2.16	2.02	1.93	1.86
80	.01	6.96	4.88	4.04	3.56	3.26	3.04
	.05	3.96	3.11	2.72	2.49	2.33	2.22
	.10	2.77	2.37	2.15	2.02	1.92	1.85
85	.01	6.94	4.86	4.02	3.55	3.24	3.02
	.05	3.95	3.10	2.71	2.48	2.32	2.21
	.10	2.77	2.37	2.15	2.01	1.92	1.85
90	.01	6.93	4.85	4.01	3.54	3.23	3.01
	.05	3.95	3.10	2.71	2.47	2.32	2.20
	.10	2.76	2.36	2.15	2.01	1.91	1.84

TABLE A-3 (cont.)

Denominator df	Significance Level	|Numerator Degrees of Freedom					
		1	*2*	*3*	*4*	*5*	*6*
95	.01	6.91	4.84	4.00	3.52	3.22	3.00
	.05	3.94	3.09	2.70	2.47	2.31	2.20
	.10	2.76	2.36	2.14	2.01	1.91	1.84
100	.01	6.90	4.82	3.98	3.51	3.21	2.99
	.05	3.94	3.09	2.70	2.46	2.31	2.19
	.10	2.76	2.36	2.14	2.00	1.91	1.83
∞	.01	6.64	4.61	3.78	3.32	3.02	2.80
	.05	3.84	3.00	2.61	2.37	2.22	2.10
	.10	2.71	2.30	2.08	1.95	1.85	1.78

TABLE A-4
Cutoff Scores for the Chi-Square Distribution

df	Significance Level		
	.10	*.05*	*.01*
1	2.706	3.841	6.635
2	4.605	5.992	9.211
3	6.252	7.815	11.345
4	7.780	9.488	13.277
5	9.237	11.071	15.087
6	10.645	12.592	16.812
7	12.017	14.067	18.475
8	13.362	15.507	20.090
9	14.684	16.919	21.666
10	15.987	18.307	23.209

TABLE A-5
Index to Power Tables and Tables Giving Number of Participants Needed for 80% Power

Hypothesis-Testing Procedure	Chapter	Power Table	Number of Participants Table
Correlation coefficient (r)	3	73	73
t test for dependent means	8	173	173
t test for independent means	9	193	194
One-way analysis of variance	10	217	218
Chi-square test of independence	11	247	248

Answers
to Selected Practice Problems

Answers are provided here for selected practice problems, including at least one example answer to an essay-type question for each chapter. For answers to the remaining questions see the *Test Bank and Answers to Practice Problems* supplement.

Chapter 1

1. **(a)** Frequency table.

Number of Hours	Frequency	Number of Hours	Frequency
18	1	8	5
17	0	7	11
16	0	6	4
15	1	5	2
14	0	4	3
13	2	3	4
12	1	2	2
11	3	1	1
10	5	0	1
9	4		

(b) Frequency polygon based on table in (a).

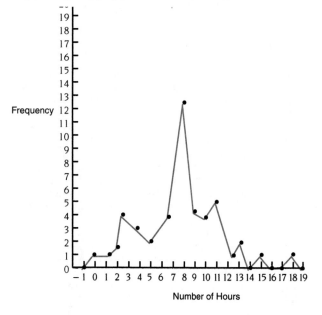

(c) General shape of the distribution: unimodal, somewhat skewed to the right (positively skewed).

4. (a) A distribution is the way a group of numbers is spread out over the different possible values they can have. One way to describe such a distribution is with a graph, called a histogram. A histogram is a kind of bar graph with one bar for each possible value, in order from lowest to highest, and one unit of height of a bar for each time its particular value occurs, with the bars arranged in order according to the different values. In this kind of graph, a symmetrical distribution has a symmetrical shape, meaning that the right and left halves are mirror images. Loosely speaking, this means that there are about as many high numbers as there are low numbers, and the way the number of instances at each value decreases as you move from a middle value to the highest value is the same as the way the number of instances at each value decreases as you move from a middle value to the lowest value. A unimodal distribution is one in which this graph has a single high point, with the other values gradually decreasing around it.

Chapter 2

1. Set A.
   (a) $M = 261/9 = 29$
   (b) Median = 28
   (c) $\Sigma(X-M)^2 = (32-29)^2 + (28-29)^2 + (24-29)^2 + (28-29)^2$
       $+ (28-29)^2 + (31-29)^2 + (35-29)^2 + (29-29)^2 + (26-29)^2$
       $= 3^2 + (-1)^2 + (-5)^2 + (-1)^2 + (-1)^2 + 2^2 + 6^2 + 0^2$
       $+ (-3)^2$
       $= 9 + 1 + 25 + 1 + 1 + 4 + 36 + 0 + 9 = 86$
       $SD^2 = \Sigma(X-M)^2/N = 86/9 = 9.56$
   (d) $SD = \sqrt{9.56} = 3.09$

2. The average temperature, in the sense of adding up the 10 readings and dividing by 10, was –7 degrees Celsius. This is called the mean. However, if you were to line the temperatures up from lowest to highest, the middle two numbers would both be –5 degrees. This middle number is called the median. So the median temperature is –5 degrees. Another way of figuring the typical temperature would be to take the specific temperature that came up most often, which is called the mode. In this case, there were two modes, two temperatures that came up most often, –1 and –5. Both of these temperatures came up twice, but the mode is not very useful information in this case.

   As for the variation, one approach is called the variance. You begin by figuring how much each temperature differs from the average. Then you square each of these "deviation scores." (This gets rid of the minus and plus signs so that you are finding the amount of difference from the average regardless of the direction of difference.) Next, take the average of these squared deviation scores. For example, the first temperature's deviation is 2 (–5 minus –7), which squared is 4. Squaring each deviation and adding up all the results gives 468. Dividing this by 10 gives an average squared deviation of 46.8. This is the variance. The variance is one way of describing how spread out a group of numbers is. The variance is an important part of many statistical calculations. Unfortunately, however, it does not give a very direct sense of how much numbers vary.

You can get a more direct sense of how much a group of numbers vary among themselves if you take the square root of the variance. In this case, the square root of 46.8 is 6.84. (The square root of the variance is called the standard deviation.) This means, roughly, that on an average day the temperature differs by 6.84 degrees from the average of –7 degrees.

5. Wife: $Z = (X - M)/SD = (63 - 60)/6 = 3/6 = .5$
   Husband: $Z = (X - M)/SD = (59 - 55)/4 = 4/4 = 1$
   The husband has a higher Z score, so he has adjusted better in relation to other divorced men than the wife has adjusted in relation to other divorced women.

   Explanation to person who has never had a course in statistics: For wives, a score of 63 is 3 points better than the average of 60 for divorced women in general. (The "mean" in the problem is a statistical term for the ordinary average—the sum of the numbers divided by the number of numbers.) There is, of course, some variation in scores among divorced women. The approximate average amount that women's scores differ from the average is 6 points: This is the SD referred to in the problem. (Actually, SD, which stands for standard deviation, is only approximately the average amount that scores differ from the average. To be precise, SD is the square root of the average of the square of the difference of each score from the mean.)

   The wife's score is only half as far above the mean of wives as wives' scores in general differ from the mean of wives' scores. This gives her what is called a Z score of +.5, which gives her location on a scale that compares her score to that of divorced women in general. Using the same logic to examine the husband's divorce adjustment compared to other divorced men, he is as much above the average as the average amount that men differ from the average; that is, he has a Z score of +1. Therefore, the conclusion is that although both have adjusted better than the average for their gender, the husband has adjusted better in relation to other divorced men than the wife has adjusted in relation to other divorced women.

Chapter 3

1. (a)

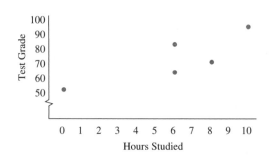

   (b) Positive linear correlation: as hours studied goes up, so do test grades.

(c)

Hours Studied		Test Grade		
Raw X	Z_X	Raw Y	Z_Y	$Z_X Z_Y$
0	−1.79	52	−1.41	2.52
10	1.19	95	1.48	1.76
6	0.00	83	0.67	0.00
8	0.60	71	−0.13	−0.08
6	0.00	64	−0.60	0.00
				$\Sigma = 4.20$
$M = 6$		$M = 73$		
$SD = 3.35$		$SD = 14.90$		$r = 4.20/5 = .84$

(d) The first step in a correlation problem is to make a graph, putting one variable on each axis, then putting a dot where each score falls on that graph. This is called a scatter diagram, and it gives a picture of the degree of relationship between the two variables. In this case, high scores seem to go with high, and low with low, making this what is called a positive linear correlation. (The basic idea of correlation is the extent to which high scores go with high scores and low scores go with low scores.) Also, because the dots fall roughly near a straight line, this is an example of a linear correlation.

The next step in the process is to convert all scores to Z scores. This makes it easier to compute the extent to which highs go with highs and lows with lows. Z scores make this easier because they are the best indicator of the extent to which a score is low or high relative to the other scores in its distribution.

The correlation coefficient is a number that indicates the degree of association. You figure it by multiplying the two Z scores for each person times each other, totaling up these products, and then averaging this total over the number of people. This will be a high number if highs go with highs and lows with lows, since with Z scores, highs are always positive (and the higher they are, the more positive), and positive times positive is positive. Also, lows with Z scores are always negative (and the lower the score, the more negative the Z score), and negatives times negatives become positives too.

Statisticians can prove that by following this procedure, the highest number you can get, if the scores for the two variables are perfectly correlated, is +1. If there were no linear relationship between the variables, the result of this procedure would be 0 (that would happen if highs were sometimes multiplied with highs and sometimes with lows, and lows sometimes with highs and sometimes with lows, giving a mixture of positive and negative products that would cancel out).

In the present situation, the total of the products of the Z scores was 4.2, which when divided by the number of people is .84. This is called a Pearson correlation coefficient (r) of .84 and indicates a strong, positive linear correlation between hours studied and test grade.

(e) Three logically possible directions of causality: (i) Studying more hours causes improved test grades; (ii) getting a better test grade causes more hours studied (note that although this is theoretically possible, it is not possible in

reality to have a future event, the score on the test, cause a previous event, hours studied); or (iii) a third factor, such as interest in the subject matter, could be causing the student to study more and also to do better on the test.

(f) Formulas: Predicted $Z_Y = (\beta)(Z_X)$
Predicted $Y = ($Predicted $Z_Y)(SD_Y) + (M_Y)$

$Z_X = -2$: Predicted $Z_Y = (.84)(-2) = -1.68$
Predicted $Y = (-1.68)(14.90) + 73 = -25.03 + 73 = 47.97$

$Z_X = -1$: Predicted $Z_Y = (.84)(-1) = -.84$
Predicted $Y = (-.84)(14.90) + 73 = -12.52 + 73 = 60.48$

$Z_X = 0$: Predicted $Z_Y = (.84)(0) = 0$
Predicted $Y = (0)(14.90) + 73 = 0 + 73 = 73$

$Z_X = +1$: Predicted $Z_Y = (.84)(+1) = .84$
Predicted $Y = (.84)(14.90) + 73 = 12.52 + 73 = 85.52$

$Z_X = +2$: Predicted $Z_Y = (.84)(+1) = 1.68$
Predicted $Y = (1.68)(14.90) + 73 = 25.03 + 73 = 98.03$

(g) $r^2 = .84^2 = .71$

6. This study used a statistical procedure called multiple regression. This procedure determines a formula for predicting a person's score on a dependent variable (in this case, the manager's effectiveness) from his or her scores on a set of predictor variables (in this case, the three types of influence strategies). The formula is of the form that you multiply the person's score on each of the predictor variables by some particular number, called a regression coefficient, and then add up the products. The procedure produces the most accurate prediction rule of this kind.

In this case, the prediction rule for the Z score for manager's effectiveness is −.66 times the Z score for "hard," plus .14 times the Z score for "soft," plus .09 times the Z score for "rational." (These are the numbers in the table under each predictor variable in the row for manager effectiveness.)

These regression coefficients suggest that manager effectiveness is most strongly related in a negative direction to using "hard" influence strategies. (That is, the more hard influence strategies, the less effective the manager.) Use of soft and rational influence strategies has a positive but slight relation to effectiveness. It is important to note, however, that the regression coefficients for each of these types of strategies reflect what the scores on each strategy contribute to the prediction, over and above what the others contribute. If we were to consider ordinary correlations between each of the predictor variables with the dependent variable, their relative importance could be quite different. (Those correlations, however, were not provided.)

Another important piece of information in this table is the "Adjusted R^2," which is approximately the same as what is usually just called "R^2." (I will describe it here as if it were an ordinary R^2, as per the instructions for the problem.) This number tells the proportion of variance accounted for in the dependent variable by the three predictor variables taken together. That is, 23% of the variance in manager effectiveness is accounted for by the three kinds of influence styles. This is equivalent to a correlation between manager effectiveness and these three variables, which is .48.

Chapter 4

1. (a) 50%, (b) 16%, (f) 84%, (g) 2%, (i) 50, (j) 45.
   Note: It will be much easier to answer problems like this if you draw a picture of a normal curve and mark it as shown here.

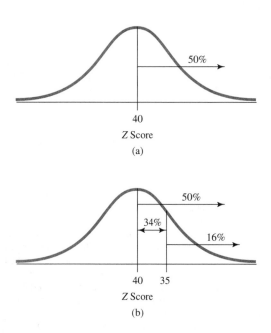

40
Z Score
(a)

50%

40   35
Z Score
(b)

34%
50%
16%

2. (a) From the normal curve table in Appendix A, 3.98% (.398) have Z scores between the mean and .10. By definition a total of 50% have Z scores above the mean. Thus 50% minus 3.98% have Z scores above .10. 50% minus 3.98% is 46.02%.
   (b) 3.98% are between the mean and .10. 50% are below the mean. Thus 50% + 3.98% are below .10, for a total of 53.98%.
3. (a) Top 10% means 90% are below; of those, 50% are below the mean, so that the top 10% is the point where 40% of cases are between it and the mean. Looking up 40.0 in the normal curve table (the closest actual value is 39.97), you find that this is equivalent to a Z score of +1.28.
4. Needed $Z = 1.64$ corresponds to raw score of $50 + (10)(1.64) = 66.4$.
   Explanation: Many things in nature occur in numbers that approximately follow a particular pattern shown here, called a

normal curve, in which most of the cases occur near the middle and fewer but equal numbers at each extreme. Because it is mathematically defined, the precise proportion of cases that fall at any particular section of it can be calculated, and these have been listed in special tables.

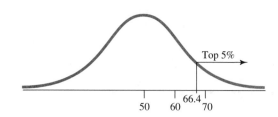

Top 5%

50   60   66.4   70

The normal curve tables are based on what are called Z scores. Z scores are in turn based on the mean and the standard deviation. The mean is the ordinary average—the sum of the numbers divided by the number of numbers. The standard deviation is a measure of how spread out a group of numbers are. Roughly speaking, it indicates the average amount that scores differ from the average. (To be exact, it is the square root of the average of the squared amounts by which each score differs from the average.) The Z score is the number of standard deviations a score is from the mean. The normal curve table tells the percentage of cases in the normal curve that fall between the mean and any particular Z score.

Because the coordination test scores are known to follow a normal curve, you can look up in the table the Z score that corresponds to the point on the normal curve at which 45% of the cases fall between it and the mean. (Because the normal curve is completely symmetrical, 50% of the cases fall above the mean, leaving 5% above 45%.) This turns out to be a Z score of 1.64. (Actually, there is not an exact point on the table for 45%, so I could have used either 1.64 or 1.65.)

With a standard deviation of 10, a Z score of 1.64 is 16.4 points above the mean. Adding that to the mean of 50 makes the score needed to be in the top 5% turn out to be 66.4.

5. (a) 10/50: $p = 10/50 = .2$

Chapter 5

1. (a) A research hypothesis is a statement of the predicted relationship among populations (for example, the prediction that they will have different means).
   (d) The comparison distribution is the distribution for the situation if the null hypothesis is true; it is the distribution to which you compare the score in your sample.
2.(i)(a) Population 1: Canadian children of librarians; Population 2: All Canadian children.
   (b) Research hypothesis: Population 1 children have generally better reading abilities than Population 2 children.
   (c) Null hypothesis: Population 1's reading abilities are not better than Population 2's.
   (d) One-tailed, because the question is whether they "do better," so only one direction of difference is of interest.
3. (a) Z score cutoff on the comparison distribution = +1.64

Z score on the comparison distribution for the sample score = 2

Conclusion: Reject null hypothesis

4. Reject the null hypothesis: Not having a sense of smell makes for fewer correct identifications.

In brief, you solve this problem by considering the likelihood of the scenario in which being without a sense of smell makes no difference. If the sense of smell made no difference, the probability of the student studied getting any particular number correct is simply the probability of students in general getting any particular number correct. Because we know the distribution of the number correct that students get in general, that probability can be determined. It turns out that it would be fairly unlikely to get only 5 correct, so the researcher concludes that not having the sense of smell does make a difference.

To go into detail a bit, the key issue is determining these probabilities. We are told that the number correct for the students in general are "normally distributed." This tells us that the probabilities of getting any particular number correct follow a specific mathematical pattern, the normal curve, sometimes called "bell-shaped," in which most of the cases fall in the middle and progressively fewer occur as the numbers get higher or lower. There are tables showing exactly what proportion of cases fall between the middle and any particular point on the normal curve. These tables use "Z scores," transformed versions of the original scores that are the number of standard deviations above the mean. The mean is the ordinary average (the sum of the numbers divided by the number of numbers). The standard deviation can be thought of as the average amount by which scores differ from the mean. (Strictly speaking, it is the square root of the average of the squares of each score's difference from the mean.)

When evaluating the outcome of an experiment, many researchers use a convention of deciding that if a result could have occurred by chance less than 5% of the time under a particular scenario, that scenario will be considered unlikely. The normal curve tables show that the top 5% of the normal curve begins with a Z score of 1.64. Because the normal curve is completely symmetrical, the bottom 5% includes all Z scores below −1.64. The researcher, even before doing the experiment, would probably set the following rule: The scenario in which being without the sense of smell makes no difference

will be rejected as unlikely if the number correct (converted to a Z score using the mean and standard deviation for students in general) is less than −1.64.

The actual number correct for the student who could not use the sense of smell was 5. The normal curve for the students in general, we are told, had a mean of 14 and a standard deviation of 4. Getting 5 correct is 9 below the mean of 14; in terms of standard deviation units of 4 each, it is 9/4 below the mean, for a Z score of −2.25.

Because −2.25 is lower than −1.64, the researcher concludes that the scenario in which being without smell has no effect is unlikely. This is shown in the following illustration.

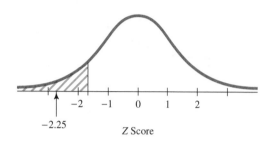

Chapter 6

2. (a) $SD^2 = 10^2 = 100$; $SD^2_M = SD^2/N = 100/2 = 50$; $SD_M = \sqrt{SD^2_M} = \sqrt{50} = 7.07$

3. (a) Characteristics of the distribution of means: $M = 100$; $SD_M = 7.07$; shape = normal
   Z score for top 2.5% = 1.96; Z score for bottom 2.5% = −1.964
   Upper confidence limit = (1.96)(7.07) + 100 = 13.86 + 100 = 113.86
   Lower confidence limit = (−1.96)(7.07) + 100 = −13.86 + 100 = 86.14

4. Because the distribution of the population of individual cases is normal, so will be the distribution of means. Based on the normal curve table, a Z score of at least 1.64 is needed to be in the top 5%. For sample (a): $SD_M = \sqrt{(36/10)} = 1.90$. Z (on the distribution of means) = (44 − 40)/1.90 = 4/1.90 = 2.11. Because 2.11 is more extreme than 1.64, this sample is less likely than 5%. The distributions are shown in the following graphs.

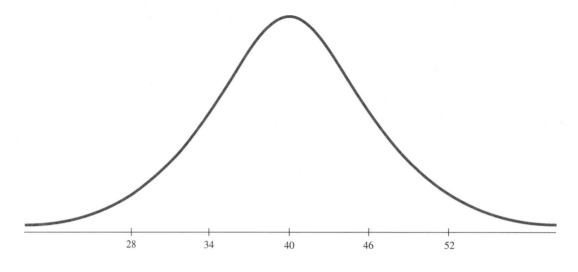

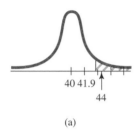

(a)

5. This is a standard hypothesis-testing problem, except that you cannot compare directly the accuracy rating result for the group of 50 North Americans tested to the distribution of accuracy ratings for individual North Americans when rating members of their own culture. This is because the distribution for those rating members of their own culture is a distribution of individual cases, and we have an average of a group of 50 people's ratings. The probability of a group of scores having an extreme mean is much less than any one individual having an extreme score just by chance. (This is because when taking scores at random, when you take several scores, any extreme scores are likely to be balanced out by less extreme or oppositely extreme scores.) The proper distribution to use to compare the mean of the group of 50 ratings is a distribution of what would happen if you were to take many random sets of 50 ratings and find the mean of each set of 50 ratings.

Such a distribution of many means of samples has the same mean as the original distribution of individual ratings, because there is no reason for it to be otherwise. It is a narrower curve, because the chances of extremes are less. In fact, it is known mathematically that its variance will be exactly the variance of the original distribution of individuals divided by the number of ratings in each sample. This makes a distribution of means with a mean of 82 and a standard deviation of .63 (that is, $\sqrt{20/50} = .63$). This will be a normal distribution

because a distribution of many means from a normally distributed population is also normal.

The cutoff for significance, using the .05 level and a two-tailed test, is ± 1.96. The mean rating of the group of 50 North Americans tested, 78, is 6.35 standard deviations below the mean of the distribution of means, making it clearly more extreme than the cutoff. Thus we can reject the null hypothesis and conclude that the data support the hypothesis that North Americans are not as accurate rating emotions of Indonesians as they are when rating the emotions of other North Americans.

6. Suppose the population of North Americans when rating Indonesians has a mean of 78, its variance (like that of North Americans when rating North Americans) was 20, and that it was a normal distribution. In this case the distribution of means for groups of 50 people would have a mean of 78 and standard deviation of .63 (as seen in the previous problem). Because this distribution is a normal curve, the chance of getting a mean more than 1.96 standard deviations above the mean of 78 is 2.5% and the chance of getting a mean more than 1.96 standard deviations below 78 is also 2.5%. That is, the chance of getting a mean more than 1.96 standard deviations above *or* more than 1.96 standard deviations below is 5%. The points 1.96 standard deviations above and below work out to 79.23 and 76.77. This is called the 95% confidence interval.

Chapter 7

1. (a)

Conclusion from Hypothesis Testing	Real Status of the Research Hypothesis	
	True	False
Research Hypothesis Supported (Reject null)	*Correct Decision* Decide more recess time improves behavior and it really does	*Type I Error* Decide more recess time improves behavior but it really does not
Study Inconclusive (Do not reject null)	*Type II Error* Decide effect of recess time on behavior is not shown in this study; actually, more recess time improves behavior	*Correct Decision* Decide effect of recess time on behavior is not shown in this study; actually, more recess time does not improve behavior

3. Effect size = (Population 1 M – Population 2 M) / Population SD
   (a) Effect size = $(91 - 90)/4 = 1/4 = .25$
4. (a) Not affected. (That is what the significance level tests.)
   (b) Probably of small importance (due to small effect size).
6. (a) Increases power; **(b)** decreases power

Chapter 8

1. (a) t needed ($df = 63$, $p < .05$, one-tailed) $= -1.671$
   $S_M = \sqrt{(S^2/N)} = \sqrt{(9/64)} = \sqrt{.141} = .38$
   $t = (M - \text{Pop. } M)/S_M = (11 - 12.40)/.38 = -1.40/.38 = -3.68$
   Reject null hypothesis.
3. (a) t needed ($df = 19$, $p < .05$, one-tailed) $= 1.729$
   $S_M = \sqrt{(S^2/N)} = \sqrt{(8.29/20)} = \sqrt{.415} = .64$
   $t = (M - \text{Pop. } M)/S_M = (1.7 - 0)/.64 = 2.66$
   Reject null hypothesis.
   Effect size $= (M - \text{Population } M)/S = 1.7/\sqrt{8.29} = .59$
4. t needed ($df = 3$, $p < .01$, one-tailed) $= 4.541$
   Change scores $= 7, 6, -1, 8$; $M = 20/4 = 5$; $S^2 = 50/3 = 16.67$;
   $S_M = \sqrt{(S^2/N)} = \sqrt{(16.67/4)} = \sqrt{4.17} = 2.04$; $t = (5 - 0)/2.04 = 2.45$
   Do not reject null hypothesis.
   Explanation: The first thing I did was to simplify things by converting the numbers to "change scores"—postprogram (1996) litter minus preprogram (1995) litter for each city. Then I found the mean of these change score, which was 5 (meaning a decrease of five pounds of litter per block per day).
   The next step was to see whether this result, found in these five cities, means some real difference more generally due to being in this program. The alternative is the possibility that this much change could have occurred in four randomly selected cities just by chance even if in general the program had no real effect. That is, we imagine that the average change for cities in general that implement this program is actually 0, and maybe this study just happened to pick four cities that would have decreased this much anyway.

I then determined just how much a group of four cities would have to change before I could conclude that they have changed too much to chalk it up to chance. This required figuring out the characteristics of this hypothetical population of cities in which on the average there is no change. Its mean would be 0 change (that is, a mean change of 0 is just how you would describe an average of no change). Because I did not know the variance in this hypothetical distribution of cities that don't change, I estimated it from the information in the sample of four cities. If the sample was just a chance draw from the hypothetical population, its variance should be representative of the hypothetical population. But because a sample of four is less likely to have quite as high a proportion of extreme cases as the hypothetical infinite population it was drawn from, I had to modify the variance formula to take this into account: Instead of dividing the sum of the squared deviations by the number of cases, I divided it instead by the "degrees of freedom," which is the number of cases minus 1—in this case, 3. As shown in the calculations, this gave an estimated population variance (S^2) of 16.67.

I was interested not in individual cities but in a group of four. What I really needed to know was the characteristics of a distribution of all possible means of samples of four drawn from this hypothetical population of individual city change scores. Such a distribution of means will have the same mean (because there is no reason to expect the means of such groups of four drawn randomly to be systematically higher or lower than 0). Such a distribution will have a much smaller variance (because the average of a group of four is a lot less likely to be extreme than any individual). Fortunately, it is known (and can be proven mathematically) that the variance of a distribution of means is the variance of the distribution of individuals divided by the number in each sample. In our example, this works out to 16.67 divided by 4, which is 4.17. The standard deviation of this distribution is thus the square root of 4.17, or 2.04.

It also turns out that if we can assume that the hypothetical population of individual cities' change scores is normally distributed (and we have no reason to think otherwise), the distribution of means of samples from that distribution can be thought of as having a precise known shape, called a t distribution (which has slightly higher tails than a normal curve). Looking in a table for a t distribution for the situation in which there are 3 degrees of freedom used to estimate the population variance, the table shows that there is a less than 1% chance of getting a score that is 4.541 standard deviations from the mean of this distribution.

The mean change score for the present sample of four cities was 5, which would be 2.45 (that is, 5/2.04) standard deviations above the mean of 0 change on this distribution of means of change scores. Because this is not as extreme as 4.541, there is more than a 1% chance that these results could have come from a hypothetical distribution with no change. Therefore, the researcher would not rule out that possibility, and the study would be said to be inconclusive.

The various distributions are illustrated.

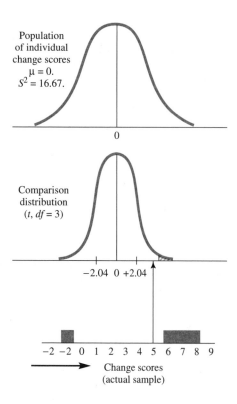

Population
of individual
change scores
$\mu = 0$.
$S^2 = 16.67$.

0

Comparison
distribution
$(t, df = 3)$

-2.04 0 $+2.04$

-2 -2 0 1 2 3 4 5 6 7 8 9

Change scores
(actual sample)

6. From Table 8–7: **(a)** .22; **(d)** .77
7. From Table 8–8: **(a)** 156; **(b)** 196

Chapter 9

2. **(a)** t needed ($df = 58$, $p < .05$, two-tailed) = ± 2.004;
$S^2_{Pooled} = S^2_1(df_1/df_{Total}) + S^2_2(df_2/df_{Total})$
$= 2.4(29/58) + 2.8(29/58) = 1.2 + 1.4 = 2.6$;
$S^2_{M1} = S^2_{Pooled}/N_1 = 2.6/30 = .087$; $S^2_{M2} = .087$;
$S^2_{Difference} = S^2_{M_1} + S^2_{M_2} = .087 + .087 = .174$;
$S_{Difference} = \sqrt{S_{Difference}} = \sqrt{.174} = .417$;
$t = (M_1 - M_2)/S_{Difference} = (12 - 11.1)/.417 = .9/.417 = 2.16$
Conclusion: Reject the null hypothesis.
The difference is significant.
Effect size: = $(M_1 - M_2)/S = (12 - 11.1)/\sqrt{2.6} = .9/1.6 = .56$
(approximately medium effect size). Power (from table) = .47 (However, a significant result must have power of at least .50. Thus, the approximation underestimates the true power to some extent.)

3. t needed ($df = 80$, $p < .01$, two-tailed) = ± 2.639
TV group: $N = 61$; $M = 24$; $S^2 = 4$
Radio group: $N = 21$; $M = 26$; $S^2 = 6$
$S^2_{Pooled} = (4)(60/80) + (6)(20/80) = 3.0 + 1.5 = 4.5$;
$S^2_{M_1} = 4.5/61 = .074$; $S^2_{M_2} = 4.5/21 = .214$;
$S^2_{Difference} = .074 + .214 = .288$; $S_{Difference} = .54$;
$t = (24 - 26)/.54 = -2/.54 = -3.70$. Reject the null hypothesis; conclude that the theory is supported by the experiment.
Effect size = $(24 - 26)/\sqrt{4.5} = -2/2.12 = -.94$; large effect size.

Explanation: The mean is the arithmetic average (the sum of the numbers divided by the number of numbers). In this case, the radio group had a higher average on the test than the TV group. S^2 refers to the estimate of the variance of scores in the general population based on the variance of scores in the group of people studied (called the sample). The variance is a measure of the amount of variation in a group of scores. When estimating the population variance from the variance of the sample, each score's difference from the mean is squared and the sum of these squared differences is divided by the degrees of freedom—the number of subjects in the sample minus 1. (The degrees of freedom represents the amount of unique information available in the sample to use in estimating the population. Using the sample's variance, which is the sum of squared differences divided by the number of cases, would give too small an estimate of the population variance.) In this case, I have two estimates, one from each sample.

Now that I have considered the results given in the problem, let us turn to the issue of how to draw conclusions. The way I frame the question is to ask what is the probability of getting this much difference in knowledge scores between the two groups even if radio versus television made no difference. That is, if the TV and radio groups actually represented two larger populations that were not different, how likely is it that I could have drawn a sample from each population that is this different from the other?

To answer this required figuring out what such nondifferent populations would look like. The estimates of the population variance that I made apply here. In fact, even if the two groups represented different populations, only the means would be different. The variance is assumed to be the same. These are two estimates of the same population variance, and I can average both estimates to get a better estimate still. In averaging, however, I want to give more weight to the estimate based on larger degrees of freedom; so I compute a weighted average, multiplying each estimate by its proportion of the total degrees of freedom and adding up the results. This pooled estimate of the population variance (S^2_{Pooled}) comes out to 4.5. At this point, I had estimated the variance of the populations of individuals' knowledge scores.

Now, because I was interested not in individual scores but in the difference between the mean of a group of 61 and the mean of another group of 21, I needed to figure out what would be the characteristics of a distribution of all possible differences between means of groups of 61 and 21 that are randomly drawn from the two identical populations whose variance I just estimated. This required two steps.

First, I needed to figure out the characteristics of an intermediate distribution for each sample—the distribution of means of all possible samples of that size drawn from its population. For the TV group, this would be a distribution of means of samples of 61 each. Such a distribution will have a variance much smaller than the variance of the population of individuals from which the samples were drawn because any one mean is less likely to be extreme than any single score. (The mean of several scores is likely to include some scores that balance out or reduce the effect of any extremes.) In fact, it can be shown mathematically that the variance of a distribution of means of all possible samples will be exactly the variance of the parent population of individuals divided by the number in each sample. For the TV group, this distribution's

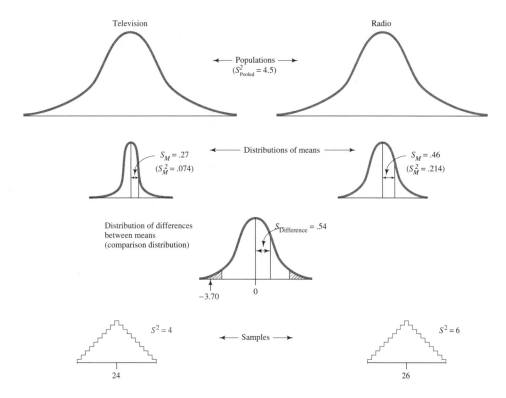

variance would be 4.5 divided by 61, or .074. The corresponding figure for the radio group is .214.

The second step refers directly to the distribution of differences between means. It is like a distribution that would arise if you took a mean from the distribution of means of all possible samples from the TV group and took one from the comparable distribution for the radio group and computed their difference. After doing this many times, the distribution of the differences so obtained would create a new distribution, of differences between means. Because we are assuming (if radio versus TV made no difference) that the two original populations have the same means, the two distributions of many means of samples should have the same mean. On the average, the difference between a sample drawn from the TV group and a sample drawn from the radio group should come out to 0. (Sometimes one will be bigger and sometimes the other, but in the long run these random fluctuations should balance out.) The variance of this distribution of differences between means will be affected by the variation in both distributions of means. In fact, it will be simply the sum of the two. Its variance will be .074 plus .214 or .288. Actually, the variation in such distributions is most often described in terms of what is called the standard deviation (the square root of the variance), which in this case is the square root of .288, or .54.

It also turns out that such distributions of differences between means have a precise known shape, so it is possible to look up in a table the probability of being a certain distance from its mean. The distance is measured in standard deviations. In this case, the table shows that for my distribution (with my total of 80 degrees of freedom), there is less than a 1% chance of getting a score (a difference between means) that is 2.639 or more standard deviations from the mean in either direction. (I took into account both directions because I was studying whether there was a difference in either direction between the TV and radio groups. The "1% level" refers to the conventional point at which researchers who are very concerned about the risk of concluding in error that an experiment has made a difference decide that something is too unlikely to have happened by chance.) I have illustrated these various distributions.

The difference between my particular two means was –2 (that is, 24 – 26 = –2). This would be 3.70 (that is, 2/.54 = 3.70) standard deviations below the mean in the distribution of all possible differences between means of groups of this size. Since this is more extreme than –2.639, I could reject as too unlikely the possibility that I could get a difference this large by taking any two groups of subjects at random regardless of whether they had been getting their news through TV or radio. The researcher can take the results of this study as support for his or her prediction.

Further, the researcher wanted to know not just that results were not by chance but also how big an effect there was of getting news from radio versus TV. The difference between the two means was 2 points on the knowledge measure. The typical amount of variation in scores on any scale is described by the standard deviation (the square root of the variance, the variance being the average of the squares of each score's difference from the mean). In this case, the standard deviation we would estimate uses the data from both samples, the pooled estimate. The pooled estimate of the variance was 4.5. Its square root is 2.12. A difference of 2 points on the scale is a difference of nearly 1 standard deviation. (To be exact, it is .94 standard deviations.) In social and behavioral science research in general, an effect size of .80 is considered large, so this is clearly a large effect. In addition to the conclusion that the result is not likely to have arisen just by chance, the researcher can also conclude that the advantage of radio over TV is quite substantial.

5. (a) Effect size = $(107 - 149)/84 = -42/84 = -.5$. Medium Effect Size.

Number of participants per group needed for medium effect size, $p < .05$, one-tailed (from Table 9–5) = 50; 100 subjects total.

Chapter 10

1. (a) F needed $(df = 2, 27; p < .05) = 3.36$

$GM = (7.4 + 6.8 + 6.8)/3 = 7$

$S^2_M = \Sigma(M - GM)/df_{Between}$
$= [(7.4 - 7)^2 + (6.8 - 7)^2 + (6.8 - 7)^2]/(3 - 1) = .24/2 = .12$

$S^2_{Between} = (S^2_M)(n) = (.12)(10) = 1.2$

$S^2_{Within} = (S^2_1 + S^2_2 + \ldots + S^2_{Last})/N_{Groups}$
$= (.82 + .90 + .80)/3 = .84$

$F = 1.2/.84 = 1.43$

Do not reject the null hypothesis; groups are not significantly different at the .05 level.

Estimated effect size = $S_M/S^2_{Within} = \sqrt{.12}/\sqrt{.84} = .35/.92 = .38$

This is a large effect size. Power (from Table 10–6) = .45

2. (a) F needed $(df = 2, 9; p < .01) = 8.02$

Group 1: $M = 8$, $S^2 = .67$; Group 2: $M = 6$, $S^2 = .67$; Group 3: $M = 4$, $S^2 = .67$

$S^2_{Between} = (4)(4) = 16$; $S^2_{Within} = .67$; $F = 16/.67 = 23.88$

Reject the null hypothesis, groups are significantly different at the .01 level.

Estimated effect size = $S_M/S^2_{Within} = \sqrt{4}/\sqrt{.67} = 2/.82 = 2.44$

This is a (very) large effect size.

4. F needed $(df = 2, 9; p < .05) = 4.26$

Affective: $M = 6$, $S^2 = .67$; Cognitive: $M = 10$, $S^2 = 3.33$

Drug: $M = 10$, $S^2 = 2.67$

$S^2_{Between} = (5.33)(4) = 21.32$; $S^2_{Within} = 2.22$; $F = 21.32/2.22 = 9.60$

Reject the null hypothesis; there is a significant difference.

Explanation: The null hypothesis is that the three groups represent populations of length-of-stay scores with equal means (and, as with a t test, we must be able to assume that they have equal variances). If this null hypothesis is true, then you can estimate the variance of these equal populations in two ways:

(1) You can estimate from the variation within each of the three groups and then average them. (This is just what you would do in a t test for independent means, except now three are being averaged instead of just two. Also, in a t test we would weight these variances according to the degrees of freedom they contribute to the overall estimate. However, because all samples have equal numbers, we can simply average them—in effect, weighting them equally.) In this example, the three variance estimates were .67, 3.33, and 2.67, which gave a pooled estimate of 2.22. This is called the within-group estimate of the population variance (S^2_{Within}).

(2) You can estimate the variance using the three means. If we assume the null hypothesis is true, the means of the three

groups are based on samples taken from identical populations. Each of these identical populations will have an identical distribution of means of samples taken from that population. The means of our three samples are thus all coming from identical populations, which is the same as if they were all coming from the same population. The amount of variation among our three means should be representative of the variation in the distribution of means from which they can be thought of as coming. We can thus use these three means (6, 10, and 10) to estimate the variance in this distribution of means. Using the usual formula for estimating a population variance, we get 5.33.

However, what we want is a distribution of individuals. So the question is, what would be the distribution of individuals that would produce a distribution of means (of four cases each) with a variance of 5.33. To find the distribution of means from a distribution of individuals, you divide the variance of the distribution of individuals by the size of the samples. In this case, we want to do the reverse, so we multiply the variance of the distribution of means by the size of the samples to get the variance of the distribution of individuals. This comes out to 5.33 times 4, or 21.32. This is called the between group estimate of the population variance ($S^2_{Between}$).

If the null hypothesis is true, the two estimates should be about the same because they are estimates of essentially the same populations. The ratio of the between-group estimate divided by the within-group estimate should be about 1.

If the null hypothesis is false and the three populations these groups represent have different means, the estimate based on the variation among the group means will be bigger than the one based on the variation within the groups. The reason it will be bigger follows. If the null hypothesis is true, the only reason that the means of our groups vary is because of the variance inside each of the three identical distributions of means. If the null hypothesis is false, each of those distributions of means also has a different mean. The variation in our means is due to *both* the variation inside of each of these now *not* identical distributions of means, but also to the differences in the means of these distributions of means. There is an additional source of variation in the means of our groups. If you estimate the variance of the population using these three means, it will be larger than it should if the null hypothesis were true. When the null hypothesis is false, the ratio of the between-group variance to the within-group variance (which is not affected by whether the three groups have different means, because it only considers variation within each of the groups) will be more than 1.

The ratio of the between-group estimate to the within-group estimate is called an F ratio. In this example, our F ratio is 21.32 to 2.22: $21.32/2.22 = 9.60$.

Statisticians have constructed tables of what happens when you compute F ratios based on the situation in which you randomly take a group of four cases from each of three identical populations. This is the situation in which our null hypothesis is true. Looking at these tables, it turns out that there is less than a 5% chance of getting an F ratio larger than 4.26. Because our actual F ratio is bigger than this, we can reject the null hypothesis.

7. (i) Main effects for class and age; interaction effect. Income is greater in general for upper-class and for older individuals, but the combination of older and upper class has a higher income than would be expected just from the effects of either variable alone.

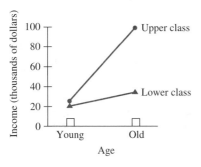

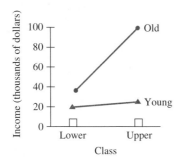

Chapter 11

1. (a) Needed $X^2(df = 3 - 1 = 2, \; p < .05) = 5.992$.

Category	O	Expected (E)	O – E	$(O - E)^2$	$(O - E)^2/E$
1	5	$(1/3)(20) = 6.67$	–1.67	2.79	.42
2	10	$(1/3)(20) = 6.67$	3.33	11.09	1.66
3	5	$(1/3)(20) = 6.67$	–1.67	1.79	.42
					$X^2 = 2.50$

Conclusion: Do not reject the null hypothesis.

3. (a) $df = (N_{\text{Columns}} - 1)(N_{\text{Rows}} - 1) = (2 - 1)(2 - 1) = 1$
Needed $X^2 \; (df = 1, p < .01) = 6.635$
Do not reject the null hypothesis.

10 (13)	16 (13)	26 (50%)
16 (13)	10 (13)	26 (50%)
26 26	26 26	52 (100%)

$$X^2 = \frac{(10-13)^2}{13} + \frac{(16-13)^2}{13} + \frac{(16-13)^2}{13} + \frac{(10-13)^2}{13} =$$
$$.69 + .69 + .69 + .69 = 2.76$$

Do not reject the null hypothesis.
$\Phi = \sqrt{(X^2/N)} = \sqrt{(2.76/52)} = \sqrt{.053} = .23$

4. $df = (N_{\text{Columns}} - 1)(N_{\text{Rows}} - 1) = (3 - 1)(2 - 1) = 2$
Needed $X^2 \; (df = 2, p < .05) = 5.992$

Device Used in Their Room

	Typewriter	Word Processor	Neither	
Pen	42 (39)	62 (65)	26 (26)	130 (65%)
Pencil	18 (21)	38 (35)	14 (14)	70 (35%)
	60 (60)	100 (100)	40 (40)	200 (100%)

$$X^2 = \frac{(42-39)^2}{39} + \frac{(62-65)^2}{65} + \frac{(26-26)^2}{26} + \frac{(18-21)^2}{21} + \frac{(38-35)^2}{35} + \frac{(14-14)^2}{14}$$
$$= .23 + .14 + 0 + .43 + .26 + 0 = 1.06$$

Do not reject the null hypothesis.
Cramer's $\Phi = \sqrt{[1.06/(200)(1)]} = \sqrt{.0053} = .07$. Small effect size.

Explanation: In this example, 65% of all subjects uses pens when taking notes. If pen versus pencil and device used in their room are not related, 65% of the people in each in-room category should use pens when taking notes. For example, you would expect 39 of the 60 students who use a typewriter to write with a pen when taking notes. Are the survey results so discrepant from these expectations that we should conclude that in general what students use to take notes with is related to the device that they use to write with in their room?

Chi-square is a measure of the degree of difference between observed and expected results. For each combination of the 2 x 3 arrangement, you compute that discrepancy between observed and expected, square it, and divide by the expected number; then you add up the results. In the pen-typewriter combination, 42 minus 39 is 3, squared is 9, divided by 39 is .23. Doing the same for the other five combinations and adding them all up gives 1.06. (Chi-square uses squared discrepancies so that the result is not affected by the directions of the differences. It is divided by the expected number to adjust for the impact of relatively different numbers expected in the combinations.)

Statisticians have determined mathematically what would happen if you took an infinite number of samples from a population with a fixed proportion of people in each of several groupings and computed chi-square for each such sample. The distribution of such chi-squares depends only on the number of groupings free to take on different expected values. (For each in-their-room category, if you know the figure for students who take notes with a pen, the figure for those who take notes with a pencil is easily determined. Of the three in-their-room categories for the pen group, if you know two of them, the third is easy to determine because they must add up to the total who use a pen. So only two combinations are "free to vary.")

A table of the chi-square distribution when two groupings are free to vary shows that there is only a 5% chance of getting a chi-square of 5.992 or greater. Because our chi-square is smaller than this, the observed numbers in each category differ from the expected numbers less than they would have to before we would be willing to reject the idea that in general the implement that people use to take notes is unrelated to the device that they use to write with in their room. The survey is inconclusive.

We can, however, estimate the actual degree of linkage between implement use in class and device use in their room. The procedure is called "Cramer's phi," calculated in this case by dividing the computed chi-square by the number of people included in the analysis, then taking the square root of the results. In this example, this comes out to .07.

This statistic ranges from 0 (no relationship) to 1 (a perfect relationship—knowing a person's status on one of the dimensions, such as what they use to write with in class, would let you perfectly predict their status on the other dimension, such as what they write with at home). Thus, .07 is a quite low figure. (In fact, Cramer's phi is comparable to what is called a correlation coefficient; and in the social and behavioral sciences .07 is very low compared to the correlations found in most studies.)

Looking at this another way, we can ask, if there really is a moderate relationship among students in general, what is the chance that this whole process would have led to a positive conclusion in this study? Statisticians have provided tables that give this probability. In this case, it turns out that there would be a 97% chance. Given the result of this study, if any relationship exists, it is almost surely fairly small.

7. t needed (two-tailed, $p < .05$, $df = 8$) = 2.306

Square-Root Transformed Scores

Group A	Group B
1.1	1.4
1.6	3.0
2.1	2.4
1.9	2.6
<u>2.7</u>	<u>2.2</u>
$M = 1.88$	2.32
$S^2 = .35$	.35

$S^2_{Pooled} = .35$

$S^2_M = .07$ .07

$S^2_{Difference} = .14$

$S_{Difference} = .37$

$t = (1.88 - 2.32)/.37 = -1.19$; do not reject the null hypothesis.

Explanation: It would not have been proper to carry out a t test on the numbers as they were (without transforming them), because the distributions of the samples were so skewed for both language groups that it seemed likely that the population distribution was also seriously skewed. That would clearly violate the assumption for a t test that the underlying population distributions are normal. So I took the square root of each score. This had the virtue of creating a sample distribution that was much closer to normal and, therefore, probably suggests that the population distribution of square roots of family sizes is nearly normally distributed. I realize that taking the square root of each family size distorts its straightforward meaning. The impact for the individuals in the family of each additional child is probably not equal. That is, going from no children to 1 child has a huge impact. Going from 1 to 2 has less, and going from 7 to 8 probably makes very much less difference for the family.

In any case, having taken the square root of each score, I then proceeded to conduct an ordinary t test for independent means. The result was inconclusive: The null hypothesis could not be rejected. (Because the sample size was so small, the power was also probably low, making it hard to draw any kind of conclusion from the failure to reject the null hypothesis.)

Chapter 12

1. A hierarchical multiple regression is a variation of ordinary multiple regression in which each predictor variable is added to the prediction rule, one at a time (or sometimes a set of variables is added as a group). The additional contribution of that variable (in addition to the variable added in the previous step) is computed. The order in which the predictor variables are entered is determined by the researcher in advance. In this case, the dependent variable was symptoms. The first predictor variable considered was gender, which, Meier reports, accounted for 15% of the variance in the dependent variable. This is an ordinary prediction situation with one predictor and one dependent variable. The next predictor variable added was social desirability. The researcher reports that it did not add anything. That means that the overall variance accounted for in symptoms, using both predictor variables together, would still be about 15%. The next variable added was score on the Meier Burnout Assessment measure. This improved the prediction slightly, accounting for another 2% of the variance (that is, with these three measures as predictor variables, R^2 was up to 17%). However, the addition of the Maslach test made a big contribution to the accuracy of prediction, accounting for an additional 10% of the variance in symptoms. (That is, the overall R^2 was now 27%.) Adding the anxiety measure accounted for another 3% of the variance, and adding depression made no further addition, so that with all variables considered, the total variance accounted for was 30%.

4. Path analysis is a technique in which the researcher specifies a pattern of causal relationships among variables, diagrammed with arrows connecting each cause to its effects. The statistical aspect of path analysis involves computing a "path coefficient" for each arrow. The path coefficient tells the degree to which changes on the variable at the tail of the arrow are associated with changes in the variable at the head of the arrow (under conditions in which all other causes for that effect variable are held constant). That is, the path coefficient is a standardized regression coefficient (a "beta") for the causal variable in an equation in which the effect variable is the dependent variable and all of the causal variables are predictor variables.

The figure is an example of a path diagram, and the numbers shown along the arrows are the path coefficients (ignore the numbers in parentheses). For example, the arrow from Self-Satisfaction (at the top left, which is for the second phase of the study) to Performance (in the middle, which is performance in the second phase) tells you that the researchers hypothesized that in the second phase of the study, Self-Satisfaction would have a causal effect on Performance. The .28 means that after controlling for the other three variables also hypothesized to have a direct causal effect on Performance (Analytic Strategies, Self-Efficacy, and Past Performance), an increase of 1 standard deviation on Self-Satisfaction predicts an increase of .28 of a standard deviation on Performance.

7. (a) Causal modeling (path analysis or latent variable modeling)
   (c) Reliability statistics, such as Cronbach's alpha and test-retest reliability
   (i) Hierarchical multiple regression

Glossary

Numbers in parentheses refer to chapters in which the term is introduced or substantially discussed.

Alpha (α). The probability of a Type I error; same as *significance level*. Also short for *Cronbach's alpha*. (7, 12)

Analysis of covariance (ANCOVA). An analysis of variance that is conducted after first adjusting the variables to control for the effect of one or more unwanted additional variables. (12)

Analysis of variance (ANOVA). A hypothesis-testing procedure for comparing means in studies involving two or more groups. (10)

Assumption. A condition, such as a population's having a normal distribution, required for carrying out a particular hypothesis-testing procedure; a part of the mathematical foundation for the accuracy of the tables used in determining cutoff values. (8)

Beta (β). Standardized regression coefficient (3).

Between-group degrees of freedom ($df_{Between}$). Same as *numerator degrees of freedom*. (10)

Between-group estimate of the population variance ($S^2_{Between}$). In an analysis of variance, the estimate of the variance of the population distribution of individuals based on the variation among the means of the groups studied. (10)

Biased estimate. An estimate of a population parameter that is likely systematically to overestimate or underestimate the true population value. For example, SD^2 would be a biased estimate of the population variance (it would systematically underestimate it). (8)

Bimodal distribution. A frequency distribution with two ap-proximately equal frequencies, each clearly larger than any of the others. (1)

Categorical variable. Same as *nominal variable*. (1, 11)

Causal analysis. A procedure, such as path analysis or structural equation modeling, that analyzes correlations among a group of variables in terms of a predicted pattern of causal relations among them. (12)

Ceiling effect. The situation in which many scores pile up at the high end (creating skewness) because it is not possible to have a higher score. (1)

Cell. In a factorial design, a particular combination of levels of the independent variables; also, in chi-square, the particular combination of categories for two variables in a contingency table. (10, 11)

Cell mean. The mean of a particular combination of levels of the independent variables in a factorial design. (10)

Central limit theorem. A mathematical principle that says that the distribution of the sums (or means) of scores taken at random from any distribution of individuals will tend to form a normal curve. (4, 6)

Central tendency. The typical or most representative value of a group of scores. (2)

Chi-square distribution. A mathematically defined curve that is used as the comparison distribution in chi-square tests. It is the distribution of the chi-square statistic. (11)

Chi-square statistic (X^2). A statistic that reflects the overall lack of fit between the expected and observed frequencies; the sum, over all the categories or cells, of the squared difference between observed and expected frequencies divided by the expected frequency. (11)

Chi-square table. A table providing cutoff scores on the chi-square distribution for various degrees of freedom and significance levels. (11)

Chi-square test. A hypothesis testing procedure that uses the chi-square distribution as the comparison distribution. (11)

Chi-square test for goodness of fit. A hypothesis-testing procedure that examines how well an observed frequency distribution of a nominal variable fits some expected pattern of frequencies. (11)

Chi-square test for independence. A hypothesis-testing procedure that examines whether the distribution of frequencies over the categories of one nominal variable are unrelated to the distribution of frequencies over the categories of another nominal variable. (11)

Comparison distribution. The distribution describing the population situation if the null hypothesis is true; the distribution to which a sample statistic is compared in hypothesis testing. (5)

Computational formula. An equation mathematically equivalent to the definitional formula that is easier to use for hand computation but does not directly display the meaning of the procedure it symbolizes. (2)

Confidence interval. Roughly speaking, the region of scores (that is the scores between an upper and lower value) that is likely to include the true population mean; more precisely, the region of possible population means for which it is not highly unlikely that one could have obtained one's sample. (6)

Confidence limits. The upper and lower values of a confidence interval. (6)

Contingency table. A two-dimensional chart showing frequencies in each combination of categories of two nominal variables. (11)

Controlling for. In multiple regression, partial correlation, or analysis of covariance, removing the influence of a variable from the association among other variables; same as *partialing out* and *holding constant*. (12)

Conventional levels of significance ($p < .05, p < .01$). The levels of significance widely used in the social sciences. (5)

Correlation. The association between scores on two or more variables. (3)

Correlation coefficient (r). The average of the cross-products of Z scores of two variables; a measure of the degree of linear correlation ranging from –1 (a perfect negative linear correlation) through 0 (no correlation) to +1 (a perfect positive correlation); the square root of the proportion of variance accounted for. (3)

Correlation matrix. A common way of reporting the correlation coefficients among several variables in research articles; a square table in which the variables are named on the top and along the side and the correlations among them are all shown (only half of the resulting square, above or below the diagonal, is usually filled in, the other half being redundant). (3)

Covariate. A variable controlled for in an analysis of covariance. (12)

Cramer's phi statistic. A measure of association between two categorical variables; an effect-size measure for a chi-square test of independence with a contingency table that is larger than 2×2; also known as *Cramer's V* and sometimes written as Φ_c or V_c. (11)

Cronbach's alpha (α). A widely used index of a measure's reliability that is equivalent to the average of the split-half correlations from all possible splits into halves of the items on the test. (12)

Cross-product of Z scores. The result of multiplying a person's Z score on one variable times the person's Z score on another variable; for a group of individuals, the average of the cross-products of Z scores between two variables is the correlation coefficient for those two variables. (3)

Curvilinear correlation. A relation between two variables that shows up on a scatter diagram as dots following a systematic pattern that is not a straight line; any association between two variables other than a linear correlation. (3)

Cutoff sample score. The point on the comparison distribution in hypothesis testing at which, if reached or exceeded by the sample score, the null hypothesis will be rejected. (5)

Data transformation. The application of a mathematical procedure (such as taking the square root) to each score in a sample, usually done to make the sample distribution closer to normal. (11)

Definitional formula. The equation directly displaying the meaning of the procedure it symbolizes. (2)

Degree of correlation. The extent to which there is a clear pattern of some particular relationship (usually linear) between two variables. (3)

Degrees of freedom (df). The number of scores free to vary when estimating a population parameter; it is usually part of an equation for making that estimate—for example, in the formula for estimating the population variance from a single sample, the degrees of freedom is the number of scores minus 1. (8)

Denominator degrees of freedom (df_{Within}). The degrees of freedom used in figuring the within-group estimate of the population variance in an analysis of variance (the denominator of the F ratio); the number of scores free to vary (number of scores in each group minus 1, summed over all the groups) in computing the within-group population variance estimate; also called the *within-group degrees of freedom*. (10)

Dependent variable (usually Y). A variable that is considered to be an effect; also used in regression for any variable that is predicted about. (3)

Descriptive statistics. Procedures for summarizing a set of scores or otherwise making them more comprehensible. (1)

Deviation score. A score minus the mean of all scores in that distribution. (2)

Difference score. The difference between a person's score on one testing and the same person's score on another testing; often an after score minus a before score in which case it is also called a *change score*. (8)

Direction of causality. The path of causal effect; if X is thought to cause Y then the direction of causality is from X to Y. (3)

Directional hypothesis. A research hypothesis predicting a particular direction of difference between populations (for example, a prediction that one population has a higher mean than another). (5)

Distribution-free test. A hypothesis-testing procedure making no assumptions about the shape of the underlying populations; approximately the same as a nonparametric test. (11)

Distribution of differences between means. The distribution of all possible differences between means of two samples such that for each pair of means, one is from one population and the other is from a second population; the comparison distribution in a *t* test for independent means. (9)

Distribution of means. A distribution of all the possible means of samples of a given size from a particular population (also called a sampling distribution of the mean); the comparison distribution when testing hypotheses involving a sample of more than one individual. (6)

Effect size. The separation (lack of overlap) between populations due to the independent variable; it increases with greater differences between means and decreases with greater standard deviations in the populations, but it is not affected by sample size. (7)

Effect size conventions. Standard rules about what to consider a small, medium, and large effect size, based on what is typical in social and behavioral science research; often known as *Cohen's conventions*. (7)

Effect size for the analysis of variance. An effect size measure based on the overall variation among the means of the groups being compared in relation to the average within group variation. (10)

Expected frequency. In a chi-square test, the number of cases in a category or cell expected if the null hypothesis were true. (11)

Expected relative frequency. The number of successful outcomes divided by the number of total outcomes you would expect to get if you repeated an experiment a large number of times. (4)

Factor. In a factor analysis, a subset of variables that correlate maximally with each other and minimally with variables not in the subset. (12)

Factor analysis. An exploratory statistical procedure, applied in situations where many variables are measured, that identifies groupings of variables correlating maximally with each other and minimally with other variables. (12)

Factor loading. In a factor analysis, the correlation of a variable with a factor. (12)

Factorial analysis of variance. An analysis of variance for a factorial research design; an analysis of variance for the differences among the means over the levels of each independent variable and for the interaction of the independent variables. (10)

Factorial research design. A way of organizing a study in which the influence of two or more variables is studied at once by setting up the situation so that a group of people are tested for every combination of the levels of the variables; for example, in a 2×2 factorial research design there would be four groups, those high on variable 1 and high on variable 2, those high on variable 1 but low on variable 2, those high on variable 2 but low on variable 1, and those low on variable 1 and low on variable 2. (10)

***F* distribution.** A mathematically defined curve that is the comparison distribution used in an analysis of variance; the distribution of *F* ratios when the null hypothesis is true. (10)

***F* ratio.** In the analysis of variance, the ratio of the between-group estimate of the population variance to the within-group estimate of the population variance; a score on the comparison distribution (an *F* distribution) in an analysis of variance; also referred to simply as *F*. (10)

***F* table.** A table providing cutoff scores on the *F* distribution for various degrees of freedom and significance levels. (10)

Fit index. In structural equation modeling, a measure of how well the pattern of correlations in a sample correspond to the correlations that would be expected based on the hypothesized pattern of causes and effects among those variables; usually ranges from 0 to 1, with 1 being a perfect fit. (12)

Floor effect. The situation in which many scores pile up at the low end of a distribution (creating skewness) because it is not possible to have any lower score. (1)

Frequency distribution. The pattern of frequencies over the various values; what a frequency table, histogram, or frequency polygon describes. (1)

Frequency polygon. A line graph of a distribution in which the values are plotted along the horizontal axis and the height of each point is the frequency of that value; the lines begin and end at the horizontal axis, and the graph resembles a mountainous skyline. (1)

Frequency table. A listing of the number of individuals having each of the different values for a particular variable. (1)

Grand mean (*GM*). In analysis of variance, the overall mean of all the scores, regardless of what group they are in; when groups are of equal size, the mean of the group means. (10)

Grouped frequency table. A frequency table in which the number of individuals is given for each interval of values. (1)

Haphazard selection. A procedure of selecting a sample of individuals to study by taking whoever is available or happens to be first on a list; should not be confused with true random selection. (4)

Harmonic mean. A special average that is influenced more by smaller scores; in a *t* test for independent means when the number of scores in the two groups differ, the harmonic mean is used as the equivalent of each group's sample size when computing power. (9)

Heavy-tailed distribution. A distribution that differs from a normal curve by being too spread out so that a histogram of the distribution would have too many cases at each of the two extremes ("tails"). (1)

Hierarchical multiple regression. A method of multiple regression in which predictor variables are added, one or a few at a time, in a planned sequential fashion, allowing the researcher to calculate the contribution to the prediction of each successive variable over and above those already included. (12)

Histogram. A barlike graph of a distribution in which the values are plotted along the horizontal axis and the height of each bar is the frequency of that value; the bars are placed next to each other without spaces, giving the appearance of a city skyline. (1)

Holding constant. In multiple regression, partial correlation, or analysis of covariance, removing the influence of a variable from the association among the other variables; same as *partialing out* and *controlling for*. (12)

Hypothesis testing. A procedure for determining whether results of a study (which gives data for a sample) provide support for a particular theory or practical innovation (which is thought to be applicable to a population). (5)

Independence. The situation of no systematic relationship between two variables; a term usually used in relation to two nominal variables in the context of the chi-square test for independence. (11)

Independent variable (usually *X*). A variable that is considered to be a cause; also, in regression, sometimes any predictor variable, whether or not it is regarded as a cause. (3)

Inferential statistics. Procedures for drawing conclusions based on the scores collected in a research study (sample scores) but going beyond them (to conclusions about a population). (1, 4)

Interaction effect. Situation in the factorial analysis of variance in which the combination of variables has a special effect that could not be predicted from knowledge of the effects of the two variables individually. (10)

Interval. In a grouped frequency table, the range of values which are grouped together. (For example, if the interval size was 10, one of the intervals might be from 20.00 to 29.99.) (1)

Interval estimate. A region of scores (that is the scores between some specified lower and upper value) that is estimated to include a population parameter; this is in contrast to a *point estimate;* a *confidence interval* is an example of an interval estimate. (6)

Interval size. In a grouped frequency table, the difference between the start of one interval and the start of the next. (If one interval was 20.00 to 29.99 and the next was 30.00 to 39.99, the interval size would be 10.) (1)

Inverse transformation. A data transformation in which the researcher uses the inverse (1 divided by the number) of each score. (11)

Latent variable. In structural equation modeling, an unmeasured theoretical variable assumed to be the underlying cause of several variables actually measured in the study. (12)

Latent variable modeling. Same as *structured equation modeling.* (12)

Level of significance (α). The probability of obtaining statistical significance if the null hypothesis is actually true; the probability of a Type I error. (5, 6, 7)

Light-tailed distribution. A distribution that differs from a normal curve by being too peaked or pinched so that a histogram of the distribution would have too few cases at each of the two extremes ("tails"). (1)

Linear correlation. A relation between two variables that shows up on a scatter diagram as dots roughly following a straight line; a correlation of *r* unequal to 0. (3)

LISREL. A computer program for structural equation modeling; sometimes used as a name for the procedure itself. (12)

Log transformation. A data transformation in which the researcher uses the log of each score. (11)

Long-run relative-frequency interpretation of probability. Understanding of probability as the proportion of a particular outcome that you would get if the experiment were repeated many times. (4)

Main effect. The difference between groups on one variable in a factorial design; the result for a variable, averaging across the other variable (sometimes used only for significant differences). (10)

Marginal mean. In a factorial design, the mean score for all the subjects at a particular level of one of the independent variables; often shortened to *marginal.* (10)

Mean (*M*). The arithmetic average of a group of scores; the sum of the scores divided by the number of scores; also symbolized as $\overline{X}$. (2)

Mean of a distribution of means. Equal to the mean of the population of individuals from which the samples are taken. (6)

Median. The middle score when all the scores in a distribution arranged from highest to lowest. (2)

Meta-analysis. A statistical method for combining the results of independent studies, usually focusing on effect sizes. (7)

Mode. The value with the greatest frequency in a distribution. (2)

Multimodal distribution. A frequency distribution with two or more high frequencies separated by a lower frequency; a bimodal distribution is the special case of two high frequencies. (1)

Multiple comparisons. Hypothesis testing procedures for testing the differences among particular means in the context of an overall analysis of variance. (10)

Multiple correlation. Correlation of one variable with a set of variables. (3)

Multiple correlation coefficient (*R*). A measure of the overall association between a dependent variable and the combination of two or more predictor variables; the positive square root of the proportion of variance accounted for in a multiple regression analysis. (3)

Multiple regression. The prediction of scores on one variable (the dependent variable) based on scores of two or more other variables (predictor or independent variables). (3)

Multivariate analysis of covariance (MANCOVA). An analysis of covariance in which there is more than one dependent variable. (12)

Multivariate analysis of variance (MANOVA). An analysis of variance in which there is more than one dependent variable. (12)

Multivariate statistics. Statistical procedures involving more than one dependent variable. (12)

Negative correlation. A relation between two variables in which high scores on one go with low scores on the other, mediums with mediums, and lows with highs; on a scatter diagram, the dots roughly follow a straight line sloping down and to the right; a correlation of *r* less than 0. (3)

95% confidence interval. A confidence interval in which, roughly speaking, there is a 95% chance that the population mean falls within this interval. (6)

99% confidence interval. A confidence interval in which, roughly speaking, there is a 99% chance that the population mean falls within this interval. (6)

No correlation. No systematic relation between two variables. (3)

Nominal variable. A variable with values that are categories with no numerical relation (that is, they are names rather than numbers); same as *categorical variable*. (1, 11)

Nondirectional hypothesis. A research hypothesis that does not predict a particular direction of difference between populations. (5)

Nonparametric test. A hypothesis-testing procedure making no assumptions about population parameters; approximately the same as a *distribution-free test*. (11)

Normal curve. A specific, mathematically defined, bell-shaped frequency distribution that is symmetrical and unimodal; distributions observed in nature and in research commonly approximate it. (1, 4)

Normal curve table. A table showing percentages of cases in a normally distributed distribution that fall between the mean and various numbers of standard deviations above the mean. (4)

Normal distribution. A frequency distribution following a normal curve. (4)

Null hypothesis. A statement about a relation between populations that is the opposite of the research hypothesis; a statement that in the population there is no difference (or a difference opposite to that predicted) between populations; a contrived statement set up to examine whether it can be rejected as part of hypothesis-testing. (5)

Numerator degrees of freedom ($df_{Between}$). The degrees of freedom used in the between-group estimate of the population variance in an analysis of variance (the numerator of the F ratio); the number of scores free to vary (number of means minus 1) in computing the between-group estimate of the population variance; between-group degrees of freedom. (10)

Numeric variable. A variable whose values are numbers (as opposed to a nominal variable). (1)

Observed frequency. In a chi-square test, the number of individuals actually found in the study to be in a category or cell. (11)

One-tailed test. The hypothesis-testing procedure for a directional hypothesis; the situation in which the region of the comparison distribution in which the null hypothesis would be rejected is all on one side (tail) of the distribution. (5)

One-way analysis of variance. An analysis of variance in which there is only one independent variable (as distinguished from a factorial analysis of variance). (10)

Outcome. A term used in discussing probability referring to the result of an experiment (or virtually any event, such as a coin coming up heads or it raining tomorrow). (4)

Outlier. A score with an extreme (very high or very low) value in relation to the rest of the scores in the distribution. (2, 11)

Parametric test. An ordinary hypothesis-testing procedure, such as a *t* test or an analysis of variance, that requires assumptions about the shape and other parameters of the populations. (11)

Partial correlation. The procedure of determining a partial correlation coefficient. (12)

Partial correlation coefficient. A measure of the degree of linear correlation between two variables, over and above the influence of one or more other variables. (12)

Partialing out. In multiple regression, partial correlation, or analysis of covariance, removing the influence of a variable from the association among the other variables; same as *holding constant* and *controlling for*. (12)

Path analysis. A method of analyzing the correlations among a group of variables in terms of a predicted pattern of causal relations; usually the predicted pattern is diagrammed as a pattern of arrows from causes to effects. (12)

Path coefficient. The degree of relation associated with an arrow in a path analysis (including structural equation modeling); same as a standardized regression coefficient from a multiple regression prediction rule in which the variable at the end of the arrow is the dependent variable and the variable at the start of the arrow is the predictor, along with all the other variables that have arrows leading to that dependent variable. (12)

Perfect correlation. A relation between two variables that shows up on a scatter diagram as the dots exactly following a straight line; a correlation of $r = 1$ or $r = -1$; a situation in which each person's Z score on one variable is exactly the same as that person's Z score on the other variable. (3)

Phi coefficient (Φ). A measure of association between two dichotomous nominal variables; equivalent to a correlation of the two variables if they were each given numerical values (for example of 1 and 0 for the two categories); an effect-size measure for a chi-square test of independence with a 2×2 contingency table. (11)

Point estimate. Estimate from a sample of the most likely single value of a population parameter. (6)

Pooled estimate of the population variance (S^2_{Pooled}). In a t test for independent means, a weighted average of the estimates of the population variance from two samples (each estimate weighted by the proportion of the degrees of freedom for its sample divided by the total degrees of freedom for both samples). (9)

Population. The entire group of subjects to which a researcher intends the results of a study to apply; the larger group to which inferences are made on the basis of the particular set of people studied. (4)

Population mean. The mean of the population (usually not known). (4)

Population parameter. The actual value of the mean, standard deviation, and so on, for the population (usually population parameters are not known, though sometimes they are estimated). (4)

Population standard deviation. The standard deviation of the population (usually not known). (4)

Population variance. The variance of the population (usually not known). (4)

Positive correlation. A relation between two variables in which high scores on one go with high scores on the other, mediums with mediums, and lows with lows; on a scatter diagram, the dots roughly follow a straight line sloping up and to the right; a correlation of r greater than 0. (3)

Power. Same as *statistical power*. (7)

Power table. Table for a hypothesis-testing procedure showing the statistical power of a study for various effect sizes and sample sizes. (7, 8)

Prediction model. A formula for making predictions; that is, a formula for predicting a person's score on a dependent variable based on the person's score on one or more independent variables. (3)

Predictor variable (usually *X*). In multiple regression, a variable that is used to predict scores of individuals on another variable; sometimes called *independent variable.* (3)

Probability (*p*). The expected relative frequency of a particular outcome; the proportion of successful outcomes to all outcomes. (4)

Proportion of variance accounted for (*r²*). The measure of association between variables used when comparing associations in different studies or with different variables; the correlation coefficient squared; the variance of the predicted scores (based on a regression formula) divided by the variance of the actual scores. (3)

Protected *t* tests. In analysis of variance, *t*-tests among pairs of means of groups after finding that the *F* for the overall difference among the means of the groups is significant. (10).

Quantitative variable. Same as *numeric variable.* (1)

Random selection. A method for selecting a sample that uses truly random procedures (usually meaning that each person in the population has an equal chance of being selected); one method is for the researcher to begin with a complete list of all the people in the population and select a group of them to study using a table of random numbers; should not be confused with haphazard selection. (4)

Rank-order test. A hypothesis-testing procedure that makes use of rank-ordered data. (11)

Rank-order transformation. Changing a set of scores to ranks, so that the highest score is rank 1, the next highest rank 2, and so forth. (11)

Raw score. An ordinary measurement (or any other number in a distribution before it has been made into a *Z* score or otherwise transformed). (2)

Raw-score prediction formula. A prediction rule using raw scores. (3)

Raw-score regression coefficient (*b*). The regression coefficient in a prediction rule using raw scores. (3)

Rectangular distribution. A frequency distribution in which all values have approximately the same frequency. (1)

Regression coefficient. The number multiplied by a person's score on the independent variable as part of a formula (prediction rule) for predicting scores on the dependent variable. (3)

Regression constant (*a*). In a prediction rule using raw scores, a particular fixed number added into the prediction. (3)

Reliability. The degree of consistency of a measure; the extent to which, if you were to give the same measure again to the same person under the same circumstances, you would obtain the same result. (12)

Repeated-measures analysis of variance. Analysis of variance in which each individual is measured more than once so that the levels of the independent variable(s) are different times or types of testing for the same people. (10)

Repeated-measures design. A research strategy in which each person is tested more than once; same as *within-subject design.* (8)

Research hypothesis. In hypothesis testing, a statement about the predicted relation between populations (usually a prediction of difference between population means). (5)

Sample. The scores of the particular group of people studied; usually considered as representative of the scores in some larger population. (4)

Sample statistic. A descriptive statistic, such as the mean or standard deviation, computed from the scores in a particular group of people studied. (4)

Scatter diagram. A graph showing the relationship between two variables; the values of the predictor or independent variable are along the horizontal axis, the values of the dependent variable are along the vertical axis, and each score is shown as a dot in this two-dimensional space. (3)

Score. A particular person's value on a variable. (1)

Shape of a distribution of means. The contour of a histogram of a distribution of means, such as whether it follows a normal curve or is skewed; in general, a distribution of means will tend to be unimodal and symmetrical and is often normal. (6)

Skewed distribution. A distribution in which the scores pile up on one side of the mean and are spread out on the other side; a distribution that is not symmetrical. (1)

Skewness. The extent to which a frequency distribution has more cases on one side of the middle as opposed to being perfectly symmetrical. (1)

Split-half reliability. One index of a measure's reliability, based on a correlation of the scores from items from two halves of the test. (12)

Square-root transformation. A data transformation in which the researcher uses the square root of each score. (11)

Squared deviation score. The square of the difference between a score and the mean. (2)

Standard deviation (*SD*). The square root of the average of the squared deviations from the mean; the most common descriptive statistic for variation; roughly (but not exactly) the average amount scores in a distribution vary from the mean. (2)

Standard deviation of a distribution of means (Population SD_M). The square root of the variance of the distribution of means; same as *standard error (SE).* (6)

Standard deviation of the distribution of differences between means ($S_{\text{Difference}}$). In a *t*-test for independent means, the square root of the variance of the distribution of differences between means. (9)

Standard error (*SE*). Same as *standard deviation of the distribution of means;* also called *standard error of the mean.* (6)

Standard score. A *Z* score in a distribution which follows a normal curve; sometimes used to refer to any *Z* score. (2)

Standardized regression coefficient (beta, β). Regression coefficient in a prediction rule using *Z* scores; also called a "beta weight." (3)

Statistical power. The probability that the study will yield a significant result if the research hypothesis is true. (7)

Statistical significance. A situation of being statistically significant. (5)

Statistically significant. A conclusion that the results of a study would be unlikely if in fact there were no difference in the populations the samples studied represent; an outcome of hypothesis testing in which the null hypothesis is rejected. (3, 5)

Stepwise multiple regression. An exploratory procedure in which all the potential predictor variables that have been measured are tried in order to find the predictor variable that produces the best prediction, then each of the remaining variables is tried to find the predictor variable which in combination with the first produces the best prediction; this process continues until adding the best remaining variable does not provide a significant improvement. (12)

Structural equation modeling. A sophisticated version of path analysis that includes paths involving latent, unmeasured, theoretical variables and that also permits a kind of significance test and provides measures of the overall fit of the data to the hypothesized causal pattern; also called *latent variable modeling* and *LISREL.* (12)

Subjective interpretation of probability. A way of understanding probability as the degree of one's certainty that a particular outcome will occur. (4)

Sum of squared deviations. The total over all the scores of each score's squared difference from the mean. (2)

Symmetrical distribution. A distribution in which the pattern of frequencies on the left and right side are mirror images of each other. (1)

t **distribution.** A mathematically defined curve that is the comparison distribution used in a *t* test. (8)

t **score.** On a *t* distribution, the number of standard deviations from the mean. (It is like a Z score.) (8)

t **table.** A table providing cutoff scores on the *t* distribution for various degrees of freedom, significance levels, and one- and two-tailed tests. (8)

t **test.** A hypothesis-testing procedure in which the population variance is unknown; it compares *t* scores from a sample to a comparison distribution called a *t* distribution. (8)

t **test for a single sample.** A hypothesis-testing procedure in which a sample mean is being compared to a known population mean and the population variance is unknown. (8)

t **test for dependent means.** A hypothesis-testing procedure in which there are two scores for each person and the population variance is not known; it determines the significance of a hypothesis that is being tested using difference or change scores from a single group of people. (8)

t **test for independent means.** A hypothesis testing procedure in which there are two separate groups of people tested and in which the population variance is not known. (9)

Test-retest reliability. One index of a measure's reliability, obtained by giving the test to a group of people twice; the correlation between scores obtained at the two testings. (12)

Two-tailed test. The hypothesis-testing procedure for a nondirectional hypothesis; the situation in which the region of the comparison distribution in which the null hypothesis would be rejected is divided between the two sides (tails) of the distribution. (5)

Two-way analysis of variance. Analysis of variance for a two-way factorial research design. (10)

Two-way factorial research design. A factorial design with two independent variables. (10)

Type I error. Rejecting the null hypothesis when in fact it is true; obtaining a statistically significant result when in fact the research hypothesis is not true. (7)

Type II error. Failing to reject the null hypothesis when in fact it is false; failing to get a statistically significant result when in fact the research hypothesis is true. (7)

Unbiased estimate of the population variance (S^2). An estimate of the population variance, based on sample scores, which has been corrected (by dividing the sum of squared deviations by the sample size minus 1 instead of the usual procedure of dividing by the sample size directly) so that it is equally likely to over or underestimate the true population variance. (2,8)

Unimodal distribution. A frequency distribution with one value clearly having a larger frequency than any other. (1)

Value. A possible number or category that a score can have. (1)

Variable. A characteristic that can have different values. (1)

Variance (SD^2). A measure of how spread out a set of scores are; the average of the squared deviations from the mean; the standard deviation squared. (2)

Variance of a distribution of differences between means ($S^2_{Difference}$). One of the figures computed as part of a *t* test for independent means; it equals the sum of the variances of the distributions of means corresponding to each of two samples. (9)

Variance of a distribution of means (Population SD^2_M). The variance of the population divided by the number of scores in each sample. (6)

Weighted average. An average in which the scores being averaged do not have equal influence on the total, as in figuring the pooled variance estimate in a *t*-test for independent means. (9)

Within-group degrees of freedom (df_W). Same as *denominator degrees of freedom.* (10)

Within-group estimate of the population variance (S^2_{Within}). In analysis of variance, the estimate of the variance of the distribution of the population of individuals based on the variation among the scores within each of the actual groups studied. (10)

Within-subject design. Same as *repeated-measures design.* (8)

Z score. The number of standard deviations a score is above (or below, if it is negative) the mean in its distribution; an ordinary score transformed so that it better describes that score's location in a distribution. (2)

Z test. A hypothesis-testing procedure in which there is a single sample and the population variance is known. (6)

Glossary of Symbols

α Significance level; probability of a Type I error. Also Cronbach's alpha, a measure of reliability. (7, 12)

β Standardized regression coefficient. (3)

Σ Sum of; add up all the scores following. (2)

Φ Phi coefficient; effect size in chi-square analysis of a 2×2 contingency table. (11)

X^2 Chi-square statistic. (11)

a Regression constant. (3)

b Raw score regression coefficient. (3)

df Degrees of freedom. (8–10).

df_1, df_2, and so on.   Degrees of freedom for the first group, second group, and so on. (9, 10)

df_{Between} Numerator degrees of freedom in analysis of variance. (10)

df_{Smaller} Degrees of freedom for the nominal variable (the row or column in the contingency table) with the smaller number of categories in a chi-square test of independence. (11)

df_{Total} Total degrees of freedom over all groups. (9, 10)

df_{Within} Denominator degrees of freedom in analysis of variance. (10)

F ratio   In analysis of variance, ratio of the between-group estimate of the population variance to the within-group estimate of the population variance. (10)

GM Grand mean; in analysis of variance, mean of all scores regardless of what group they are in. (10)

M Mean. (2)

M_1, M_2, and so on.   Mean of the first group, second group, and so on. (9, 10)

n In analysis of variance, number of scores within each group. (10)

N Number of scores. (2)

N_1, N_2, and so on.   Number of scores in the first group, second group, and so on. (9, 10)

N_{Columns} Number of columns in a contingency table. (11)

N_{Rows} Number of rows in a contingency table. (11)

p Probability. (4)

r Correlation coefficient. (3)

r^2 Proportion of variance accounted for. (3)

R Multiple correlation coefficient. (3)

R^2 Proportion of variance accounted for in multiple regression. (3)

S Unbiased estimate of the population standard deviation. (2, 8)

S^2 Unbiased estimate of the population variance. (2, 8)

S_1^2, S_2^2, and so on.   Unbiased estimate of the population variance based on scores in the first sample, second sample, and so on. (9, 10)

S^2_{Between} Between-group estimate of the population variance. (10)

$S_{\text{Difference}}$ Standard deviation of the distribution of differences between means. (9)

315

$S^2_{\text{Difference}}$ Variance of the distribution of differences between means. (9)

SE Standard error (standard deviation of the distribution of means). (6)

S_M Standard deviation of the distribution of means based on an estimated population variance. (8)

S_M^2 Variance of a distribution of means based on an estimated population variance; variance of a distribution of means estimated from the variation among means of groups in analysis of variance. (6, 10)

$S_{M_1}^2$ and $S_{M_2}^2$ Variance of the distribution of means based on a population variance estimated from data in the first sample and in the second sample. (9)

S_{Pooled} Pooled estimate of the population standard deviation. (9)

S^2_{Pooled} Pooled estimate of the population variance. (9)

S^2_{Within} Within-group estimate of the population variance. (10)

SD Standard deviation. (2)

SD^2 Variance. (2)

t score Number of standard deviations from the mean on a t distribution. (8)

X Score on a particular variable; in regression X is usually the independent or predictor variable. (1–3)

X_1, X_2, and so on. First predictor or independent variable, second predictor or independent variable, and so on. (3)

$\overline{X}$ Mean of variable designated X. (2)

Y Score on a particular variable, usually the dependent variable in regression. (3)

Z Number of standard deviations from the mean. (2)

Z_X, Z_Y, and so on. Z score for variable X, for variable Y, and so on. (3)

References

ARON, A., ARON, E. N., & SMOLLAN, D. (1992). Inclusion of Other in the Self Scale and the structure of interpersonal closeness. *Journal of Personality and Social Psychology, 63,* 596–612.

ARON, A., ARON, E. N., TUDOR, M., & NELSON, G. (1991). Close relationships as including other in the self. *Journal of Personality and Social Psychology, 60,* 241–253.

ARON, A., PARIS, M., & ARON, E. N. (1995). Falling in love: Prospective studies of self-concept change. *Journal of Personality and Social Psychology, 69,* 1102-1112.

ARON, E. (1996). *The highly sensitive person.* New York: Carol/Birch-Lane Press.

BAER, J. (1991). Generality of creativity across performance domains. *Creativity Research Journal, 4,* 23–39.

BANDURA, A., & JOURDEN, F. J. (1991). Self-regulatory mechanisms governing the impact of social comparison on complex decision making. *Journal of Personality and Social Psychology, 60,* 941–951.

BANKSTON, W., THOMPSON, C., JENKINS, Q., & FORSYTH, C. (1990). The influence of fear of crime, gender, and southern culture on carrying firearms for protection. *Sociological Quarterly, 31,* 287–305.

BAROCAS, R., SEIFER, R., SAMEROFF, A. J., ANDREWS, T. A., CROFT, R. T., & OSTROW, E. (1991). Social and interpersonal determinants of developmental risk. *Developmental Psychology, 27,* 479–488.

BARON, R. S., BURGESS, M. L., & KAO, C. F. (1991). Detecting and labeling prejudice: Do female perpetrators go undetected? *Personality and Social Psychology Bulletin, 17,* 115–123.

BERSCHEID, E., SNYDER, M., & OMOTO, A. M. (1989). The Relationship Closeness Inventory: Assessing the closeness of interpersonal relationships. *Journal of Personality and Social Psychology, 57,* 792–807.

BIERMAN, K. L., & SMOOT, D. L. (1991). Linking family characteristics with poor peer relations: The mediating role of conduct problems. *Journal of Abnormal Child Psychology, 19,* 341–356.

BIERNAT, M., & WORTMAN, C. B. (1991). Sharing of home responsibilities between professionally employed women and their husbands. *Journal of Personality and Social Psychology, 60,* 844–860.

BINER, P. M. (1991). Effects of lighting-induced arousal on the magnitude of goal valence. *Personality and Social Psychology Bulletin, 17,* 219–226.

BLASS, T. (1991). Understanding behavior in the Milgram obedience experiment: The role of personality, situations, and their interactions. *Journal of Personality and Social Psychology, 60,* 398–413.

BOWMAN, R. A., & BOWMAN, V. E. (1995). Academic courses to train resident assistants. *Journal of College Student Development, 36,* 39–46.

BUCK, J. L. (1985). A failure to find gender differences in statistics achievement. *Teaching of Psychology, 12,* 100.

CAPALDI, D. M., & PATTERSON, G. R. (1991). Relation of parental transitions to boys' adjustment problems: 1. A linear hypothesis 2. Mothers at risk for transitions and unskilled parenting. *Developmental Psychology, 27,* 489–504.

CARLIN, M. F., & SANIGA, R. D. (1990). Relationship between academic placement and perception of abuse of the voice. *Perceptual and Motor Skills, 71,* 299–304.

COHEN, J. (1988). *Statistical power analysis for the behavioral sciences.* Hillsdale, NJ: Erlbaum.

CONOVER, W., & IMAN, R. L. (1981). Rank transformations as a bridge between parametric and nonparametric statistics. *American Statistician, 35,* 124–129.

COOPER, S. E., & ROBINSON, D. A. G. (1989). The influence of gender and anxiety on mathematics performance. *Journal of College Student Development, 30,* 459–461.

DANE, F. C., & WRIGHTSMAN, L. S. (1982). Effects of defendants' and victims' characteristics on jurors' verdicts. In N. L. Kerr & R. M. Bray (Eds.), *The psychology of the courtroom.* Orlando, FL: Academic Press.

DELUGA, R. J. (1991). The relationship of subordinate upward-influencing behavior, health care manager interpersonal stress, and performance. *Journal of Applied Social Psychology, 21,* 78–88.

DIXON, W. A., HEPPNER, P., & ANDERSON, W. P. (1991). Problem-solving appraisal, stress, hopelessness, and suicide ideation in a college population. *Journal of Counseling Psychology, 38,* 51–56.

DRAKE, C. C. & MICHAEL, W. B. (1995). Criterion-related validity of selected achievement measures in the prediction of a passing or failing criterion on the National Council Licensure Examination (NCLEX) for nursing students in a two-year associate degree program. *Educational and Psychological Measurement, 55,* 675–683.

DWINELL, P. E., & HIGBEE, J. L. (1991). Affective variables related to mathematics achievement among high-risk college freshmen. *Psychological Reports, 69,* 399–403.

EPPLEY, K. R., ABRAMS, A. I., & SHEAR, J. (1989). Differential effects of relaxation techniques on trait anxiety: A meta-analysis. *Journal of Clinical Psychology, 45,* 957–974.

EVANS, R. (1976). *The making of psychology.* New York: Knopf.

EYSENCK, H. J. (1981). *A model for personality.* Berlin: Springer-Verlag.

FRANZ, M. L. VON. (1979). *The problem of puer aeternus.* New York: Springer-Verlag.

FREUND, R. D., RUSSELL, T. T., & SCHWEITZER, S. (1991). Influence of length of delay between intake session and initial counseling session on client perceptions of counselors and counseling outcomes. *Journal of Counseling Psychology, 38,* 3–8.

FRICK, R. W. (1995). Accepting the null hypothesis. *Memory and Cognition, 23,* 132–138.

FRISCH, A. S., SHAMSUDDIN, K., & KURTZ, M. (1995) Family factors and knowledge: Attitudes and efforts concerning exposure to environmental tobacco among Malaysian medical students. *Journal of Asian and African Studies, 30,* 68–79.

FRODI, A., GROLNICK, W., BRIDGES, L., & BERKO, J. (1990). Infants of adolescents and adult mothers: Two indices of socioemotional development. *Adolescence, 25,* 363–374.

GALLUP, D. G. H. (1972). *The Gallup poll: Public opinion, 1935-1971.* New York: Random House.

GOIDEL, H. K., & LANGLEY, R. E. (1995). Media coverage of the economy and aggregate economic evaluations: Uncovering evidence of indirect media effects. *Political Research Quarterly, 48,* 313–328.

GREENWALD, A. G. (1975). Consequences of prejudice against the null hypothesis. *Psychological Bulletin, 82,* 1–19.

HAZAN, C., & SHAVER, P. (1987). Romantic love conceptualized as an attachment process. *Journal of Personality and Social Psychology, 52,* 511–524.

HENDRICK, C., & HENDRICK, S. S. (1989). Research on love: Does it measure up? *Journal of Personality and Social Psychology, 56,* 784–794.

HINDLEY, C., FILLIOZAT, A., KLACKENBERG, G., NICOLET-MEISTER, D., & SAND, E. (1966). Differences in age of walking in five European longitudinal samples. *Human Biology, 38,* 364–379.

HOBFOLL, S. E., & LEIBERMAN, J. R. (1987). Personality and social resources in immediate and continued stress resistance among women. *Journal of Personality and Social Psychology, 52,* 18–26.

HUBER, V. L. (1991). Comparison of supervisor-incumbent and female-male multidimensional job evaluation ratings. *Journal of Applied Psychology, 76,* 115–121.

HUNSLEY, J., & LEFEBVRE, M. (1990). A survey of the practices and activities of Canadian clinical psychologists. *Canadian Psychology, 31,* 350–358.

HUSSERL, E. (1970). *The crisis of European sciences and transcendental phenomenology: An introduction to phenomenological philosophy* (D. C. Carr, Trans.). Evanston, IL: Northwestern University Press.

INTROINI-COLLISON, I. B., & McGAUGH, J. L. (1986). Epinephrine modulates long-term retention of an aversively motivated discrimination. *Behavioral and Neural Biology, 45,* 358–365.

JUNE, L. N., CURRY, B. P., & GEAR, C. L. (1990). An 11-year analysis of black students' experience of problems and use of services: Implications for counseling professionals. *Journal of Counseling Psychology, 37,* 178–184.

KAGAN, J. (1994). *Galen's prophecy.* New York: Basic.

KILHAM, W., & MANN, L. (1974). Level of destructive obedience as a function of transmitter and executant roles in the Milgram obedience paradigm. *Journal of Personality and Social Psychology, 29,* 696–702.

KIRBY, R. R., & DAS, J. P. (1990). A cognitive approach to intelligence: Attention, coding and planning. *Canadian Psychology, 31,* 320–333.

KRAEMER, H. C., & THIEMANN, S. (1987). *How many subjects? Statistical power analysis in research.* Newbury Park, CA: Sage.

LYNN, S. J., WEEKES, J. R., NEUFELD, V., ZIVNEY, O., BRENTAR, J., & WEISS, F. (1991). Interpersonal climate and hypnotizability level: Effects on hypnotic performance, rapport, and archaic involvement. *Journal of Personality and Social Psychology, 60,* 739–743.

MANNING, C., HALL, J., & GOLD, P. (1990). Glucose effects on memory and other neuropsychological tests in elderly humans. *Psychological Science, 1,* 307–311.

McCRACKEN, G. (1988). *The long interview.* London: Sage.

McLEOD, D. M., EVELAND, W. P. & SIGNORELLI, N. (1994). Conflict and public opinion: Rallying effects of the Persian Gulf War. *Journalism Quarterly, 71,* 20–31.

MEIER, S. T. (1991). Tests of the construct validity of occupational stress measures with college students: Failure to support discriminant validity. *Journal of Counseling Psychology, 38,* 91–97.

MILGRAM, S. (1974). *Obedience to authority: An experimental view.* New York: Harper Collins.

MIRVIS, P., & LAWLER, E. (1977). Measuring the financial impact of employee attitudes. *Journal of Applied Psychology, 62,* 1–8.

MOONEY, S. P., SHERMAN, M. F., & LO PRESTO, C. T. (1991). Academic locus of control, self-esteem, and perceived distance from home as predictors of college adjustment. *Journal of Counseling and Development, 69,* 445–448.

MOOREHOUSE, M. J., & SANDERS, P. E. (1992). Children's feelings of school competence and perceptions of parents' work in four sociocultural contexts. *Social Development, 1,* 185–200.

MORIARTY, S. E., & EVERETT, S-L. (1994). Commercial breaks: A viewing behavior study. *Journalism Quarterly, 71,* 346–355.

OLTHOFF, R. (1989). *The effectiveness of premarital communication training.* Doctoral Dissertation, California School of Family Psychology, San Rafael, CA.

PECUKONIS, E. V. (1990). A cognitive/affective empathy training program as a function of ego development in aggressive adolescent females. *Adolescence, 25,* 59–76.

PETERS, W. S. (1987). *Counting for something: Statistical principles and personalities.* New York: Springer-Verlag.

PETTIGREW, T., & MEERTEN, R. W. (1995). *European Journal of Social Psychology, 25,* 57–75.

RIEHL, R. J. (1994). Academic preparation, aspirations, and first-year performance of first-generation students. *College and University, 70*(1), 14–19.

ROWE, B. H., THORSTEINSON, K., & BOTA, G. W. (1995). Bicycle helmet use and compliance: A northeastern Ontario roadside survey. *Canadian Journal of Public Health, 86,* 57–61.

RUSBULT, C. E., VERETTE, J., WHITNEY, G. A., SLOVIK, L. F., & LIPKUS, I. (1991). Accommodation processes in close relationships: Theory and preliminary empirical evidence. *Journal of Personality and Social Psychology, 60,* 53–78.

SHAH, H., & GAYATRI, G. (1994). Development news in elite and non-elite newspapers in Indonesia. *Journalism Quarterly, 71,* 411–420.

SKINNER, B. F. (1956). A case history in scientific method. *American Psychologist, 11,* 221–233.

SOLANO, C. H., & KOESTER, N. H. (1989). Loneliness and communication problems: Subjective anxiety or objective skills? *Personality and Social Psychology Bulletin, 15,* 126–133.

STASSER, G., TAYLOR, L. A., & HANNA, C. (1989). Information sampling in structured and unstructured discussions of three- and six-person groups. *Journal of Personality and Social Psychology, 57,* 67–78.

STEEN, L. A. (1987). Forward. In S. Tobias, *Succeed with math: Every student's guide to conquering math anxiety* (pp. xvii-xviii). New York: College Entrance Examination Board.

STIGLER, S. M. (1986). *The history of statistics.* Cambridge, MA: Belknap Press.

TABACHNICK, B. G., & FIDELL, L. S. (1996). *Using multivariate statistics* (3rd ed.). New York: Harper Collins.

TANKARD, J., JR. (1984). *The statistical pioneers.* Cambridge, MA: Schenkman.

THOMAS, A., & CHESS, S. (1977). *Temperament and development.* New York: Bruner/Mazel.

TOBIAS, S. (1982, January). Sexist equations. *Psychology Today,* pp. 14–17.

TOBIAS, S. (1987). *Succeed with math: Every student's guide to conquering math anxiety.* New York: College Entrance Examination Board.

U.S. BUREAU OF THE CENSUS. (1990). *Statistical abstracts of the United States.* Washington, DC: U.S. Government Printing Office.

U.S. DEPARTMENT OF EDUCATION. (1990). *The condition of education.* Washington, DC: U.S. Government Printing Office.

WHITLEY, B. E. (1990). The relationship of heterosexuals' attributions for the causes of homosexuality to attitudes toward lesbians and gay men. *Personality and Social Psychology Bulletin, 16,* 369–377.

YUKL, G., & FALBE, C. M. (1991). Importance of different power sources in downward and lateral relations. *Journal of Applied Psychology, 76,* 416–423.

ZEIDNER, M. (1991). Statistics and mathematics anxiety in social science students: Some interesting parallels. *British Journal of Education, 61,* 319–329.

Index

C

Interaction effects, 219–220
    defined, 219
    graphs for, 222, 223f, 224f
    interpretation of, 220–222, 221t
    main effects and, 223–225
Intervals
    defined, 6
    estimates of, 120
Inverse transformation, 254

J

Jung, Carl, on statistics, 35b

K

Kendall's tau test, *t* test for correlation vs., 257t
Kruskal-Wallis *H* test, analysis of variance vs., 257t

L

Latent variable modeling, 275–276, 276f, 277f, 280t
Levels of measurement, 4n
Lindquist, E. G., 207b
Linear correlation
    computation of, 52–59
    defined, 449
    degree of, 53–54
LISREL program, 275
Loading, factor, 272
Long-run relative-frequency interpretation of probability, defined, 82
Love scales study, 272–273, 273t

M

Main effect
    defined, 220
    interaction effect and, 223–225
MANCOVA. *See* Multivariate analysis of covariance
MANOVA. *See* Multivariate analysis of variance
Man-Whitney *U* test, *t* test vs., 257t
Marginal means, defined, 220
Marriage communication study, 165–168, 166t, 168f, 174
Matched pairs, *t* test for, 165n
Maternal antisocial behavior study, 276, 277f
Maternal teaching style study, 267, 267t
Math anxiety, 2–3, 10b–11b
    gender/ethnicity and, 16b–17b
Matrix, correlation, 65
Mean(s), 23–28
    as average, 23
    as balancing point, 24, 24f–26f
    cell, 220
    defined, 23
    differences between. *See* Differences between means
    distribution of, 109–117, 110f–112f, 116f, 117f, 118t, 181

examples of, 25–26, 26f, 27f
formula for, 24–25
harmonic, 193
marginal, 220
normal curve and, 76–78, 77f
in research articles, 40, 40t, 41t
of samples, hypothesis tests with, 108–123
standard error of, 114n, 123
symbols for, 24–25
tyranny of, 34b–35b
to Z score, 287t–289t
Measurement, levels of, 4n
Median
    defined, 27
    example of, 27–28, 28f
Meditation research study, 138b
Meta-analysis
    defined, 137
    effect size and, 137
    of relaxation research, 138b
Mode
    defined, 26
    examples of, 27f, 28f
Modeling
    causal, 273–277, 274f, 276f, 277f
    latent variable, 275–276, 276f, 277f, 280t
    structural equation, 275–276, 276f, 277f, 280t
Moorehouse, Martha, 5t–7t, 5–7, 9f
Multimodal frequency distribution, 13, 13f, 14f
Multiple correlation, 265–266
    coefficient, 64
    defined, 63
Multiple regression, 266–269, 267t, 268t, 280t
    correlation and, 63–65
    defined, 63
    hierarchical, 266–267, 267t
    stepwise, 268t, 268–269
Multivariate analysis of covariance, 279
Multivariate analysis of variance, 278–279

N

Negative correlation, defined, 50–51, 51f
News coverage study, 18–19, 19t
Nominal variable, 4
    chi-test and, 232
Nondirectional hypothesis, 99–100
Nonparametric test, defined, 256
Normal curve, 15–16, 17f, 75–81
    commonness of, 76
    defined, 75
    probability and, 83f, 83–84
    standard deviations and, 76–78, 77f
    table, 78–81, 80f–82f, 287t–289t
    t distribution vs., 159f
Normal distribution. *See* Normal curve
Null hypothesis. *See also* Hypothesis testing
    acceptance of, problem with, 100b
    defined, 94
    rejection of, 97–98